American EDUCATION
A Social History

Dennis R. Herschbach
University of Maryland

Kendall Hunt
publishing company

Cover images © 2014, Shutterstock, Inc.

Kendall Hunt
publishing company

www.kendallhunt.com
Send all inquiries to:
4050 Westmark Drive
Dubuque, IA 52004-1840

Copyright © 2014 by Kendall Hunt Publishing Company

ISBN 978-1-4652-1201-6

Printed in the United States of America
10 9 8 7 6 5 4 3 2 1

To Mary, with love

CONTENTS

CHAPTER FIVE: Education, the War, and Its Aftermath   85

PART THREE: Expansion and Schooling   101

Introduction   101

CHAPTER SIX: The Emerging Pattern of Public Education   105

ACKNOWLEDGMENTS

In a real sense this book is a result of a collective effort over many years to grasp the complexity of American education. Its structure and substance is an outcome of many hours of class discussion with University of Maryland students as we puzzled over the uses society makes of education, and how the forces of people, politics, and social change impact education. I look on this new generation that will go about shaping the educational world with hope and gratitude.

I am also indebted to the scholarship of the many individuals whose work served as resources for this small volume. There is a wide range of wonderful source material that added to the scope of this work. Finally, writing is a lonely craft, and one can lose a sense of perspective. Outside comment is useful. I appreciate the collaboration of Molly Dunn. She read all of the chapter drafts and provided many useful suggestions. Her judgments were very helpful on places to cut, refine, or add material. Her sharp editorial suggestions helped to produce a more focused, clean, and readable text.

PREFACE

This book is about society and education. It is about how society uses education to achieve social stability, maintain order, and transmit its national values to the young. Similarly, this book is about education's political underpinnings: how schools are constituted to build political consensus and accommodate the demands of various constituencies. The book also is about how education is used for economic development, a key element in the economic progress of the nation. Finally, this book is about the use of education as a great equalizer, a tool individuals use to navigate along the path into mainstream America.

There are many textbooks on the history of American education and it is not the intention in this volume to faithfully reproduce how others tell the story. Many contemporary accounts follow a time-worn pattern that traces its origins to the early-20th-century work of the Stanford University education historian Ellwood Cubberley. The early Puritans are considered the primary influence on the formation of American education. Cubberley envisioned the following extension of American education as part of a long process of working out the ideals of democracy established by the Puritans. It is true that embedded in contemporary educational thought are vestiges of Puritan thought: public support for common education; education opportunity being widely available; education for both boys and girls; education used as a tool of social stability and control. But there also are marked differences, and similarities end when the reasons behind what appear to be common elements with contemporary educational practices are understood. A limited, focused perspective cannot capture the fullness of American education that is a product of the ethnic richness that makes up the mosaic of the American population.

In this volume the view is taken that American public education evolved from a rich variety of influences. We tend to view the history of American education from an English perspective. The conqueror gets to write history, and this is true of education history. Some of the long-standing major beliefs underpinning education, however, derive from the European Enlightenment that extended considerably beyond the English orbit of influence. Again, the Spanish were in North America for almost 300 years and they left a legacy of ideas, educational practice, culture, and bloodlines. The early French cannot be overlooked. To best view the long journey toward our present system of public education requires a broad and inclusive view of educational history.

Taking a broad view of education history means stepping back from a limiting perspective of America and recognizing the multiple influences of ethnic groups. America always has been a pluralistic geographical, cultural, and political entity. The Amerindians themselves represent an extensively diverse, complex population, and the unity as a people in our minds stems primarily from a rather anemic understanding of the original inhabitants of America. Similarly, the early

Blacks brought to North America represented people of distinct historical, language, and cultural heritage, and as individuals they struggled to retain an identity that eventually was stripped away through a system of slavery that made them "Africans." The early European population that came to America was diverse, representing practically all of the ethnic and national populations characterizing Europe today. But even within one national group, such as the French or English, there were distinct ethnic divisions represented by bloodlines, internal conflict, dialect, and religion. To speak of the "English" influence on education, for example, has to be tempered with the knowledge that there is not one "English" perspective. From the very beginning, the American nation confronted the challenge of creating unity out of diversity, a challenge that profoundly shaped education, and continues to do so today.

Educational history is American history. Education is a product of society, it is a social institution shaped by its larger historical context. Societies at specific times use education to achieve certain ends, and it is these uses that are important to understand. A distinguishing characteristic of this volume is the nesting of the study of education within its larger historical context.

This volume is divided into six parts. Part One examines the colonial, pre-Revolution period. An extensive treatment of the historical background is given because to a surprising degree the fundamental educational, economic, and population characteristics that continue to define the nation were established. The present does not necessarily repeat the past, but it evolves out of it, thus the importance of understanding this early period of educational history.

Part Two covers the time immediately following the Revolutionary War and independence. The issue of schooling quickly came to the fore as leaders confronted building a unified nation out of what was formerly a loose collection of colonies separate by economic, demographic and religious differences. Education was considered a potential tool of national unification. The local community school was the dominant educational force, but in the effort to transform many local voices into a voice of national unity, an intellectual and institutional framework progressively emerged that influenced the shape of American education.

Part Three covers the pivotal period when the foundation was erected for the framework of a comprehensive "system" of public education. Schooling of all types and at all levels was founded and expanded in response to the pressures of immigration, westward expansion, and emerging industrialization. The common, tax-supported school became a reality, the public high school was in its infancy, and hold of the classical curriculum on higher education was broken by science and technology. More women searched out educational opportunity. But in a real sense, national expansion was accomplished at the expense of slaves, eastern Amerindians, and inhabitants of the southwestern Mexican territories.

Part Four is an educational account of the remarkable period following the Civil War when the nation industrialized and urbanized at a dizzying pace. Immigration was overwhelming. At the same time our "modern" school system began to emerge in full form. Educational change is linked with social and economic change and we examine both together. The purpose of schooling altered, as children of different classes, ethnicity, and religion were absorbed into the kindergartens and common schools in increasing numbers. The lower grades became institutions of social reconstruction. The public high school became permanently rooted in American education, and higher education solidified its form as a major institution of nation building.

At the same time, the nation struggled with the moral, political, and educational issues surrounding the discrimination, exploitation, and violence that engulfed the immigrant and non-European populations making up an increasing proportion of the population.

Part Five covers the time between 1900 and the 1930s, a period of remarkable population and economic growth, but also of social uncertainty and dislocation. This was the time when the form of our present school system was fleshed out. Major ideas that influenced the form and practice of American education are examined. The national education focus shifted to the high school; it became recognized as an important institution to address some of the social and economic ills that became increasingly visible. Throughout the 1920s and 1930s the nation struggled to maintain its equilibrium in the face of social conflict and economic uncertainty.

Part Six is an overview of education from the close of World War II to the present. It is an account of the continuing struggle to response to complex, diverse, and changing society through a redefinition of public education. It examines the efforts of the more "conservative" factions of society to strengthen mathematics and science achievement in order to spur on economic growth and build a formidable military machine. It also examines the conflicted 1960s, the civil rights moment, and the war on poverty. These were years during which social consciousness dominated educational thought. This final part concludes with a discussion of public education and its "capture" by the marketplace.

A different approach to the study of American education might focus on teachers, class-rooms, and school administrative structures. This volume takes a broader view: how education relates to people and society, and how it is used and misused to achieve social and economic ends. At the same time, public education is viewed as a wonderful tool of society, one of the truly momentous accomplishments of men and women concerned about the individual and collective welfare of the nation's citizens.

Part One
The Coming of Change

Introduction

As Columbus and his band of adventurers waded ashore on a small, outlying Caribbean island they were not the first Europeans to land in the "New World," but they were the most consequential. Five hundred years earlier Vikings had established a settlement at L'Anse aux Meadows on the northwestern coast of Newfoundland, but the little colony did not last. Exploration and trade, nevertheless, continued with archaeological evidence indicating Viking presence throughout the Canadian Arctic and as far south as New England, eventually ceasing around the mid-1300's. Norse artifacts are found in Nova Scotia, Maine, New York, and Pennsylvania. Before Columbus the Basques probably ventured as far as Newfoundland in the search for cod. There may have been other early voyages. But these early explorations were largely isolated adventures and stimulated little interest among other Europeans (Diamond, 2005 Flannery, 2001). It was not until after Columbus made landfall in the Caribbean that Europe became inflamed with the allure of the New World.

The purpose of his voyage was to find wealth, and on his very first voyage Columbus encountered Arawak Indians wearing ornaments of pure gold. The wealth of the silver mines in Mexico and the gold of the Aztecs and Incas quickly projected Spain into a world power. But the land itself also was enormously rich in forests and timber, minerals, fertile soil, game, food crops, vast open expanses, harbors, and flowing rivers and lakes. And land was abundant. The promise of the enormous windfall wealth that would follow brought adventures and settlers from all over Europe: a trickle at first, then in rapidly increasing numbers, and then finally an unstoppable flood that progressively overwhelmed and conquered the land and original peoples.

The Spanish struck the first successful permanent settlement a decade after the landfall in 1492, and a full century before the French and English. Among other European powers resources were too limited to support colonization and they had to be content with lesser adventures. Explorers and traders cruised along the coastlines of North America, into bays and up rivers, and trekked inland, establishing vast claims for the European powers to land that was already claimed and occupied by indigenous inhabitants. Trading posts and fishing ports were established; but domestic troubles and intense continental rivalries kept other European powers away from establishing more permanent settlements. Europe was in a state of protracted upheaval as the old order was breaking down. It was not until the early 1600s that both France and England capitalized on previous claims to found permanent colonies.

This was a time referred to as the "Enlightenment," a period of intellectual flowering, of the emergence of secular rationalism, of a growing challenge to the arbitrary power of church and state, and of an expanding confidence in human capacity and science to harness the forces of nature. Technical innovations in shipbuilding and navigation made it possible for explorers to sail to the New World, and the opening of the mind created the desire and confidence. There were new intellectual, spiritual, scientific, and physical worlds to conquer, and this inspired men to journey 3,000 miles from their homelands to subdue the wilderness and the indigenous inhabitants. They brought with them ideas inspired from the Enlightenment. They also brought with them what they knew of home, and attempted to reproduce a distant lifestyle in an unfamiliar and alien context. They could never entirely escape from the home influence that was itself characterized by the excitement but yet uncertainty of the revolution in thought sustained by the Enlightenment. The resulting colonies were an amalgam, a blend of what the colonists took from home and a reshaping to accommodate the uncertain and unfamiliar circumstances that they confronted.

Colonization was not easy. Not only did settlers have to confront the wilderness and Amerindians, but also they clashed with other Europeans in a brutal contest for control of the new continent. The Enlightenment also was a time of great social, political, military, and religious conflict. Continental wars became colonial wars. Political, social, and religious differences spilled over into the colonies. Some colonies were more successful than others, and eventually settlements took root, prospered, and expanded as European influence pressed ever outward.

The Focus of Part One

In Part One we examine the colonization of North America up to the revolutionary war period. During this time, the social and religious dimensions that stamped an identity on what was to become the new nation were established; an intertwined, multiethnic population emerged; and economic lines were developed that continued to influence the character of the nation. Institutional forms, ideas, beliefs, and social and economic practices brought from Europe were transformed. New cultural and political forms emerged. And, importantly, schools emerged out of the struggle to found colonies.

Societies rely on schools. Schools are a mark of social and economic stability. Schools provide the essential level of education necessary to sustain communities. The establishment of schools means that citizens have enough security and resources to invest in the future of their children. While schooling in colonial America was provided in various forms, its functions remained fairly constant. Colonists were interested in cultural transmission, both for their own children and to pacify Natives. In the case of their own children, they wanted to preserve and pass on to the young their history, literature, beliefs, and values. But the colonial powers, particularly the Spanish, also used education as a means of forced cultural assimilation to bring the indigenous populations under control. Schooling functioned as a tool of deculturalization. Religion played a major part in this effort. In Part One we examine the intersection of family, church, and school.

Schools also function as an agent of social control. Colonial societies struggled to maintain social stability and order. They were besieged by outside forces as well as internal dissent. Schools helped to preserve the social structure, maintain beliefs, and teach the young to accept and obey authority. Children—whether European or Native—learned to take their place in the social and economic order. Therefore we examine the social control function of education in early colonial America in Part One, as well.

Schools also provide an important skill development function. The colonies were always short of human resources. It was vital that the skills and learning that members possessed were passed on to later generations. It was also expected that Native populations could learn how to contribute to the European society colonists were attempting to reproduce. For this reason, in Part One, we look at how schools functioned as an instrument of skill development.

Early European occupation and settlement left distinct footprints. Part One is organized around the five major ethnic groups that were most involved in the coming of change. First, Chapter One examines the early Spanish experience in colonial America. The Spanish developed the earliest and most widespread empire. Of all the colonizing European powers, they made the most extensive use of schooling as a means of bringing the Amerindians under their control. Next, we briefly examine early French efforts to stake a claim in the New World. They left a legacy of Catholic education. Chapter Two examines the English colonial experience. English colonization is characterized by substantial variation between the Puritans of New England, for example, and the Quakers of Pennsylvania or the Anglicans of the Virginia tidewater. The change imposed by the English on the New World was much broader in scope and varied more than other European colonists. It is instructive to examine how social class, religion, occupation, and environment influenced the establishment of schools. In Chapter Three the focus is on the introduction of slavery and the impact of Africans on the evolving ethnic mosaic that was to characterize America. We also will discuss the Amerindians, the occupants of the land invaded, overrun, and conquered by the Europeans.

Chapter One

The Spanish and French in Early Colonial America

The Spanish were the first Europeans to sink roots in the New World. They were also the first to build settlements and use armies, churches, and schools to evolve ways to rule and coexist with the Native populations. After subduing the inhabitants of the densely populated Caribbean basin in the early 1500s, conquest was extended to Mexico, Peru, and the coastal areas of Latin America. Spanish exploration, conquest, and settlement moved into what is North America in the 1530s. It basically took two directions. From roughly the mid-1500s, and increasingly for 150 years up through the early 1700s, settlement efforts were mainly directed to the southeastern region of North America. After 1700 the major focus for over a hundred years was on regions west of the Mississippi, encompassing the southwestern and far western parts of the territory. This was a difficult area to bring under Spanish domination because of the vast distances and rugged terrain. Large parts of the territory were hot and arid, and two major mountain ranges towered over 14,000 feet, among expansive plains and large deserts. The Indians were a mixture of widely diverse groups living in uneasy alliance with one another. Nomadic bands roamed the region.

Spanish Settlement in the Southeast

The first permanent Spanish settlement in what today is the United States was established in 1565 in St. Augustine, Florida. The Spanish wanted to have an Atlantic coastal base to protect their treasure ships on the run up the Bermuda channel and across the Atlantic. Raiders coming down from the north could be blocked. A school started in 1606 was for Spanish children. Of the 600 original settlers, 26 families were included among the 500 soldiers. The Franciscans also started a classical school and preparatory seminary for Spanish youth. The Jesuits and Franciscan missionaries who were part of the settlement turned their attention to the Native American populations in the surrounding region. Initial attempts to convert and educate met with mixed results, however. The attempt to eliminate the Indian language and culture was resisted. A revolt in 1597 killed the Franciscans friars. Nevertheless, by 1650, there were 50 missions and around 25,000 converts in the "La Florida" region, which also encompassed the Carolinas and Gulf Coast areas over to Louisiana. A pattern of settlement was established early by the Spanish that was also followed in the West. Soldiers comprised the largest number of individuals; a few accompanying priests established missions and ran schools, and there was a limited number of women and few families. St. Augustine was an exception in the number of Spanish families.

The southeastern settlements eventually collapsed. The indigenous Amerindian population was drastically reduced through diseases introduced by the Europeans, war, slavery, and forced relocation. By 1700, only two missions were left and by 1710 only one remained, located in St. Augustine (Webb, 2006). Attacks by the English and allied Indians decimated the settlements. Amerindians and the Spanish settlements along the Gulf coast all the way to Louisiana experience similar decline (Gallay, 2002).

The major overall reason for the decrease in Spanish influence along the southeastern seaboard was the ongoing clash with the southward expansion of Anglo settlers. Both sides used the local Indians to war against the other, a pattern repeated in the conflict between the French and English. By the late 1600s a robust slave trade among the Indians was underway. For over a hundred years the southeastern region was kept in state of protracted conflict as groups of Natives confronted the danger of extermination from each another. The European antagonists armed competing groups. Whole tribes vanished (Butler & Watson, 1984; Gallay, 2002; Wilson, 1998).

The settlements eventually became untenable for the Spanish against the numerically superior Anglo, American, and allied Indian forces that could be mustered. The Spanish were also caught in a struggle with the French for domination of the lower Mississippi region. By the 1700s the Spanish empire in North America had become extended beyond its capacity to support and defend the southeastern settlements against the flood of encroaching Anglos and French (Remini, 2001). Given the extensive Spanish occupation throughout the Americas, there were not enough resources in men and money to protect all of its claims. The Spanish retrenched into enclaves in Florida and in strategic locations along the Gulf coast.

The process of disengagement from the southeastern region was slow, but took a final, decisive turn in the early 1800s. In 1803, Spain lost large chunks of its possessions when they were absorbed into the Louisiana Purchase. The Americans argued that they had a solid claim because the land was part of the territory ceded from France. In the aftermath of the War of 1812, additional Spanish territory was lost along the Gulf coast. American soldiers and settlers simply moved in and occupied areas. In 1819, Andrew Jackson forced the Spanish to cede, to the United States, Florida and its remaining southeastern territory. Jackson had been commissioned by the federal government to put down a Seminole rebellion along the Georgia and Alabama borders, but he continued southward. The warring Indians and runaway slaves were using Spanish settlements as a refuge, and Jackson used this as a justification to invade and force Spanish capitulation. With the resulting Adams–Onis treaty and payment of $5 million, Spanish presence in the southeastern United States ended (Gonzales, 2000, p. 35; Remini, 2001).

Indirect Spanish influence in the southeastern areas nevertheless continued. In the immediate term, strong ties had been built with the Creek, Choctaws, Cherokees, and Chickasaws. The knowledge and skills learned from the Spanish did not leave when they departed. The local Indians used what they learned from the Spanish to build towns and farms. They had also honed their warfare skills under the Spanish and gave the Anglos stiff resistance. Presently, throughout the region, many of the place names reflect early Spanish origins. Spanish cultural influence continues in the form of speech, architecture, food, literature, and song. Spanish bloodlines flow through the veins of citizens. In an ironic twist of history, individuals from the extended Spanish empire in America are repopulating south Florida today and the surrounding region.

Western Conquest

Settlement efforts were more extensive further west. The distances were vast. Missions were at the heart of settlements, and they tended to be located at the borderlands on the "Rim of Christendom" in sparsely populated regions. Soldiers conquered and controlled and the missionaries converted and educated. What set off Spanish settlements from other later European colonization effort was that they were primarily populated by indigenous natives rather than Spanish immigrants. The Spanish could not conquer and hold such a large area without use of Indian labor. Buetow (1970) observe, "Spanish missions extended, held, and promoted the frontier. Spain utilized her missionaries as a means of changing the social order of the natives in order that, lacking colonists, she would colonize the frontier with aborigines" (p. 2). There were four fundamental objectives: bring the Natives in the surrounding area together into aggregated villages where they would collectively form a "Spanish" community; convert the locals to Catholicism; "civilize" the Indians; and promote "ethnic fusing" among the Spanish and Indian populations (Buetow, 1970). The Spaniards consciously set out to form a new mixed ethnicity fully immersed in Catholicism. They also used the Indians as a workforce, often under brutal conditions. In New Mexico, the second oldest permanent settlement in the United States was established at San Gabriel in 1598 and another settlement in Santa Fe in 1609, about the same time the first English settlement was established in Virginia. A network of settlements and missions followed that eventually in the 1700s stretched through Texas, New Mexico, Arizona, and California. Major towns of today such as San Diego, Los Angeles, Monterey, San Francisco, Pueblo, Las Cruces, El Paso, San Antonio, and Corpus Christi were founded.

As in the southeastern areas, priests followed soldiers and had wide responsibilities. Of first order of importance was to build stable settlements and convert the local populations to Catholicism. This was a Crown mandate, and missions and schools were used. Priests had the major responsibility to found and run schools as well as knit the community together. They controlled money, established missions, built and operated schools, monopolized religious teaching, approved marriages, commanded obedience, and administered to the physical needs of families. The Spanish introduced fruit trees, vegetable crops, grain cultivation, horses, cattle, pigs and chickens, and new and better ways of farming, all of which resulted in greater food security. The making of iron, and the forging of tools and weapons were introduced. Spaniards taught locals how to make bricks and build houses, barns, and bridges. The local inhabitants also benefitted from the trade for European goods; housing and food was available in settlements; and the Church offered the promise of a better afterlife.

Escaped Spanish horses and cattle soon populated the interior Plains states. The early bloodlines are still present in livestock herds throughout the Southwest. The Amerindians found a new and powerful means of transportation and warfare and another source of food. The power relationships among tribes were profoundly altered (Hamalainen, 2008). The

Native populations, however, suffered. Disease devastated local tribes; they had no immunity to European sicknesses. The death rate was astronomical in some Indian settlements, reaching up to 90% or 100%. Severely weakened tribes were open to subjection, enslavement, or annihilation by warring neighbors. Some tribal groups simply disappeared; no living members could be found. In a pattern that was to repeat itself, severely weakened tribes often forged alliances with the Europeans in an attempt of find protection and aid.

Of Mixing and Heritage

The Spanish attitude toward ethnic mixing contrasted significantly with the English who drew sharp lines between White, Brown, and Black. The Spanish soldiers and settlers took the local women as concubines, some men engaged in consensual unions, and some in marriage. As suggested, "racial fusion" was encouraged (Buetow, 1970, p. 3). The mixing with the Amerindians, and later Blacks, resulted in a rainbow of ethnic types ranging from mestizo (white and Indian), to mulatto (white and black), to coyotes (mestizo and Indian), to zambos (black and Indian)— and to every other imaginable combination (Gonzales, 2000, p. 20). This mixing was largely out of necessity. The Spanish brought conquering armies and priests, with a limited number of women accompanying the men to the New World; mixed children increasingly became a greater portion of the population (a fact that continues to be true). "Since about 90 per cent of Spanish colonist were unmarried men," Harold Driver (1969) observed, "they cohabited with and married Indian women in large numbers." A new ethnicity was created. Indian genes today make up about 80% of the ethnic mixture (pp. 476–477). The Spanish were always in the minority, and they relied on the indigenous Indians as well as the newly generated mixed population to perform the tasks required to sustain the new settlements. Sometimes the settlements were comprised of as few as one or two priests, a few Spanish soldiers, and 2,000 or 3,000 Indians and mixed children (Gonzalez, 2000).

"Race relations" were complex (Brooks, 2002; Gonzalez, 2000). The Spanish had a tradition of ethnic mixing because of Spain's own historical development. It was accepted for Spanish male settlers to engage in sexual unions with both Native populations and Africans, and as previously suggested, the offspring were afforded greater acceptance than found among the Anglo population (Gonzalez, 2000). But acceptance was not equality. There was a distinct class structure. A small, wealthy White population tended to limit its range of marriage options primarily to secure inheritance lines, although it was common for "lower class" Whites to mix. Consensual unions rather than marriage were common primarily because they did not disturb the class structure. However, for purposes of securing land and wealth, the elite Whites married into elite Amerindian families. The mixed offspring of elite Whites and concubines occasionally would be admitted to "higher society" if they did not unduly subvert the class structure. The large and growing mestizo class tended to occupy one of a number of social positions above full-blooded Indians, but below Whites (Gonzales, 2000).

A class of free Blacks, zambos, and mulattos developed within the Spanish settlements. Along the southeastern seaboard this was largely comprised of runaway slaves from the Anglos who found refuge and freedom among the Indian and Spanish settlements. In the Southwest and West, mixed populations were formed primarily by individuals fleeing from along the fringe of the Caribbean basin. Although racism existed, it was in more of a muted form than found in the English colonies mainly because of the large mixed populations present among the Spanish. As Gonzales (2000, p. 20) observed, within the Spanish settlements, "mestizos and mulatos, no matter how dark, were invariably regarded as part of white society, although admittedly second-class members."

The framework for the beginning of a class system was thus established—one that exists today. Pure-blood Southwest Indians tend to occupy the bottom rung of the economic and social ladder, with the top rung reserved for individuals who can trace their genetic heritage back to European ancestors. Various other mixes hold the rungs somewhere in between.

Education in the Settlements

Of all of the European powers, the Spanish made the widest use of schools as a tool of colonization. The Spanish settlements became centers for the conversion and education of the Native and mixed populations. Particular emphasis was placed on teaching Catholic doctrine, along with reading and writing. Trades and technical skills, agriculture, fine arts, singing, and instrumental music were also taught (Webb, 2006). As part of the cultural conversion, the arts and classical music were valued. Rather than try to eliminate the technical skills that the local population already possessed, the Spanish tended to add European technique to the existing skills of the Indians. They needed to develop a population of skilled locals who could perform the work of the new settlements. The friars mainly made up the teaching staff, but it was not uncommon to bring special teachers from Mexico. Boys showing promise also were groomed to be teachers, clerics, and mission assistants. In some cases there were separate schools for girls where they concentrated on domestic science skills. The Spanish, in contrast to the later English settlers, tended to learn and preserve the local languages. In some cases, written alphabets were formulated and catechisms crafted in the local tongue (Buetow, 1970; Shea, 1969.

Some European offspring attended mission schools, but the general practice was for children of Spanish settlers to be home schooled by tutors, perhaps followed by additional schooling in Mexico or Spain for the very wealthy. Mixed blood and Indian boys made up the population of mission schools.

A number of practices characterized mission schools. The discussion of two polar opposites follows. The mission school at Loreto, California, in 1697 devised an innovative system duplicated elsewhere to reach talented mixed and indigenous boys in scattered, outlying areas. The mission served as the central school, and Jesuit teachers in surrounding schools recruited promising boys to attend what we would term today the "magnet school" at Loreto where they received training to prepare as teachers and mission assistants (Buetow, 1970). In a sparsely populated area lacking transportation, this was a way that talented youth could be identified and given educational opportunity that they otherwise would not have. The Loreto innovation instigated what we today refer to as "creaming": the best school performers are selected (i.e., creamed off) to continue on to the next level, where high performers are again selected to go on to an additional, more advanced level of education, and so on. Thomas Jefferson later made creaming a central idea in his scheme to cultivate a "natural aristocracy" of leaders, a concept that we practice today with scholarships and financial aid for exceptional students.

The school in the El Rosario mission in Texas took the opposite tack. It focused primarily on training workers. Agriculture was the principal focus, but also trades such as pottery making, carpentry, masonry, blacksmithing, and spinning were taught. Reading was taught so that the catechisms and primers of Christian doctrine could be followed. Many schools failed, however. Hostile Indians killed the friars and destroyed the missions. In some cases, schools had to close because the local tribes gradually disappeared through sickness and disease. There was no longer a population to educate (Buetow, 1970; Shea, 1969).

One legacy of the mission schools is the emphasis on formal vocational preparation. For centuries formal schooling in Europe tended to focus on cultivating an elite. The technical skills essential for maintaining a society were passed down, often from father to son, through an apprenticeship system associated with craft guilds. It was not possible to do this with Amerindians. The Spanish turned to mission schools. This was a giant step away from the elitism characterizing classical formal European education. The Spanish used schools to maintain the religious as well as the social and economic order of the community. This idea found favor with Robert Molesworth and others in 18th-century England: Education could serve a useful social and economic development function by equipping the young to fill productive work roles (Spring, 1994). Benjamin Franklin echoed similar views as he implemented the idea in the mid-1700s of providing both an "ornamental" and "useful education" through the academy, a transplant from England (Morgan, 2002). Today, the practical objective of preparing the young for economic roles in society dominates American education. The Spanish came to this conclusion much earlier.

The importance of the early mission schools cannot be overemphasized. They were central to the establishment and maintenance of settlements. The Spaniards were so few in numbers that they had to rely on the local Indian population to perpetuate community life. The settlements could not prosper unless there were inhabitants with the skills essential to feed, clothe, house, nurse, and protect members. While it was of primary importance to teach essential technical skills fundamental to maintaining and protecting the community, the mission school was also used to cultivate among the Indian population allegiance to the Crown, the Catholic Church, and local authority. The cultural transmission and social control functions of schooling were enforced. The settlements could not survive under Spanish rule unless the local Amerindian population was taught to obey the rules, accept discipline, acknowledge authority, and accept the religious and social norms imposed.

Spanish colonial schools are an early example of using education as an instrument of social control, a practice later followed by other colonial powers: The civic authority, the Church, and the school worked in consonant to establish and maintain social stability. The civic authority supported the Church, commanded allegiance to its beliefs, and punished dissention; the Church in turn bestowed legitimacy on the civic authority, supported the laws, rules, and norms of society, and upheld the right of the leaders to rule; schools taught allegiance to both state and church and prepared the young to play a constructive social role.

Spanish mission schools also are an example of the early use of education as a tool for deculturalization. The dominant culture seeks to replace the culture of the dominated through the use of language and the beliefs, values, and norms of behavior that it transmits through schooling. The assertion on the part of the dominant group that it is culturally superior gives it justification for imposing domination and rule. Cultural transmission continues to be a major education objective in societies

Power of the Gun

In the newly established settlements, much of the indigenous population tended to be reduced to a subservient state. The Spanish settlers tended to be the landowners, overseers, and skilled artisans. The Indians were primarily laborers and servants. The Crown advanced the policy of allotting large tracks of land to Spaniards. They would rule and the Indians would labor. In return for protection and teaching, the Spaniards had the right to extract labor. This was known as the "encomienda system," and it was subject to abuse. It was not uncommon for authority to be harshly enforced, life minutely regulated, labor involuntary, social stratification maintained, and civic liberty restricted. In some cases, several generations were kept in a stage of semi-servitude. Those who disobeyed where put into stocks or flogged. This was "good" for the soul. Escapees were tracked down and punished. Intransients were sold into slavery (Furnas, 1969, pp. 368–369). Hardship, in fact, was intensified by the fact that Spanish slave hunters preyed on unexpecting settlements.

Few subjected populations, however, quietly submit to abuse for long without organizing against repression. It is not surprising that priests and soldiers met death in the hands of what they though were pacified flocks. Abused Indians put up with only so much before they turned to massacre. At different intervals, organized and widespread rebellions broke out that required the intervention of troops and took years to subdue. In New Mexico, for example, there was an Indian revolt in 1680; at least 400 Spaniards were killed, including 21 Franciscans, and the mission was destroyed. It took 11 years for the Spaniards to reassert authority. Settlement authorities at times had to tread lightly to thwart rebellion and build support. Ranchers and settlers in outlying regions had to be particularly on guard to maintain peaceful relations with the local Native inhabitants. In the sparsely populated regions of the Southwest and West, it was often difficult to maintain control. Missions, schools, and settlements fell into ruin as Spanish government support waned (Buetow, 1970, p. 7; Furnas, 1969).

Conquerors tend not to be gentle toward those being subjugated. This is true of the Spanish. But why did the Amerindian population tolerate Spanish conquest, abuse, and domination? Some did not, and 250 years of Indian resistance drained the Spanish treasury and sapped its political will, setting the stage for early 19th-century rebellions throughout Spanish-America. The Comanche Confederation itself put so much pressure on the Spanish that it almost single-handedly forced withdrawal from the Southwest (Anderson, 1999; Brooks, 2002; Hamalainen, 2008). At the same time, however, a dependency developed so that local populations came to view the Spanish occupiers as protectors. The forcible capture of women and children for marriage, adoption, and servitude was widespread among the southwestern Amerindians before the Spaniards arrived and continued into the late 1800s. There were slave exchange networks through which captives were sold or traded (Brooks, 2009; Hamalainen, 2008). Stronger tribes raided and devastated weaker groups. The Spanish introduced a new element as masters who gave protection to the tribal groups that became members of the newly formed settlements. There was shared interest in mutual protection. The Spanish offered a measure of security and stability. They also offered European goods that were in high demand.

Contrary to what is often the "conventional view," Spanish influence in North America did not simply disappear without discernible impact. North America of today continues to be profoundly influenced by its Spanish roots. The United States is populated by citizens who can trace their lineage back to the ethnic mixes that were generated over 250 years of Spanish presence. Countless American citizens retain family ties to surrounding Spanish countries and share a common cultural heritage. "Latin" culture has enriched the country in countless ways: literature, religion, food, song, customs, art. Our geography carries Spanish marks: towns, cities, roads, rivers, and mountains across America today have place names that are testimony to the extradinory range of influence.

Americans restlessly pushing west across the Mississippi River in the 1800s did not have to fight Spain for domination. A markedly weakened Spain left North America in 1821 when victorious rebels established the new country of Mexico. It was from this new country that we took possession of the land that was to define the southwestern and western boarders of the United States.

Settlement and Education in "New France"

Early French presence in North America was slow to form but was eventually expansive in territory while proportionally low in population. The French attempted to control a vast area but they simply did not have the available human resources to permanently hold on to their expansive claims. French fishermen in the 1500s began to ply the same waters off the Grand Banks that the Basques had centuries before. But unlike the Spanish, they were not interested in permanent settlements. They wanted places where they could come ashore to recuperate and dry cod. Increasingly, as the century progressed, the French found themselves in competition with the English. Both nations established trading settlements on Nova Scotia, New Foundland, and Labrador. To fend off English competition, the French were motivated to expand exploration and establish more permanent settlements. Expeditions up the St. Lawrence revealed the unanticipated finding that the waterway was the doorway to what turned out to be the richest source of beaver fur on the North American continent. Trappers and traders pushed inland to reap the benefits of the newfound bounty (Morrison, 1965).

The great French explorer Samuel de Champlain, considered the father of "New France," traversed a wide area, going as far south as Cape Cod looking for a suitable place to establish a secure French colony. He turned north and west and eventually settled on a rocky cliff above the St. Lawrence, establishing Quebec as a trading post in 1608. He went on to found Montreal in order to strengthen the French hold on North America and secure the river passage from the east coast to the heart of what was to become the French-speaking Province of Quebec today.

The French and the Indians

In the meantime, trappers and traders continued to push inland along rivers and streams in search of wealth. They explored throughout the north and on down the Ohio and Mississippi valley to the Gulf of Mexico, followed by Franciscan and Jesuit priests bent on saving Indian souls. Along fur trapping and trade routes, chains of small settlements and trading posts were established, some eventually turning into towns and cities that dot the landscape of America today with French names.

Unlike the Anglos, however, the traders and trappers strongly resisted expanded settlement so the French population remained small through the better part of the 17th century. The fur merchants wanted no interference by White settlers with their monopolies. Exclusive of Nova Scotia, in 1643, there were only 300 French in the rest of Canada; two decades later Quebec, the largest town and center of population, had only 550 individuals. A quarter of these were associated with religious orders. By 1700 the population of New France had reached only 6,200, compared to 130,000 in New England alone (Morrison, 1946, pp. 131–132).

Also unlike both the Spanish and Anglos, the French did not dispossess the Indians of land. To be sure, they had to bargain and barter for land to establish forts, settlements, and small farms, but there was no drive to take over large tracks of land from the Indians for their own use and profit. The French did not force Indians from the land. The French mainly wanted to trade, and this appealed to the Indians because they now had a source of European goods. Also, the French were not dogmatic about religious conversion, so those Indians that resisted were not subjected to harsh consequences. The French in the north were also unlike both the Spanish and Anglos regarding slavery. There were a few early attempts to import slaves, but the practice did not catch on. An economy based on small farms and trading could not make use of slave labor, and few had money to purchase slaves even if they could be used (Morrison, 1945).

To say that relative good relations existed between the local Indian populations does not mean the there was an absence of deadly conflict. Throughout the northern area, the French were caught in the middle of a struggle between the warring Iroquois Confederation and other tribes, and this conflict intensified with the increasing number of clashes between the French and competing Anglos. No one could stay neutral. In addition, misunderstanding and outright treachery resulted in sporadic killing, sometimes on a wide scale. As in the case of Spaniards, the greatest destruction of human lives, however, resulted from the contact between Indians and Europeans. Amerindian populations were wiped out on a massive scale everywhere the French traveled because of imported European diseases, of which they had neither resistance nor immunity (Diamond, 1997, p. 210).

In a remarkable feat of exploration Robert Cavelier de La Salle gave France claim to a large part of what eventually became the United States and left a legacy of French place names, culture, and ethnic inheritance. With a small band La Salle traveled in 1679 through what today is Ohio, Michigan, Wisconsin, Illinois, and Indiana; two years later his party undertook the journey down the Mississippi in the dead of winter, arriving at the Gulf in April 1682, and laying claim to a vast territory of what was to be included in the "Louisiana Purchase" by Thomas

Jefferson. As he traveled, La Salle came across the remains of the Mississippian agriculture economy that had succumbed to Old World germs.

Throughout its 200-plus years of existence, the French colony in North America floundered primarily because of the relative small population and an inability to bring under control the Iroquois who were allied with the English and wrecking the fur trade. This was the major source of revenue for the colony and its loss was catastrophic. The Iroquois were a powerful and well-organized confederation that hindered settlement. Centered mainly in New York, they protected their position as middlemen in the fur trade by killing rival Indians working with the French and blocking transportation down the Ottawa and St. Lawrence rivers. Frenchmen who got in the way were killed. For the most part, when the French were in armed conflict with the English, the Iroquois gave the English a decisive edge.

The Iroquois were kept in the English fold mainly through the supply of West Indies rum and superior trade goods. They continued to be a major hindrance to French conquest and settlement. The alliances with the Indians were complex and changing, however, and continued to play a role in the protracted and bitter conflict with the English that eventually ended with the French exit from North America.

Conflict and Exit

Taking hold of the situation, Louis XIV in 1663 converted the region into a Crown colony and appointed Marquis de Tracy as military governor. He immediately acted against the Iroquois Confederation by bringing an 1,100-strong regiment from France. Although not able to completely subdue the Indians, an uneasy peace was achieved for 20 years. In order to build up settlements, soldiers who remained were given land and wives. Over the next decade, 961 young French women were imported and the Crown offered dowries. Every young woman was married within two weeks of arrival. The offspring of these bountiful unions, when combined with the children of the unconsecrated unions of French trappers and traders with Indian women, made up a large proportion of what became the French Canadian population of today (Morrison, 1965).

The French attempts at colonization of North America took place against a backdrop of protracted, ugly war throughout western and central Europe. As the largest continental power, France was pitted against England with shifting alliances among the other powers, changing the dynamics of the ongoing conflicts. Hostilities extended throughout the Atlantic, Caribbean islands, and North American continent. This conflict reverberated throughout the shifting borderlands between the English and French settlements, with a constant seesawing back and forth as one side encroached on what was claimed by the other. Each side worked to thwart the designs of the other with intermittent warfare that enlisted the Indians.

In Europe, a divided France struggled with a population that went to war with each other. The French Protestants, known as "Huguenots," bore the brunt of brutality. They were intermittently but continually persecuted over a 200-year period. Early on, alarmed by the growing influence of the Protestants, Charles IX ordered a massacre on Saint Bartholomew's Day, August 24, 1572 (MacCulloch, 2009). Thousands of unsuspecting Huguenots were slaughtered. This lead to a mass, ongoing exit over the years to the New World, enriching the early religious and ethnic mix of the continent. To escape the religious tensions in France, Huguenots earlier had already settled in Canada, but now they came to North American in droves. More went to Canada, but many settled in New England and throughout the mid-Atlantic region. The English colonies profited greatly. This was an educated class that brought with them many skilled craftsmen, and importantly, women. Successive Huguenot migrations went on to swell the strength of the Anglo-American colonies (Johnson, 1997; Morrison, 1965).

The French dreams for a North American empire came to an end with the Seven Years War (1756–1763). The conflict was a showdown over control in North America, but it spread to both sides of the Atlantic; to North, Central, and South America; to the Caribbean; and as far as India and the East. Contempories termed the conflict the "war that set the world on fire" (Johnson, 1997, p. 124), and it finished the French in Canada. The capture of Quebec by the English general, James Wolfe, along with gains up and down the Hudson and St. Lawrence, and in Ohio and Allegheny, brought the French to the peace table. With the Peace of Paris in 1763 the French surrendered their North American claims and ceded all of Louisiana to Spain. After concluding that it could not hold the territory against certain future American advancement, Spanish retroceded Louisiana to France in 1800 and its presence in North America ended with the sale by Napoleon in 1803 of the Louisianan claim to Thomas Jefferson. But the English also lost. To pay for the massive debt incurred in the protracted conflict with the French, taxes were assessed on the colonies, which fed the already growing discontent; and thus began the colonists' first round in their fight for independence.

Colonial Education in New France

What was the French legacy in North America? Unlike the Spanish, the Catholic priests who worked among the Indians had considerable less success in establishing missions and schools (Buetow, 1970). The education that the Indians received tended to be incidental to religious instruction. The greatest success was in teaching the French language and in formulating alphabets and translations of religious material in the local dialect. They gave some tribes a written language (Buetow, 1970). As the priests followed the trail of trappers and traders, however, attempts to form permanent missions and get the Indians to inhabit the French forts and settlements generally met with failure. There were some successes, but the converted Indians prefered to live outside in their own communities. As Jaenen (1987) observed, "[T]he French never colonized the Amerindians. They co-existed, so to speak, within their areas, and while bound together by military pacts, trade, social communication, and often religion, they each maintained their own viable society under French sovereignty" (p. 59). For this reason, while it was essential for the Spanish to establish schools to train an Indian workforce that could sustain an integrated community life, the French did not consider this a need. The Indians continued to maintain their own settlements and the French maintained their own.

In the larger settlements populated by the French it was a different matter. Considerable informal training took place to prepare the blacksmiths, brick makers, carpenters, roof thatchers, wheelwrights, and other workers in jobs that benefited from the systematic transfer of skills from the experienced to the novice. The children of French settlers, offspring of mixed unions and Indians, made up the workforce.

The priests played a major role in establishing Catholic schools for French settlers—an educational legacy that remains. In Quebec, for example, the first elementary and secondary schools in New France were established in 1616 by the Jesuits and in 1642 the Ursuline teaching order of sisters founded a school for women. In Quebec in 1663 seminary training was established that foreshadowed the spread of the Catholic religion present today in the regions occupied by the early French. Again, in New Orleans the Ursuline Sisters founded in 1727 a school for young women irrespective of social or economic class that served as a model of instruction up into the 19th century (Buetow, 1970; Watras, 2002).

The New Orleans school included a day school, boarding school, and an academy. The daughters of Whites, Blacks, Indians, and mixed races, both rich and poor, were accepted. The children of the more impoverished families attended the day school free of charge, daughters of the "better classes" attended the boarding school, and the "cream" attended the academy to prepare them for life at the social and economic top. Religious instruction was central. Reading was the subject around which all other secular instruction revolved. Spelling was taught in the context of reading and penmanship was taught by copying model letters written by the teacher. Arithmetic and "industrial training" made up the remainder of studies. The vocational work was thought to be essential in an environment of uncertainty and want. To learn how to sew, knit, weave, and prepare food and nurse was mandatory to survival.

A model of instruction was devised by the Ursuline teaching order that was later duplicated by Joseph Lancaster in the United States in 1806 and popularized throughout the charity school movement. The scheme was simple and effective: the best behaved and highest achieving girls were chosen as pupil-teachers and charged with helping younger students by conducting drill and review sessions, maintaining discipline, and distributing and accounting for class materials. Each of the "dixainieres," as they were termed, was assigned a group of 10 younger girls to guide spiritually and academically (Buetow, 1970). The scheme was effective, and in the day when women were held to second-class status the school has to be considered a forward-looking exception.

Ethnic and Cultural Impact

Clearly the most profound and lasting influence of the French colonial effort was on the ethnic and cultural mix of the United States. In what is the upper New England region, in New York, and along the St. Lawrence waterway, many families trace their origins to French heritage, and in some parts, such as in the state of Maine, a dialect rooted in 17th century French is spoken to this day. Some French settlers pushed down into New England and even lower, fleeing war, religious persecution, or forcible deportation. Families of French heritage are scattered around the Great Lakes region and throughout the upper Midwest and down the Mississippi waterway.

The French Huguenots played a particularly large role in populating the mid-Atlantic seaboard. In 1685 alone, as many as 400,000 Protestants were expelled from France by Louis XIV. They scattered across Europe with thousands fleeing to the Anglo colonies. As suggested earlier, they brought a rich mixture of skills with them, enriching the intellectual, commercial, and agriculture life of fledging communities from New York to the Carolinas. In South Carolina, the French Huguenot refuges were welcomed, where they established the labor-intensive cultivation of rice in the coastal lowlands. Slaves were imported for this purpose, resulting in, as Morrison observed (1965, p. 97), "the first step in the conquest of South Carolina by slave economy." The Huguenot families of South Carolina continued to highly influence "southern" culture.

French Huguenots also populated the Louisiana area, including settlements in Biloxi and Mobile and surrounding hamlets in the Gulf states. To escape from the growing intolerance and war in the North, they fled by boat on the long voyage down the eastern coastline to the Gulf region and settled among the polyglot mixture populating the most southern French colony. Other French that were forcibly deported by the English following the conquest of French northern territory in the 1740s joined them. Thousands were deported by the English from French Acadia (Nova Scotia), giving us southern Cajun food.

The French Crown, realizing the strategic importance of the Mississippi gateway to its northern regions, sent permanent settlers to Louisiana, but Louis XIV was reluctant to send "useful" citizens. The continental wars had depleted the population of France. Instead, he instituted a practice also duplicated by the English, and cleaned out the prisons of France. Some of the forced immigrants had been arrested for crimes of violence, others for theft, debauchery, drunkenness, or begging, and others because they were troublesome neighbors or incorrigible sons and daughters. As expected, they proved to be poor additions to the struggling colony. "The French colonization of Louisiana became to a great extent a penal colonization" composed of the "rejects" of French society, Hall (1992, p. 5) suggested. These individuals joined a multiethnic population of Spaniards, Portuguese, Germans, Indians, and Africans that made up the bustling, disorderly, and largely lawless Gulf centers (Hall, 1992; Morrison, 1965, p. 137).

There was always a shortage of women. The early Louisiana settlers forged close relationships with Indians in the surrounding villages by marrying their women. The desertion rate among soldiers and sailors was high, as many fled to Indian villages where they sought refuge and took concubines and wives. Africans were imported in high numbers. By the latter 1720s African slaves outnumbered Europeans two to one. The French authorities viewed the African as a much better worker. Mulatto women were prized for their beauty. Most slaves came from the area between the Senegal and Gambia rivers (Senegambia), an area in Africa controlled by the French. Louisiana's Afro-Creole culture is rooted in the Senegambia, and in particular is linked to the Bambara people from the upcountry captured and sold into slavery by the coastal tribes (Hall, 1992, pp. 34, 40). Crops from the area such as indigo, corn, and rice found their way to Louisiana as did highly skilled metalworking, crafts, and weaving. A rich cultural heritage evolved, centered on New Orleans. The ethnic mixture known as "Creole"—indigenous French and Spanish offspring often mixed with African and possibly Indian—produced a dialect of mixed linguistic heritage spoken today (Hall, 1992). The descendants of Acadian French immigrants of the late 1600s produced the colorful Cajun dialect and flavorful cuisine that today is associated with Louisiana.

With the Louisiana Purchase, for a price of $12 million, the United States gained an area that would embrace 14 states comprising the major breadbasket of the country and a major source of coal and petroleum reserves. The French barrier to unrestricted traffic on the Mississippi was removed, and the way was opened for the conquest of the West and expansion to the Pacific.

Chapter Two
The Enduring English

The English impact on what was to become the United States was extensive, varied, and decisive. In 1700 few would predict that England would eventually dominate colonization. They were a relatively small nation, less powerful than either Spain or France. Their 18th-century naval power, however, was superior. The common element among the several dozen colonies established along the eastern seaboard was that from the very beginning they were intended to be permanent settlements for Europeans. The Plymouth and Massachusetts Bay colonies set the pattern for subsequent development throughout New England. The population was largely made up of farmers, merchants, and artisans; families were formed and nurtured; religion and schooling were seen as major social stabilizing factors; and an educated laity was viewed as essential to economic self-reliance and civic participation. A diverse population dominated the mid-Atlantic region, comprised of individuals fleeing Europe for religious, political, or economic reasons to join the English colonies: Dutch, French, Swedish, German, Swiss, Belgian, among a mix of other nationalities and ethnicities. The religious mix was equally varied: Puritans, Huguenots, Moravians, Quakers, Presbyterians, Hebrews, Lutherans, Baptists, Dunkards, Mennonites, Ranters, and Anglicans, among others (Johnson, 1997; Phillips, 1999). The diversity in population was reflected in the diversity among systems of governance, religion, and education.

The southern colonies were primarily formed from royal grants for commercial purposes under the administration of governors responsible to the king. The Crown and the Church of England had greater authority and influence than in the other colonies. Anglicans tended to dominate southern religion. They tended to be royal supporters in the English civil war starting in 1641, and mourned the loss of King Charles I's head. The Puritans in England were the ones who cut it off, so it is not surprising that religious tensions with the Anglicans existed with New England right up into the Revolutionary War period (Phillips, 1999). The economies were based on a plantation system that produced export crops of tobacco, rice, indigo, and eventually cotton, overseen by a small upper class of planters and a large lower class of indentured servants, unskilled workers, and slaves. The middle class was small, and in general the population throughout the southern colonies was small, poor, and highly dispersed among rural plantations and small farms. For middle-class children, limited schooling was obtained through the church; for the upper-class children, tutors were enlisted. Poor children had next to no opportunity for schooling. Indians and Blacks had none. In the case of all of the colonies, in the North and South, tensions with the Crown continued to frustrate colonists. The Mother Country itself was going through political and religious convulsions.

A strong base of secure settlements along a relative concentrated area was essential to gaining domination over both other European powers and Amerindians. These settlements provided the resources, communication networks, manpower, and stability for military success and economic growth and expansion. Schools became important to towns. They were a source of stability. Those founded in New England were among the first and most important.

Of God and Man: Education in Colonial New England

From the initial settlement at New Plymouth in December 1620 and subsequent voyages and settlements in the years 1623, 1628, and 1629, the Puritan foothold in New England was established. But it was the "great migration" of the 1630s that was the crucial turning point. As Morrison (1946, p. 61) observed, what probably would have remained a poor, isolated, and insignificant colony of small farms, trading posts, and fishing stations was transformed into a political and economic force. There was an influx of over 20,000 settlers alone in the first half of the 1630s before the Crown called a halt to the exodus. Similar to the French Huguenots, the large Puritan migration of that time was driven by the growing intolerant conditions at home and on the continent. Charles I of England was intent on checking Puritan influence and reestablishing "high church" practices that continue to characterize the Anglican church of today. Puritans were purged from high positions and isolated from economic opportunity. At the same time, the counterreformation sweeping the continent was suppressing Protestants. Life was becoming uncomfortable both in England and on the continent and it was time to go.

Leaders such as Thomas Dudley, Thomas Leverett, Richard Saltonstall, Theophilus Eaton, and John Winthrop set into motion the mass migration that resulted in populating New England with a substantial number of permanent settlements, adding a critical mass to the original colonies. Settlement spread south into Connecticut and Rhode Island and north into New Hampshire and Maine. As the century progressed, the population expanded much faster than it would have in the home country through high birthrates and relatively low infant mortality rates. Many children died, but simply put, many more children were born and more survived than could normally be expected. By 1700, the population had swelled to 130,000, which was 40% of the total Anglo colonial population in America (Johnson, 1997; Morrison, 1946). The Puritans fully carried out God's command to Adam to "fill the earth and subdue it." Any southern French migration along the costal area was effectively prevented by the expanding Puritan settlements.

The Puritans set out to build a new society, a "city on the hill" that would radiate God's will on earth as revealed in the Bible and through His covenant with them as His chosen people. The new colony provided the chance to establish a truer form of church, one that would point the way for the regeneration of Christendom. However, in order to preserve and perpetuate their beliefs they had to be always on guard and engaged in an endless struggle against the forces of corruption and evil, and against harsh environmental conditions. They had succeeded in leaving behind the religious disarray found in Europe, but they could not escape the struggle with pestilence, hunger, sickness, and death that surely were signs of the Devil's work. Dissention also developed among the colonists; and under the harsh conditions of the wilderness it was difficult to keep the colony together.

The family was the first line of defense. It looked after the physical and spiritual needs of its members. Adults and children collectively contributed to securing food, clothing, and housing. Children worked alongside adults in the fields, shops, and at home. Parents had the responsibility to bring up their children to be moral, pious, civil citizens engaged in an honest "calling." Church attendance was essential but instruction and religious observance at home played the larger part. Training in respect, duty, and morality was centered in the home. Also, the more affluent families had libraries of works on divinity, health, agriculture, law, and literature and their homes became lending centers for the communities to enhance both practical and cultural learning. Household manufacture was also common and a mainstay of the economy. When coupled with the fact that a large part of the economy was also rural and subsistent, this meant that boys and girls received considerable instruction by their mothers and fathers in the management of households, farms, and shops. Overall, a considerable amount of both formal and informal intellectual, technical, and spiritual education took place in the home (Cremin, 1970).

The church worked hand in hand with the family. Standards of behavior, and moral and religious values were established, the lives of community members closely monitored, justice dispensed, and church doctrine rigidly enforced. Formal schooling, however, was initially considered of secondary importance but steadily gained in importance as the colony grew and expanded. Formal schooling became recognized as an essential link in the effort to preserve and perpetuate the religious and cultural heritage of the colony, establish and maintain social and class lines, and foster economic progress (Curti, 1959). Formal schooling, even in limited form, provided assurance that a similar set of beliefs and behaviors were perpetuated, and formal schooling also addressed the concern that some parents were lax in carrying out their educational duties and responsibilities. Neighborhood households increasingly banded together to support education for the young. Out of necessity, community schools became established.

Governing in the Name of God

The Puritans dominated the spiritual and civil life of New England for over a hundred years before their influence crumbled through unreconcible internal conflict and outside pressures. But the impact on American civic, religious, and educational thought continues. During the colonial period Puritan intellectual influence took three major forms: the character of government, religion, and schools. On the very first voyage a "social compact" was formulated which established the framework for civic governance. The passengers were organized as a community divided into households with collective responsibilities independent of masters or the Crown. Additional decisive steps were taken in 1629 and 1630 when the colony backers formed the Massachusetts Bay Company under royal charter that granted a large degree of self-governance.

As long as the communities remained within the boundaries of English law they could elect officials, formulate laws, and "correct, punish, pardon, and rule" all inhabitants (Johnson, 1997, p. 32). Town meetings, neighborhood churches, and general courts provided a way through which considerable local self-governance was exercised. This eventually included running schools.

The pattern of organizing families by households was extended to neighborhood groupings, which reinforced local involvement. Very early, then, the practice of local, collective government was established which set New England off from the centralized, autocratic rule of the home country. More than two decades of intense political and religious conflict in England punctuated by a civil war that did not end until the 1660s gave New England additional breathing space free from interference to shape the colony along the lines defined by the leaders. The Crown and parliament were simply too occupied to intervene. A tradition of relatively independent governance was developed that inevitably spawned conflict as New England became a leading player in the events eventually leading up to the American Revolution (Johnson, 1997; Morrison, 1965).

Even though a small oligarchy ruled the colony from the top, their rule, nevertheless, had to be balanced against local representation. Families, neighborhoods, and local congregations were powerful political entities and could not simply be ignored in councils. To ensure that the rule of law would prevail over the power of individuals, a representative form of government was established, with towns sending deputies to lawmaking councils. In 1641 two remarkable documents were adopted: "General Fundamentals" and "Bodies of Liberties." The basic rights of citizens were established, including trial by jury; no taxation without representation; free elections; the protection of the right of life, liberty, and property through the due process of law; protection against self-incrimination; prohibition against cruel punishment and torture; and protection for foreigners. Cruelty toward wives was also forbidden unless the husband was defending himself from her assault. Cruelty toward animals was also punished (Johnson, 1997; Morrison, 1946). These and other safeguards of individual liberty were copied and spread throughout the region, their preservation becoming in a little more than a hundred years later a "cause" for the rebellion against the Mother Country. Similar safeguards also became the backbone of the Bill of Rights of the new nation. Early Puritan New England helped to give us a representative form of government and the rule of law that we have today.

But the New England Colony was not a democracy in the modern sense. It was a form of theocracy with the church functioning and intertwined side by side with the secular government. In order to fully participate in the running of the colony individuals had to be elected by all of the full members of the congregation. The church elders determined who were fit to be considered for nomination to full membership as "freeman," and kept the numbers at a minimum. This meant that political power tended to be concentrated in a small minority of ministers and church elders. The congregation also appointed, supervised, and removed clergy. While the clergy was influential, its influence was limited. The laws and norms of the community were shaped by religious belief, but there never developed a clerical hierarchy that defined with certainty church doctrine because the Puritans believed that salvation came directly to them through individual study of the Holy Book. Ministers were important as uniting leaders of the congregation, but ultimately the authority of God was to be found in the Bible, not the minister's words. This placed the center of religious instruction and education in the family, as suggested earlier. It was the responsibility of the home to ensure that the young could read, understand, and live by the Word of God. The Bible was studied daily both individually and collectively, and religious discussion dominated domestic life. The significance of specific biblical passages was debated endlessly, and events—good and bad—were attributed to God working out His will.

Dissention and Challenge

It took but a few years, however, before the colonists begin to squabble among themselves over what were considered doctrinal differences and repressive measures to control community behavior. Puritan communities became conflicted over the incongruity of an authoritarian oligarchy at one level and a form of representative, self-government at another. How could the two be reconciled? As the population increased, more families moved out into the fringe of wilderness areas where they fended for themselves away from centralized authority. It was difficult to maintain control. As Johnson (1997) notes, "[T]he elites proposed—and the people disposed themselves otherwise. Sermons, tracts, and laws say one thing; town and church records often show that quite different things actually happened. The New England rank and file contained many individualists who would not be curbed by Puritan leaders" (p. 6).

Societies attempt to curb dissention in a number of ways. Some early leaders, such as John Winthrop, increasingly turned to authoritarian rule in order to quell dissent and enforce beliefs. Those who would flaunt civic and religious order were severely dealt with. By today's standards, punishment was brutally executed. One could be hung for idolatry, blasphemy, adultery, perjury, theft, cursing a parent, or rebellion against parental control. A host of other "crimes" were punished by time in the stocks, whippings, shunning, banishment, and fines. Religious dissent was not tolerated and was checked by banishment, whipping, ear cropping, burning, or hanging.

The fact that there was no central authority to establish doctrine orthodoxy invited challenge and dissent. Very early both Roger Williams and Anne Hutchinson were banished and forced to flee, Williams going south to found Rhode Island and Hutchinson from Rhode Island on to what today is New York, where hostile Indians killed her and her family. Her "sin" was to think that as a woman she could speak out, express views on doctrine, challenge the clergy, and rally others, especially women to her views, and hold religious services. Williams challenged the belief that God covenanted with a society of like believers rather than with individuals, and that the church and state should be one rather than separated. His argument for the separation of church and state threatened the rule of the oligarchy; and his views on church and state separation were later reflected in the constitution of the new nation.

Rhode Island soon became a haven for the discontented, and the alarmed Boston oligarchy began referring to the colony as the "latrina of New England." Outsiders especially encountered the wrath of the Puritans. A Baptist was whipped in 1651 for trying to preach. Three Quakers in October 1656 dared to returned to the colony to preach their version of religion after repeatedly being warned and expelled. They were hung for the crime of "pestilential and disruptive" behavior (Johnson, 1997; MacCulloch, 2009; Morrison, 1965). The most notorious action against an imagined threat was the Salem witch trials of 1692, and the conviction and hanging of 18 men and women and the pressing to death of one man stemming from hearsay evidence of witchcraft. The motivation appears to be petty hate and envies and the desire to clean the community of "troublemakers," rather than any evidence of the Devil's work (Starkoy, 1949).

One fear that the Puritan constantly lived with was corruption from the outside. Isolated from the Motherland, facing a wilderness considered the abode of the Devil with the hostile Indians instruments of destruction, and lacking a police force or army to enforce law, the Puritans felt besieged and vulnerable. They lived with a continuing sense of insecurity.

From the very beginning Puritans lived with "outsiders." Among the 1620 voyage there were 66 nonbelievers included, and over the years there was a continuous influx of outsiders who did not share their beliefs. "Vice and corruption" was considered spread by outsiders who visited their seaports, traded with merchants, established shops, staked out farms and homes, and introduced new ideas. They struggled as a governing majority to retain civic control and protect their way of life. By the 1730s they had lost the struggle. If their laws were extreme they were in defense of the new home under threat. The potential loss of community control had to be countered. Flannery (2001) contended that within a decade "the religious fanatism of Puritan society had become extreme" (p. 274). MacCulloch (2009) suggested that the protection of home and community required explicitly defined laws and harsh, if not brutal, justice. Sin had to be contained for the good of all so individual liberty itself was circumscribed.

Puritisum was attacked by other believers for being extreme, but today there is hardly a Protestant domination in the United States that does not reflect the influence of the early New England theocracy. Whispers of their doctrine permeate Protestant belief: the Bible is the source of individual salvation; by faith and not works alone one is saved; redemption is a gift from God; life is to be lived in a way that reflects the Kingdom of God on earth; and self-governance is the foundation of the church community. The beliefs of early Puritans defined in large part what a Protestant is. No other single source probably has had a more lasting impact on American Protestants (MacCulloch, 2009; Morrison, 1965; Phillips, 1999).

Schools and God

How could the young be brought up in the light of God? How could the temptation of sin be held in check and the young armed against the invading influences from the outside? Schools were at least a partial answer. Lawrence Cremin (1970) suggested that schooling "was viewed by the colonists as the most important bulwark after religion to their incessant struggle against the satanic barbarism of the wilderness" (pp. 176–177). Education and religion worked together. One could not participate in religious life without knowing the "word of God," and for Puritans, this meant the ability to read and study the Bible. The scriptures were the key to personal salvation, so the young (both boys and girls) had to learn to read. And as suggested earlier, education also was a way to build a common understanding of shared community values and norms of behavior. The catechisms that the children studied taught them what to believe and how to behave. Daily behavior could be kept under control and individuals could find their way to personal salvation.

While initially homes and churches were left to themselves to provide for schooling, as noted this did not last and soon towns started to impose rents, cede land, enlist subscriptions, and allocate stipends to support schools and teachers. Barnard Bailyn (1960) observed the growing concern that not enough was being done to guard against the moral deterioration of the community. In the wilderness environment the old order was starting to crack: Dissenters challenged authority, family discipline appeared to be weakening, and Satan, always lurking in the shadows, threatened personal salvation by deceiving untutored minds. In 1642 the Massachusetts Bay Colony made parents legally responsible to provide elementary instruction. This law was intended to counter the neglect of parents in training the young in learning, labor, and worship. Five years later, in what is known as the "Old Deluder Satan Law," towns of 50 or more inhabitants were required to appoint and support a school master, and towns of 100 families or more both an elementary school and a grammar school. Apprenticeship was also made a legal requirement. This law was intended to check the threat of "that ould deluder, Satan." Without strengthening the support for education, the young would be kept from knowledge of the Scriptures.

In rapid follow-up, a 1648 law requiring compulsory literacy and job training was given enforcement teeth. The law provided for the appointment in local communities of "selectmen" who would keep a "vigilant eye over their brethren and neighbors." Parents found lacking were subject to fines, and parents that continued to be negligent could have their children taken away and placed in apprenticeship with responsible masters (Tyack, 1967). Similar laws were enacted throughout New England.

The importance of education was reinforced by religious beliefs. In early Puritan eyes purity of beliefs and behavior was essential, and they lived in constant fear of community corruption. The major argument that revolved around the banishment of Roger Williams was the issue of community guilt. If God, indeed, covenanted, with the community of believers, then the collective membership itself had to remain pure. This in itself justified Draconian measures to control individual behavior. The sin of a few could bring down God's wrath on all and it had to be stamped out. It was considered not only a right but also a necessity for the community to impose its will on society. The church, as well as the school, was essential to do this (Johnson, 1997, p. 67).

Kinds of Instruction

At the most basic level, the "common folk" parents either instructed children at home or placed them in a "dame" or "petty" school. Early dame schools were but a "normal" complement to the training by parents that was already taking place. A woman, often a widow, would undertake teaching the neighborhood children, usually for a small contribution from the parents. Primarily, children below age 7 or 8 attended and they learned the basics of spelling and reading encased in religious instruction, which revolved around memorizing a series of questions and answers set out in a catechism guiding the child through set lessons. Boys learned simple writing, arithmetic, grammar, and perhaps geography if a qualified "marm" could be found. The little girls learned needlework and cooking; but it was thought that they required little else beyond basic reading and the ability to count and work simple sums (Cremin, 1970; Webb, 2006).

As time went on, formal town schools were established. They were open to all children, but a fee was charged, often supplemented by the town. Often dame schools were simply transformed into town schools in order to conform to the legal requirement to establish schools. By the 1700s, the towns themselves began to directly pay teachers rather than rely on parental support. The precedent of public-supported common school education was thus established for the lower grades. The town schools also started to extend instruction into the upper elementary grades and eventually branched out into fee paying "reading and writing" schools. The reading school focused on the ABCs and religious instruction; the writing school was more advanced and comprehensive, with instruction useful for commerce (bookkeeping and arithmetic) along with reading and writing. Girls could attend, but usually did not. Many boys did not go very far in formal schooling, but rather went to work or followed the apprenticeship road.

For those who by choice or necessity wanted to pursue preparation for work outside of the home, apprenticeship was the main option. The apprenticeship system was patterned after long-established continental practice. Since the Middle Ages in Europe craft guilds were maintained which controlled entry into occupations and sustained quality standards. Unlike the Spanish and French, this institutional form was transferred to the New England colonies and was a major way the young prepared for work. For a fee, primarily boys (and sometimes girls) as young as 6 or 7 were bound by contract to a master typically for seven years. The master was considered a parental surrogate and had the duty to feed, clothe, and nurture the spiritual needs of the apprentice in addition to skills training. By law, reading had to be taught so that the young could become immersed in the scriptures. By the 18th century, the responsibilities of the master had extended to the teaching of writing and cyphering, and in some cases the youth was even sent to night school. Girls focused on learning domestic occupations such as weaving and quilt making while boys followed more technical or professional pursuits that would lead to wage or self-employment. It was not unusual for those wishing to go into "more learned" fields to have periods of apprenticeship mixed with periods of school attendance. In periods of critical labor shortage, it was not unusual for the time of apprenticeship to be reduced (Tyack, 1967; Vassar, 1965).

The colonial apprenticeship system was essential to the business, technical, and commercial life of the community, and without it the colony probably would have seriously floundered. Until complemented by academies beginning in the 1750s, apprenticeship was the primary way that the practical knowledge fundamental to the smooth working of the society was transferred to the young. Generations of lawyers, clerks, bridge builders, printers, soap makers, and wheelwrights learned and passed their skills on to the next generation through apprenticeship.

For those who had the means and inclination, grammar school was an option. For a fee, the boy could study the reading, writing, and speaking of Latin in addition to instruction in ancient Greek and occasionally Hebrew, accompanied by "appropriate training in piety and civility" (Cremin, 1970, p. 187). The course was for as long as seven years, but most boys attended intermittently, withdrawing for a period and reenrolling when circumstances and money permitted. Most did not complete the entire course, but used what they learned to gain admission to Harvard or to embark on a civic or religious career. The grammar school was intended to create the leadership of society.

The distinction between petty reading and writing and the learning in grammar schools, however, became less clear as financially hard-pressed schools opened enrollment to all and adjusted instruction accordingly. Most schools were small so they had to take what enrollment they could find. In practice, hard lines could not be clearly drawn. Students were mixed from different levels and kinds of schools, in addition to variation among students in a given grade level. Petty school students may work side-by-side with reading and writing students along with a couple of grammar school boys receiving individual tutelage. It was necessary to accommodate small enrollments by grouping students together under one school master in addition to the fact attendance may be irregular for individual students so that progress was not uniform. Institutional forms were blurred.

In order to maintain the religious character of the colony and to provide similar advantages experienced in England to their children, yet another educational layer was added in 1636: Harvard College. Privileged young men could prepare for the ministry or for leadership positions in civic society. Between 1642 and 1689, approximately half of the 368 completers became clerics and 42 public servants, including judges, councilors, governors, and permanent officials (Spring, 1994, p. 12). The first president, Henry Dunster, established such high standards of quality that soon Harvard became known for its liberal arts studies throughout the colonies and even attracted students from the Caribbean and as far away as England. Youth throughout the colonies seeking additional education went to Harvard, which Morrison (1946, p. 72) observed "set both the pace and the pattern for higher education in North America," both of which continue today. Other colonies eventually followed, so that by the Revolutionary War period, nine colonial colleges were founded, making up today's "Ivy League."

The concentration of educational institutions in the Northeast contributed to an emerging social and economic pattern that propelled political and economic development forward. Human resources and capital established the foundation for urbanization and industrialization. Cities and towns became important as commercial centers. By 1760, the Northeast had four of the nation's five urban centers, the South had one, and it (Charleston, South Carolina) had a population of only 8,000. Skilled and educated businessmen, technicians, and craftsmen established manufacturing capacity. Farming became less important and business activity, commerce, small manufacturing, and shipbuilding became the mainstays of the economy. Farms tended to be small and fed local markets. There was less social stratification than in the South and a bigger and growing middle class. The south increasingly became a supplier of raw materials in exchange for manufactured goods from the North, an economic pattern that was only finally broken in the mid-20th century. The North cultivated its own skilled labor, the South relied on indentured servants and Indian and African slave labor, an economic model from which it could not extract itself (Dinnerstein, Nichols, & Reimers, 1996).

Of Status and Class

Education provided opportunity in the North, despite a hierarchy of educational forms and practices, although caution has to be used in drawing sharp distinctions. Different clusters of educational experiences served specific populations and dovetailed with a particular social and economic notch. For the children of the common farmer and worker, instruction in the home and church imparted discipline and morality; work skills were learned from the father or mother, and loosely organized dame schools taught the mechanics of reading. The reading and writing schools afforded boys the opportunity to acquire greater proficiency in the skills of reading, writing, and cyphering and for some opened the way for jobs beyond the home into the expanding business and commercial fields. Children of the affluent attended private dame schools followed by tutors or reading and writing schools. The lucky poor boy found an attractive apprenticeship; the son of the wealthy attended a private grammar school with the promise of a prestigious job placement or admission to Harvard.

Education historians Merle Curti (1959) and Lawrence Cremin (1970) drew attention to the class character of colonial New England education. Curti argued that elite groups of dominate religious leaders and ruling authorities used the schools as a means to reinforce their authority and maintain social control. Joel Spring (1994) took a less sharp view and recognized that colonial schools for some "assumed the role of providing a degree of upward mobility" (p. 11). He suggested that different levels of schooling confirm status for a particular social class, and for those boys that are able to advance in schooling beyond what is expected of their social and economic class, higher status was conferred. The colonial grammar school was at the top of the status hierarchy and was mandatory to preserve or to achieve status. An educational hierarchy existed that functioned to both confirm and confer status.

Coping with the "Red Devils"

A particular worrisome source of outside corruption was the Native Indians. Not only were they nonbelievers, but they were considered to be infected by the Devil who worked through them to destroy God's "city on a hill." In contrast to the French and Spanish, there was little ethnic mixing. The indigenous population tended to be considered inferior, a feared subspecies that threatened their very existence. The untamed wilderness was considered a God-forsaken, infected place where the way of the Devil was manifested though the marauding Indians. The Puritans, however, were so focused on ensuring their own salvation that there was little interest in Indians except to guard against unexpected violence and to divest them of land. If, as Calvinists' beliefs asserted, only a minority of "chosen believers" were to be saved, then there was little chance that there would be any "elect" among savages. Why even bother to attempt to convert (Wilson, 1998, pp. 93–94)? Conversion, in contrast to the Spanish and French, was not an objective; it was best to eliminate Indians. And this elimination took a heavy toll, through catastrophic disease and conquest.

An early and particularly brutal way that the indigenous population was dealt with was the Perquot War of 1638. The outcome set the pattern for reducing native populations in the future. The war was based on the assumption that Native American and European societies could not coexist (Wilson, 1998, p. 94). The savagery of the Pequot War was shocking to Indians and Europeans alike.

Alarmed by the intrusion of colonists into their traditional lands in the Connecticut valley, the Pequot went about organizing resistance. In 1636, two English traders were killed, and the response of the colonists was swift, misdirected, and disproportionate. At a place called Block Island, 90 Indians were killed but most of them were not even Pequots. Retaliation and counterretaliation followed, with a decisive encounter by the colonists on Mistic, a major fortified Pequot settlement. A surprise dawn attack in conjunction with rival Indians wiped out the settlement and the inhabitants—600 or 700 old men, women, and children were burned out, with only a handful of surviving captives. Attacks by avenging Pequots were fought off and the remaining were hunted down and killed or captured. Surviving women and children were sold into slavery in Rhode Island and the surviving men shipped to a Puritan colony in Bermuda where they were sold into slavery. The Pequots were exterminated as a people. The Puritans rejoiced in God's sign of favor, and a pattern was set for the elimination of the Native population from New England (Wilson, 1998).

The Puritans took an eventual shift in balance away from the indigenous population as a sign of God's favor for thwarting the Devil's work (Flannery, 2001; LaFeber, 1989; Wilson, 1998). There were exceptions, however, as some viewed the indigenous inhabitants as more than unredeemable barbarians (Szasz, 1988). To counter criticism mainly from England, a strategy was developed that appeared to address religious duty but at the same time kept Natives isolated. "Praying towns" were established, separate enclaves under the control of the authorities where the Native inhabitants agreed to live. They were taught English and technical skills so they could enage in the manufacture of simple objects to sell to the colonists. Fish, venison, and berries were also sold. Religious instruction was stressed, but conversion was voluntary.

In a direct attack on the cultural and spiritual life of the Indian, however, any outward evidence of the denial of the Christian God or of a show of the Indian's spiritual worship was punishable by death. For an Indian, residence in a praying town meant nothing less then reputing an individual's ritual life; isolation from his kin network, community, and culture; and indeed, the loss of a sense of identity. The real or pretended conversion rate was low, but as Wilson (1998, pp. 94–95) suggested, the overall impact was lasting. Thus, another pattern developed among the English colonies: The way to deal with a troublesome presence of the Native American was through segregation, isolation, and control. The ghettoization of the "misplaced" became a practice of successive American settlements as they attempted to deal with ethnic conflict. Elimination, as with the Pequots, was also an option.

Cremin (1970) suggested that by 1650 there were some Indian children attending schools side-by-side with Whites. Also, in its charter, Harvard College mentions the education of both English and Indian youth. In 1653, a preparatory program was started for Indian children with college potential but there is little evidence of success. For Blacks, a few may have attended school, but there is no evidence of an all-Black school. For all of these endeavors little is known, and they probably remained at the margin. In 1755, Elizer Wheelock established a charity school for Indian children in New Hampshire, but it never got off the ground. Wheelock founded Dartmouth College in 1769 for both European and Indian youth, but few "children of pagans" ever attended.

Slavery was practiced in New England. The number of slaves was relatively small, but supporting the slave trade and supplying others made great fortunes. With an abundance of quality timber, New England became a vital center for shipbuilding. Ships out of New England ports bought, transported, and sold cargoes of slaves, primarily to the Caribbean plantations, but human cargos were also delivered to the Carolinas and Chesapeake region to feed the developing slave economy of the South. New England shippers also engaged in two-way trade with the Caribbean in rum and goods, contributing to their great fortunes.

The number of slaves in the North was limited because of the character of the economy—that is, fewer slaves were needed. Like the French in the North, the small farms could not use slaves. Slaves in the North tended to be used as domestic servants, laborers, farm workers, and helpers. Some engaged in fishing and building. Some Africans were given what amounted to as an apprenticeship and became skilled craftsmen. The increasing industrialization used skilled slave labor. There was a small, early population of free Blacks that came as indentured servants and achieved release, and some slaves were able to purchase their freedom, but the numbers remained small. While slaves in New England were considered property, unlike in the South, they had certain rights, the most important probably being their entitlement to a jury trial and their right to buy property. Overall, however, Africans tended to fare not much better than Native inhabitants: They were denied freedom and looked down on as an inferior species.

The triangle of religion, civic authority, and education also repeats itself among the Puritan colonies of New England. As in the Spanish colonies, schools were used to legitimatize the church and state. Instruction was designed to enforce allegiance to civic authority and adherence to the religious beliefs of the community. The church reinforced civic authority, and the civic authority in turn required undissenting allegiance to religious teaching. Church attendance was made mandatory in 1635, and even those who did not hold formal church membership had to contribute to the support of the ministry. Education at all levels performed a critical social control function. The social, economic, and political hierarchy was maintained; societal norms and beliefs were reflected through instruction; law and order was fostered; and work attitudes and skills were taught to the young.

Some Puritans went south to settle in the mid-Atlantic colonies. Some founded a colony in Virginia, and others settled in the Carolinas and Georgia. As Phillips (1999) observed, many more settlers from New England eventually worked their way west, populating areas across upstate New York and on through the Great Lakes region and upper Mississippi valley and eventually on to the Pacific Northwest. They carried with them a regional religious and cultural heritage derived originally from areas of Puritan influence in south and east England. This heritage set New England off from the mid-Atlantic region with its ethnic and religious diversity, and particularly from the Greater South, with its population influx primarily from Africa, Scotland, Ireland, Germany, and the north and west upcountry of England. These differences would continue to play out, and regional differences in America today continue to be deeply rooted in the colonial past. The Puritans also projected an educational heritage that would profoundly influence events as the new nation after the revolution struggled to define itself and forge a national identity. The common school movement of the early 1800s reached back to the colonial era, emulating both ideology and practice.

New York: Bridging the Private and Public

A year after the Puritan settled in Plymouth, the Dutch founded New Netherland, encompassing the Hudson Valley, Long Island, and the Delaware Bay shore, including what is today New Jersey. Trading posts were established in Albany in 1624 and New Amsterdam (New York City) in 1626 on Manhattan Island. The Dutch claim was based on Henry Hudson's voyage in 1609. In Dutch employ, he sailed up the Hudson River to Albany, where rapids blocked him. Trappers and traders established the commercial value of the area, and the Dutch West Indian Company was founded to exploit the potential wealth. The United Providences of the Netherlands (Holland) was small in population, however, and did not have enough potential colonists to press its claim. The colony quickly became multicultural in character as others were encouraged to immigrate. A religious cosmopolitanism also emerged. The major port of the colony, New Amsterdam was on the direct route from Boston to Virginia, and like most ports attracted a mixed population, including French Huguenots, Flemish and Walloons, English, Irish, German, and a smattering of Africans along with a sprinkling of other ethnicities. By 1664, when war with the English broke out, the population of New Amsterdam was over 2,000 (out of a total colony population around 5,000).

The province remained small and heterogeneous under the Dutch. The area surrounding New Amsterdam had Dutch farms, Long Island had a few dozen English farms, and to the west in the area of the Delaware River and south into what is today is New Jersey were a scattering of Swedish, Finish, German, and Dutch farms. The settlers were attracted by free land and concessions offered by the Dutch government. The Dutch West Indian Company promised to the colony that it would supply enough African slaves "as they conveniently can." North along the Hudson River valley was the domain of the great estates. Rich Dutch merchants and bankers profited by the "Charter of Privileges to Patroons," issued in 1629. In exchange for bringing over 50 people, a 15-mile stretch of riverfront along the Hudson was granted. These became feudal domains, ruled by the Patroon, generating immense wealth from rents, sharecropping, the monopoly of milling, the fur trade, and the issue of licenses and privileges. The wealth solidified their political and economic power, extending to after the English conquered and beyond. Dutch farmers, shopkeepers, and clerks of more modest means used the commerce of New Amsterdam or the rich surrounding farm land to amass wealth and work their way up the economic and social ladder, joining the Patroons as a ruling class (Morrison, 1965, pp. 75–76). An "American aristocracy" evolved, with its decedents continuing to be prominent in finance, commerce, and government. The small Dutch colony gave the nation three presidents: Martin Van Buren in the 19th century, and Teddy and Franklin Roosevelt in the 20th century.

Private, Public, and Church

The Dutch West Indian Company ran the colony, and its objective was to make money. Nevertheless, the Company was expected to promulgate the official church religion through schools. Schools also would attract additional settlers. From the very beginning the schools in New Netherland were the most complete example in colonial America of the marriage between private, state, and church interests. In New Amsterdam the Company established schools in 11 of 12 communities, paying for teachers; the city financed the school house and teacher's dwelling; the local government administered the schools; and school operations were carried out by the Dutch Calvinist Church, which also oversaw the licensing and supervision of teachers. Over time the financial mix was extended to voluntary and enforced subscriptions and tuition (Cohen, 1974; Cremin, 1970; Spring, 1994; Webb, 2006).

There was high public demand and support for schools. As Protestants, learning to read was essential to their faith, but schooling did not extend beyond the primary level. At the primary level, children of different social and economic class and ethnicity were in the same schoolhouse, and there appears to be little religious friction. Individual villages increasingly absorbed more of the cost, but there continued in both New Amsterdam and individual villages an ongoing struggle over financing. Any additional level of support was obtained through private means. Over time, in New Amsterdam additional private schools were started that offered a range of studies. Some private schools were connected to specific religious interests, but attendance tended not to be restricted (Cohen, 1974; Cremin, 1970; Spring, 1994; Webb, 2006).

English Conquest and Control

The Dutch had money, they were powerful, and they had the most advanced navy at the time. But their population was small. What was a friendly rivalry on the surface soon turned into a power struggle, with the English regarding the Dutch as potential enemies. War broke out over foreign commerce and was disastrous for the Dutch in New Netherland. A small English fleet commissioned by Charles II sailed into the New Amsterdam harbor in August 1664 and obtained surrender from the Dutch governor, Peter Stuyvesant. Both the city and province were renamed "New York." A new Anglo-Dutch war broke out again in 1673, and the Dutch briefly reoccupied New York, but with defeat in 1674 they made a permanent exit from North America. The Netherlands with a small population did not have staying power, and as in the case of most wars, by simple attrition they lost to an enemy that had deeper reserves. With the English triumph, the population swelled and continued bringing diversity with it. This set a future pattern in North America for the mid-Atlantic states.

The English, however, had to apply a light hand to a highly heterogeneous population accustomed to having its own way. The English tended to control the top offices while letting the machinery of government established by the Dutch continue to run. Schools continued to operate, but eventually the English authorities removed state responsibility and support. Some town schools continued, but in most cases parents had to rely on tutors, private schools, or the few domination schools established. For the very poor, a limited number of charity schools were started, and a strong apprenticeship system emerged, but overall, educational opportunity in New York became more limited, especially for those without the means to support opportunities for their children. Fewer children went to school, and illiteracy rates turned high (Webb, 2006).

Even though of relative short duration, the Dutch system of a combination of private and public financing coupled with multiple layers of support, administration, and operation appeared highly effective in a very diverse population. But the system eventually fell apart with

English rule and population growth. Support became more restricted and limited. This is perhaps unfortunate for the system was ripe with innovative possibility for the financing and governance of education in colonial America. Among a highly diverse population, the system was open to all children irrespective of social class, ethnicity, or wealth.

Pennsylvania: Diversity and Schools

When William Penn settled Pennsylvania in 1682, from the very beginning he was intent on fostering ethnic and religious tolerance. In Europe, he was subject to persecution for his Quaker beliefs and he was determined that the new colony would be free from discrimination. A gift from Charles II to settle a royal debt owed Penn's father, Pennsylvania already had a scattering of settlers by the time Penn arrived to stake his claim. Swedes, Finns, and Germans had moved in from the surrounding areas and established flourishing farms in the fertile soil. Philadelphia was a town of a couple of hundred. The early non-English-speaking settlers retained their claims. Penn also widely recruited new settlers from Europe among the Dutch, French, and Germans, and especially from among the English and Welsh Quakers who soon made up the majority of new colonists. Others came from Barbados, Jamaica, New York, and New Jersey to form an ethnic and religious mix that brought their rich variety of skills as clerks, accountants, brick makers, wheelwrights, tanners, glass workers, carpenters, and ironmongers to the new colony. Philadelphia and surrounding towns were quickly transformed into flourishing population centers. Within two years, Pennsylvania had a population approaching 9,000, and Philadelphia alone had 357 houses as it became a bustling port (Johnson, 1997; Morrison, 1965).

Trade prospered and farming was highly productive. There seemed to be unlimited land as farmers pushed westward along the river valleys and on to the low hills of the Piedmont and into the interior across the first ridges of the Appalachians. Trails went north and up to Pittsburgh, destined to become an industrial center of the nation, and west to the Ohio Valley. Pennsylvania eventually became the crossroads to the south and west. Settlers left ship at the Philadelphia port and went west, traversed gaps in the Appalachians, and traveled down the Shenandoah Valley to exit and populate southwest Virginia and the Carolinas. There was a heavy influx of Germans, Scots, and Scots-Irish. Others crossed the Cumberland Gap over the Appalachians and on to southern Ohio, Kentucky, and Tennessee. Still others went further north to cross into upper Ohio (Johnson, 1997; Morrision, 1965).

Early settlers as well as later immigrants and travelers brought their religious beliefs with them. Philadelphia became a center of religious diversity. To be sure, Quakers dominated, but others flourished. Presbyterians had a strong presence; the national headquarters of American Baptists was centered in Philadelphia; Anglicans, Catholics, and German Lutherans found a home; smaller sects, such as the Moravians, Schwenkfelders, and Mennonites were welcome, as were the Amish who continue to have an enduring presence today. In time, the African Methodist Episcopal Church, the first independent Black denomination, located in Philadelphia (Johnson, 1997; Morrison, 1965).

The Quakers are an offshoot from the English Puritans. This may be why they were harshly abused in New England. Apostates are not treated kindly. George Fox and his followers in

England broke from the mainline Puritans around 1650 over the use of the Bible and ministry. The direct word of God through prayer and how it touched the human soul is what was important to the Quakers. The ministry was not useful; listening to God was. All men were considered equal, and they refused to give allegiance to authority and even to have clergy. They called themselves "The Friends," but Fox's admonition to "quake before the word of God" apparently gave them the name by which they are best known. They followed the commandment "Thou shalt not kill," which continues to invite trouble from governments. Military service was refused. Like the French Huguenots and the Puritans, the Quakers fled to the colonies to escape persecution and the corruption of English society. They found a lukewarm reception in Rhode Island, settled in Nantucket at the back door of Plymouth Colony, and formed a colony in North Carolina. Within Penn's settlement they found a friendly home, and the Quaker population swelled in Pennsylvania (Johnson, 1997; Morrison, 1965; Phillips, 1999).

With a rich, vibrant population mix, freedom of expression and belief, advantages of geography and abundant natural resources, coupled with the security of wealth, in a remarkably short time Pennsylvania was transformed into a thriving province that illustrated the belief among early leaders that "man could lead the good life without monarchy, feudalism, or religious conformity" (Morrison, 1945, p. 131). The success of Pennsylvania was not lost later on those who were fomenting rebellion against the Crown. As Pennsylvania demonstrated, they did not need a king. Pennsylvania became a center of rebellion against the English Crown. Philadelphia itself was soon transformed into the cultural capital of the English colonies. It became a dynamic, affluent, and wonderfully complex city. It is not surprising that Benjamin Franklin, seeking to flee from what he considered an oppressive apprenticeship, went to the "City of Brotherly Love."

But the very diversity and tolerance also spawned challenges. This manifested itself through government and also schools. The Quakers controlled politics but they continually struggled to retain domination in the face of diversity. Granting the vote to others meant that they could contest for power. The Anglican settlers in Philadelphia soon formed political opposition to the Quakers. The troublesome Germans were the greatest challenge. After 1720, large numbers arrived in the colony. By the mid-1700s they collectively constituted one third of the population, the Quakers a third, with the remaining third spread among other ethnicities. At the same time, there were around 5,000 enslaved Blacks and a couple hundred freemen (Cremin, 1970, pp. 259–260). The fact that the Germans were divided among four or five different sects saved the Quakers. They could split the opposition.

The Germans formed schools in their own communities in order to maintain their language and culture. They also established newspapers. The Quakers countered. Laws were passed in 1727 requiring from male Germans an oath of allegiance and levying a 20-shilling tax on immigrating "foreigners." They were ineffective. Additional laws were proposed to restrict German immigration, prohibit the importation of German books, and suppress German printing presses. It was also proposed to establish public-supported English schools and require an English literacy test for suffrage. A measure was introduced to encourage intermarriage between English and Germans; in this way ethnic and religious differences would be fused. None of these measures passed the provincial assembly or Parliament, but they no doubt influenced attitudes toward the German population, growing, in the eyes of some, at an alarming rate.

Benjamin Franklin expressed fear that unless something could be done, the province would be "Germanized" (Cremin, 1970, p. 261).

One endeavor to check German influence was the founding of charity schools. Benefactors contributed money to support schooling for the children of the poor. The target was mainly the child of the immigrant German population arriving in large numbers after the 1720s. To the Quakers, they were a different class: poorer, uneducated, of questionable morality, and of suspect religious beliefs. Cremin (1970) contended that the charity schools were "agencies of deliberate Anglicization" (p. 261). Children were taught the English language, and "conformity to manners, and customs and culture." The effort was to counter home and community influence. The importance of this enterprise can be gauged by the fact that considerable sums of money were raised in Holland, London, and Scotland. In London the Society for the Propagation of Christian Knowledge among the Germans in Pennsylvania was established by an elite philanthropic organization. These efforts came to naught. By 1759 the charity school movement peaked out, and by 1764 the last school closed. The German communities simply would not send their children to the charity schools. They did not want them Anglicized. The Germans continued to maintain separate schools and churches.

Despite efforts to thwart German influence, Quakers asserted that they believed in equality. It is not surprising that they established early schools for girls, Blacks, and Indians, but we know little about these schools. Girls also attended mixed schools. The Quakers did not restrict the effort of others to found schools, and the Germans as well as other ethnic and religious groups did so in order to preserve their language and culture. Children had the option of apprenticeship, private, or church-sponsored schools. The Germans organized Franklin College at Lancaster in 1787 to train their own religious and civic leaders (Cremin, 1970, p. 268). But Pennsylvania continued to lack public-supported education until the common school movement in the 1830s. Religious and ethnic diversity appears to be a barrier against rallying support for the public financing of common schools for all children.

Pennsylvania illustrates the challenge of diversity. The Americas have always been diverse. When Columbus waded ashore he permanently introduced European diversity into a land already characterized by a very diverse indigenous population. America is even more diverse today. The Puritans attempted to combat diversity by stamping it out: Indians were to be converted or eliminated; foreigners would be controlled or banished; and religious doctrine and civic codes scrupulously observed and rigidly enforced. Dissenters were punished, eliminated, or driven away. Schools would be used to create a harmonious, homogenous society. The English in New York solidified rule at the top while letting diversity flourish at local levels. They could not do otherwise. As minority rulers in an established society they continued local practices. The variation in schools mirrored the variation in the population of New Amsterdam.

Pennsylvania is another early example of the attempt to use schools as an instrument of deculturalization. In variations that continue to find application in American schools, the politically dominant Quakers attempted to use charity schools as a way to blunt German influence. The charity schools were political in purpose and practical in outlook. They failed for the same reason that the charity schools established in the 1820 for poor children of factory workers failed. Parents perceived them as instruments of a dominant group trying to impose their will on the dominated. But early schooling in Pennsylvania is also an example of accommodating diversity. From the very beginning the colony was multiethnic and characterized by religious tolerance. Private and domination schools flourished.

Education in the South

The southern colonies represent a diverse mixture, differing in the history of settlement and in the characteristics of the land and indigenous and European populations. The South always lacked the human resources to carve out and maintain the large plantations. A considerable number of laborers and indentured servants were imported from England, and the population grew rapidly, but the mortality rate was markedly higher than in the more northern colonies. Edmund Morgan (2004) observed that "death was the most common feature of life (p. 77)." Extremely poor living conditions, endemic disease, and brutal and often forced labor took a heavy toll. Increasingly, Indian slave labor was used, and after 1720, a large proportion of the population was derived from Africans transported against their will and forced into labor.

A common characteristic of southern colonies was that they primarily were established by Crown grants and intended to generate profit. Most of the grant holders lived in England and relied on sons, relatives, or governors to produce a profit from the vast landholding. George Calvert, for example, the benefactor of a slice of Virginia from Charles I extending from the south bank of the Potomac to Pennsylvania, intended to use the province he named "Maryland" as the means to rebuild his family fortune. He used methods that were applied elsewhere—a "head-rights system" which granted land to everyone who brought out settlers at their own expense. In the case of Maryland, the grant was 100 acres for each man and 50 for each woman or child. African slaves counted toward head-rights. Wealth was generated by the quitrent, an annual assessment per 100 acres. Large grant holders also obtained manors, titles, and judicial powers over tenants, servants, and slaves. The incentive to populate the colony was so great that a recruiting office was maintained in London. The Calvert fortune was restored (Johnson, 1997; Morrison, 1965).

The Carolinas, obtained from Charles II in 1663, were so attractive that no less than 40 great landowners acquired titles, most of them absentee landlords; but Virginia passed all with 63 grant holders. They tended to carve out large plantations in the tidewater region. As in other southern states, in Virginia a wealthy landowning class was created that viewed itself as a New World version of the English aristocracy (Morgan, 1975). The basis was established throughout the southern colonies for an economic system of large plantations worked by indentured servants and slaves that generated great wealth for a few but brought undescrible suffering to many. There was a small upper class, a small middle class, and larger poor White class, many of whom were members of what was considered the "vulgar herd," and a growing and rapidly expanding population of slaves. The system was so fundamental to the southern economy that it could not be altered without the bloodshed of a civil war.

There was always a shortage of English immigrants in the early southern colonies, in addition to an early smattering of sons from the upper crust and self-made men as well as yeoman farmers. But for the first 50 years, the most influential proved to be men of middle-class origins who worked their way up to wealth and power. The largest class of Europeans that came to the southern colonies was known as "servants." A servant could be anyone from a wheelwright and construction labor to a fieldhand, candle maker, mason, tinsmith, or maidservant. The defining characteristic was that they were indebted for passage and once they worked this off, which took between five and seven years, and sometimes longer, they could revert to "freemen" and seek wage employment or become small farmers. Those with conditions specified in a contract were referred to as "indentured servants." But as Kolchin (1993) observed, most servants in Maryland and Virginia ended up as field workers where they had hard lives. Almost half died before their terms of labor were completed; many more ran away, but if caught and brought back they were subject to harsh punishment: whippings, branding, bodily mutilations, and extended servitude terms (pp. 10–11).

It was not uncommon for servants to be given help to reestablish themselves as freemen. In Maryland, for example, each was given 50 acres of land, a suit of clothes, farm implements, and three barrels of corn. Proprietors wanted to induce individuals to come and settle. Impoverished "gentlemen," poor laborers, failed farmers, "wayward" women, fleeing criminals, youth, and in fact anyone seeking opportunity or escaping home conditions used the servant path to a new life in the colonies. This was the main way that the southern colonies were populated and up until 1700 the major way that labor was supplied. But still shortages of workers remained. To establish plantations, found towns, and build road networks required immense amounts of human labor (Johnson, 1979; Kolchin, 1993; Morrison, 1965).

Below the servant class were prisoners of war, criminals, and kidnapped persons. Duplicating the French, under James I the practice was started and continued until the mid-1700s of transporting to the colonies Scottish and Irish prisoners of the extended British conflict at home. Most were sent to the West Indies, others to Maryland, Virginia, and New England. To clean out what was perceived as a growing criminal class, under Charles II, the practice started of transporting convicted criminals to the southern colonies. They were enrolled as indentured servants for seven years, but they were disliked because they were hard to control and shirked hard labor. Slackers were punished, and runaways were whipped, assigned to harsh taskmasters and more time was added to the terms of indenture, but they continued to be a troublesome addition to the colonies. A less fortunate, but apparently a substantial group over time, were victims of "trepanning." Young boys and girls were kidnapped off the streets by London crooks, hustled on board a ship leaving to the colonies, where upon arrival they were sold by the shipmaster to recoup the kidnapper's fee, transportation costs, and gain profit (Bremner, 1970; Morrision, 1945 p. 120). To this mix were added French Huguenots fleeing from persecution in Canada and France, a scattering of other European nationalities, and Barbadians expanding into the Carolinas from the crowded conditions on the Caribbean island. By the early 1700s, Germans and Scots-Irish were working their way south from the North along inland routes to settle in the low hills of the Appalachians and flat lands along river bottoms. Nearly a half million arrived in the colonies during the 18th century, constituting the largest European immigrant group. Many settled in the South.

Toward a Slave Society

Some enterprising colonists and local Indians formed alliances to kidnap individuals from weaker tribes to use as forced labor. As will be discussed later, this was not a reliable supply of labor, but its practice spread. It was next to impossible to keep individuals from escaping to join their brothers, and retaliation could be expected to follow. The practice of enslaving Indians inflamed the region. Indians were pitted against Indians, with settlers caught in between. Conflict came to a head with the Carolina Tuscarora uprising and Yamasee War in the first decades of the 1700s. The loss of land and fear of enslavement resulted in widespread conflict that bloodied both Europeans and Indians. The destruction of the colonies in the Carolinas was in balance. In the end, the settlers bargained for peace, but slaving among the Native population continued on a large scale with two significant shifts. English slave merchants turned to enslaving the Indians allied with the Spanish and French. And they also focused on exporting Indian captives to the Caribbean island plantations in exchange for African slaves. As the price of African slaves went up, exported American Indian slaves were in demand because they could be purchased in the West Indies for half as much. Carolina Indian slaves were also in demand in the northern colonies because they were less expensive than Africans (Gallay, 2002).

Slaving among the Indians had two long-term consequences. Enslavement and the collateral damage along with it significantly contributed to the depopulation of the southeastern region of indigenous Indians and made more room for Whites. Large numbers of Indian villages were wiped out, the food supply destroyed, many died, many were killed, and many fled out of the region. Butler and Watson (1984), for example, observed that the most significant factor about the North Carolina Indians is how quickly they disappeared. Another consequence was that the region also was kept in a heightened state of turmoil for over 100 years, and both the Spanish and French were weakened and their exit hastened.

The Carolinas became an early user of African slave labor. As briefly recounted earlier, in the 1660s labor-intensive rice plantations were established in the South Carolina tidewater. A slave economy was established as Africans were brought in to clear and work the land. The value of the plantation system based on African slave labor was demonstrated. Other colonies followed. By 1720, every colony south of Maryland had an African population that outnumbered the population of White "servants." African slave labor replaced White field labor (Johnson, 1997). The South became a slave society—that is, a society that uses slaves. Its economic and social developments were dependent on slave labor. Great wealth for a few was generated from the labor and sacrificed lives of slaves, Indians, and Africans.

In Virginia it was not until the 1680s that slavery took root. Virginia, as in other colonies, drifted into African slavery. The labor of White "servants" in the fields initially surpassed Blacks. Up until the 1680s Whites were the major supply of workers. Blacks worked alongside Whites, and the substitution of Black for White labor was not a big jump. Initially, in Virginia, African laborers were treated as indentured servants with a set period of indenture. Until the 1660s, baptized Blacks were eligible to be freed after their term of service was over. Some even gained head-rights, and some accumulated hundreds of acres and even had slaves and employed White servants from England. Mixed unions between Whites and Blacks were not uncommon (Johnson, 1997; Kolchin, 1993; Morrison, 1945).

But as the value of labor increased, slavery became lifetime bondage for Africans. By the 1680s, laws were made to keep Africans permanently enslaved. Laws were also made to free European men from the responsibilities of fathering mixed offspring. The racial designation of the child was asserted to derive from the mother, not the father, so that unlike among the Spanish, the mulatto child would remain a slave with no possibility to integrate into White society. Again, a child born from the union of a White woman and Black or mulatto was considered bound to conditions of servitude.

By the 1720s, the economies of the southern colonies were firmly dependent on African slavery. White labor was scarce and simply too expensive. In 1714, there were 60,000 slaves of African decent in all of the mainland English colonies. The number grew to 78,000 by 1727; 263,000 by 1754; and 697,000 by 1790 (Johnson, 1997, p. 74). Money was the factor. In the long term, African slaves yielded greater profit than did the use of White indentured servants; and women slaves were valued because they could produce more chattel labor. But this was not true until after the 1680s when the mortality rate among Africans started to significantly drop. It was not a good investment to buy a slave that would die after a few years (Morgan, 1975, p. 297). The supply of indentured servants from England also precipitously dropped while at the same time the acreage under cultivation increased. The labor squeeze caused planters to engage both Amerindian and African forced labor.

Similar to New England, it was a challenge in the southern colonies to keep law and order. Local militias were used to put down disturbances but there was no way to check defections by disgruntled workers. They could simply pack up and go off to somewhere else. Women were also in short supply so fewer stabilizing families could be established, and men complained that they could not find mates and settle down. Women were imported and sold by brokers but there were simply too few of them. Some men and women never escaped their servitude. Kolchin (1993) observed that "within the colonies men and women were bound out for indebtedness and crime, and a small floating underclass of laborers lived perpetually in the margins of servitude, serving multiple terms of indenture (p. 10). New England had the advantage of community units held together by common beliefs. Church and school were unifying factors, but this was not the case in southern colonies.

Schooling for Some but Not for All

Although Anglican doctrine dominated among the ruling hierarchy, there was no uniting religious belief, class solidarity, or feeling of political unity to knit the diverse population together. It is not surprising that the institution of schooling was approached with less enthusiasm in the South. For the most part, the population was scattered, and people in the small towns and farms tucked away in mountain valleys and along streams and in flatlands exercised a high degree of autonomy and independence (Morgan, 1975). They were also poor, and private schooling was out of reach. The large plantations in the tidewater and piedmont operated largely as independent fiefdoms, and landlords generally had little inclination or interest in wider education opportunity. Voicing what may have been a popular sentiment, the governor of Virginia, William Berkeley, thanked God that there were no free schools or printing presses in Virginia because an educated population "only brought disobedience and heresy and sects into the world." There was virtually no public supported education until the common school movement in the 1830s; and even then, the South lagged behind other parts of the country (Morrison, 1965).

The wealthy plantation owners educated their children mainly through tutors, and they sometimes extended this opportunity to wealthy neighbors. They also educated their daughters, thus confirming their social class, but most women remained uneducated and illiterate. The relatively small middle class relied on fee-paying private schools for their children. In some of the larger towns there were clusters of like-minded believers who took it upon themselves to support petty and reading and writing schools. Churches were used: The Catholics in Maryland; the Presbyterians and Moravians in Virginia, the Carolinas, and Georgia; and the Anglicans in all of the southern colonies sponsored schools for their followers. In Maryland the Jesuits supported through mission funds and tuition a school for teaching the humanities. In some communities, benefactors gave money for "endowed free schools," but usually the efforts fizzled, as the funds were directed elsewhere. There were a few pauper schools, and apprenticeship training was available and was a major way that poorer children acquired exposure to instruction. Webb (2006) stated, "Virginia was the most active of the southern colonies in attempting to ensure the education of apprenticed children, especially orphaned children (p. 85)." But overall apprenticeship opportunity tended to be limited.

"Old field schools" were the major way that most children in the South received a smattering of education. On depleted farmland, sheds and barns that were still standing were cleaned up and used to teach local children. Fees were charged to supply supplemental income to a local clergyman to teach the few students that could be mustered from the surrounding rural area. The field schools served children in isolated rural areas with a small population density. A no less illustrious person as George Washington acquired most of his early education at an old field school (Webb, 2006, p. 86).

The very wealthy plantation "aristocracy" sent their sons to New England or Britain for secondary or more commonly university education. Colleges in Edinburg, London, Oxford, or Cambridge, or Harvard in the colonies were typical options. After 1693, the first college established in the South, William and Mary in Virginia, was available, but it was probably not until around 1729 that it taught at the collegiate level (Tyack, 1967, p. 34). Most inhabitants in the southern states, however, had very little education, if any; the illiteracy rate was high; girls tended not to go to school; a small middle class acquired some skills through reading and writing schools, and some attended grammar schools. For some boys from families of modest means apprenticeship was an available option.

There was wealth in the South sufficient to support a broadly based education system, but it was concentrated in a relatively few families, reflecting the class system in England. The upper crust, largely of self-made men, had no reason to support education for the class of freemen. The wealthy took care of education for their children, and they wanted workers to stay on the land. Why support education for "common people"? The purpose of plantations was to make money for the landlords, not to support the creation of an enlightened citizenry; and as Governor Berkeley observed, education could be considerably disruptive of the social order.

There also was a lack of social cohesion fed by the ethnic, religious, and class diversity. Small groups of like-minded, middle-class citizens provided some education for their own, but there was little sentiment for the establishment of a more comprehensive system to address the larger population. The 'bawdy" lower class in particular seemed incapable, if not undeserving, of community support for education. Under conditions of scattered settlement and low population density, just the practical need to form large enough instructional groups was a challenge.

Very early there were attempts to educate Indians. The Virginia company and later the colonial government advanced the establishment of two schools, Henrico College and the East India School. Both were to be largely supported through donations from European sources, and they followed an administrative pattern later duplicated throughout post-revolution America. The church was brought into a partnership to run the schools. Resistance was encountered among the European population from those who thought that it was not a good idea to educate Indians. The Powhatan Indians went against the schools. Rightly, they viewed the stress on English customs and Christianity as nothing more than an attempt to undermine Indian tradition and religion and turn youth away from their elders (Szasz, 1988). The experiment came to a quick end with the Indian uprising in 1622 and the killing of George Thrope, the director. Uprisings in 1644 and again in 1676 put a stop to any education attempts among the indigenous populations. The Indians had little interest in adapting to what they considered a "foreign" culture," Szasz (1988, p. 62) suggests.

Chapter Three
Slaves, Amerindians, and Colonization

By the time slavery took hold in the colonies, the Atlantic slave trade had been marketing humans for over 200 years. Around the early 1400s, the Portuguese began establishing a sugar industry at various locations along the African coast, expanding in the mid-1400s to the Biafran islands off what is West Africa, and eventually on to the Cape Verde islands 300 miles out into the Atlantic. The enterprise, based on African slave labor, was immensely profitable. The practice of slavery expanded, and the Portuguese established markets that sold captives by the thousands, both in Europe and to plantations throughout the coastal Atlantic region. The Spanish occupied the Canary Islands and established a sugar industry. The labor force of slaves was purchased from the Portuguese, and by the time Columbus used the islands as a restocking call on his western voyage a slave pipeline from sub-Sahara Africa had been established. It was a matter over time of enlarging and extending it across the Atlantic to the eastern and northern fringe of South America and to the Caribbean (Johnson, 1997; Kolchin, 1993).

Slavery in Africa is old, the practice reaching far back in time. Prior to the Atlantic slave trade, Arab traders off the eastern African coast amassed fortunes in human trafficking. Suppliers reached deep into the heart of the eastern part of the continent for captives, a practice that continued during the time of the Atlantic slave trade. But the flow also went the other way. For over 300 years, Moroccan corsairs terrorized coastal villages along Brittany, and around Ireland and the England coast. In lightly armed, fast, small craft they struck villages in the very early waking hours before defenses could be erected, and carried away captives and loot. Merchant ships not yet far out to sea were captured. People and plunder were taken back to Morocco to enrich the kingdom (Milton, 2004).

Women and children were enslaved as concubines and servants; the men had an option of converting to Islam and serving in the Sultan's army, or facing a lifetime of hard labor. The extensive, beautiful royal complex that stands in Marrakesh today, for example, was primarily built with European slave labor over a 100-year period. It is estimated that over a course of time that roughly corresponds to the colonial period in America, 1 million slaves were taken from European shores.

A robust slave center also was maintained in Algeria for centuries. Captives from throughout the eastern Mediterranean area, the Balkans, and the Ukraine were auctioned off to European, African, and mid-East buyers. The number of slaves sold added up to millions (Drescher, 2009; Milton, 2004). By the time Thomas Jefferson became president, one fifth of the annual revenue of the new country was paid to the North African states of Morocco, Algiers, Tunis, and Tripoli as ransom or tribute money. Raids against American shipping and the consequential enslavement finally were stopped by military action both on land and sea between 1803 and 1805. The British finally stamped out slaving in the eastern Mediterranean around 1850 (Johnson, 1997).

The trans-Atlantic slave trade was different. The long Middle Passage was cruel and deadly, and on a larger scale than had been seen before. It was not uncommon for one fourth of the "cargo" to be lost through death, mutiny, or suicide. Also, the slaves in the Western Hemisphere were integrated into an economic system that itself depended on forced labor. It took a sobering toll on human lives. The average life span of a Caribbean sugar plantation worker was as little as three years (Shepherd & Beckles, 2000). The forced labor was hard and long, living conditions unhealthy, and there was no effective medical treatment. The smallest cut from the sharp edges of sugar cane could mean infection and death. Brazil and the Caribbean, in the words of Peter Kolchin (1993), "became graveyards for Africans and their descendants" (p. 22). "Within months of arrival," Ira Berlin (2010) observed, "many of the new immigrants . . . were dead. In all, perhaps as many as one-quarter to one-third perished in the first year from overwork, exposure, and disease to which they had but scant resistance" (p. 77). The high replacement rate generated a continuous flow of slaves.

Between 10 and 11 million humans from Africa transversed the Middle Passage. This forced migration exceeded the immigration of Europeans to the New World until the 1830s. Most slaves went to the coastal areas of Brazil and along the northern coast of South America, and to the Caribbean islands. A relatively small proportion went to the northern colonies, with around 600,000 to 650,000 individuals of African heritage distributed primarily in the South by the time of the Revolutionary War. But the slave population in the colonies grew from indigious expansion, becoming the largest in the hemisphere (Kolchin, 1993; Morgan, 1975).

Slavery in the Colonies

After the 1720s, the expansion of African slavery in the colonies was primarily home grown. African slaves in the northern colonies tended to live longer than slaves in the Caribbean, more had families, and women had more children, but the fact that stands out is that locally born Creoles lived even longer yet and they reproduced at an even higher rate. In the Chesapeake tidewater region, for example, African women had on average three children, the Creole women six. Elsewhere, slave deaths exceeded births, particularly in the Caribbean, but in the North American colonies it was the opposite. This increase in population no doubt was due in large part to the fact that women formed a higher percentage of the slave population in North America than elsewhere, more reproduced, and they had more children. Diets and climate probably also played a part in the population growth. For reasons not fully understood, the mortality rate among all slaves of African ethnicity dropped after the 1720s. Africans experienced after the 1720s, interestingly, the same population multiplication experienced earlier among New England settlers (Berlin, 2010; Kolchin, 1993; Morgan, 1993).

It was in America that Africans became "Africans," Ira Berlin (2010) observed. Africa was then, and remains today, an extremely ethnically diverse continent. Mandinga and Bambara differ substantially in culture from Ewe, Yoruba, Ashanti, Wolof, or Kongo, among the large number of diverse ethnic groups populating the West African slaving grounds. Ship captains cruised north and south as far as a thousand miles over months picking up a few captives at each stop until they had a full enough "cargo" for the transatlantic voyage. The coastal slave kingdoms reached far inland for captives, adding to the already diverse mixture in the holding pens waiting purchase and transport. In North America, slaves were intentionally sold in mixed groups to prevent the clustering of one ethnic clan. This was thought to prevent the building of solidary and rebellion. But the American slave masters had little understanding of culture differences, and referred to all slaves as "Africans." This was strange to a Benin Ibo, Angolan or Efik who thought in terms of a specific cultural heritage. It is as if Lithuanians, Greeks, Basques, Swiss, and Scotts were all lumped together with no recognition of their individual historical, language, and cultural legacies, not to mention physical differences. Transatlantic slaves lost their individual freedom as well as their identity; no longer were they defined by the language that they spoke; by the hills, forests, valleys, and streams surrounding where they had lived; by the stories that were told from the time of their ancestors; or by songs, dances, dress, and food that they remembered—or, in fact, by the very name that they were given at birth to reflect their ancestral bloodline. They were lost souls indiscriminately referred to as "African," exchangeable commodities to be exploited.

Newly arrived slaves were given Anglicized names. They were thrown together into groups where collectively they had to sort out among different dialects and English a way to communicate. African words and pronunciations penetrated deeply into everyday talk, and a speech patois developed that profoundly influenced the local dialect used by Whites and Blacks. To this day, in some sections of the country there are distinct language patterns that reflect words, pronunciation, and forms that are distinctively African in character (Blassingame, 1972).

The widespread practice of using imported African slaves initially emerged along the Chesapeake tidewater region (Maryland, Virginia, and the northeastern fringe of North Carolina). The inlets and riverfronts provided easy access for shipping; the land was rich and fertile; water was available and the climate suitable for growing export crops, primarily tobacco. After the 1720s, slave importation stepped up rapidly. In the Chesapeake region during the 1730s as many as 2,000 imported slaves flowed annually to the plantations. Between 1700 and 1750, Virginia alone imported 45,000 slaves, roughly doubling the slave population. By the time of the Revolutionary War, the slave population in Maryland and North Carolina totaled one third of the overall population, and in Virginia two fifths. In some areas, the population of slaves was as high as 40% of the total population, excluding Native Americans. Most of the Black population was located on large plantations along the tidewater. By the 1750s, however, the importation of slaves dropped as locally born Creoles increasingly replaced Africans (Berlin, 2010, pp. 68–70; Kolchin, 1993, pp. 24–25; Morgan, 1975, p. 301).

In the lower South along the coastal areas of South Carolina and Georgia, and in southeastern North Carolina, the use of slaves lagged until rice cultivation expanded, then spiraled upward, surpassing the slave population of the Chesapeake with more than 250,000 Africans imported. In 1708 there were 3,960 free Whites, 4,100 African slaves, and 1,400 Indian slaves in South Carolina. Indentured servants numbered a small 120. The preponderance of Africans remained, so that on the eve of the Revolutionary War the slave population throughout the lower South was in the majority. The increase continued as the lower South became the largest slave-importing region following the Revolutionary War (Berlin, 2010, pp.70–71; Kolchin, 1993, pp. 24–26).

Almost a third of the African slave population in North America, however, was in the Spanish and the southern French territory. There were a few Spanish African slaves scattered throughout the southwestern region, but the large majority were concentrated in the Gulf region, and in particular in Louisiana, where slaves eventually outnumbered Whites two to one. The first slave ships arrived in Louisiana from Africa in 1719, and by 1731 an additional 23 ships had followed. African slaves also were procured from the Caribbean islands where two Indian slaves were exchanged for one African (Hall, 1992, p. 59). As a general rule, Blacks were preferred over Whites because they were considered superior workers and their mortality rate was considerably lower. Disease, lack of sanitation, and malnourishment struck down Europeans in droves. It was also hard to get the motley collection of Europeans to work, many preferring to strike off to live with the Indians or to use their own whit in smuggling and thieving. The French and Spanish ruling classes also lacked cohesion and control, resulting in fractionalization (Hall, 1992, pp. 73, 160).

The importation and growth of African and Creole populations in the mideastern seaboard and New England states was limited. As suggested earlier, slaves were used in much smaller numbers because the farm economy was on a much smaller scale. There were exceptions, such as the plantations along the Hudson River valley and in New Jersey, but the much smaller family farms that grew limited commercial crops did not need slave labor. The slaves in the mid-Atlantic and northern colonies also tended to be used in more skilled capacities as craftsmen, household service workers, stable tenders, construction workers, or as day laborers. Slavery was not fundamental to the economy. Slaves were used in society, but they were not slave societies. By the 1750s, the already modest level of slavery slackened (Kolchin, 1993, p. 27).

Throughout the country, north and south, a considerable number of slaves lived dispersed on small land holdings, but at the same time there was a high proportion of the White population that owned no slaves or were against the practice. According to Kolchin (1993), 77% of the South Carolina backcountry households in 1790 had no slaves, with even fewer slave owning households in the backcountry of Virginia and North Carolina. "Although the South was a slaveholding society, substantial numbers of southerners had no direct interest in or experience with slavery (p. 33)." Those not owning slaves, moreover, were kept powerless by laws that included slave-owning and property ownership as voting qualifications, thus generating much friction between groups. Slaveholders had a limited and unsure hold on society, and potential conflict within the White population was never far from the surface. Slaves threatened to undermine the supply of jobs that non-property owning, lower class Whites relied on, thus hardening racial lines (Kolchin, 1993, p. 34).

Slavery threw different peoples together, but this did not prevent small groups from forming and plotting rebellion and escape. Plantation owners were constantly on guard to thwart runaways. Small- and large-scale rebellions were always a threat. A major source of fear was the alliances formed with Indians. Both were united by the abuse of Whites. Slavery was coercive and brutal, and barbarous repression and punishment only brought more bitter resentment. Rebelling runaway Africans joined with Native Americans as they formed raiding parties and fought neighboring Indian slavers and Europeans. They became a lethal combination and a constant source of resistance (Gallay, 2002, pp. 348–349). The Seminoles, for example, with numbers strengthened by Africans were never completely conquered and subdued. Africans and Indians tended to intermix, so that today there is throughout the Southeast an ethnicity formed by the two along with European blood to produce a distinct people. Future DNA sampling will unravel the complexities of this distinctly American combination.

Early on, Europeans also mixed so that there are bloodlines that incorporate West African lineages in combination with English, French, and Spanish. Some unions were sought after and voluntary, particularly prior to the 1700s; others were forced, brutal unions; and still others consensual. Recent DNA testing, for example, shows that a small ethnically similar group living on the Appalachian Tennessee-Virginia border, referred to as "Melungeon," descended from unions of Black and White mid-1600 indentured servants from Virginia before slavery took hold. The Montauks and Mantinecocks in New York; the Pools in Pennsylvania; the Lumbees, Waccamaws, and Haliwas in North Carolina; the Redbones, Buchkheads, Yellowhammers, and Creels in South Carolina; and the Redbones and Creoles in Lousinana are examples of mix-ancestry people. During the 1600s and 1700s it was not uncommon for Whites and Blacks to marry but a release had to be obtained from the slave owner and permission from the civic authorities. Among "upper class" men, it was common practice to take African concubines. The legal structure partly promoted this. If a wife died, her children were left with no inheritance if the father remarried; the offspring of the new union received all. As Annette Gordon-Reed (2008) documented, this is the case with Thomas Jefferson when he took Sally Hemmings as a concubine followings the death of his wife, fathering seven children, four surviving. Sally herself was a half sister to Jefferson's wife and her four other slave siblings were similarly related. Millions of Americans are of mixed heritage. Of all of the ethnic heritages that make up the mosaic of what is America, that of the west coastal Africans is among one of the most consequential.

The education of slaves was almost nonexistent. In a self-serving argument, Europeans deemed Africans "brutish people" only fit for labor. "Having Africans judged intellectually and spiritually inferior to all other humans, the slavers devoted little thought to elevating Africans' status or incorporating them fully within European or colonial societies" (Gallay, 2002, p. 47). Craft skills were taught to some, but in colonial America there appears to be no successful record of any systematic effort to provide education to individuals of African heritage. There was no incentive: They were meant to work and remain on the fringe of society. The teaching of reading was discouraged and eventually made illegal because a literate population was more likely to rebel. There were a few efforts in the northern colonies to provide schooling for freemen, but we know little about how successful they were or how long they lasted. Some educational opportunity was extended after the Revolutionary War, and as many as 5% of the slave population had learned to read by the time of the Civil War. But most Americans of African heritage had to wait until the 20th century before educational opportunities opened on a wider scale.

The Original Occupants

There is still only partial understanding of the origins of the first occupants of the Americas. The ancestors of most Amerindians apparently crossed over from Asia on a land bridge formed in the narrows of the Bering Strait linking Asia and Alaska. At different times a number of small bands crossed and worked their way down the northern continent, perhaps along the coast or though a divide formed about 13,000 years ago in the great ice sheet covering what is Canada today. But this cannot be the full story, or even the correct story. In 1997 an archaeological dig in southwestern Chile found evidence of human habitation over 12,000 years ago, making an earlier date when there was no longer a gap in the ice sheet necessary to account for the long traverse from the north. Subsequent diggings show evidence of habitation even 20,000 to 30,000 years ago. Did early inhabitants come from a southern Pacific origin along a route passing through Australia? Along the eastern U.S. coast at the Meadowcroft Rockshelter in western Pennsylvania, artifacts dating to more than 19,000 years ago were found, pointing to early habitation. In Richmond, Virginia, stone tools more than 15,000 years old have been found; and near Charleston, South Carolina, small tools of a similar age were unearthed (Olson, 2002). Is a European origin possible? The Clovis point, a mainstay of the supporters of the Asian crossing theory because of its date of origin, has no counterpart in Asia, but its distinctive fluted spearhead is similar in size and design to the work of the Solutrean people in southwest France and Portugal dating to 22,000 years ago. The Clovis point culture also appeared in southern North America before spreading north (Olson, 2002). Did these people work their way along in a long arch across the Atlantic through the frozen north to become among the first inhabitants of the Americas?

Recent DNA evidence also is throwing light on the complexity of the origins of Amerindians. In work by Douglas Wallace and his group, almost all Amerindians are found to belong to one of four mitochondrial haplogroups, three of which are common to Asia. But in Asia there is wide geographical dispersion among the matching haplogroups, ranging from the coast of China and Southeast Asia to the border of Mongolia and Siberian Russia and farther west to Lake Baikal. Others belong to the fourth group, but the origins in Asia are not completely clear. An additional haplogroup has been found among the Algonquian-speaking population around the Great Lakes in the United States, but surprisingly, there is a relationship with haplogroups among the Druze, Italian, and Finnish populations. The mystery deepens. Additional analysis of mitochondrial DNA by others shows dates of origin at 30,000 to 40,000 years. The story of the Amerindians is not complete (Mann, 2005; Olson, 2002).

Linguistics provide clues to the Amerindians, but distinctions remain clouded. Wilson (1998) suggested perhaps there are "twelve quite distinct and apparently unrelated linguistic groups" (p. 21). This diversity probably supports a multiorigin thesis. Others hypothesize an even larger number of language groups. In California alone there appears to be 86 "tongues" divided into between 5 and 15 larger family groups. Across the continent, 180 different linguistic families have been identified (Mann, 2005, p. 164). Yet others refute the claim of many distinct language groups. Joseph Greenberg and his colleagues at Stanford University analyzed over four decades thousands of Indian vocabularies and grammars and came up with three large groupings: Aleut, spoken by people along the northern tier of the continent; Na-Dene', common to western Canada and the Southwest; and an extremely large grouping, Amerind, the most common and widely spoken throughout the remainder of the continent, and Central and South America. Greenberg sees these groups as corresponding with major Amerindian migrations (Mann, 2005, pp. 164–165). His contentions are not widely accepted, and debate, some heated, continues.

America's largest linguistic and ethnic stock (20% of Amerindians) appears to be the Algonquians who occupied a large area from east of the Rockies to the Atlantic coast, and from the Great Lakes to the Carolinas. Thousands of dialects spoken by related tribes are nested within the mother language. A smaller language group, Iroquoian, is the language of the Iroquoian confederation centered in New York and the surrounding area, spilling over into the Ohio Valley and into parts of Kentucky and Tennessee. There is a narrow band of Iroquoian-related groups that knifes through Pennsylvania, Maryland, Virginia, and on down to the Carolinas. There is a smaller eastern language group comprising Siouan. They are in the Dakotas and Plains states, but the same linguistic family extends east of the Mississippi along the Appalachians and down into the Carolinas. Similar wide ranges in language groups can be found among western Indians and illustrates the considerable dispersal of people within a similar ethnic grouping. Offshoots of parent groups are found hundreds of miles apart and relatives apparently traveled great distances to see one another. Restrictions on marriage within the tribe means that the extended networks of related groups probably were tapped for wives and husbands (Butler & Watson,1984; Wilson, 1998).

It is not clear how many Amerindians peopled the continents when the Europeans came following Columbus's landfall. Fifty years ago it was common to estimate around 9 million or less in North America, with some estimates as low as 1 million (Olson, 2003; Wilson, 1998). These figures surely are low and serve to reinforce the argument that the continent was largely an undeveloped wilderness free for the Europeans to take, subdue, and populate. More recent estimates establish figures between 75 and 100 million, including both continents and Central America. At the time Europe had a population of 70 million, and the British Islands itself had a population of around 5 million (Olson, 2002; Wilson, 1998). But the gruesome death rate among the Amerindians quickly decimated the indigenous population. Traders plying the New England coast before the Europeans settled report that on return voyages they found whole villages wiped out by the diseases that the Europeans brought along with them on prior voyages. Mortality rates of 90% to 100% were not uncommon in areas of early European contact (Diamond, 1997; Wilson, 1998).

Following Columbus's landfall, the Caribbean Indians were quickly annihilated through slavery, war, and disease. Death followed Hernando de Soto as he and his troop tramped through Florida, up into the Carolinas, across Georgia and Alabama, and up the Mississippi Valley in 1541. A maturing agriculture economy was wiped out as the inhabitants along the waterway disappeared. What remained of the great Mound Builders society was obliterated. Disease and death spread into the upper Mississippi and Ohio valleys and the upper Midwest as infected Indians traveled north and west. The Southwest, Plains, and Western Indians experienced catastrophic human losses as the Spaniards advanced. The French, Dutch, and English spread death through infectious microbes everywhere they went. Overall, the Amerindian population was reduced on a massive scale never experienced before in recorded history through the introduction of European killer diseases for which there was no natural immunity: smallpox, measles, influenza, and typhus were the four big killers. Smallpox was almost always fatal. Diphtheria, malaria, mumps, yellow fever, tuberculosis, cholera, and plague also spread death (Diamond, 1997). The Amerindians did get a small degree of revenge. Syphilis was introduced (or reintroduced) into Europe where it ravaged the population with no distinction between social class and wealth (Olson, 2002).

Estimates of the New England population before European colonization are as high as 140,000; by 1670 the numbers were reduced to an estimated 8,600. At the same time, the European colonial population was over 50,000. The Massachusetts tribe was reduced from 24,000 to 750 by 1631, during the time when 20,000 new Puritan colonists arrived. By 1640, both the Huron and Iroquois populations in the Northeast were reduced by half. In the Deep South, the Indian population was drastically reduced through the spread of disease by early Spanish explorers the 1500s. The region was hit a second time just as it was recovering as the English brought death by disease in the 1600s. Whole Indian towns were destroyed throughout the region. Explorers, trappers, and missionaries were leading carriers of infection. They pushed into areas of no previous contact with Europeans with catastrophic results. The arrival of Jesuit missionaries among the Huron in 1634, for example, was followed by extreme reduction of the population (Starkey, 1998).

The overall mortality rate over time among Amerindians may have been as high as 90%, but we do not know for sure. But we do know that it was incredibly high. Europeans did not have to be present. All there had to be was an initial infection for deadly microbes to spread. Jon Reyner and Jeanne Eder (2004) estimated that by the beginning of the 20th century there were only a little over 200,000 indigenous citizens in North America. This does not count mixed populations. Millions of Americans have Amerindian genes in their DNA, even if only in small amounts, and the Native American population has recovered somewhat, but as a society it is difficult to escape from the human and cultural loss that cannot be replaced.

The Indians were continually at war with rival populations. The clan structure was so tightly knit that outsiders were not recognized except as potential captive additions to increase tribal numbers. Young males, women, and children were targets for capture. Young male captives were prized as replacements for war losses, captive women reproduced, and as little children grew they could be fully integrated into the clan. As discussed previously, the Europeans capitalized on Indian warfare by aligning themselves with different warring groups. The Native Americans were superior at frontier fighting and could not be beaten by Europeans alone. By arming one Indian group against another the Europeans could win. The Puritan war with the

Pequot was won by the intervention of the Narragansett and Niantic Indians, for example, and the Tuscarora and Yamasee were only defeated when the English were able to muster Indian allies. The power of Indian alliances was also used against other Europeans. The English used Indian allies to attack the Spanish missions in Florida, for example, and 90 of 92 missions were wiped out (Gallay, 2002). It was not until the period of the Revolutionary War that tactics and firearms improved to the point that Europeans could battle Indians head-to-head and win. But by this time, Native power had been severely reduced. Starkey (1998) argued that successful settlement by the colonists was not a triumph of arms but rather conquest by the stealth of microbes. He states that "war may have been the least important vehicle of European conquest. Epidemic disease killed far more native people than did muskets or cannon and undermined the resistance of many tribes... waves of European epidemic diseases devastated Indian communities" (p. 7).

The contention that North America was a big, open, largely empty space waiting for the civilizing influence of the Europeans is a myth. Every inch of the continent was claimed and used by tribal groups. The Europeans were puzzled by the fact that there appeared to be no neatly defined boundaries, and large areas that were claimed were apparently left unsettled. A typical comment by Europeans was that Native Americans roamed over the land rather than inhabiting it. There were boundaries that the tribal groups understood, but they followed the contours of rivers, valleys, and mountains and they were marked by trails, streams, rocks, and mountains; the areas lacked the geometrical shape from surveying that Europeans expected. To be sure, the Native Americans had permanent settlements, but whole villages tended to leave for months at a time to harvest seasonal nuts and berries, follow fish runs, and hunt migrating animals. These food-gathering excursions were essential to stock up for the winter. Throughout the year, small individual hunting parties would forge hundreds of miles for game. Moreover, whole villages would periodically move. Indians lacked large domestic animals to use for plowing so they resorted to intensive, dense farming methods that exhausted soil fertility. Game also became depleted. It was necessary to move considerable distances in order to let land and animals regenerate. The new location could not overlap the former farming and hunting areas (Diamond, 1997; Wilson, 1998). A hunting-gathering culture required vast amounts of land in contrast to a permanently rooted farming economy, and only a part of it was used on a semipermanent basis for any length of time. Even in settlements, Morrison (1945, p. 107) estimated that it took 20 times more land to support an Indian than it did an Englishman.

Land was at the center of the conflict with Europeans. Amerindians did not individually own land. Unlike the Europeans, they did not have the concept of private property, and individuals had very few personal possessions. Property permanently belonged to the larger clan and use was allocated with each generation. Work was communal; the harvest was communal; and the bounty of the hunt was communal. Children belonged to the clan rather than to the parent. Native Americans were surprised and puzzled over land transactions with Europeans. In the eyes of Native Americans, this was an exchange to cement a reciprocal relationship, an exchange of gifts that would draw the two parties closer together. But the Europeans erected fences, kept the Indians off, and continually wanted more land. They freely encroached on hunting grounds and killed off the game that was essential to Indian survival. They destroyed a way of life. When formal treaties were agreed upon, they were quickly broken with Europeans occupying land that was to be set aside for Indian use. The major root of conflict was that the invasion of Europeans could not be stopped. They kept coming. The only way to expand was onto Indian land.

In addition to economic exploitation, a clash of cultures was central to the conflict between the encroaching Europeans and the Native populations. The Europeans ardently believed that they were superior to the "savages" that they confronted. They were more culturally advanced, their technology was better, and certainly, their God was superior. The colonists viewed what they considered grotesque religious rites of the Indians with a mixture of disgust and foreboding. The Indians appeared to be paying homage to a pantheon of devils that if unleashed could bring destruction to a colonial existence that already was tenuous (Terrell, 1979; Furnas, 1969). The very fact that Indians had darker skins also cast them as imperfect humans.

The Indians in turn were perplexed by practices of the Europeans. Colonial women, for example, were considered subservient to men and they had few rights. Indian women had clearly defined rights and power that men could not abridge. Marriage was not a property transaction, like it is among European societies. Some tribes were matriarchal, with women picking the male tribal leaders. In some cases, women became tribal leaders. Norms of sexual behavior were starkly different. In some tribes, marriage was communal. European men marrying Indian women had to adjust to the fact that women were free to select additional partners whenever and if they wanted. Wilson (1996) observed that Indians in the Southwest "regarded pre-marital sex, serial monogamy . . . and polygamy as normal and acceptable" (p. 198). Changing partners was easy. All that the woman had to do was to put the man's shoes and clothes outside of the door.

Indians believed in cleanliness, and they were surprised by the lack of hygiene among Europeans (Spring, 1994). They selected settlement sites along streams and lakes and bathed daily. Europeans did not bathe often and washed clothing even less often. To the disgust of Indians, they smelled. The Indians could live and survive in the wilderness, and certainly did not feel second in status; the Europeans struggled. And Indians considered their way of war superior.

The Europeans considered Indians unreliable in war because they fought only enough to gain loot, prisoners, and domination before retreating with their gains. They fought in a way to avoid causalities and withdrew when the battle became too hot. They were opportunists, and took whatever advantages they saw to exploit conditions. They would not adhere to the ridged and inflexible discipline practices by the Europeans trained in set-piece continental war. To Indians, it was best to raid, ambush, and retreat. The Indians also would not observe the "rules of war" by which Europeans thought "civilized" wars were fought. On the other hand, Indians were shocked by the violence of the Europeans. Taking prisoners was more important than killing. It was not unusual for Indians to leave the field rather than participate in slaughter (Starkey, 1998).

Amerindian Slavery

Another major source of conflict was slavery, as was previously discussed. The Amerindians engaged in slavery before the Europeans arrived and they continued afterwards (Brooks, 2002; Butler & Watson, 1984; Gallay, 2002). The major difference is that afterwards slavery became a commercial venture practiced with the Europeans. Native American groups used trade in slaves as a major way to acquire European goods. Weaker tribes were subject to attack, capture, and extinction. Anxiety and fear quickly spread among lesser vulnerable tribes. Some moved into more protected areas, and in some cases large settlements were broken up and populations dispersed into smaller units that could more easily evade slave traffickers in mountainous areas (Gallay, 2002).

The most widely extended practice of slavery among Amerindians was in the Plains and southwestern regions. Because of the large, open distances settlements were often small and isolated which made them vulnerable to slave raids by more powerful enemies. There was no place to hide or flee. Also, because of the large distances and harsh travel conditions it was difficult for captives to escape. This made the practice all the easier to engage in by the more powerful. Some captives were incorporated into the social unit as adopted sons and daughters; some served as "kin" replacements for those lost in war in order to replenish the fighting power of the tribe; a few others were sacrificial replacements; and most were "servants" or kept for ransom. Women and children in particular were forcibly seized for marriage and adoption. Tribes had to maintain or add to their strength and this was an effective way to do it (Anderson, 1999; Brooks, 2002).

After the Europeans came, Amerindian slavery took a commercial turn. As Brooks (2002) recounted, increasingly, market-driven conduits developed that extended north and east into the upper Midwest and Great Lakes through which individuals were fed into captive exchanges. To the south the exchanges supplied labor to the Spanish mines of Mexico and the plantations of the Spanish Caribbean. With the addition of Spanish horses and weapons, the relationships between tribes altered so that the more aggressive grew in power as they decimated rivals in the quest for marketable captives. The Comanche, for example, descended out of the plains to grow into a powerhouse that for over four generations controlled the Southwest. Trade, tribute, and slavery produced their power. They raided, terrorized, subdued, and subjected surrounding Native groups and Spanish settlements. Their ascendancy to power in the mid-18th century marked the beginning of the long decline of the Spanish empire in the American Southwest (Hamalainen, 2008). The Comanche confederacy united the southwestern Native population in the successful effort to marginalize, isolate, destroy, and ultimately drive the Spanish from North America.

As earlier recounted, the Southeast became a primary slaving ground of Europeans. The plantation system needed labor. Initially Europeans aligned with local Indians to supply slaves, providing weapons and goods in exchange for humans. Capturing and selling their neighbors was a quick way for Amerindians to acquire European goods (Dinnerstein, et. al, 1996). As expected, warfare between Indians and settlers and between Indians and Indians resulted. Unlike in the Southwest, Native groups were more densely compacted so they were open to retaliatory raids. The Indian slave trade, Gallay (2002) observed, "infected the South: it set into motion a gruesome series of wars that engulfed the region. For close to five decades, virtually every group of people in the South lay threatened by destruction in these wars. Huge areas became depopulated, thousands of Indians died, and thousands more were forcibly relocated to new areas in the South or exported from the region" (p. 6). Slaving and the accompanying retaliatory wars contributed substantially to the reduction of the Amerindian population of the South.

The use of Indian slaves became increasingly more untenable. Not only did it generate deadly conflict between Native groups but it also brought down on European settlements the wrath of avenging kin. It was also difficult for Europeans to maintain forced Amerindian labor because of the relative ease of escape. There was no way to keep individuals physically bound and still extract useful labor, but at the same time field workers not constrained could run off and find their way home in a landscape in which they had extensive knowledge of the terrain. A following assault by kin could be expected. Then again, over time the need for labor outstripped the available supply of Indian slave labor.

Enterprising entrepreneurs turned to the exportation of Indian slave labor, and the importation of Africans. The expectation was that if the captives were transported far enough away they could not return and would submit to enslavement. Also, the inability to find their lost kin made retaliation more difficult. The Puritans had done this in 1638 with the Pequot and it worked: A troublesome tribe was eliminated. Southern seaboard ports became shipping points for captured Native Americans to Caribbean plantations where they could not escape or be found. They were exchanged for African slaves. An estimated 50,000 Indians were sent into permanent bondage in the Caribbean islands from Charleston, South Carolina, alone, as the port became a major collection and shipment center. Some Indian captives were also shipped to the northern colonies. Africans trans-shipped north from the Caribbean began exceeding by far Indian slaves, but nevertheless, at the heart of the African slave trade in the initial stages was the Indian slave trade. The early establishment of the southern plantation system was largely financed by Amerindian lives (Gallay, 2002; Wilson, 1998).

The Indians got trapped in the European mercantile system, which contributed greatly to their destruction. The Indians wanted European goods; they made life easier and contributed a decisive edge in warfare. But how was a hunting-gathering society to pay? At first, as we have seen among the northern Indians and the French, beaver pelts were exchanged. The demand became so great that trappers went all the way to the Pacific coast in search of the furry animal that was rapidly becoming wiped out. Similarly, in the Southeast and Southwest, hundreds of thousands of deer hides annually were exchanged for European goods to satisfy the continental craze for the wonderfully soft leather. When the deer were gone, bear, wolf, and every other kind of game were killed for hides. But at the same time, the food supply that the local populations had depended on for generations was wiped out. As a way to finance European goods, slavery came next, but also there was a limit and the supply became exhausted. Those that were slave brokers even became captives. Some groups began to sell land and the consequences were irreversible. The homeland that the indigenous population shared was gone forever. Finally, Indians went to war. Unable to eliminate debt and cut off from new goods, armed conflict became the solution. Both the Tuscarora and Yamasee wars in the Carolinas, for example, were an outcome of unsuccessful attempts by the Indians to negotiate heavy debt obligations. They felt that the European traders were unfair, took advantage of them, cheated, and were unreasonable in the refusal to negotiate (Gallay, 2002).

Anderson (1999) observed that some groups of Plains Indians were successful in resisting the Spanish largely because they worked outside of the European market system. They had an existing political economy before the European presence. "Native groups competed for control of this economy, which always remained outside of Spanish control, and created social and political relationships with other Indian groups to defend themselves and their economic interests" (p. 5). They turned, in the words of Anderson, the plains into a "center of production" through horse and mule breeding, dried meat processing, tanning, basket making and a host of other productive activities. Different Indian communities "often became mobile markets, making adaptation crucially important to economic success" (p. 5).

Indian Education

The Indians did not have to rely on formally organized European education because they had their own way of instructing the young. There were basically three groups of skills that had to be mastered before the young could gain entrance as a full tribal member. Economic skills were considered key to survival. Over a period of years the young were taught how to find and use resources. At an early age children were instructed on how to use the bow and arrow, knife, and club; they learned the ways of game, the migratory patterns of fish, and the availability of berries, nuts, acorns, and edible plants. Horticultural and food preservation practices were taught. Weaving, tanning, basketry, and pottery making were perfected. The construction of shelter, building of fortifications, and the fabrication of watercraft were learned, and warfare mastered. These and other survival skills were taught at an early age up until adulthood when the individual was expected to assume full tribal responsibilities. Training was interwoven with spiritual and cultural instruction, and given by families and clan members as well as by religious and secular leaders of the tribe (Szasz, 1988).

Spiritual instruction was crucial. Well-being depended on maintaining the right relationship with and respect for the spiritual world. Some groups worshipped a single creator, such as the "Great Spirit," but others saw multiple creative forces, but what was common is that they did not separate the spiritual and material worlds and saw the creative force in all things—natural, supernatural, human, and animal. They were puzzled why the Europeans had so little regard for the natural world that they indiscriminately destroyed. In some tribes members worshipped daily. Children were exposed to the rituals and expected behaviors early.

Puberty was a dividing line, that when crossed signaled adulthood, but required significant rituals on the journey to adulthood. In some cases, individuals had to complete a quest so that they could acquire a guardian spirit. Great weight was placed on a successful guardian spiritual quest. As (Szasz, 1988) observed, the guardian spirit "whether in the form of an animal or some other living creature . . . would aid and guide the youth for the remainder of his or her life" (p. 17). Names such as "Running Bear," "Little Crow," or "Morning Star" had considerable significance for the individual. Some groups tested boys to find which ones should be considered for priesthood; some groups initiated youth into secret societies, and they engaged in endurance tests that may take months or years to complete. Youth were exposed to hardship, solitary privation, and fasting along the way to finding a vision of the guardian spirit (Szasz, 1988).

When the Europeans attempted to convert Indians they clashed with spiritual beliefs and practices that were central to defining what an Indian was. To the Indian, spiritual worship, Szasz (1988) observed, "provided the matrix for the native American groups, pervading their cultures and giving shape to common life" (p. 15). A major point of conflict with Europeans was over religion. John Terrell (1979) suggested that Amerindians were guided every waking and sleeping hour by religion. "It is improbable that in all of recorded history any people of any race on earth was guided more by religious tenants" (p. 17). Most Europeans would simply not acknowledge the importance of the spiritual life of the Indian.

The Native populations also transmitted a rich cultural heritage. In a culture without a written language, storytelling was advanced to a high level. Designated members of the oldest generations were responsible for retaining knowledge of the past and transmitting it to the younger clan members. Nightly storytelling reinforced cultural ideals, lessons of morality, and appropriate behaviors. A detailed and rich history was conveyed, and community responsibilities and roles reinforced. The transmission of cultural heritage was a shared community event, enriching group identity. When large-scale death occurred from disease and war, the band lost its tribal heritage. There was no one left to pass on to the young what it meant to be a tribal member.

As we have seen, different colonial settlements struggled to bring the indigenous populations under the influence of European education. To the Native Indian, however, European education was devoid of meaning. They considered it an attempt to strip them of their cultural heritage, to deny them of their spiritual life, and to reinforce a subservient status. It would destroy a way of life meaningful to the Indian. To be sure, individual Indians profited from European instruction, but schooling on a group scale did not take. After the Revolutionary War, national leaders turned their attention to Indian education, but as we will see in Part Three, the results continued to be mixed.

By the time of the Revolutionary War, the basic dimensions of what was to become the new nation were established. Small, urban centers primarily in the middle states and New England contained the seeds of modernization and industrialization. Farms all up and down the Eastern seaboard continued to feed an expanding population and small household manufacturing supplied goods. A plantation system based on slave labor produced immense wealth north and south as it fed northern manufacturing and Europe with raw materials. The agricultural power of the country would continue to develop as new lands were opened. Newcomers kept coming and brought labor and skills, joining regional labor forces that continued to use land and resources to advance economic growth. The Native populations along the eastern seaboard, however, were not yet subdued by the time of the Revolutionary War, and conflict continued as a restless European population pursued the journey of westward expansion. A rich ethnic mixture continued to define the nation, but tensions rooted in ethnicity, religion, and politics existed, and would continue to exist. The question of enslavement festered.

Post-revolutionary leaders faced the challenge of forging a new nation out of the divisive conflict with the English. They had to bring a diverse population together, and reconcile the national origins of the American people with an ideology that would unite. They took entrenched tradition and intellectual thought and shaped it to new purpose. They took pre-revolutionary institutional forms and attempted to mold them to fit the new nation. The political, social, and economic vision of society forged out of the Revolution had to be put into practice, and the process took time and was messy, and was accompanied with uncertainty and conflict. Schools played a big part. The post-revolutionary leaders borrowed from colonial America to form a school system that reflected national purpose and goals. The also borrowed from European Enlightenment thought. Faith was put in schools to bring about national unity. This is the subject that we turn to next in Part Two.

References for Part One

Anderson, G.C. (1999). The Indian Southwest, 1580–1830. Norman: University of Oklahoma Press.

Bailyn, B. (1960). Education in the Forming of American Society. Chapel Hill: The University of North Carolina Press.

Berlin, I. (2010). The Making of African American. Four Great Migrations. New York: Viking.

Blassingame, J.W. (1972). The Slave Community; Plantation Life in the Antebellum South. New York: Oxford University Press.

Bremner, R.H. (1970). Children and Growth in America; A Documentary History. Volume I: 1660–1865. Cambridge, MA: Harvard University Press.

Brooks, J.F. (2002). Captives and Cousins. Chapel Hill: University of North Carolina Press.

Buetow, H.A. (1970). Of Singular Benefit; the Story of Catholic Education in the United States. New York: The Macmillan Company.

Butler, L.S., & Watson, A.D. (Eds). (1984). The North Carolina Experience; An Interpretive and Documentary History. Chapel Hill: University of North Carolina Press.

Cohen, S.S. (1974). A History of Colonial Education, 1607–1776. New York: John Wiley & Sons, Inc.

Cremin, L.A. (1970). American Education; the Colonial Experience, 1607–1783. New York: Harper and Row, Publishers.

Curti, M. (1959). The Social Ideas of American Educators. Patterson, NJ: Pageant Books.

Diamond, j (2005). Collapse. New York: Viking press.

Diamond, J. (1997). Guns, Germs, and Steel. New York: W.W. Norton and Company.

Dinnerstein, et. al, 1996. Natives and Strangers; A Multicultural History of Americans. New York: Oxford University Press.

Drescher, S. (2009). Abolition History of Slavery and Antislavery. Cambridge, MA: University Press.

Driver, Harold. (1969). Indians of North America. Chicago: University of Chicago Press.

Flannery, T. (2001). The Eternal Frontier; an Ecological History of North America and Its Peoples. New York: Grove Press.

Furnas, J.C. (1969). The Americans. A Social History of the United States, 1587–1914. New York: G.P. Putnam's Sons.

Gallay, A. (2002). The Indian Slave Trade. New Haven, CT: Yale University Press.

Gonzalez, J. (2000). Harvest of Empire History of Latinos in America. New York: Penguin Putnam, Inc.

Gordon-Reed, A. (2008). The Hemingses of Monticello; an American Family. New York: W.W. Norton & Company.

Hall, G.M. (1992). Africans in Colonial Louisiana. Baton Rouge: Louisiana State University Press.

Hamalainen, P. (2008). Comanche Empire. New Haven, CT: Yale University Press.

Jaenen, C.J. (1987). Thought on Early Canadian Contact. In Calvin Martin (Ed.), The American Indian and the Problem of History (pp. 55–66). New York: Oxford University Press.

Johnson, P. (1997). A History of the American People. New York: HarperCollins Publishers.

Kolchin, P. (1993). American Slavery 1619–1877. New York: Hill and Wang.

LaFeber, W. (1989). The American Age United States Foreign Policy at Home and Abroad Since 1750. New York: W.W. Norton & Company.

Loller, T. (2012). DNA Study Sheds Light on an Appalachian Genealogy Mystery. *The Washington Post*, June 10, A7.

MacCulloch, D. (2009). Christianity; the First Three Thousand Years. New York: Penguin Books.

Mann, C.C. (2005). 1491 New Revelations of the Americas before Columbus. New York: Alfred A. Knopp.

Milton, G. (2004). White Gold. New York: Farrar, Straus and Giroux.

Morgan, E.S. (1975). American Slavery; American Freedom. New York: W.W. Norton & Company.

Morgan, E.S. (2004). The Genuine Article. A Historian Looks at Early America. New York: W.W. Norton & Company.

Morrison, S.E. (1965). The Oxford History of the American People. New York: Oxford University Press.

Olson, Steve. (2002). Mappings Human History Genes, Race, and Our Common Origins. New York: A Mariner Book.

Phillips, K. (1999). The Cousins' Wars Religion, Politics, and the Triumph of Anglo-America. New York: Basic Books.

Remini, R.V. (2001). Andrew Jackson and His Indian Wars. New York: Viking.

Reynor, J., & Eder, J. (2004). American Indian Education; A History. Norman: University of Oklahoma Press.

Shea, J.G. (1969). Catholic Missions among the Indian Tribes of the United States. New York: Arno Press.

Shepherd, V., & Beckkes, H. McD. (2004). Caribbean Slavery in the Atlantic World. Kingston, Jamaica: Ian Randel Publishers.

Spring, J. (1994). The American School, 1642–1993 (3rd ed.). New York: McGraw-Hill, Inc.

Starkey, A. (1998). European and Native American Warfare, 1675–1815. Norman: University of Oklahoma Press.

Starkoy, M.L. (1949). The Devil in Massachusetts. New York: Time Incorporated.

Szasz, M.C. (1988). Indian Education in the American Colonies, 1600–1783. Albuquerque: University of New Mexico.

Terrell, J.U. (1979). The Arrow and the Cross. Santa Barbara, CA: Capra Press.

Tyack, D.B. (1967). Turning Points in American Educational History. Waltham, MA: Blaisdell Publishing Company.

Vassar, R.L. (1965). Social History of American Education. Volume I: Colonial Times to 1860. Chicago: Rand McNally & Company.

Watras, J. (2002). The Foundations of Educational Curriculum and Diversity, 1565 to the Present. Boston: Allyn and Bacon.

Webb, L.D. (2006). The History of American Education a Great American Experiment. Upper Saddle River, NJ: Pearson Education, Inc.

Wilson, J. (1998). The Earth Shall Weep; a History of Native America. New York: Atlantic Monthly Press.

Part Two

Bring Forth a New Nation

Introduction

Revolutions usually are long in coming. They are an outcome of tensions that build up over time until they erupt in a fury that tears the social fabric apart. Such was the case of the American Revolution that commenced with the Declaration of Independence in 1776. From the founding of the very first colonies the roots of dissention existed. The Puritans themselves were self-exiles from an England that was deeply divided and would engage in a civil war over questions of religion, political power, and the character of government. The southern colonies chafed under the pressure of London investors for more profit, and everyone suffered from the high prices of imports and low return on exports. Thousands experienced grievances of exploitation, insult, and disrespect. The gradual poisoning of relationships between the two sides inevitably resulted in political crisis.

Conditions within England reverberated within the colonies up and down the eastern seaboard. The periodic shifting, but continuing conflicts with the European continental powers prevented England from consistent oversight. The colonies often were left to fend for themselves. The Crown and parliament tried intermittently to impose authority and rule, but met resistance after periods of neglect. Laws and edicts simply were ignored. The colonies had grown in population, wealth, and confidence; and they evolved more advanced ways of self-governance largely outside of the English orbit. On the eve of the war, the population of the 13 colonies was over one third that of England. Why should they accept subservience to a faraway ruling class that considered the colonies primarily as property to be exploited? Resentment grew.

The English badly played their hand. Chronically short of money to finance its military debts, they turned to what they thought was a potential rich source of revenue, the colonial economy. Schemes to tax the colonies were disastrous. The masquerading Boston merchants dumping fine tea in the salt waters surrounding Griffin's Wharf demonstrated the explosive resistance engendered by what was thought to be unfair tax schemes. Money exchange rates, interest on loans, and exports and import controls favored London and generated oppressive hardship for the colonists. Evasion, boycott, deception, and smuggling became the norm. The refusal by the English to even consider colonial views generated deep dissent. "There was arrogance by the English," Paul Johnson (1997) stated, "and arrogance bred mistakes, and obstinacy meant they were persistent in to the point of idiocy" (p. 12). Revolt followed.

With the conclusion of the Revolution, a new nation was formed that continued to have deep roots in its colonial past. The American Revolutionary leaders were not interested in the destruction of the existing social and economic order, but rather they wanted to reshape it, to restore rights that the colonists felt that they had lost, and to put into place checks to freedoms that they thought were threatened. "Americans needed to maintain, develop, and correct the state of things political and religious, which already existed," Samuel Morrison (1965, p. 270) suggested. To correct the state of things, however, required a remarkable feat of leadership and national will to knit all of the disparate forces of the Revolution together and form a new nation. By the time of the Revolution, the colonies reflected a patchwork of regional and local economic, religious, political, and ethnic differences tempered by the hardships of colonial life.

Post-revolutionary leaders faced a number of challenges. First, and primarily, was to create unity out of division. There were divisions among the colonists, some deep, and in a real sense the Revolutionary War was also a civil war. Colonists confronted colonists. About one third of the colonial population was comprised of Tory loyalists on the side of the English, and another third were neutral, but the war was always against the overseas power of England and not against home institutions or people. While Patriots and Loyalists shared a common English historical and cultural heritage, the war with the Mother Country broke this bond. With victory, they were all Americans now, and they inherited all of the economic, religious, political, and class differences that characterized the tensions within and between the colonies, and they had to forge out of these differences an American identity. Education was thought to play a big part.

The Focus of Part Two

The issue of schooling quickly came to the surface. Post-revolutionary leaders generally placed great faith in the power of education to bring about national unity through an educated population that advanced ideas of liberty. Education, even in its limited forms, was a strong tool for building the colonies and it was asserted that it could play an even bigger role in post-revolutionary America. Revolutionary ideas on government were linked with ideas on education. As the decades progressed, national leaders increasingly turned to schools as a means to knit together the new economic and political order.

In Part Two, we give attention to the condition of education in the immediate post-revolutionary period. This is commonly referred to as the "Republican era," a time of nation building before the country began politically disintegrating over unresolved sectional tensions and the question of slavery. In Chapter Four we first look at the European Enlightenment thought. Early revolutionary leaders drew heavily from the Enlightenment to shape ideas on schooling for the new nation. A number of concepts were advanced that continued over time to influence the character of American education. But the early leaders tempered Enlightenment ideas so that they were consistent with the conditions and necessities at hand. And of course, American educational leaders took from the English and French Enlightenment only those ideas that they needed, understood, and valued; and they filtered, cut, transposed, transformed, and reinterpreted the ideas of a Bacon, Locke,

Rousseau, or Erasmus to fit within the colonial experience. A unique American dimension was added (Nye, 1960)

In Chapter Four this remarkable period of Western thought is considered so we can better understand the uses Americans made of the educational ideas that were advanced. National leaders faced specific challenges not only rooted in the colonial past but also embedded in the revolutionary causes advanced. As in the case of revolutionary thought in general, ideas on education "came about as a result of the assimilation and rationalization of one hundred and fifty years of American experience, combined with the ideas of the Enlightenment" (Nye, 1960, p. 4). American education evolved out of this assimilation and rationalization, producing its own character while at the same time incorporating vestiges of its European intellectual parenthood.

The focus of Chapter Five is on post-revolutionary education at the local level. This is where community leaders made selective use of the currents of new educational ideas national leaders were promoting. They worked within the framework of existing schools and practices as they addressed local conditions. It was the literate clergy, small town lawyer, merchant, dirt farmer, landed gentry, urban craftsman, school teacher, and parent that struggled with the questions of what kind of education should be provided by the community, for whom, and how was it going to be paid for. Chapter Five presents a snapshot overview of the condition of American education in the immediate post-revolutionary years.

Individual communities, linked with religious affiliations, continued to be the strong educational element in post-revolutionary America. With few exceptions, states had only skeleton administrative structures with little direct control, and at the national level there was none. The inspirational thoughts advanced by early national leaders found only partial acceptance when confronted with the realities of local application. And as was true of other institutional forms, educational thought was caught in the interplay of ideas with shifting societal forces. Ideas were used, as they were needed. Then again, schools were too heterogeneous, scattered in different form and quality about the country to easily impress any kind of unity of purpose or practice on them. It was not until the emergence of the common school movement in the 1830s that the educational heritage of revolutionary thought could be brought into full focus on the development of a hierarchy of institutional forms approaching what the early national leaders envisaged. Conditions were set for the common school movement over the next four decades.

The educational ideas of post-revolutionary leaders, nevertheless, were powerful. What they lacked in constitutional authority and immediate, local impact was made up by staying power. The intellectual and institutional framework that emerged out of the Republican period continued to shape American education. Within two generations the ideas of early national leaders on education were absorbed in the building of public school systems, and today they are embedded in our national educational ideology.

Chapter Four
The Transforming Influence of the Enlightenment

The Enlightenment caused people to think differently. It is difficult to precisely define. No set time frame can be given, and the Enlightenment is comprised of different overlapping and intermingled influences that shifted over time. It is a movement over several centuries that by the time of the Revolutionary War resulted in a profound change in human thought and produced a wider worldview incorporating intellectual, scientific, political, and religious dimensions. Enlightenment thought fed the revolutionary ideas of a Thomas Jefferson and James Madison, the scientific experiments of a Benjamin Franklin, and the education fervor of a Benjamin Rush (Commanger, 1977).

Because of a considerable cultural lag, it was only by the mid-1700s that European Enlightenment thinking of the 1600s significantly impacted Americans. To be sure, Enlightenment influence brought European settlers east to the New World and continued from very early to impact colonial American life. Few early Americans, however, had the relative luxury of time and money to become immersed in European literary, philosophical, and social ideas. There was a class of colonists educated in European thought, but the relative isolation of the colonies, preoccupation with the challenges of the New World, and the slow pace of building extensive library collections and secular institutions of learning meant that ideas from Europe were slow in becoming widely grounded in the colonial intellectual environment.

The colonists were isolated from Europe and isolated among themselves. Carl Bridenbaugh (1964) observed that it was only in the immediate pre-revolutionary years that cities developed to the point where there were sufficient communication networks among them to focus and fuse colonial thought. But the timing could not have been better. Inspired by the Enlightenment, revolutionary thought was spawned, nurtured, and spread throughout the cities and seaport towns along the east coast from Maine to the Carolinas. "The achievement of the integration of urban elements was an essential prelude to independence" (p. 418).

The origins of the European Enlightenment extend in three directions: the Renaissance, Classical Humanism, and science. Its offspring, the Reformation, shook the European world to its core. This brought the Puritans to New England, the Quakers to Pennsylvania, and the French Huguenots to South Carolina. In a real sense, the Enlightenment marked the ending of one age and the beginning of another: the ending of the feudal social order, the ending of the domination of the Western church, and the breaking up of the system of absolute, aristocratic rule; the formation of nation states, the freeing of secular and scientific thought, the transformation of social and political systems, and the shifting to a man-centered world where "rational" thought was asserted to be a major contributor to the human condition. Our modern era of today marks its beginnings with Enlightenment thought.

A New Vision: The Rebirth

The Renaissance, a period of time roughly between the 14th and 16th centuries, refers to the great intellectual and artistic flowering in Italy that spread throughout the European world. The Renaissance was a rebirth after prolonged and repeated periods of death on a massive scale through plague, disease, poverty, and war. In the 1300s alone up to one fourth of the European population was wiped out (Tuchman, 1978).

Something significant happened. In a few short decades great masterworks by Leonardo, Michelangelo, and Raphael dazzled the world; new forms of architecture impressed; and poetry and literature blossomed. Technical invention also marked the new era: Gunpowder destroyed the old feudal order and ushered in the rise of nation states; the mechanical clock freed man from nature's rhythms and irrevocably altered the relationship of man to time, nature, work, and to each other. Perhaps most significant was the invention of the printing press, which made it possible for learning to be widely distributed to all and broke the monopoly of the clergy on learning. The magnetic compass made it possible for Columbus to find landfall in the Caribbean, Europeans to ply the coastal waters off North America, and Americus Vespucci to sail around the world. The Renaissance was a transition period into a new age that brought the Spanish friars to New Mexico, Puritans to New England, and French trappers to the St. Lawrence.

Classical Humanism and the Reformation

The Renaissance was fed in part by the rebirth of classical humanism. Ever since the 9th century, the Western church had been accumulating and studying classical texts; but with the perfection of the printing press, literature from the ancients became widely accessible. No longer was it locked away on dust-covered shelves in churches and monasteries (MacCulloch, 2009). Additional prized ancient Greek works also were available from refugees fleeing the Ottoman conquests in the East. It was a matter of translating texts and making them available.

The search was on for the wisdom of the past. The printing press fostered a great leap in learning. The way was opened to knowledge and learning on a scale never before realized. There was a resurgence of interest in the Latin language and culture. Western Europe was exposed to Roman engineering, architecture, construction, and road building. Intriguing, moreover, were works on government and politics, such as Marcus Cicero's treatise on war and government.

Combined with classical Greek literature, a rich body of thought became available that exposed thinkers to counter viewpoints that challenged the very foundations of church and state. There was fostered "intellectual pluralism, skepticism, and even revolution" (Tarnas, 1991, p. 247). The Renaissance opened a world of poetry, oratory, rhetoric, theater, art, history, and literature. The classical literature brought to light the science, architecture, philosophy, art, and theater of the ancients. Cultural roots were significantly deepened. Scholars were exposed to Cabbala, the body of Jewish literature that broadened and enriched the diversity of thought and cultural heritage. Translations of Arab works on science inspired Europeans (MacCulloch, 2009).

The challenge to the church was robust. Classical works had been used to support church teachings, but with the substantial expansion of the range of ancient works available, there was a questioning of the interpretations initially applied to establish Christian doctrine. Major errors in meaning had found their way into doctrine. Early manuscripts also revealed conflict in teachings. With more sources available, particularly troublesome were errors found in translations that placed theological constructions enforced by the Western church on shaky grounds (MacCulloch, 2009; Tarnas, 1991). The assumed purity of its expressed beliefs was at odds with the very source of those beliefs. The Reformation was an outcome.

Scientific Rationalism

A new kind of knowledge emerged. Prior to the Reformation, the Western Christian church zealously controlled knowledge as a sanctioned gift from God. Francis Bacon (1561–1627) challenged the absolutism of church doctrine, however, with the argument that it was through "rational thought" based on practical (empirical) experimentation and observation that human understanding could be best unlocked. The "Age of Reason" was launched. Similarly, echoing Bacon, Isaac Newton contended that the "lost rationality" of the past had to be uncovered with creative observation and thinking. Bacon directly influenced John Locke as he asserted that all knowledge ultimately derived from man's sensory experience, not religious revelation. These and other thinkers argued that there was a rationality connected with humanity that went beyond the constraints of Christian teachings. Human reasoning could open doors of the temporal and natural world. Tarnas (1991) suggested that this realization had a profound effect. "Christianity no longer seemed to be the driving force of the human enterprise . . . it was science and reason, not religion and belief, which propelled that progress" (p. 323). Science revealed a deeper understanding of the heavens, earth, nature, and the human body. Through science, secular thought challenged the lock the Church had on the human mind.

One of the most notable accomplishments of the French Enlightenment was publication of the *Encyclopédie*, a 28-volume compendium of knowledge arranged alphabetically. Its editor and motivating force, Denis Diderot (1713–1784), conveyed a deist and subverting tone to the work, evoking anger and censorship from government and church. But the *Encyclopédie* displayed in all of its imperfection the grand scope of man's intellectual work if left unhindered to apply the power of secular reasoning. The French philosopher Voltaire (François-Marie Arouet, 1694–1778), contemporary of Diderot, added yet further support for secular reasoning with his unsparing attack on organized religion for its self-interest conspiracy to interfere with the minds of intelligent people. Religion should be left to the "rabble," he contended, but intelligent individuals should be left uncontaminated to pursue the struggle against the "darkness" of church dogma. He was not liked by officialdom.

The scientific revolution comprised a dominant strand of thought clearly embedded in the Enlightenment. Science stirred as the natural world revealed itself through mathematical calculations, brilliant creative thinking, and innovative instrumentation. Nicolaus Copernicus (1473–1543), Johannes Kepler (1571–1630), and Galileo Galilei (1564–1642) demolished religious concepts of an earth-centered order. Isaac Newton (1642–1727) added the final touch with laws of gravity formulated through mathematical calculations. René Descartes (1596–1650) introduced reductionism and mathematical analysis as a means of breaking down and studying parts of the natural world. This continues to be a powerful tool of empirical research. The Swedish botanist Carl Linnaeus (1707–1778) gave us a way to classify the plant kingdom, opening up "God's secret cabinet," and the Dutchman Antonie van Leeuwenhoek (1632–1723) opened up the microscopic world with his study of spermatozoa. Through this and other work a scientific revolution was launched that, by the time of the War of Independence in America, irrevocably altered the way that the natural world was conceived and that stimulated inquiry and fostered technological and industrial growth. In America, the way was opened for the exploitation of the natural world for human ends.

The American colonies came into being at the inception of the great scientific discoveries that brought Columbus to America, gave us new ways to look at the universe, perfected the refinement of iron, fostered machine building, started untangling the mysteries of medicine, established laws of physics, and added rationality to conjecture about the world. The Revolutionary War, however, severely disrupted scientific development in America. Some of the leading scientists were Loyalists who chose to leave. This was a loss because they were brilliant minds. Libraries, laboratories, and equipment were destroyed, scientific organizations disbanded, and journals discontinued. Scientific work came to a standstill and had to be restarted. A first, major step was to reactivate pre-revolutionary scientific work (Nye, 1960).

Pre-war Americans were deeply engaged in science, its discoveries, and its use. Benjamin Franklin gained international fame for his scientific experiments, and was on the edge of unlocking the explanation of electricity. His is the best known of the brilliant scientific workers in America: Benjamin Rush advanced concepts in psychiatry; John Bartram advanced the field of botany; the work of Cadwallader Colden embraced medicine, mathematics, physics, and anthropology; and David Rittenhouse gained distinctions as an astronomer and mathematician. His advancements in instrumentation and theoretical knowledge were a significant scientific leap (Wright, 1957).

Americans tended to apply a practical bent to science. Thomas Godfrey improved the mariner's quadrant by perfecting a way to determine latitude. Innovative metalworkers in Pennsylvania figured out how to use bog iron and establish smelting works, freeing the colonies from English control of iron production and establishing an export trade. Eli Terry developed a system of mass production of clocks based on interchangeable parts. Shipbuilders in New England perfected innovation in quality and production, capturing world markets. John Fitch invented a workable steamboat and put it to use in 1790 with regular runs on the Philadelphia river. Scientific and industrial values, like the products they produced, spread across the new land. Americans were deeply engaged in the use of science, and economic expansion was intimately and increasingly linked with the genius citizens had for science, machinery, and technology (Furnas, 1969).

The American Philosophical Society, first organized in Philadelphia in 1743–44 largely as a result of Franklin's work, became a leading scientific force after the Revolutionary War. The

American Academy was organized later in 1780 by John Adams and fellow New Englanders and similarly became instrumental in the proliferation of scientific work during the Republican period. More specialized scientific groups were either reactivated or established, so in a relatively short time American science regained momentum. Societies for medicine, chemistry, natural sciences, agriculture, and manufacturing were among many that spurred on professional, intellectual, technical, and economic development.

By 1800, the economy was booming and unprecedented wealth was being generated; transportation networks linked communities, urban manufacturing centers sprung up, agriculture export soared, immigrants came by the thousands, and people were on the move, seeking opportunity from the great, abundant natural wealth in the opening lands. The common school movement emerged from this period of great national flux; and a challenge was mounted by science and engineering to the classical curriculum inherited from colonial days.

Constructing "American" Education

Following independence, in the spirit of youthful nationalism leaders started thinking in terms of building a system of national and universal education in a way to solidify and extend the principles and ideology of the Revolution. The church coupled with the parents had long been the dominant educational force for educating youth, but with the rise of secular rationalism and the emergence of revolutionary ideology, a new center of unity had to be found. With no centralized educational authority, how best could the "national will" be asserted? Leaders grasped at what they saw as a way to create a new unity: Formulate a common citizenship and culture outside of formal religion and embedded in the definition of Republican America. This would be done at the local level. Schooling would be bent to this purpose. A blueprint for national unity would be provided to the rural schoolmaster, city school board member, frontier teacher, southern cleric, and northern legislator. With fervor the young schoolmaster Noah Webster, for example, affirmed what other American leaders were saying when he urged the use of schools as a tool to unite the nation by forming a "national character."

The ideals and proposals of early leaders found only limited, immediate application. This early work, nevertheless, conveyed the spirit of the revolutionary age, the hopes and aspirations of the leadership, and faith in the power of education to promote both the welfare of the individual and of society. Early educational thinkers made selective use of the ideas of what was to become known as the "American Enlightenment." This early work expresses the idealism of the new nation and reflects the efforts of early leaders to address educational problems within a diverse, divided, and widely scattered population. Ideals were established that continue to influence the character of American education (Bailyn, 1960).

Diversity and Unity

Issues of class conflict ran through all of the colonies, and became one of the most important challenges that had to be addressed with Independence. It was fundamental in the effort to bring about national unity. Carl Bridenbaugh (1964) suggested that the height of "colonial aristocracy" came in the 1760s, to fall off rapidly after Independence. Following the war, both the middle class and the highly privileged were conscious of maintaining their place in society. Bernard Bailyn (1960) noted the aims of the Revolution "were not to recast the ordering of the society that had developed in the earlier years" (p. 45). The revolutionary leadership was anxious to redraw and protect the social class lines that existed prior to the conflict.

One of the very reasons for the rebellion against English rule was that the harsh economic conditions imposed on the colonists threatened to destroy the financial foundations of the elites. The great plantation owners, merchants, traders, shipbuilders, and financial manipulators struggled against financial ruin. What Bridenbaugh (1964) termed the "aristocracy" wanted to control their own financial destiny, but at the same time they wanted to maintain the organizational and class structure of the colonies that had given them a position of privilege. Following the Revolution, however, a new dimension was added. In the rapidly expanding urban areas in particular, a large segment of the working population concluded that the elite thwarted access to the benefits of the Revolution and kept them in a position of social and economic subservience. "Long-festering class antagonisms could now be detected in daily social interchanges, religious activities, the pursuits of diversions, and even in taverns and round and about towns" (Bridenbaugh, 1964, p. 332). The lower classes wanted social and economic respectability and opportunity.

Education, Privilege, Opportunity, and Class

The new ideas filtering through all social strata caused a heightened awareness of issues of wealth, class, and poverty. The new nation basically maintained existing pre-Revolution class relationships and the political power of the colonial aristocracy and upper middle class, while diminished, remained in place. The Revolution generation was aware that something had to be done to reconcile the high national ideas of equality, justice, freedom, and opportunity with the realities of everyday life. They also had to accommodate individual state interests that had so vividly shown themselves with the failure of the Articles of Confederation. A divided response ensued.

A split developed within the early national leadership. Those of a more conservative bent feared the consequences of unbridled democracy. The fact that they were greatly outnumbered was a challenge to their authority: In every state there were considerably more citizens of modest means than wealthy. If they could get organized and work as a whole, the less-well off could overrule the wealthy. To combat this, the conservatives coalesced into a political party, the Federalist.

The Federalists were primarily made up of wealthy landowners, merchants, men with capital, and the educated upper class: George Washington and Edmund Randolph of Virginia, Edward and John Rutledge of South Carolina, Charles Carroll of Maryland, Alexander Hamilton and Philip Schuyler of New York, John Adams of Massachusetts, Jonathan Trumbull of Connecticut, and Robert Morris and Edward Biddle of Pennsylvania were leading members among the powerful, privileged, and wealthy that formed the core of the Federalist Party. They were conservative in outlook. They cautioned against uncontrollable forces of change that could be released, spinning out of control in an orgy of destructive excesses. Popular uprisings had to be guarded against, and the masses kept in check.

Among the Federalist, common people tended to be held in low esteem: unreliable, ignorant, slothful, incompetent, and when organized in mass easily incited to violence. In their view, it was the duty of the few virtuous, well-bred, able, and educated custodians of wealth to preserve order, promote the general welfare, and guard the cultural heritage of the nation (Nettels, 1938). They would be the leaders. "The poor," John Adams noted, "are destine to labor, and the rich, by the advantages of education, independence, and leisure, are qualified for superior status" (Nye, 1960, p. 105).

Very early and in an effort to preserve political influence, the Federalist set out to achieve several political objectives. First, the Constitution would establish a "moderately strong" central government with sufficient authority to ensure that conflicting interests could be kept under control. This was the failure of the Articles of Confederation. At the same time, constitutional constraints on majority rule would restrain elected legislatures from enacting popular laws that would threaten upper-class interests; second, a bicameral legislature would help neutralize conflicting views; third, suffrage would be restricted to property owners, eliminating the vast mass of citizens from direct participation in electing leaders, and stacking the odds in support of the control of government by the upper class. By the time of the Constitution, only one in four male citizens qualified to vote. And fourth, as an added precaution, the president would be elected through a system of electors rather than by popular vote. Citizens should have freedom to participate in government, but not too much freedom (Nettels, 1938, pp. 660–663; Nye, 1960, 99–108; Phillips, 1999, pp. 329–339).

Education also came to be viewed as an important tool. Initially, the wealthy class opposed the use of public tax money to support education for the lower classes; they paid most of the bill. The position of the Federalist changed rather quickly, however, with the realization that public education could be used to control the population. Education for the working class and the poor could be used as a tool of social control to teach respect for authority and property, obedience, industry, and allegiance to the new political system. What Noah Webster said about forming a national character through education resonated. Education for the lower classes was a way to create national unity and maintain social cohesion and control.

The "Jefferson Democrats," variously known at the time as "Jeffersonians" or "Democrats," were another political party that was eventually formed. They held views that contrasted sharply with the Federalists, and constituted a direct challenge to the first two Federalist administrations of Washington and Adams. Their educational ideas became important in the ensuring national public debates over the role, form, and substance of education. These were men profoundly influenced by Enlightenment thought. Among the members were a handful from the southern planter class, Jefferson and George Mason the most prominent, and important lawyers such as Luther Martin from Maryland, Joseph Reed and George Bryan of Pennsylvania, Thomas Burke of North Carolina, and George Clinton of New York. Benjamin Franklin and Samuel Adams added status. Eventually, the bulk of the membership was made up of small farmers, frontiersmen (including Ethan Allen of Vermont, Thomas Person of North Carolina, and Thomas Sumter of South Carolina), artisans, mechanics and laborers in urban areas, and small free traders and merchants. These men desired a reconstruction of American society, and believed that the Revolution released currents of change that would irrevocably alter social and power relationships. Education would be used as a tool of reconstruction to ease change in a peaceful way.

They wanted to manage change in a democratic way. Unlike the Federalists, they believed that the general population if given sufficient education was capable of governing itself in a rational, orderly manner, and would make just, fair decisions; second, they believed that government too often is used as a tool of oppression and power, so it should be kept in check and limited. The powers of government should be narrowly defined. Third, they believed that the further government is removed from the people the less power it should have. For this reason, state and local government should be the most powerful. Finally, they believed that the people in the communities in which they live should impose government restraints. To the consternation of Federalists, Democrats also believed in wide public participation in the exercise of governmental powers through equal legislative representation, liberal and popular suffrage, and the right of all citizens to hold office (Nettels, 1938, pp. 660–663).

Popular education was supported. It was viewed as a way for the young to achieve social and economic opportunity, a way to create emotional allegiance to the new nation, and a necessity in a democracy in order to cultivate an enlightened citizenry. For the Democrats, however, schooling was a local matter, to be controlled and financed through local initiative.

In the immediate decades after the war these two competing visions of government dominated the American political scene as the leadership grappled with the challenge of forming a new nation. At the same time, both the Federalists and Jefferson Democrats had areas of agreement where they came together on policy. Both were children of Enlightenment thought, although both used it in different ways to advance their own ends. These two political positions, although they altered and shifted over time, nevertheless defined the political framework of the nation over the next half dozen decades.

Erasmus, Revolution, and Privilege

Schools in early America were classed based (Curti, 1959). In his study of colonial cities, Gary Nash (1979) found, "Virtually everyone of wealth or position in the port towns adhered to the axiom that rank and status must be carefully preserved and social roles clearly differentiated if society was to retain its equilibrium." He also noted, "Social stability was uppermost in the minds of most of these leaders and they believed that nothing counted for more in its achievement than a careful demarcation of status and privilege" (p. 7). Schools were expected to maintain the social order.

The revolutionary leaders recognized a class structure regardless if they were Federalists or Jefferson Democrats. Sharp distinctions were drawn between the more privileged and the underclass. Breeding and wealth made a difference, but merit in the upward social climb also was within limits recognized. It was thought that an individual could achieve the status of "gentleman" through piety, virtue, talent, and education. Thomas Jefferson thought that there was a "natural aristocracy of worth" that marked man, and it could be cultivated through education. While education was generally believed to mark class differences, it was also believed to provide an avenue of social advancement for those that demonstrated virtue and ability. In this sense social mobility was recognized, but it also was recognized that few of the poor climbed far.

The idea that schooling should be used to create and maintain an elite was cemented in Western thought by the early Enlightenment scholar Desiderius Erasmus (1466–1536). Erasmus is numbered among the most brilliant intellectuals of his age. Early Americans studied his work both before and after the Revolution. He was a firm supporter of aristocratic rule and had deep religious beliefs, but he had no qualms in criticizing both when he thought that reasoning and knowledge gleaned from the great thinkers of the past showed them in error. He sometimes had to tread lightly and backtrack in a world gripped in civic and religious strife. Running through all of his work, however, is the spirit of rhetorical humanism (Woodward, 1964).

Erasmus's scholarship was prodigious, ranging from Greek and Latin translations of ancient works, to commentaries on Plato and Aristotle, arguments on Christian doctrine, and works on education. The completion of a Greek New Testament and the translation of the Bible from Greek to Latin were probably his most influential contributions. The errors that he found in biblical interpretations from faulty translations set Europe alive with theological discussion and greatly bolstered the cause of the Protestant Reformation. There simply were no grounds for some doctrinal assertions. William Tyndale used Erasmus's work to produce the first translation of the New Testament in English, and 83% of Tyndale's unmatched, beautiful use of the language found its way into the 1611 King James Version of the Bible that Protestants have used for 400 years. Through trickery, Tyndale was caught, strangled at the stake, and his corpse burned for daring to make available an unauthorized biblical translation that could be read by common people (MacCulloch, 2009).

Increasingly, during the last 20 years of his life, Erasmus was interested in education. Works such as *Order of Study* and *The Liberal Education of Children* along with numerous letters and essays made major contributions to ideas on educational practice. His most enduring work was *The Education of a Prince*. For close to 400 years it set the standard for what was considered a high status education. When the early Puritans established Latin grammar schools to prepare a leadership class, they built from the ideas of Erasmus; when Harvard College required knowledge of ancient Greek and Latin, they were trying to maintain the foundation for an education of the privileged as advocated by the Dutch scholar, and when Thomas Jefferson filled his library at Monticello with classical works he was indebted to the scholarship of Erasmus. Throughout the 19th century, educational status was gauged by the extent curricula reflected the ideas of Erasmus, and his work set the tone and substance until recently for much of what is considered a "liberal education."

In *The Education of a Prince*, published in1516, Erasmus argued that since society was ruled by hereditary monarchies, the best assurance of a just society was to prepare a young prince to rule by wisdom, honor, and virtue. This took a gifted tutor in addition to the right kind of studies. Mastery of the elements of Greek and Latin was essential, he thought, to be followed by the study of the Bible and the work of the great ancients: Plutarch, Seneca, Aristotle, Cicero, and most importantly, Plato. Finally, the prince would be exposed to history. Since he believed in aristocratic rule, he wanted to bring together in the mind of the prince the wisdom of classical literature and the knowledge of religion as an indirect means of creating the good society (Cremin, 1970, p. 60). Like others of his time, he believed that learning was linked with virtue and morality. An educated person would be a good person. Post-revolutionary leaders in America were receptive to his beliefs.

Education and the Creation of an Orderly Society

Erasmus was not a revolutionary. He stressed the importance of education as a means of maintaining a docile and orderly society under the rule of a virtuous elite. In this sense, he appealed to post-revolutionary American leaders, particularly Federalists. In today's terms, he advocated use of education as a tool of social control. The populace when "properly" instructed would learn to follow the right course without recourse to laws and punishment. Children at an early age were exposed to the morality of religion and the literature inherited from the great thinkers of the past. Erasmus gave us the idea of the ideal public leader as well as an idea of the means by which the character of the populace could be raised through the civilizing influence of the knowledge of the past. Education could be an instrument of personal and social betterment. While early leaders rejected ideas on the inherited rights of aristocracy, without hesitation they accepted the ideas of Erasmus on how to prepare a social and political elite: immersion in the classical Greek and Latin writers and study of the scriptures would stock the mind with superior intellectual vision and cultivate virtuous behavior (Woodward, 1964).

His ideas appealed to early Americans because of the promise of advancement in social status. To early Americans his work suggested that education could produce the "cultured gentleman," the well-rounded man who knew ancient Greek and Latin, was versed in the great works of literature and philosophy, knew history and politics, and by virtue of superior being was best suited to leadership and the privilege of wealth (Karier, 1967).

Very early, George Washington, John Adams, and Thomas Jefferson proposed a national university along the ideas of Erasmus that would prepare an elite leadership class. The idea that the social status of the individual could be improved through education also was highly appealing to the middle class in America desirous of upward mobility. If their children could study the ancient Greek, Latin, and philosophy that rich children did, they too could acquire status. It is not surprising that throughout the post-colonial period and up into the early 1900s schools throughout the nation, from elementary level to the collegiate, reflected a classical curriculum.

The idea of a national university was discussed at the Constitutional Convention, advanced by Washington in his first and last annual messages to Congress in 1790 and 1796, and promoted by his four immediate successors. The argument in support was that "a national university would enable the United States to develop a class of men free from the restricting prejudices of provincialism and sectionalism" (Rudolph, 1962, p. 42). Nothing happened. The proposals ran afoul of the same parochial interests that they were intended to defeat. But a major outcome was to help shift the national discussion on education from its rather limited focus on church and family to state responsibility.

John Locke, the State, and Education

For Americans, John Locke (1632–1707) was perhaps the most influential Enlightenment writer. The very framework of American revolutionary thought is based on Locke. Born near Bristol, England, into a family of modest means he managed to acquire an education at Oxford. A contemporary of Isaac Newton, Locke gained attention through connections, travel, and brilliant writing. This was the time of the "Glorious Revolution" when in what amounted to a bloodless coup Protestants William and Mary were brought from Holland in 1688 to assume the throne of England, averting a second civil war in the same century. After political maneuvering, James Stuart, the Catholic son of Charles II, stepped aside. This quelled a potential religious war.

In the midst of considerable intellectual and political upheaval, Locke offered through writings such as *Letters Concerning Toleration* (1689–1692), *An Essay Concerning Human Understanding* (1690), and *Two Treatises on Government* (1690) a vision of mixed government based on informed experience, reasoning, and empirical experiment. Americans used his concepts of mixed government. "It was," Lawrence Cremin (1970) pointed out, "but a short step to such characteristic Enlightenment doctrine as government by the consent of the governed, education for the business of living, and the possibility of progress in the world" (p. 255). Thomas Jefferson directly took ideas and wording from Locke's writings on government and put them into the Declaration of Independence; James Madison, George Mason, Thomas Paine, as well as other revolutionary leaders fed off the words of John Locke. Our Constitution reflects Locke.

The right to govern in Locke's view is grounded in contracts freely entered into by citizens in order to enable them to live more easily and freely with each other. This viewpoint undermined the "concept of sacred monarchy" and promoted a scheme of "rights and duties" such as found in the United States Constitution and Bill of Rights (MacCulloch, 2009). Locke also supported the right of all individuals to labor and own land, but while he declared in *Two Treatises of Government* that slavery was a "vile and miserable practice," at the same time he helped to draft and revise the constitution for the Carolina colony that sanctioned slavery. John Locke also wrote and talked a lot about the rights and freedom for men, but with an exception or two he was curiously silent about the rights of the half of the human species that were women.

Locke on Education

Locke's major central educational idea is that individuals are variously endowed by nature but can be shaped through education. Put another way, man has the capacity through empirical reasoning and action to improve individuals and society, an affirmation fundamental to Enlightenment thought. Some would have to warm up to the idea, but reformers of the day used Locke's beliefs as they attempted to mold instruction around the natural unfolding of the child. They were attracted to his idea that the child was neither good nor evil, but rather an individual being that could be shaped through a proper education into a virtuous, thinking, self-directed person. This challenged more "conventional" thinking rooted in religious doctrine.

But what constitutes "proper" education? Engaging the individual in a personal observation of the natural world. "Knowing is seeing," according to Locke. He felt that knowledge of the natural world was arrived at through the sense organs. This is what he called "sensations."

But the mind also engaged in its own operations such as thinking, analyzing, believing, doubting, reasoning, and knowing, which he termed "reflections." Sensations and reflections result in "ideas." Small children start out and by degrees over time shape experiences into sensations, and then into reflections and eventually ideas. Through sense impressions and inner reflection the mind, which is conceived as a *tabula rasa,* is filled, and eventually the child is able to work independently with his own ideas. Simple sensory impressions are combined and compounded through ideas to reflect complex concepts. The capacity for what we term today "self-learning" is developed (Curtis & Boultwood, 1965).

Locke stressed a number of attributes of what he considered good teaching. Teaching should be conceived as guiding the learner toward the objective of achieving self-control; reward and satisfaction in the form of praise, help, and reinforcement are more effective than punishment, and punishment itself should be avoided. Individuals are born with different capacities and aptitude; the significant differences between students need to be recognized and instruction tailored accordingly. Early learning should be made pleasant for children, and it is essential to engage children in activity. The inability to adequately reason stems from the lack of an adequate balance in the acquisition of experiences; children need exposure to wide experiences in order to develop full understanding of their natural and intellectual environment. Balanced learning required exercise in the wide use of mental faculties. He regarded the formation of useful habits as more important than the mere acquisition of knowledge.

These are kernel ideas that underlie the thinking of Swiss educator Johann Pestalozzi, the educational practices of Francis Parker of the Quincy, Massachusetts, schools in the 1880s, of the psychology of John Dewey, of the innovative educational practices of Maria Montessori, and of the cognitive psychology of today. Locke's influence on educational thought and practice spans three centuries.

Cremin (1970) observed that running through all of Locke's ideas on education is a utilitarian flavor: the development of useful citizens who can fully participate in a virtuous civic, business, and commercial life. This appealed to Americans trying to carve out a stable life in an uncertain environment. Using Locke's reasoning, Benjamin Franklin argued in his *Proposals Relating to the Educating of Youth in Pennsylvania* (1744) for a secular, practical education including agriculture and mechanical studies along with English, rather than Greek and Latin. Locke's political ideas also had immense appealed to post-revolutionary Americans seeking to form the new nation. In a real sense, Locke's writings on government and education formed a tie between the political thought of the Revolution and the intellectual revolution of the Enlightenment. Locke's ideas on government were a direct counterpoint to Erasmus.

Locke greatly influenced educational thinking in the 19th and 20th centuries. He fed the thoughts of educators who were looking for ways to offset some of the harsh and limiting aspects of schooling. Importantly, he reinforced the belief that the individual as well as society could be shaped through education. As a nation, we could build "a more perfect union," and as well develop an enlightened citizenry that supported the goals and processes of democracy. Influenced by Locke, Thomas Jefferson contended that a virtuous natural leadership could be created through proper schooling; Noah Webster argued that the immigrant child, rural migrant, factory worker, Catholic, or former loyalist could be conditioned to be good citizens through lessons of nationalism, morality, and patriotism; and Horace Mann suggested that the influence of a system of common schools could mollify class and religious differences.

Jefferson: Class, Education, and Opportunity

Feeding off ideas of Locke, Thomas Jefferson was among the first revolutionary leaders to propose widely available public education as a way to achieve national goals. "Natural" leaders would be created while at the same time free, public supported educational opportunity would be extended to citizens. While governor of Virginia, Jefferson presented to the legislature in 1778 a *Bill for the More General Diffusion of Knowledge* outlining his scheme for a comprehensive system of education. The proposed system was composed of three tiers loosely linked. He intended to "rake from the rubbish" the truly gifted and create a "natural aristocracy" based on talent and virtue. Educational opportunity would be widely available for everyone through the first tier, free local public schools for three years. For those continuing on, fee-paying schools were available, and among those unable to afford fees the most promising male student from each school would be selected and supported. At the end of the first year, one third of the non-fee-paying students would be selected out, with the remainder continuing on for the second year. After the third year, the top student among those who could not afford to pay fees would be selected to join the rest of the students for an additional four years of education. A select number of the very best students among the poor could attend William and Mary College along with the sons of the affluent (Curti, 1959; Kaestle, 1983).

Jefferson did not believe in equality of abilities among men, and like Erasmus he affirmed the necessity of a leadership class, but he differed from Erasmus in that he wanted leaders to evolve "naturally" based on talent and virtue rather than inherited "rights." Jefferson also differed from Federalists in that he believed that within common people was the potential for leadership if it could be properly cultivated through education. But Jefferson apparently was unaware of the inconsistency of his own thinking. By his proposed system, very few poor boys would reach the top, and if they did they would join sons of the affluent, many of whom reached the higher levels of education and entered the ranks of the privilege by virtue of their family wealth despite mediocre ability and effort.

The "natural aristocracy" of leadership that he expected to evolve through his plan was not in any true sense of the word "natural," but rather primarily represented the wealthy and landed gentry. At the same time, however, Jefferson left us with the idea of "creaming," that is, selecting the more academically deserving and providing financial assistance so that they can develop their full intellectual potential. Of course, in his mind he was not considering women, Blacks, or Amerindians. Nevertheless, today we see the practice of creaming in almost all of our institutions of higher learning as fellowships and financial assistance are granted to highly deserving students regardless of class, ethnicity, or gender.

Jefferson's proposal on extending education to the masses also had lasting influence. As in the case of other revolutionary leaders, he believed that popular government rested on the foundation of an enlightened populace. This probably is his most enduring legacy. When Jefferson presented his *Plan* to the Virginia legislature in 1778 and again in 1817 it was rejected, however. Later he was to claim that this was because of "ignorance, malice, egoism, fanaticism, religious, political and local perversities"(Kaestle, 1983, p. 9). In more simple terms, rejection at the time probably was because of the opposition of the affluent. They did not feel a need for public schools for their own children, and they did not want to pay taxes to fund schools for the sons of the "vulgar" crowd. This attitude could be found throughout the new nation, and when coupled with religious differences presented a difficult barrier to surmount in the quest for public-supported schools for everyone.

In a more practical sense, the plan was considered too expensive, would cut into the hold for profit schools had on education, and disrupt the tutorial system the landed gentry relied on; in addition, the plan was thought unachievable. In the widely dispersed, sparsely populated agrarian Virginia, it would be impossible to develop and maintain the institutions and administrative structures required, critics alleged. In a mood of discouragement, he remarked "people generally have more feeling for canals and roads than education" (Kaestle, 1983, p. 199).

Like much of Jefferson's legacy, his educational influence was achieved after his death. With the onset of violent labor unrest and ugly ethnic and religious riots in the 1830s and 1840s, many of the affluent were convinced by enlightened self-interest that public-supported education was a necessary step for keeping society from collapsing and destroying any sense of social and political unity. The former Federalists, now Wigs, probably tripped the scale when they got behind public-supported education. They, too, could be destroyed in the aftermath of social dislocation (Curti, 1959).

Recognition of Jefferson's ideas on teaching and learning came late. He was out of step, indeed, probably ahead of most contemporaries. His ideas come down to us today as early American reflections on the Enlightenment ideas of Bacon and Newton, and Locke and Rousseau. He rejected institutionalized religion, the concept of original sin, and the idea of a fixed human nature, but continued to be guided by his own values of man's rights and a pragmatism tempered with realism. He promoted science and technology. He was a product of the "Age of Reason" and had faith if not in the perfectibility of man then at least in the possibility of considerable improvement through education. Unlike Federalists, he expressed confidence in the ability of an enlightened citizenry to make rational decisions and to act accordingly in the best interest of society. He strongly argued for freedom of speech and press, the right to free inquiry, and against censorship and control (Karier, 1967).

His educational ideas on teaching and learning reflected his deep sense of commitment to education as an instrument of general enlightenment. In contrast to common practice of his day, following the ideas of Locke, Jefferson wanted to use instruction to develop the essential basic tools of reading, writing, and finding information so that the young could engage in forming their own opinions and judgments. Reading newspapers and history were primary ways of gaining knowledge about humanity. The purpose of instruction was not to indoctrinate, but rather to bring out the innate moral sense and reasoning capacity an individual is born with, and help to shape this capacity in mature ways. With echoes of Rousseau, Jefferson stated that the individual is "endowed with a sense of right and wrong. This sense is as much a part of his nature as the sense of hearings, seeing, feeling; it is the true foundation of morality" (Spring, 2008, p. 55). A full moral sense, however in Jefferson's eyes, could not be developed until the youth gained enough maturity to make rational decisions. For this reason, he opposed efforts in schools to introduce small children to religious instruction. Jefferson considered this early indoctrination counter to the task of creating citizens capable of making enlightened decisions.

Like most individuals, Jefferson is inconsistent in his actions and beliefs and this is especially true in reference to slavery. He talked in elevated terms about equality, the rights of man, justice, and freedom, yet his very livelihood depended on an enslaved class that labored to keep him in fine linens and silks, fed with the best of foods and wine, housed in a superb mansion of his own design, and placed in the highest station in society. The money that he lavishly spent on a lifestyle that he could not afford, on the exquisite library that he assembled at Monticello, on the luxury goods that he shipped in from Europe, and on the political campaigns that elevated him to the highest office in the land and to a place in history, was earned from the toiling of individuals that received no recognition or expression of appreciation for their sacrificed lives. In demeaning terms he disparaged Blacks in public statements, but yet seemed to reverse his views in guarded, private moments, and for over three decades kept the Black concubine Sally Hemings, fathering seven children. He supported slavery, but yet wanted to free his own Black workforce at the time of his death, but could not because of the considerable debt that he had accumulated. His estate was bankrupt. He wanted to be known as a humanitarian, but on his instructions left the dirty work to overseers of applying brutal discipline and punishment to his plantation workforce when they were not generating enough income to support his wants (Gordon-Reed, 2008). Jefferson left a brilliant legacy that forever gives him an exalted position in the nation's history, but there are dark corners that one does not want to closely look into.

Noah Webster: Educating the Republican Citizen

Unlike Jefferson, Noah Webster had an immediate impact on the formulation of education in the new nation. His work was highly influential and set the tone for antebellum education. He was a former country schoolmaster and directly addressed classroom instruction through his widely adopted series of textbooks and spellers. As a Federalist, he had deep faith in education as a tool of social control. His objective was to create a dominant Protestant-American culture that embraced the ideals of patriotism, nationalism, and Christian morality. In contrast to Jefferson who wanted children to learn early in school basic tool subjects to equip them to later form their own beliefs out of school, Webster believed that children should be indoctrinated early through the use of catechisms, patriotic stories, lessons in morality, use of the Bible, and specifically written "American" textbooks.

Webster believed that the new nation had to achieve cultural independence from England and develop a sense of national unity. To achieve this, he argued, English texts or British reprints had to be removed from schools and replaced with American material that extolled the values of loyalty, patriotic commitment, respect for property rights, and virtues of industry and thrift. Webster set about doing this, publishing his wildly successful blue-backed speller, *The American Spelling Book in 1783,* and the *American Dictionary,* both designed to record colloquial words and Americanisms and simplify English to give it an "American" cant. A companion grammar and reader were also published. An "American" version of English would work to unify the nation.

In the first 15 years, close to a million and a half copies of the speller were sold, and by 1850 sales reached a million copies a year, with total sales reaching 75 million by 1875. In the South during the Civil War the Confederacy even made a special edition of the spelling book for its youth. This was one of the most successful secular books ever. Webster's dictionary also was highly successful and is still in use today. Others, such as Jedidiah Mores produced the bestseller, *Geography Made Easy*, keyed to the new nation, and newly published math books taught children how to figure in dollars and cents instead of pounds, shillings, and pence. In 1788, Nicholas Pike brought out *A New and Complete System* of "American" math that quickly became the standard text (Morrison, 1965, p. 288).

Webster's instructional model was widely copied. The key element was that while learning lessons on vocabulary use, reading, and writing, children at the same time also were immersed in lessons designed to make them good citizens, condition them to conform, and strengthen their emotional ties to the new nation. The textbooks and readers bulged with stories of nationalism, patriotism, and morality. The exploits of the revolutionary leaders were idealized, "love of country" was a recurring theme, a national literature was presented, and virtues of obedience, acceptance, and conformity were wrapped in a dominant American-Protestant veneer. Little children were told that one had to be content with one's lot in life. This was God's will; there was virtue in poverty, and through frugality, industry, and conformance to moral and religious teachings one could improve his/her station in life; pain, suffering, misery, and misfortune were necessary conditions that tested one's beliefs; property was the source of position and contentment; it was the best citizens that possessed the largest share of property and power, and this condition had to be respected and protected by all (Curti, 1959, pp. 32–34; Springs, 2008, pp. 51–54). It not surprising that Webster had great appeal to a fledgling nation that was insecure, that was struggling to define itself, that was undergoing rapid social, economic and political change, and that was trying to build unity among highly disparate parts. He made the upper class comfortable with the idea of education extended to the lower classes.

Webster was conservative in his social, political, and religious views, and he transferred these views to a remarkable variety of educational writings. He was successful precisely because he was conservative. At a time of great uncertainty, it was comforting to draw lessons of support from traditions of the past. The social radicalism of the Enlightenment as expressed through national leaders such as Jefferson was simply too risky for an expanding middle class. They looked for future stability in the stability that they already knew. It is in local schools where the educational forms inherited from the colonial period had to be recast and formalized in order to expand opportunity, to establish the legitimacy of law, to garner financial and political support, and to achieve fuller political meaning. And it was Noah Webster who provided what appeared to be the best balance in this transition to a more expansive and inclusive concept of public-supported education.

The Constitution, Religion, and Education

Among the most continuous issues faced by post-revolutionary Americans were those of social class, poverty, opportunity, and wealth. They presented strong impediments to the formation of national unity. Religion was an equally strong impediment. Almost all other issues were somehow eventually linked with religion.

The English colonization of America was primarily Protestant. Religious rebels carried the waving banner of Protestantism with all of its splintering factions to the colonies. The battles with the Spanish and French were over power and wealth, but they were cast in religious terms: virtuous Protestants overcoming the power of Catholic corruption, pope and church. With few exceptions, Catholics in the English colonies were not allowed to vote or hold civil office. The Pennsylvania assembly in 1705 disenfranchised Catholics, Jews, and non-believers. Even control of the only Catholic founded colony, Maryland, was seized by Anglicans in the 1690s.

The "heathen" Indians were overrun, subdued, and conquered in the name of Christianity. Their religions were stamped out in the name of salvation. The Puritans created the tightest bond between church, state, and school, but throughout all of the early English colonies religion could not be easily separated from everyday civic life, and with few exceptions from the smallest neighborhood dame school to the growing network of colleges, Protestant doctrine reigned. Churches were the founding and supporting agencies of schools, and instruction was religious based. The newly founded colleges were theological in tone.

But as the 1600s turned into the 1700s, the sectarian splintering evident among Protestants became marked. Religious differences became political differences, and sectarian rivalries between Protestants became as ugly as conflicts between Protestants and Catholics. The European battles of the Reformation begat conflict in the colonies. The shortage of clergy coupled with isolation also fed a growing pluralism. Local leaders free from central oversight crafted their own religious versions often at variance with more standard doctrine, resulting in what MacCulloch (2009) termed additional "slices in a Protestant cake" (p. 730). Religious tensions dominated 18th-century colonial America and were carried on though the Revolutionary War and up well into the 19th century (Phillips, 1999). Following the war, as settlers poured over the mountain ridges and into the frontier lands, there was a proliferation of small, loosely allied churches that would make up yet more slices of the Protestant cake.

But also, a new intellectual force came into play. The Enlightenment and Reformation opened the Bible and attendant doctrine to intense scrutiny. Catholic orthodoxy was first questioned, but all biblical theology soon came under examination. Secular thought won its independence from theology. The intellectual role of Christianity became less encompassing as scientific thought and objective reasoning came into focus on the natural and the everyday world of man. The moral and ethical precepts of Christianity were accepted, but on secular terms as human ideals. This intellectual shift spawned *deism*, the belief in a divine authority but not as commonly portrayed by the organized Church. The religious story in the Bible was thought to be just that, a nice story, a collection of writings composed and modified over time by human hands. Deist believed in a divine creator, but the world was left to go on its own way to follow the laws of the universe that were formulated by God but understandable through human reason. Reasoning itself was considered a divine gift to be used by man to seek truth as revealed through nature. Ideas of Locke, Voltaire, Rousseau, and Newton run through deist thought (Tarnas, 1991).

Eighteenth-century American colonists were attracted to deism. In New England, Puritan influence was fading, and throughout the colonies Enlightenment ideas increasingly appealed to a population that was grappling with the taming of nature. The intellectual leadership was intrigued by the idea reinforced through Locke that man can control his own destiny through a belief in science, reasoning, and progress. New knowledge in the practical arts was sweeping the land, and scientific advancement showed what human reasoning could accomplish. Also among the colonies further splintering continued as increasingly local pastors went their own way, ignoring or challenging the more mainline denominations. The considerable religious stirring throughout this period resulted in hybrid evangelical offshoots, "cool" versions of Christianity, and a substantial erosion of beliefs. It is against this backdrop that the times produced what is termed the "Great Awakening."

The Great Awakening

The Great Awakening was a response primarily by New England Congregationalists (formerly Puritans) and middle-colony and southern Presbyterians to what they saw as the considerable softening of religious belief. It was also a reaction to the challenge of secular Enlightenment thought. By the 1730s, the churchgoing population in many colonies was a minority, and many people had no religious affiliations whatsoever. In 1700, for example, Anglicans served roughly one fourth of the colonial population; by the time of the Revolution this number had dropped to one ninth (MacCulloch, 2009, p. 760). In simple terms, the message was that sin was on a rampage, and the country had to get back on the road to salvation.

Jonathan Edwards, a brilliant Massachusetts pastor, is given credit for spearheading the remarkable religious revival that rapidly spread across the colonies. He was able to capture the essence what others were saying in widely appealing terms through his sermons and writings, and give promise to the reconstruction of a near-perfect human society in anticipation of the Second Coming. Charismatic ministers in scores joined, as the movement swept through the colonies like a whirlwind; it forever changed the landscape of American religion.

The Awakening destroyed "the territorial communality which was still the assumption of most religious practice," MacCulloch (2009, pp. 759–760) observed. Religious communities were thrown into turmoil. Revivalism led to dissention as "New Light" churches broke off from established congregations, freelance preachers struck out on their own, and religious interpretation and practice became a matter of choice. New dominations emerged. Evangelical Protestantism carried the fervor of the Awakening into the frontier and separate Baptist and Methodist Black churches were established in the South, fostering an African-American Christian culture. Morrison (1965, p. 151) summed up the Awakening: "It stimulated a fresh interests in religion, caused hundreds of new churches to be founded, strengthened the movement for religious liberty, gave the common man a new sense of his significance, and thus indirectly contributed to the American Revolution." Yet more slices were added to the Protestant cake.

The Constitution and Education

Religion was a major issue that revolutionary leaders had to address. Religious divisiveness blocked national unity. Religious divisions reflected deep community, regional, class, wealth, and political differences that threatened the formation of the union (Phillips, 1999). The national leadership itself was divided. Undefined or deist beliefs were held by a number of revolutionary leaders. George Washington, for example, was ambivalent about religion, and tended to talk in terms of "providence" or "destiny" rather than of "God." Thomas Jefferson refused to support the new Constitution unless it was accompanied with a Bill of Rights eliminating the possibility of religious domination over government. Jefferson was an avowed deist, as was Benjamin Franklin, Thomas Paine, and others. Jefferson's strongest check on organized religion was his Bill for Establishing Religious Freedom, formulated in 1779 and submitted to the Virginia Assembly in 1789. James Madison used the bill to model the First Amendment to the Constitution.

At the same time, Anglican's held on to a disproportional share of influence from the fact that revolutionary leaders tended to come from the educated and wealthy class which outside of New England was heavily made up of Anglicans. John Adams, a follower of the Puritan New England beliefs that he grew up with, along with others had to find ways not only to work with nonbelievers, evangelicals, and deists but as well with the two thirds of the signers of the Declaration of Independence who were Anglicans. But Anglicans also made up the bulk of former loyalists. The strife between Presbyterians and Anglicans was particularly strong (Phillips, 1999).

But there was also a significant gap in religious zeal between the general population and the revolutionary leadership. Elite education and wealth tended to lead the revolutionary leadership away from the Awakening and to the Enlightenment and deism (MacCulloch, 2009, p. 763). The writings of the classical humanists, the science of Newton, and the revolutionary ideas of Rousseau were more engaging than the dire warnings of Jonathan Edwards or the revival ministry of the iterant preacher trekking though the valleys of the trans Appalachians. How could all of the religious differences be accommodated? They could not, so the best course of action was taken—that is, to neutralize differences.

Both the First and Tenth Amendments in the Bill of Rights address the question of religion and education. Both can be portrayed as promoting freedom of religion, but the underlying motivation of both was to protect the individual from the imposition by the state of specific religious beliefs, and to irrevocably maintain the separation of religion from the state. Revolutionary leaders were acutely aware of keeping a "wall of separation" between Church and State as a way to prevent the imposition of any one set of beliefs, and to avoid the decent into destructive religious conflict that so bloodied Europe. No one religious voice would have official government sanction.

But equally important to the principle of separation of church and state was education. The system of aristocratic rule based on assumed divine rights that the colonists had just successfully rebelled against was undergirded by the considerable coercive power that is generated through the linkage of state, church, and education. The church provides legitimacy to the state by sanctioning its authority; the state enforces adherence to the church and its beliefs; and both use education to teach allegiance and obedience. Free thought and expression is stifled.

Enlightenment thinkers such as Robert Molesworth rebelled against the use of education by state and church to create an obedient and submissive populace. Generations of Europeans over centuries were kept as serfs in a state of bondage akin to slavery by a state and church alliance that controlled all knowledge, temporal and spiritual. It was only when the lock on knowledge was broken that an explosion in secular thought occurred that helped to destroy the reinforcing bond that maintained absolute rule. Molesworth in his influential revolutionary work *Account of Denmark as It Was in the Year 1692,* along with a series of essays by his colleagues John Trenchard and Thomas Gordon published collectively in the latter 1720s as *Cato's Letters,* exerted immense influence on revolutionary thinkers. Repeated reprints were issued in the colonies over a 25-year period, stimulating rebellion by justifying independence from a system of aristocratic rule (Spring, 2008). Schools would have to be free they stressed. The questioning of the Enlightenment emancipated education from the control of church and state, and made it possible to break free from a system of hereditary absolutism that characterized Europe for close to a thousand years.

The principle of the separation of church and state was a consequence of the spread of secular thought across the leadership class and down into the middle class, of the influence of the American Enlightenment, and of prodigious growth of religious pluralism spawned by the Great Awakening. In practical terms, there was no way to maintain a single established religion.

It took almost a hundred years, however, for the principle to be widely applied in America that the state does not have the right to impose religious beliefs on citizens, that religion does not have the right to impose beliefs on the state, and that public-supported education must be kept free and separate from the coercive tendencies of both. The First and Tenth Amendments applied to the federal level, not state. Following the Revolution individual states continued to supply tax dollars to support schools operated through religious groups, but they shifted aid to multiple religious establishments in an effort to accommodate increasing pluralism. This did not work. By 1791, nine states moved to complete separation. A battle continued to play out at the state level that significantly hindered the spread of common, public-supported education. Bitter sectarian rivalries, fights over public tax dollars, growing secular views, and the continuation of the Enlightenment spirit kept the issue of religion and schools in a churning state of flux. Finally, with the passage of the Fourteenth Amendment and its interpretation by the Supreme Court, the principle of separation was made applicable to states. But the court's decision was not made until the early 20th century (Karier, 1967, pp. 37–38; MacCulloch, 2009, pp. 755–765).

Today, some continue to strongly believe that *their* religious beliefs should be imposed by the state on public education. But in a nation that is finally becoming fully conscious of its pluralistic inheritance, the question of religious values and public education has become even more complex. Religion is inextricably linked with questions of morality and values. Parents want morality and values to be reflected through schools. But the question always is "whose values?" Today, the issue of religious beliefs is co-joined and immersed in political issues of "family values" and diversity. Schooling always conveys values, and as a nation we will continue to struggle with issues of values, diversity, schools, and religion that have evaded answers, issues, moreover, that are embedded deeply in our colonial past.

Rousseau, Revolution, and the Child

Probably the most vilified opponent of organized religion was Jean-Jacques Rousseau (1712–1778). He was one of the most effective critics of organized religion. Rousseau made people angry—even today. He cast doubt on the biblical concept of original sin, threatening to destroy the very pillar of Judeo-Christian doctrine. Counter to church belief, he asserted that man is born without sin but it is society and its social institutions, including the church, that corrupt. His writings on government were revolutionary. The opening sentences of a major work, *The Social Contract*, inflamed: "Man is born free; and everywhere he is in chains." The march toward the perfectibility of man depended on the removal of the shackles of government and church, Rousseau pronounced. It was society and the church that kept man from an idealized state and deprived him natural liberty. To be sure, man gains through a state that provides services and perhaps frees him from physical wants, but in return he is subjected to abuses that degrade him, enchains him. What he has in natural liberty he gives up to civic and religious authority. It is up to man to rebel against oppressive traditional institutions in the quest for dignity and freedom.

Rousseau flouted convention and caused in his lifetime such a political and religious uproar through his writings that an arrest order was issued by the French government, and *Emile*, this major work on education, was condemned and copies ordered burned. He sought refuge in a friendlier place, but in towns across Switzerland he was either refused residency or ordered to leave after a relatively short time. He seemed to have had a talent for quarreling with others, and his life of debauchery offended. He settled in England with the philosopher David Hume, but after some time his contentious behavior ended in violent disagreement and a period of wandering. He finally returned in 1770 to Paris and remained to the end of his life after assurance that the arrest warrant would not be activated.

Counter to his published views of kindness and obligation toward children, he placed his own five children in a foundling home and neglected them. His life is one of contradiction between the way that he lived and his expressed beliefs. Nevertheless, he was profoundly influential. Will and Ariel Durant (1967) asserted Rousseau "had more effect upon posterity than any writer or thinker" of the 18th century. "Europe was ready for a gospel that would exalt feeling above thought, and Rousseau gave this and more" (p. 3). To this day his work is loved by "liberals" and hated by "conservatives."

Rousseau and Education

His influence on education is enduring and probably more far-reaching than any other later thinker. He made the contested assertion that the starting and ending point of all education is the child and its nature, not the content of instruction. It is the responsibility of the teacher to provide a protecting, nurturing environment in which, echoing Locke, the child learns through experience and discovery. Like Locke, he stressed the importance of sense impressions as fundamental to learning. In anticipating the concept of "development tasks," he advocated different educational experiences for children of different ages, divided into four stages: infant, childhood, preadolescent, and adolescence. Instruction should be laced with activity based on the abilities, interests, and outlook of the child, but the goal always is the free development of the child rather than the cultivation of skills for society.

His ideas on children and teaching stand in stark contrast to practices of the day. Children should be nurtured, not treated harshly; learning should be interesting and fun, not tedious and rote; what children learn should be cast in terms of their world, not the world of adults. Rousseau's own words best convey his ideas on education and children:

"Nature wants children to be children before they are men. If we deliberately pervert this order, we shall get premature fruits which are neither ripe nor well flavored, and which soon decay. . . . Childhood has ways of seeing, thinking, and feeling, peculiar to itself, nothing can be more foolish than to substitute our ways for them."

"We know nothing of childhood; and with our mistaken notions, the further we advance, the further we go astray. The wisest writers devote themselves to what a man ought to know, without asking what a child is capable of learning. They are always looking for the man in the child without considering what he is before he becomes a man . . . Begin thus by making a more careful study of your scholars, for it is clear that you know nothing about them" (Curtis & Boultwood, 1965, pp. 276–277).

What Rousseau said about education was not particularly new, and his debt to Locke is obvious, but it is the way that he presented thoughts on children that jolted society. Children had natural rights, and this had to be acknowledged. They were more than miniature adults, and had to be treated as such and placed in the center of educational development. Children had to be sheltered from the adult world, which is corrupting. His thoughts had immediate impact in his day, and have had a strong educational presence for over 200 years.

Rousseau's denial of original sin was explosive. It brought into question the very foundation of Christianity, and exposed him to condemnation from church and government. He was corrupting the very civilizing foundation of society it was alleged. But Rousseau argued that under the shelter of what was a theological myth there had become established a repressive, harsh concept of education that ignored the very character of childhood, did violence to all that is good in human nature, retarded "natural" development, and resulted in adults stunted and damaged. Rousseau's claim was that all deviations from virtue could be traced to the influence of the child's environment and in particular to ill-advised direction by the parent or teacher (Curtis & Boultwood, 1965, p. 278).

Rousseau's influence spread considerably beyond education. He is blamed for inciting revolutionary violence, for the bloody excesses of the French Revolution, for destabilizing society, and for debasing religion. But he also is given credit for early articulating dimensions of what we term today "Romanticism." Richard Tarnas (1991, pp. 366–394) pointed out two aspects of Enlightenment thinking. One is rooted in scientific thought and stresses the secular, the rational, and the empirical. Scientific thought tends to be skeptical toward tradition, and views the past primarily as a starting point for the pursuit and growth of knowledge. The other aspect is grounded in the Renaissance and classical Greek and Roman culture. Man is viewed as part of an organic unity engaged in the drama of human life where imaginative and creative powers come into play, where spiritual aspirations, emotional temperament, and artistic expression are outward signs of the essence of the human soul, and where self-awareness, imagination, irrationality, and emotion drive human action. Human consciousness thrives. The dark side of the human soul also is recognized. Rousseau could understand his own actions, and perhaps, Jefferson's human inconsistencies as well as his own.

First conspicuously recognized in the work of Rousseau, the Romantic vision of the late 18th and early 19th centuries is found in the philosophy of Goethe, Schiller, and German Romanticism; in the poetry of Blake, Shelley, Keats, Byron, and Whitman; and in the writing of Emerson and Thoreau, and on to the counterculture and its various forms today (Tarnas, 1991, p. 375). The crux of Rousseau's enduring legacy is found at the intersection of pedagogy with Romanticism.

Useful Education: Commonwealth Men and Benjamin Franklin

Advocates of intellectual freedom such as Robert Molesworth, John Trenchard, and Thomas Gordon were members of a group that became known as the "Commonwealth men." Other political thinkers, scientists, inventors, and early industrialists such as Matthew Boulton, James Watt, Erasmus Darwin, Samuel Galton, and Joseph Priestly were leading members (Spring, 2008). Over several decades in what were called Dissenting Academies they mobilized discussion around such issues as the form and role of government, human rights, free speech, religion in schools, and social and political freedom. As their influence spread, Dissenting Academies became a focal point for community discussion.

These were self-financed schools outside of the church or government orbit. Members paid dues and had the rights to a lending library. At a time when books were out of the reach of many, this was an important way to extend knowledge. Lectures and discussion were a source of political and social thought. Generally, a freer, open society was advocated that promoted individual liberty and economic opportunity. Arguing against a political and economic system that kept people in a state of subservience and poverty, the Commonwealth men advocated the use of schools to redirect the economy along the lines of the rapidly emerging Industrial Revolution. The technical and intellectual skills taught in the Academies would open opportunity, as well as feed prosperity. The importance of this argument cannot be overstated. It challenged the hold of the classical curriculum on education.

Similar offspring groups were formed in the colonies. These were instrumental in the progression of revolutionary thought across the colonies. Like the Commonwealth men in England, American thinkers questioned the very rights of the current aristocratic system to rule. The discussion among Americans had a profound influence on the Revolution, and their ideas continued to be reflected in the Constitution and Bill of Rights. The discussion among Americans also had a profound influence on the course of education.

Education as a Tool of Progress

Eighteenth-century schooling was tightly bound to the idea that education should focus on a classical curriculum designed to impart virtue and enhance social standing. Education was conceived primarily as a way to create an elite. It was extremely difficult to break away from the belief that all students, regardless of their station in life or probable destiny, profited from emersion in the study of Greek and Latin, the scriptures, and the great literature of the past. The extension of Erasmus's concepts of the "educated gentlemen" continued to reign. Practical, useful subjects were considered patently inferior in intellectual content, and only suitable for the toiling classes to be learned outside of formal schooling. It was extremely difficult to counter a concept of schooling that was almost exclusively defined along classical lines.

Cracks, however, appeared. As the considerable impact of scientific and technological thought increasingly became apparent in 18th-century colonial America, public perception shifted. By the mid-1700s, the evidence was becoming obvious that there was a change in attitudes of parents. The demand was for a more secular, relevant, and useful education. Enrollment in Latin grammar schools went down while at the same time more youth enrolled in fee-paying "English" schools. These tended to be small, private schools offering a range of subjects from arithmetic, English spelling and grammar, to navigation, surveying, bookkeeping and accounting, and they caught on as parents searched for ways to enhance the earning prospects for their children through useful learning. Their children were not going to become "cultured gentlemen," but at least they could become better off economically. This trend continued after the Revolution and up into and through the common school era.

The Commonwealth men helped to establish the concept that widely available, public-supported education can be used as an instrument of social and economic development. In today's terms, schooling can be used as a tool of social reconstruction. Skills are learned that contribute to individual growth and welfare, and at the same time society benefits because individuals contribute more to the common good. Schooling is conceived as a means through which to promote national social and economic objectives. The argument for the extension of public-supported schools in the mid-1800s went hand in hand with arguments over what subjects are most important to teach. There was a continuous and ongoing national struggle over whether or not "practical subjects" should be made a central part of the college and high school curriculum. In the eyes of defenders of classical languages, science was too practical and utilitarian to be worthy of consideration. By the 1850s, however, the hold of the classical curriculum on the school was breaking down, and by 1900 the battle was lost (Reese, 1995). Very early, Benjamin Franklin contributed to this transformation.

Franklin and the Academy

Among the revolutionary leaders that most effectively promoted the cause of a more practical and useful education was Benjamin Franklin. The son of a poor tallow chandler and soap maker and himself a printer, Franklin understood and had a deep respect for working men. He was sensitive to class barriers. As a product of the Enlightenment, he had little respect for religious doctrine, authoritarianism, class privilege, and aristocracy. He was a remarkable multidimensional genius with outstanding accomplishments in business, publishing, science, diplomacy, and government. He played a major role in the advancement of science in America. He participated in revolutionary activities and was a guiding voice of maturity and wisdom in formulating the governing framework of the new nation (Morgan, 2002).

He grew up in poverty and experienced class discrimination. He spent his life working for the interests of the emerging middle class, advancing schemes of self-education, founding self-improvement clubs, publishing *Poor Richard's Almanac*, supporting charity schools, advancing a plan for an academy and founding a college, which later became the University of Pennsylvania. The impact of his ideas on the later academy movement was far reaching, and he pointed to a model for the spread of similar institutions throughout America during the antebellum period.

In his *Proposal Relating to the Education of Youth in Pennsylvania* (1749), Franklin sketched the outline of an instructional program for the state. No doubt influenced by the work of the English Commonwealth men, instruction would be practical and useful. But he basically dropped the dissenting part, and included exposure to classical works. Always a compromiser, Franklin's ideas accommodated a secular practical education, including agriculture, mechanics, and technical subjects, and a grounding in works from the strong 18th-century classical tradition. He asserted, students should "be taught *every Thing* that is useful, and *every Thing* that is ornamental: But Art is long, and their Time is short. It is therefore propos'd that they learn those Things that are likely to be *most useful* and *most ornamental*, Regard being had to the several Professions for which they are intended" (Vassar, 1965, p. 67).

The academy appealed to parents wanting their child to climb the path of social status as well as to parents concerned that instruction for their child be orientated more toward preparation for adult life. A wide variety of fee-paying subjects were available: English grammar, composition, rhetoric, and oratory; foreign languages, science, and geography; writing, arithmetic, and drawing; agriculture, mechanics, and accounting, among others. Reflecting the influence of Locke, Franklin argued that learning should be both meaningful and useful.

The plan was put into practice in 1753 with the issue of a charter, but it did not develop as Franklin envisioned. The Philadelphia Academy had both an "English School," the site of practical subjects, and a "Classical Department." After returning from a long period abroad, he found that the Classical Department gained dominance over other aspects of the Academy and the school was under control of the "Latinists." His attempt to formulate an alternative to the classical curriculum was premature. Following the Revolution, however, the idea of the academy took hold and spread through both urban and populated rural areas, as parents wanted more educational choices. At a time when the pattern of organized school districts caught hold and the common school movement gained momentum, fee-paying academies spread, becoming part of the remarkable expansion of education opportunity in the early 1800s.

Chapter Five
Education, the War, and Its Aftermath

The revolutionary leadership was primarily made up of the wealthy upper class. As largely a product of European thought, they drew heavily from the Enlightenment ideas that had been fueling the breakdown of the old religious, political, and military order in Europe and that were instrumental in guiding the American Revolution. But educational ideas were slow in taking root in local communities across post-revolutionary American. It took time for the ideas of the national leadership to filter and extend down to the level of community and state school reform. Bernard Bailyn (1960) put it best when he suggested:

> Most of the major statesmen had sweeping schemes for national systems of education and national universities, or other programs by which the new nationalism and its republican spirit might properly be expressed. But the efforts to realize these plans came to nothing. They rose too far above the needs and interests of the scattered, variegated, semi-autonomous communities that comprised the new nation; they placed too concrete a meaning on national life and a national society. The forces shaping education had never been closely related to the higher political organization; they had if anything, grown up in deliberate opposition to them. They owed little to political independence (pp. 45–46).

The educational ideas of a Washington, Jefferson, Rush, or Franklin were important, but they had a long-term rather than an immediate impact. Individual states and communities in post-Revolution America were the focal point of education. Both the Articles of Confederation and the Constitution sidestepped the issue of education responsibility by ignoring it at the national and state levels. The Federal Constitution, however, gave states residual responsibility for education by stipulating that powers not specifically expressed were retained by states, opening the door for state governments to expand their educational role. This is where the impetus for change worked itself out in the opening years of the new century.

Local and State Efforts

Following the Revolution, education was addressed primarily through individual and community initiatives; opportunity was uneven and limited. Some states had embryonic administrative structures. But there was no such thing as a "system" of national education, as continues to be the case today, and even to talk of "state systems" was premature. Great variation in the mix of schools, quality, and opportunity continued to characterize education across the country. Revolutionary leaders talked of instituting national systems, but this did not happen. They argued for a number of proposals, but ideas were slow in taking root. Some never did. Nevertheless, education in all of its incompleteness and variation in the immediate post-revolutionary period significantly contributed to building the national character. The ideals of the revolution filtered into schools, helping to build faith in the new form of government, promote a sense of national unity, and sustain belief in education as a means through which individual and national welfare is promoted.

Across the country, there was widespread rudimentary learning provided primarily through parental initiative, churches, and fee-paying schools of all kinds. The majority of White males appeared to be able to read and write at some level. But public-supported education was limited, and actually in decline. When towns and villages provided schools they tended to be co-financed with parents paying part of the cost. This limited availability, but the more common pattern was to leave the option to parents to find ways to educate their children. In the remote backcountry, on isolated farms, and along the frontier fringe, the ability to read and write typically had to be attained at home or through friends. In larger towns and cities parents could find privateventure, fee-paying options for their children if they could afford the cost, and church-sponsored charity schools existed for the poor. In the South, the literacy rate lagged behind the North, and educational opportunity became even more limited by the time of the Revolution as it had across the country. Poor working class Whites, women, Blacks, and Native Indians in particular had limited if any educational opportunity. In New England, the practice of public funding of schools for everyone had considerably eroded away in the immediate post-revolutionary years to be replaced by more private schools.

The Revolutionary War drained away financial resources otherwise used for education. Parents trying to regain their economic footing in the uncertain post-war years had less to spend for schooling. State and local governments were financially pressed. By 1807 in New York, parochial and private schools were practically the only kinds left, and as late as 1828 more than 24,000 children between the ages of 5 and 15 still did not have available schooling of any kind. A similar situation could be found in Delaware, New Jersey, and Maryland (Curti, 1959).

The lack of educational opportunity also characterized the movement west. The results of the Revolution pushed the line of settlement beyond the western slope of the eastern mountain chains, but as communities established footholds there were few resources left for schools. Indiana did not have a general school law until 1824, and schools were not made free in Indiana, Ohio, and Illinois until the 1850s (Curti, 1959, pp. 24–26). In Virginia, "the handful of free school foundations, so far as they survived the Revolution, hardly touched the masses, and the same was true, with few exceptions, of the old field schools (p. 26)." Virginia only established a public-supported school system as late as 1870.

As for colleges, children of the clerical, professional, merchant, and planting classes mainly made up the student body, further widening the opportunity gap between the well-off and the less-fortunate. At the same time, expanding industrial and commercial development required the provision of a higher level of formal educational preparation that was not readily available to many. For the poor, some educational substitutes were found in infant and charity schools supported through philanthropic efforts but these hardly expanded opportunity. The quality of instruction was low (Curti, 1959, pp. 24–28).

Division, Diversity, and Unity

The country was faced with addressing divisions brought to the surface by the Revolution. And this went beyond the division between the rich and the poor. About 200,000 Tories left and went to Canada or England. In Canada they tipped the balance from a predominately French to an English-speaking nation and cemented English rule. Johnson (1997) observed that those who left were among the biggest losers of the war: "they lost everything—jobs, houses, estates, savings, often their lives" (p. 171).

But the new nation also lost. Those fleeing often were the cream of society and they took their skills with them: landowners, lawyers, merchants, government officers, and learned men. Also skilled craftsmen left: wheelwrights, shipwrights, blacksmiths, builders, printers, coopers, and brewers, among other skilled fields. This was a considerable loss to the new nation that community leaders struggled to mend with expanded forms of skill training. To rebuild and expand the new nation required skills. The demand for a more "practical" education grew. Support for Latin grammar schools dropped as enrollments dived, and enrollments shot up in the "English" school, a private school giving instruction beyond the elementary level in "useful" subjects. Franklin's admonition for more practical education had listeners. Even with its limitations, apprenticeship was attractive and academies attracted attention.

The largest concentration of loyalists in relation to population was in Georgia, New York, and South Carolina, reflecting original immigration, religion, and ethnicity patterns. They were also strong in New Jersey and Massachusetts but almost nonexistent in Virginia, Maryland, and Delaware. Scots tended to be loyal because the Crown gave them generous land grants, and they clashed with patriot militia in South Carolina, Georgia, and the North Carolina backcounty. Catholic Irish and Scotch-Irish were fanatically anti-English, as were other Catholics and the same with Presbyterians. The Huguenots were with the Revolution, but the Germans attempted to stay neutral; the revolutionaries also had to contend with the large number of German mercenaries hired by the English to fight the war in the colonies. Many of the former German combatants elected to stay, swelling the German population in America. The Quakers tried to keep out of the war since they were against all war. The Congregationalists were among the most avid patriots. Anglicans tended to be loyalists and made up the New York Tory stronghold, but they were revolutionaries in Virginia, and a number of wealthy, educated Anglicans played essential roles in the Revolution and its aftermath. They made up the majority of the revolutionary leadership (Johnson, 1997). As efforts were made to generate public support for the financing of common schools, one of the most intractable issues, in fact, was religion. Denominational differences surfaced, but perhaps more contentious were religious differences allied with political differences (Phillips, 1999).

Most loyalists elected to stay in the United States after the war, but they tended not to stay where they originally lived. Perhaps to mask their former allegiance, they moved. Those in the southern states tended to go north into Pennsylvania, New York, and the surrounding states. Others crossed the Appalachians and traveled into the Ohio Valley, Kentucky, and Tennessee. This movement was highly significant according to Johnson (1997). It "diluted the pure English stock of the American population somewhat but, more importantly, it mixed everyone up more . . . transforming people from innumerable ethnic and religious backgrounds into full-blooded American citizens" (p. 174). It is easy to understand why Noah Webster with great urgency advocated that schools should be used to form a "national character"; he wanted to create and solidify a unity that did not fully exist. A major argument for the creation of public-supported schools was to promote allegiance to the new republic.

Issues of diversity were compounded with increased immigration. Following the war immigrants started coming, few at first with the numbers increasing so that by the beginning decades of the 1800s there was an almost continuous flow. Oscar Handlin (1969) reported that between 1815 and the Civil War over 5 million arrived. These were deserters from foreign ships, adventures seeking fortunes or a better life, criminals hiding, and "strays" with no known purpose. Families came, and increasingly groups came in mass to join others from the same European villages that had established a foothold in the new nation. Labor brokers recruited large contingencies of potential workers from poverty-stricken European towns with the lure of jobs and economic security. About 200,000 French came after the revolution of 1789; following the abortive Irish insurrections against the English in 1798 and again in 1803, scores fled to America. Later driven by poverty and starvation, millions of Irish came between 1830 and 1860. As the century wore on, European political upheaval brought Polish, French, Hungarian, Italian, and German exiles to America by the thousands. Large contingencies of Scotch-Irish and Germans came between the early 1800s and the Civil War. In the immediate post–Revolutionary War years, the immigration mix became so varied that "[o]ne could find enough natives of Switzerland, the Azores, Armenia, Poland, Sweden, Spain, China, and Russia to credit the claim that twenty-seven different languages were spoken in Boston" (Handlin, 1969, p. 26).

The promise of a better life escaped many. In cities new arrivals were lost in a swirling sea of labor unrest, economic hardship, poverty, crime, and dirt and disease. New immigrants were despised, robbed, cheated, exploited, and mislead. For many it was difficult to find secure permanent employment, and when jobs were found they often were the least skilled and the lowest paid. Kaestle (1973) observed that by 1790 slum areas were developing in New York, a pattern repeated in other growing cities. New immigrants were paid as little as the employer was able to get away with, and they undercut the wages of more established workers. Immigrants were desperate and would take just about any wage that was offered. Labor strife grew, and to quell it became a cause of the common school movement.

As the nation began to industrialize at a quickened pace in the decades immediately following the turn of the century, violent labor clashes broke out at an alarming rate. Public-supported schools, educational reformers asserted were vital to check unrest and bring the young of the nation together. The voices of educational reformers became more strident as they urgently reasserted that public-supported schools could be used to teach the young nationalism, patriotism, and morality; develop allegiance to the political system; bring the social classes together; and impart skills that would enhance the potential earning power of the young. It is easy to see why Webster's work became so popular, and the practical side of education promoted by Franklin gained adherents. Others moved to establish privately financed charity schools. The more affluent recognized that they had to quell the social dissent and violence in the cities and in the newly industrializing towns in order to thwart the possible collapse of the economic and political system. They put their own money to work founding private charity schools for the working poor.

The Expanding Frontier

Not all immigrants faced poverty. Benjamin Franklin, appealing to Europeans, wrote a pamphlet on the eve of his death extolling the great promise awaiting immigrants. America was a good place for those who worked hard. They could become rich, he said, but countering his exuberance he added "nowhere else are the laboring poor so well fed, well lodged, well clothed and well paid (Johnson, 1997, p. 283). Apparently one could work 14 hours a day, be "well paid," and still be poor.

He was at least partly right in the case of those leaving the port cities and migrating into the sparsely populated rural areas and the opening frontier. Land was abundant and cheap. Land taken from the Indians was sold for $2 an acre, and in some cases as low as $1.25 following a 1796 act of Congress, with up to four years given to pay off the debt. Approximately 3,400,000 acres were sold to individuals in the Northwest during the first 11 years of the 1800s, and another 250,000 acres in Ohio. By 1815, half a million acres annually were being purchased in Illinois. In Alabama, government sales increased from 600,000 acres annually to 2,280,000 acres by 1819. Georgia gave free 200-acre plots to lottery winners (Johnson, 1997, p. 290). This ensured that the country would remain agrarian and an agriculture power for the next 100 years.

In the newly opened lands, schools were needed to address the exceedingly rapid population increase. Rural families were large, and to have 10, 12, 14, or more children was common; families of 20 or 25 children were not unusual, but the mortality rate was high (Nettels, 1938, pp. 441–442). The population throughout the country nevertheless increased at a prodigious rate. Although rural families had little cash, they could barter and had a degree of food security not available to many urban residents. To provide education to a highly dispersed population with limited family and government resources, however, was a challenge that early 19th-century schoolmen faced. Ignorance and illiteracy were commanding issues.

School Districts in Rural America

It was in rural areas where the idea of public-supported common schools got the greatest early boost. Perhaps divisive class and religious differences were less dominant; most rural Americans lived in small, scattered communities that were relatively homogenous when compared with cities. In 1795, for example, around 95% of the population lived in places with less than 2,500 residents and the percentage only edged down to 91% by 1830. The new nation was solidly agrarian in character. It was not until the early 1900s that the nation became urban with more people living in cities than in rural areas.

But how could the early school leaders oversee the many small schools dispersed throughout isolated areas and staffed with a single, young, inexperienced teacher? School districts were formed. Gradually the rural schools were linked into a central administrative district with school inspectors regularly riding a circuit of visitations. Districts schools were financed through school fees, income from public land rent and sales, special levies, and taxes. It was common for communities to provide food and lodging, as part prepayment in a practice termed "boarding around." But the proportion of public support increased over time as more pupils enrolled, many from the poorer families that could not afford cash outlays of any kind. Public money increasingly carried an increasing proportion of support. The move toward tax-supported common schools was underway (Curit, 1959; Kaestle, 1983).

Rural schooling was irregular and diverse. Rural children typically began working around age 8 to 10, and enrollment swelled in the summer and winter months when they were no longer needed to work in the fields. It was not unusual for class attendance to double from 30 students or so to 60 or 70, further crowding the already full one room, and then drop off again. It was a herculean task to maintain learning groups and order, let alone impart learning.

There was no set age for beginning school. Parents sent very young children, as little as 2 or 3 years old to join older children of up to 14 years in the ungraded class. Apparently this was a way to free mothers for work in the home or fields. One disgruntled teacher referred to the tots as "trundle bed trash." Standard practice was to have the little ones seated in the front in easy range of the eyes of the teacher. School attendance consisted primarily of custodial care, and little instruction time was given the toddlers. But apparently some learned to read at an early age through observing lessons for the older pupils (Kaestle, 1983).

Classes were roughly grouped by age, but the text material varied greatly. Children brought with them to school the material that they had at home and this varied from child to child. Instruction tended to center around a smattering of reading, writing, and arithmetic, with the Old and New Testaments serving as source material. There may be some grammar and geography instruction, and the use of catechisms as a learning tool was common. The percentage of students attending for very long fluctuated greatly from community to community. Most of the young did not continue in school for long. Smaller communities had higher and longer attendance rates. Overall, gross enrollment and attendance rates were higher in rural school districts then in urban (Kaestle, 1983).

Urban Impetus for Schooling

In urban areas primarily throughout the North there were multiple education options, if one had money. The merchant and privileged classes primarily viewed education as a way to confirm one's social and economic status through a classical curriculum that imparted cultural polish. The continuing influence of Erasmus is evident. Some of the rich sent sons off to expensive boarding schools or hired tutors. Some of the more forward thinking realized that their children could benefit from a more timely education and sought out private schools that offered "modern subjects." Their sons would still be at the top among the privileged, but now they acquired skills useful to run business enterprises and industrial establishments in an economy that was transforming America. In Boston, for example, by 1800 private classical schools lost their edge to private schools offering such practical subjects as mathematics, bookkeeping, accounting, and navigation to middle- and upper-class families in search of useful education for their sons (Reese, 1995). Academies also became an increasing attractive mode of instruction, competing with Latin grammar school enrollments.

Those aspiring to upward mobility sought out independent pay-schools. These varied greatly in cost and quality, so that there was a school that fit the pocket of just about anyone except the poor: Proprietors, clerical workers, skilled craftsmen, cartmen, carpenters, and mariners paid fees ranging from as little as $3 or $4 a term to as much as $30 or $40. Apprenticeship was a diminishing option for the working class, however. There was lax enforcement of regulations for teaching reading and writing and the system itself was coming apart in the face of increased industrialized production. Concern over the education of girls continued to feed the support for dame schools. At the same time, the working poor were thwarted by school fees, even when minimal or partial, and in some cases they could not qualify for public-supported options because the reading requirements were not met. Charity and orphan schools continued to be the major educational option for the urban poor. At best, a minimum of literacy was achieved. It was out of the growing effort to provide schooling for the less well off, however, that additional voices were added to the drive for public-supported elementary education for all (Curti, 1959; Kaestle, 1983; Reese, 1995).

Immigration and Religion

Immigration irrevocably altered the religious mix of the country. With the exception of Catholic Maryland, English colonization was Protestant. With the English victory in the Seven Years War, Catholic French influence was effectively checked. In the southeastern region along the Gulf and in Florida, Catholic Spanish influence continued until extinguished by Andrew Jackson in 1819. The large southwest region was lost to Spain in the revolt of 1821 when the new nation of Mexico was formed, with Mexico losing out to the United States in the war of 1846. Mexican Catholics were largely treated with distain and isolation, as were Catholics in general. The nation had been and continued to be primarily Protestant. In the immediate post-Revolution years there were only 24 Catholic priests and around 25,000 followers in the new nation, mostly in Maryland and Philadelphia (Morrison, 1965, p. 293). Immigration following the Revolution, however, stamped a Catholic presence on what was English Protestant territory and it continued to grow in the cities of the major eastern ports. Protestants had to confront Catholicism in their own front yards. Clashes ensued primarily over questions of the moral content of education. There was a close tie with schooling and religion throughout all of the colonial period, and this tie continued after the Revolution.

Schooling and religion were inextricably linked. The major purpose of schooling, in fact, was considered moral (Kaestle, 1973, p. 112), not economic or political. As more attention was given to public education the central question became "Who would establish and control the moral content of schooling?" The religious differences among Protestants already created social and political tension, and now Catholics were added. A major impediment to the expansion of public-supported education for all continued to be religious differences (Phillips, 1999).

Amerindians and the Revolution

The Amerindians tended to side with the British in the Revolution or else tried to stay neutral, which became impossible. They were inevitably drawn into the conflict that ended up in a disaster for them. Treaty barriers erected by the British to westward expansion fell with victory, and American settlers scrambled west, only to be temporarily stopped by the French and the Mississippi River, an obstacle removed by the Louisiana Purchase in 1803. The Indians were driven out. One outcome of the conflict was the Northwest Land Ordinances of 1785 and 1787, which set out provisions for statehood in areas of the upper Midwest where the Indians were forced to leave. The states of Michigan, Ohio, Indiana, Illinois, and Wisconsin were formed. In the first federal act for aid to schools, the ordinances provided for the support of public education through land grants.

In the border and southern states and along the southern Gulf areas, the newly minted "Americans" felt no restraints to moving into territory occupied by Amerindians, French, and Spanish. The unrelenting pressure of westward population expansion capped with military clashes simply could not be stopped. And with Jefferson's triumph of land purchase in 1803 the way was open for westward expansion eventually to the Pacific.

Throughout the new nation leaders were confronted with the task of resolving the "Indian problem." The pressure of population growth and western expansion brought conflict with the indigenous inhabitants to a head. There was a slow dance of conflict, death, destruction, submission, and possession that worked its way across the nation. In sure but erratic steps the Amerindian population was disposed of and almost eliminated. There was not room for both. As we have seen in Part One, throughout the colonial period the European occupiers employed four basic approaches to confronting and conquering the indigenous populations. All four were applied in the post-revolutionary years: elimination through disease and war; slavery; "civilizing" populations and forcing them into restricted areas; and removal to a remote location. In the immediate post-revolutionary period and up through the remainder of the 19th century, schools and churches were used to encourage Natives to settle in communities, and along with removal became a large part of the effort to resolve issues with the Native populations. Elimination was also an unspoken policy.

Slavery, Its Spread, and Education

The possibility of removing the blight of slavery was lost with the victory of the Revolution. Resistance to the "organic sin" of slavery that had been growing both north and south was put on hold, and differences were held in check in a united opposition to the British. Even the garrulous John Adams agreed to omit an anti-slavery passage from the Declaration of Independence. Southerners, in an effort to rebuild the impoverished post-war economy restored and expanded slavery. Thousands of slaves were lost to the British and had to be replaced. In addition, with victory land opened and as slave owners populated the Carolinas, Georgia, and Alabama and pushed westward into former Amerindian land in Kentucky, Tennessee, and along the Mississippi, they needed slaves to work the fields. Over 100,000 Africans alone were imported between 1783 and 1807. Natural increase through birth and extended longevity significantly increased the slave population (Johnson, 1997). After 1800, the coastal southern states started selling slaves to plantation owners in the newly opening lands; 120,000 were sent southward and westward by 1820 (Berlin, 2010).

At the same time, in northern states resistance to slavery had been growing and came to a head following the Revolution. Prior to this, Pennsylvania, Rhode Island, and Connecticut passed laws prohibiting the slave trade. In a promising act, the first Continental Congress in 1774 adopted in its General Articles of Association an anti-slave trade clause that member states, north and south, agreed on. Between 1786 and 1801, five states, including the slave states of Kentucky and Tennessee, passed laws permitting manumission. Both Virginia and Maryland acted even earlier with manumission laws in 1782 and 1783, respectfully; 10,000 slaves were immediately freed in Virginia and 20% in Maryland over the next 20 years. During the course of the war, all of the northern states except New York and New Jersey directly outlawed slavery, and the two reluctant states followed with "gradual abolition" after 1799 and 1804. Pennsylvania enacted in 1780 the first emancipation law. These movements were inspired by the rhetoric of the Revolution: freedom, justice, and equality (Johnson, 1997; Morrison, 1965).

Many southerners were conscious that slavery was morally wrong, had a corrupting influence on society, and was counter to the very principles that the Revolution fought for, and they said so. But the practice was so essential for holding up the social and economic structure of society that it was impossible to eradicate (Morrison, 1965). The wealth of the elite was based on slavery. Efforts to halt slavery became particularly divisive and ineffective with the great forced migration in the first half of the new century of over 1 million slaves from the eastern seaboard to the southern interior to tease crops and fortunes from the rich soils for the slave-owning planters (Berlin, 2010). The new nation embarked on an economic course that could only change with the tragedy of civil war.

In the South, Blacks basically were denied education since it was considered dangerous to equip an enslaved population with the ability to read and write. In the North, as the free population increased, schooling emerged as a challenge. Blacks tended to attend integrated schools on a limited basis, but often met with resistance and discrimination. In some cases, provisions were made for the establishment of separate schools for Blacks. Diane Ravitch (1974), for example, reported on the founding of a nonreligious free school in 1787 for Black children by the Manumission Society of New York, supported through private funds. Such prominent men as John Jay and Alexander Hamilton were supporters of the campaign to mitigate "the evils of slavery, to defend the rights of blacks, and especially to go give them the elements of education" (p. 6). A second school was opened in 1794. Other schools were opened in other cities, but the numbers attending were usually low and instruction restricted. They certainly were not given the "polish" that Erasmus prescribed for the education of a "gentleman."

Educational Opportunity in the South and North

In the South, educational opportunity for poor, working class Whites and small farmers became even more restricted after the Revolution. From the early 1600s and up to and beyond the revolutionary period, the southern population was basically stratified into four main groups: a relatively small, wealthy planter class; a small group of merchant and skilled craftsmen of modest means; the poor consisting of White servants but also including subsistence farmers and day workers; and slaves. The White population throughout the South continued to be relatively small.

Following the war a "higher planter class" controlled political, economic, and social development by virtue of the land and wealth that they amassed. This small group controlled educational legislation and they were reluctant to support public education. They could take care of their own class through private means, but public support for middle- and lower-class education only meant more taxes, the bulk of which they would pay. But in a practical sense, the population was small in the scattered coastal plantations and small farms throughout the backlands, and there was a lack of towns and villages that made it almost impossible to have schools. In the isolated farms tucked away in mountain hollows and along river flat lands and rolling hills there was not the inclination or opportunity to work with neighbors to start schools even if groups of children could be formed. People had little spare money, and communication and travel was difficult. In places where there was sufficient population density it was generally dispersed among "lesser planters," small farmers, workers, and servants. Individually and collectively they had little wealth or political power. Some owned as little as an acre or two and perhaps a slave or two, if any. As a group they lacked the influence needed to secure public support for education. Generally children of poorer families had very little in the way of formal education (Jernegan, 1931).

Public support for abandoned, orphaned, and destitute children was an exception. Throughout the South, and particularly in Virginia, laws were established for the education of very poor children. This was also true in the North. It was feared that left unattended these children would embark on a lifetime of crime and moral decay. The community itself would suffer. This certainly was a possibility that made the Federalists shutter. The churches typically played an active community role, and they were afraid that they would be left with the support and schooling of children of the very poor unless public education was legislated. Similar legislation was passed in the North and South. Religious groups did not want, in the words of Jernegan (1931), "the burden of maintaining certain classes, such as the children of the poor, idle, dissolute, or vagrant parents, or of those of illegitimate birth" (p. 140). Throughout the nation, high illegitimate birthrates, in fact, appeared to be common, particularly in the South. Illegitimate children among mixtures of White, mulatto, and Black were not uncommon (Jernegan, 1931).

Women and Schooling

Women suffered from the war and its aftermath. They were the ones who mourned the loss of brothers, husbands, and sons during the Revolutionary War and had to carry on broken lives. They were the ones who struggled over the long war years and beyond to coax from the fields enough food to keep families alive, to nurse sick children, to hide from danger, to bury the dead, and to endure the brunt of suffering poverty. The war created thousands of single-parent and orphan homes. In addition, as a result of the war thousands of families already living on the edge were reduced to conditions of poverty that took years to overcome, if ever.

After the war schooling opportunity was very limited for women. In 1790, literacy among women was roughly about half of the rate among men (Tyack & Hansot, 1990, p. 46). The Revolution was fought to free the colonies from the yoke of England; but it did little to free half of the population from sexist discrimination. Following the war, women still did not have the legal rights of men, and the common perception continued that females required little in the way of education. Convention also kept women from speaking in public. They could not participate in public life, and they could not vote. They had to let men do this.

It was accepted that women had to have enough exposure to education to enable them to read and write, and perhaps in individual cases, to figure, but little else in education was thought necessary. Curti (1959, pp. 169–170) noted, "They were trained for the state of matrimony, which economic necessity forced on almost every girl." Curti reported that as late as 1820 the mayor of Boston closed the girls' school on the pretext that the city could not afford the expense. The place of females was considered to be in the home taking care of the children and men. This perception had not changed since colonial times. For the poor, women had to work and this usually involved long, physically hard, drudgework outside of the home. In rural areas on small farms fieldwork was the expected norm. Of course, slave women endured a life of forced labor.

Cottage industries still characterized manufacturing, and many women contributed substantially to household income: making and assembling small, hand manufactured goods, spinning and weaving, dressmaking, tailoring, washing, and preserving food. After the turn of the century, industrialization increasingly replaced cottage industries, and working-class women along with men and children were forced into the factory. Perlmann and Margo (2001), in fact, noted the success of northern manufacturing was due in part to the low wages paid to women and children relative to the wages of men. At the same time, attitudes about women and education started shifting. A common perception was that women did not have the intellectual capacity to profit from education beyond rudimentary skills. While this attitude was changing, it would take several decades before there was general acknowledgment that women were intelligent, even if "not quite on par with men" (p. 56).

In the immediate post-revolutionary years, nevertheless, perceptive changes were at hand. Some argued that it was only logical that the revolutionary principles of justice and natural rights apply equally to women. Enlightenment thought also fostered the view that human capacity was malleable and could be shaped through education. Both Locke and Rousseau fostered this perception. Why did this not also apply to women?

Quakers from the late 1600s had fostered education for women based on the insistence of equality, and they continued to add to the intellectual mix challenging repressive conventions. Fundamentally important was that as the frontier opened, the public perception of women markedly altered. They shared equally in hardships with men and occupied a central position in the survival of the family. There was an increased recognition of the abilities of frontier women, and these extended considerably beyond knowing how to embroider fancy lace and pour tea. In a real sense, women were the backbone of frontier life. Curti (1959) observed, "It is hardly an accident that the first co-educational colleges sprang up in the West" (p. 172). Then again, along the frontier areas young women increasingly stepped in and took position as teachers when schools were established.

The way was opened for "respectable" employment as well as the opportunity to gain education by preparing to become a teacher. As the movement for the improvement of teaching gained greater attention in the 1820s and 1830s, young women had the opportunity to obtain an education in the many newly founded rural schools and beyond the elementary level in the newly opened teaching academies, female seminaries, and normal schools. By 1840, the literacy rate among women equaled that of men. Along primarily the northern tier of states, the one-room schoolhouse characterizing communities increasingly became coeducational. Why? There is no good answer. Attitudes toward the education of women took a dramatic turn. Perhaps it was the belief that if women shared the work in rural America they should at least share the opportunity for learning. Also it was less costly and more practical to have coeducation schools rather than separate ones. "The adoption of coeducation seems to have been one of those major transitions in practice in which citizens moved gradually from *why* to why *not*" (Tyack & Hansot, 1990, p. 47).

Some women, however, had privileged access to education. In the immediate post-Revolution years, the early education advancement by women was primarily confined within the upper and upper-middle classes. Wealthy men wanted their wives and daughters to display the "showy graces" that affirmed wealth and status. Only the wealthy could afford to send their girls to the private schools designed to groom them for the privileged life they were expected to enter. Instruction itself was "designed to promote taste and propriety, and to provide a veneer of artificial graces and superficial knowledge of drawing, painting, modern languages, and music" (Curti, 1959, p. 175). In this way, the young woman could "embellish" the home of her future husband. In time, there was more interest in including exposure to the natural sciences, history, geography, classics, and mathematics because they were an addition to a curriculum that was already overly "ornamental," but the tendency was to offer such subjects in a simplified form to combat the danger that the young woman would be rendered unfit for home and social duties by too heavy of a concentration on intellectual matter.

Change in attitude was slow, nevertheless, and throughout the antebellum period, women continued to struggle to achieve not only political rights but also educational opportunity. In urban areas, the debates over coeducation schools were particularly continuous and intermixed with issues of class, poverty, and ethnicity. Arguments against coeducation generally revolved around the issue that daughters needed protection from the sons of the poor, and especially the sons of immigrant families. To guard against unwanted coupling and imagined dangers, parents did not want their daughters to mix with boys of unknown virtue and means. More affluent families preferred to send daughters to the shelter of private schools, making the idea of common schools decidedly uncommon. Separate-sex public schools were most common in cities such as Boston, New York, and Philadelphia and in southern cities and towns where there was wealth (Kaestle, 1973; Tyack & Hansot, 1990).

Charity and Pauper Schools

There was growing concern in urban areas, however, over what appeared to be increased crime, worsening living conditions, and social friction. In New York City, for example, mixed neighborhoods were disappearing to be replaced by segregated slum areas, but these were still in close proximity to the more affluent areas so that social strife became a common concern. Increasing population density packed a struggling lower class into alleys, cellars, backyard shacks, rented hovels, and crowded tenements. Streets were narrow, unpaved, and filled with rotting garbage and filth. Disease and dirt spread everywhere. French and Irish immigration alarmed "native" citizens not only because they appeared "different," but also they were associated with radical political ideas, poverty, and crime. Give them the vote and they will take over, some warned. A disproportionate number of the city's paupers and destitute were Irish, and it was alleged in 1802 by the *American Review* that three fourth of the criminals in New York City were foreign born. Religious differences between various Protestant groups as well as between Catholics and Protestants began to come to the fore in ugly ways. In 1794, the new Society for Promoting Christian Knowledge and Piety was formed under the presidency of Presbyterian minister John Rogers; in the same year a Society for the Information and Assistance of Persons Emigrating from Foreign Countries was started. Other cities experienced similar pains of growth and change and turned to similar ways to cope.

The concept of public schools emerged out of urban chaos. Private social reform groups thought that it was better to counter potential crime and moral degeneration through the influence of early schooling rather than to pass crime laws and build jails. Poverty, and the accompanying degenerate lifestyle, was considered primarily a consequence of ignorance that, in the spirit of Enlightenment thinker John Locke, could be ameliorated though education and religious exposure. Locke had argued that human behavior was amenable to change but it was necessary to start with the very young. This is one reason why charity and pauper schools became an early focus of public support. Schools could intervene at an early age for the common good. It was not a large shift to advocate the extension of public funding to urban, public-supported common schools, but this required addressing the question of religious differences and overcoming barriers of class and status, and poverty and ethnicity (Dinnerstein, Nichols, & Reimers, 1996; Kaestle,1983; Ravitch, 1974).

As the new nation entered the new century, there was a general belief in the power of education to forge national unity. The Enlightenment conviction in the worth and perfectibility of the individual was strong; there was faith in government's pursuit of the common good; education was conceived as a tool to master the physical world, and there was little doubt that the mastery of science and technology were keys to progress. However, the belief that education should serve as an instrument of church and state, and should be used to impose religious and moral values and enforce control was vigorously contested. Religious forces were not yet ready to let go, however. And the nation was not yet ready to accept the premise that only through state responsibility could all citizens be sufficiently prepared for personal, civic, social, economic, and intellectual responsibilities. Benjamin Rush noted that the Revolution was only "the first act of the great drama. We have changed our forms of government, but it remains yet to effect a revolution in principles, opinions, and manners so as to accommodate them to the forms of government we have adopted" (Vassar, 1965). This was true of education. In the immediate formative years after the Revolution, the players were only engaged in the first act. The second act commenced with the drive to extend the national scope of education, the subject of Part Three.

Part Two References

Bailyn, B. (1960). Education in the Forming of American Society. Chapel Hill: The University of North Carolina Press.

Berlin, I. (2010). The Making of African Americans. Four Great Migrations. New York: Viking.

Bridenbaugh, C. (1964). Cities in Revolt; Urban Life in America, 1743–1776. New York: Capricorn Books.

Commanger, H.S. (1977). The Empire of Reason. London: Phoenix Press.

Cremin, L.A. (1970). American Education the Colonial Experience, 1607–1783. New York: Harper & Row Publishers.

Curti, M. (1959). Social Ideas of American Educators. Totowa, NJ: Littlefield, Adams & Co.

Curtis, S.J., & Boultwood, M.E.A. (1965). A Short History of Educational Ideas. London: University Tutorial Press.

Dinnerstein, L., Nichols, R.L., & Reimers, D.M. (1996). Natives and Strangers: A Multicultural History of Americans. New York: Oxford University Press.

Durant, W., & Durant, A. (1967). Rousseau and Revolution. New York: Simon and Schuster.

Furnas, J.C. (1969). The Americans A Social History of the United States, 1587–1914. New York: Putnam's Sons.

Gordon-Reed, A. (2008). The Hemingses of Monticello; An American Family. New York: W.W. Norton & Company.

Handlin, O. (1969). Boston's Immigrants, 1790–1880. New York: Atheneum.

Jernegan, M.W. (1931). Laboring and Dependent Classes in Colonial America, 1606–1783. Chicago: The University of Chicago Press.

Johnson, P. (1997). A History of the American People. New York: HarperCollins Publishers.

Kaestle, C.E. (1973). The Evolution of the Urban School System. Cambridge, MA: Harvard University Press.

Kaestle, C.E. (1983). Pillars of the Republic. New York: Hill and Wang.

Karier, C.J. (1967). Man, Society, and Education. Glenview, IL: Scott, Foresman and Company.

MacCulloch, D. (2009). Christianity. New York: Penguin Books.

Morgan, E.S. (2002). Benjamin Franklin. New Haven, CT: Yale University Press.

Morrison, S.E. (1965). The Oxford History of the American People. New York: Oxford University Press.

Nash, G.B. (1979). The Urban Crucible. Cambridge, MA: Harvard University Press.

Nettels, C.P. (1938). A History of American Colonial life. New York: Appleton-Century-Crofts, Inc.

Nye, R.B. (1960). The Cultural Life of the New Nation, 1776–1850. New York: Harpers & Row.

Perlmann, J., & Margo, R.A. (2001). Women's Work. American School Teachers, 1650–1920. Chicago: The University of Chicago Press.

Phillips, K. (1999). The Cousins' Wars; Religion, Politics & the Triumph of Anglo-America. New York: Basic Books.

Ravitch, D. (1974). The Great School Wars, New York City, 1805–1973. New York: Basic Books Publishers.

Reese, W.J. (1995). The Origins of the American High School. New Haven, CT: Yale University Press.

Rudolph, F. (1962). The American College and University; A History. New York: Alfred A. Knopf Inc.

Spring, J. (2008). The American School. New York: McGraw-Hill.

Tarnas, R. (1991). The Passion of the Western Mind. New York: Ballantine Books.

Tuchman, B.W. (1978). A Distance Mirror the Calamitous 14th Century. New York: Alfred A. Knopf, Inc.

Tyack, D., & Hansot, E. (1990). Learning Together: A History of Coeducation in American Schools. New York: Russell Sage Foundation.

Vassar, Rena L. (Ed.). (1965). Social History of American Education. Volume 1: Colonial Times to 1860. Chicago: Rand McNally & Company.

Woodward, W.H. (1964). Desiderius Erasmus Concerning the Aim and Method of Education. New York: Bureau of Publications, Teachers College.

Wright, L.B. (1957). The Cultural Life of the American Colonies, 1607 to 1763. New York: Harper & Brothers.

Part Three
Expansion and Schooling

Introduction

The first half of the 19th century was marked by remarkable expansion. The physical boundaries of the new nation were extended west to the blue of the Pacific, north to the 49th parallel with British Canada, and south to the Rio Grande and Colorado rivers on land forcibly taken from the new nation of Mexico, carved out in 1821 from the crumbling Spanish Empire in the New World. Alaska was added in 1867 and the continental dimensions were set. The vast new territory tripled the landmass of the United Sates and set into motion massive westward migrations that continued well up into the 20th century. Population expansion was remarkable. Large-size families continued to be the norm with a dozen or more children common, so the multiplication effect across generations resulted in five times the number of grandchildren, with an astounding increase to 200 or 300 great-grandchildren by the time of the third generation. Domestic increases were compounded by immigration: millions came to the eastern seaports, driven by poverty, social and religious conflict, and war. America with its strengthening industrial potency and vast opening lands offered hope. It is not surprising that the population of the country doubled approximately every 22 years (Berthoff, 1971).

Immigrants came to America in increasing numbers. There was a slake period during and immediately following the Revolution, but the flow of Europeans seeking a new life picked up in the early 1800s. The total population increased from under 4 million in 1790 to almost 8.5 million by 1815. During this period, over three fourths of a million immigrants came, the largest group Irish Catholics. Almost all of the early immigrants came to one of the five eastern seaboard cities, New York and Boston being the most common points of disembarking because of the promise of jobs. Most stayed in the cities because they were too poor or uncertain to go further (North, 1966). After 1820 they came in larger numbers, with a rapid increase after 1840. Immigration was encouraged because cheap labor was needed to support the increasing pace of industrialization (Dinnerstein, Nichols, & Reimers, 1996).

By the time of the common school movement, the ethnic mix was changing rapidly, and resistance to the movement was mounted in part by those objecting to the use of tax money to fund the education of non-English, "foreign" children (Kaestle, 1983). The number and the diversity of immigrants also created a political backlash as a result of violent clashes between the new arriving workers and the established workforce. A labor surplus was created that drove down wages. A contentious, short-lived political party (American Party) emerged in the form of the "know-nothings," a collection of conservatives bent on violence against foreigners. When questioned by outsiders over violent acts they "knew nothing." Their arrival signaled what was to become a growing nativist movement that ultimately achieved the passage of federal immigration restriction laws in 1921 and 1924. The know-nothings among others contributed to the breakup of the Whigs by polling large numbers in the early 1850s elections, but as a political party they splintered over the question of slavery (Schlesinger, 1946).

The Irish and Germans constituted the two largest immigrant groups during the 1850s. Each had a distinctive impact on the country. Combined, 2 million came. During the same time, 300,000 British came. The Irish were the largest group, and when combined the high immigration numbers of the earlier decades with the 1850s, the total number of Irish was around 3 million. The Irish settled primarily in the northeastern seaboard industrial cities where they found low-wage, unskilled employment. They lived in squalid slum conditions. They arrived poor, downtrodden, and physically and spiritually beaten by the harshness of a life on the edge of poverty and starvation in Ireland. They brought with them their Catholic faith—a shock to Protestant America (Berthoff, 1971). The core values of Catholicism were in direct conflict with ideas of the Enlightenment that undergirded the ideology of the Revolution. Anxiety and hostility on the part of Protestants derived from the Catholic doctrine that the state is subordinated to the Church, and that the sovereignty of the Church is manifested through its supreme authority over individuals as well as the state (MacCullogh, 2009). Hatred and conflict also resulted from the willingness of Irish workers to accept low wages and poor working conditions. They "worked like brutes at what ever menial tasks were available," one contemporary observed (Dinnerstein et al., 1996, p. 94). The Irish were fast becoming a large part of the low-wage, working-class population, and undercut the efforts of others to find jobs at the very time when industrial workers in America were attempting to unionize. Irish parents also resisted sending their children to school. They also were the largest recipients of charity, and they had the highest crime rate (Ware, 1964).

The Germans were a diverse group, coming from a region that was not yet a united country and still divided in many relatively small fiefdoms. The immigrant population was mixed: laborers, farmers, skilled craftsmen, artisans, and professionals of every sort. Most were from peasant stock. As a group, they outnumber each of the other groups, had significant influence, and settled in relatively large numbers over a more varied number of locations. After entering the port cities, the German immigrants tended to move inland, and many settled in the western opening frontier on both sides of the Mississippi, in the plains and upper midwestern areas. They worked hard, were thrifty and helped each other, and at the same time retained as much as they could of their home culture. In communities they supported athletic clubs, theaters, concert halls, singing societies, bands and beer gardens, breweries, and schools. Education was highly valued. They prospered economically (Dinnerstein et al., 1996).

The Germans were a religious mix: Jews, conservative Catholics, Lutherans, Dunkers, Mennonites, Moravians, Baptists, and Brethren, among others. They also brought with them radical political ideas, participated in labor conflict, and played a major role in the struggle to organize workers. They flirted with Marxist doctrine. Many supported socialism. From Germany they brought ideas of the Enlightenment, and educational offshoots in the form of the kindergarten, child-centered education and graduate school.

It was in cities where change was most evident. In the two decades between 1840 and 1860 the population of Philadelphia almost doubled from 360,000 to 670,000 and that of New York more than doubled from 410,000 to 910,000. At the same time, the number of smaller cities of over 8,000 inhabitants increased from 44 to 141. Most of this increase was in the northern Atlantic states. Overall, the population in cities increased 90% from 1840 to 1850 and another 75% from 1850 to 1860 (Ware, 1964, p. 12). The movement from rural to urban was stronger in numbers than the westward migration. This increase coincided with the period of the greatest push for public-funded common schools.

Industrialization was driving growth in cities. Textiles were an important source of early growth. By 1830, about 70,000 factory workers were employed. The figure tripled again by 1860. The mills tended to hire young women off the farm, between the ages of 15 and 30; by 1840, employers in New England switched to young Irish women at lower wages. Strikes, resentment, and violence against the Irish ensued. The iron industry grew. Boots and shoes, paper, equipment, clothing, and food products were manufactured. The demand for stoves spawned an industry. Agriculture and mining products found their way to domestic and European markets. Shipbuilding continued to prosper. American ships carrying cotton and agriculture and manufactured goods to Europe brought back immigrants and manufactured goods. A technological revolution was underway. The growing demand for public education followed this revolution (Ware, 1964).

Westward expansion was no longer contained by the Mississippi. Easterners spilled over the river, settling along the fertile fringes of the western Mississippi bank, along the bottomlands of the Missouri and other great rivers and into areas of the upper Midwest. The population continued to move west over the plains, on through mountains and across desert barriers and on to the immensely rich Pacific valleys and coastlands. The westward migration was set into motion that continued for over a hundred years. Kentucky and Tennessee became states in 1792 and 1796. Ohio followed in 1803, and by 1820 all of the area east of the Mississippi became states except for Florida in the south, recently taken from Spain, and Michigan and Wisconsin in the north. States west of the Mississippi followed in a hodgepodge patchwork formed around conflicts over the curtailment of slavery, war with Amerindians already possessing the land, and international border disputes. To internally connect the markets of the country east and west, and north and south, cannels and roads were built in rapid succession. Key junctions often became sites of towns and eventually cities. Roads were flung across the west, and railroads were built to span the great distances and bind cities, regions, and eventually the country together into a transportation and commercial network.

Small farmers tended to populate the newly acquired Northeast Territory and down into Kentucky, Tennessee, and beyond. Small farming communities also made up the bulk of the population in the newly settled western territories, but the great distances, harsh environmental conditions, and rough terrain that characterized the plains and much of the west presented stubborn challenges. It is not surprising that the territory was sparsely populated. At the same time, there were large pockets of unmatched beauty, great woods, streams and lakes, large expanses of fertile soil, and expansive pasturelands.

In addition to small farmers, the population that went west of the eastern mountain chains was an assortment of small businessmen, millers, tanners, meat packers, blacksmiths, wagon makers, builders, and bankers who provided the services and goods required for the survival of the relatively isolated settlements and farms. They produced or supplied the flour, farm tools, woven cloth, hinges, and nails that men and women relied on to build homes, maintain families, and eke out a living. They bought the products of the farm to resell; they preserved, packed, stored, and shipped products of the farm; they made available goods transported from elsewhere; and importantly, they produced goods for the local market. A small nucleus of skilled workmen and rudimentary manufacturing capability was nurtured, and this served communities as they embarked on the road to industrialization. Manufacturing in the eastern urban areas began spilling over into the upper Midwest.

The Focus of Part Three

Schooling of all types and all levels expanded during the antebellum period. A range of educational institutions emerged that formed the foundation of American education. The expansion of schooling was in response to the emerging industrialization; it was in response to the mass of immigrants pouring into the seaport cities, and to the social dislocation accompanying the growth of cities; and it was in response to the relocation of the population as thousands went west to an uncertain future in the opening frontier. And schooling was in response to the deepening cleavage between sections of the country, and between ethnic, economic, and social classes. Questions surrounding the expansion of schooling reflected the apprehension expressed by the earlier Revolutionary leaders that a nation so diverse had to be bound together by a sense of national purpose, of unity, and by the ideology of the Revolution or it would face the fate of disunion.

Schooling could create unity, but what form? Early educational ideas of a Jefferson or a Benjamin Rush resonated among antebellum schoolmen. School opportunity had to be spread widely. The ideas of a Locke, Rousseau, or a Molesworth were argued over. What was the state's responsibility for the welfare of all of its citizens? Franklin's sponsorship of a practical education found advocates. The use of Noah Webster's patriotic readers spread with surprising rapidity as children attended the schoolhouse in increasing numbers. Science broke the hold the classical curriculum had on instruction, and schoolmen debated how to put into the school instruction that was more attuned to the class of children attending. More women searched out educational opportunity.

In Part Three the educational opportunities that developed are examined. In Chapter Six we focus on charity schools for the poor, the expansion of state administrative systems, and the common school movement. This is a time when the decisive debate over the use of public resources resulted in the national expansion of educational opportunity to populations not otherwise fully served. In Chapter Seven we turn attention to academies and the remarkable expansion and transformation of colleges. Following, in Chapter Eight, we look at three ethnic groups that lost out in the course of social, economic, population, and geographical change: southern slaves, eastern Native Indians, and the inhabitants of the former southwestern Spanish and Mexican territory. National expansion in every sense was largely accomplished at their expense.

Chapter Six
The Emerging Pattern of Public Education

Public acceptance of the idea that the state should use taxpayer's funds to support schooling for the children of all of its citizens was slow in forming. There was over a 200-year history in the country of placing the responsibility of educating a child squarely on the shoulders of the parent. To be sure, there was community involvement, and this was mainly through churches, neighborhoods, and community groups, but initiatives primarily were for children of the same ethnic, religious, and social and economic mix, not for children of the migrants, immigrants, and working poor who were part of the moving human tide that was populating the cities and industrial areas, and flowing out and into the expanding frontier regions. A broader view of public responsibility was required. In addition, public statutes and laws were lacking. In community after community, initiatives for public-supported common schooling were an outcome of political action by voters. Charity schools, long supported through public funds, were an important step along the way in forming public opinion.

Charity Schools

Following the Revolution the colonial practice of using public money to support charity schools for the poor continued, so that by 1820 practically every state constitution had some stipulation for education of the "dependent classes." The long trail of support for charity schools was sustained by three related beliefs: First, the poor constituted the dangerous classes, and it was necessary for society to intervene in order to safeguard the interests of all. There was fear of vice, crime, and moral corruption. Second, human behavior, in the spirit of Locke and other Enlightenment thinkers, was thought to be malleable and changeable, particularly in the young. Children had to be brought under the redeeming influence of education early. And third, poverty and human degradation were thought an outcome of the lack of virtue and morality, which could be taught. If little children could be brought early under the guiding influence of the school and church, then they could learn to become virtuous, moral adults capable of working themselves out of poverty. The poor were poor because they lacked virtue and morality, and this could be overcome through education. Charity school instruction was thought to counter an unwholesome family and community environment.

Charity schools typically were supported through churches, private philanthropy, and public contributions. However, support increasingly shifted to public funding as the increased demand for charity schools exceeded the interest or capacity of religious and private sponsors to yet carry more of the charity school load. Churches in particular balked at the prospect of providing full support for children outside of their own denomination that were among the immigrant and rural migrant families populating the urban slum centers in increasing numbers. Protestant churches particularly objected to supporting education for Catholic children. There was little interest in providing communal education for all.

Nevertheless, voluntary associations of all kinds continued to provide outreach education to the poor not served by denominational charity schools, with public sources filling in the breach. These groups proliferated in places with the greatest need, such as in New York, Philadelphia, and Boston, in addition to smaller, expanding cities on the verge of economic transformation. Along with education they provided other services to the needy: food, clothing, and help with finding shelter and medical assistance. Abandoned children and deserted women found help. Women played a large part in providing services. The Quakers filled a large role, not hesitant to provide outreach outside of their religious fold. Benevolent social and education societies and mutual aid societies became important instruments of social regeneration (Cremin, 1980; Kaestle, 1983; Ravitch, 1974).

The Monitorial System of Lancaster

Of the many forms of charity education, the monitorial (better known as the "Lancastrian system") quickly became popular and widespread. Similar to what the Ursuline Sisters had implemented more than a hundred years earlier in New Orleans, Joseph Lancaster devised an instructional system that made use of student monitors to keep students competitively engaged. Older, advanced students were used to drill younger students who advanced through assignments on a rotating basis. The head monitor would give a group of students an assignment, and the students would take their place at the back of the room where they would undergo drill and recitations. A second group would receive instruction, march to the back and replace the former group who then moved up and engaged in a new drill by the assisting monitor. The next group did the same, in a process of rotation as each of the groups received instruction, drilled, recited; received additional instruction, drilled, recited, and continued on with the cycle. Students were tested, and individual children progressed at their own rate, electing to remain at the same lesson by not moving up. With one teacher, master, and additional group monitors, up to 500 students could be assigned to one class.

The Lancastrian system received immediate acclaim by charity school supporters. It was inexpensive to operate. No other system could accommodate so many students at such a low cost, a fact quite important to charity donors. Students learned strict discipline; they had to conform to participate. Students had to pay attention, follow lock-step directions, and follow routine. What was perhaps most appealing was the emphasis on nonsectarian morality. If the offspring of indigent parents needed anything, it was a solid moral grounding, as emphasized by one charity school advocate. For the first 30 years of the new century, the Lancastrian system dominated charity school teaching, extending to both the south and west and even spilling over into schools established for the Native Indians.

The Transition to Public Education

Charity schools typically took care of immigrant children, but with the spiraling increase in the number of poor children from high birthrates and rural migration to the cities, as suggested, the overall general increase of children simply overwhelmed the capacity of benefactors, churches, and community organizations to provide education through charity. The number of children particularly in urban areas not attending school was alarmingly high. Living conditions were so stressful and uncertain that education was deferred. School fees, even modest, could not be paid. The population that particularly wanted help were those at the margin: They were struggling just to stay ahead and had no extra money to support schooling of any kind for their children, but yet they did not qualify for public help. One contemporary publication (*Mechanic's Free Press*, March 6, 1830) noted that public support for schools is confined exclusively to the children of the poor, "while there are, perhaps, thousands of children whose parents are unable to afford for them, a good private education, yet whose standings, professions or connexions in society effectively exclude them from taking the benefits of a poor law" (Vassar, 1965, p. 172).

It was just a short step to demand the extension in the use of public money to support public schooling for all. The stigma associated with the use of public money to fund pauper education quickly fell away in the face of the stark realities confronting an increasing large segment of the population that needed public help. As parents struggled, public attitude shifted and they, too, demanded support for the education of their children. This is what happened in the case of the Free School Society in New York. Schooling for the poor used public funding, so why not extend its use to all children? Politically, it became an advantageous move.

The Free School Society and Public Education

The Free School Society started out sponsoring a small charity school for poor boys, but within a decade it became the forerunner of the New York public schools (Ravitch, 1974). Motivated by the success of a group of Quaker women who established a free school for poor White girls in 1801, two wealthy Quaker men, John Murray, Jr. and Thomas Eddy, assembled a group of highly influential and wealthy men to found in 1805 a similar school for boys. The Society wanted the school to be free from religious conflict, so it was clearly stated in its charter that enrollment was open to poor children unaffiliated with any religious group, a stance that eased obtaining public funding. Also, the Society membership was comprised of some of the most rich and powerful men in New York, so not only were they able to solicit ample private funds but they were able to build a strong political case for public local and state funding so that by 1817 the Society was getting a good share of a school fund established by the state. The work of the Society was highly successful. By 1817, school attendance reached 1,000; by 1834, 12,000; and by 1839, 20,000 in a network of schools amply supported with public funds. In 1826, the state granted a new charter to the organization making it the Public School Society. Enrollment was extended to all children in the city, and the Society was transformed into a "quasi-public agency, with public funds, public facilities, and public duties, under the immediate supervision of a private, unpaid board" (Ravitch, 1974, p. 22).

The work of the Society was important to the early common school movement in three ways: (1) The schools were effectively and efficiently run, demonstrating how public money could be used constructively; (2) the Society effectively conveyed to the public the importance of public-supported education, and through its political power was able to obtain tax revenue for public school support; and (3) its emphasis on limiting the use of public funds to secular educational uses contributed to a practice that still applies today. By being neutral it could attract broad-based support.

Educational work among the poor through the various charity school schemes was thought to teach honesty and respect toward superiors, instill loyalty to country, and expose the young to Christian morality and values. The young learned the discipline of the classroom that was thought to eventually carry over into work. Some skills taught, such as simple arithmetic and rudimentary reading and writing, provided an employment advantage. Some of the young were able to benefit from apprenticeship opportunities, and it was not unusual for pauper children as young as 4 or 5 to embark on apprenticeship. Much of the thinking since colonial times about the purpose of charity work was carried over in the educational applications for the poor: The primarily economic objective of preparing a malleable workforce was combined with character formation as well as humanitarian and civic motives. These purposes manifested themselves in the common school movement.

The Common School Movement

The common school movement in its simplest terms was the effort by citizens in communities across the country to secure financial support for free public schools through public taxation. This effort took several decades. It is no easy task to get the public to tax itself, so in many ways it was a remarkable accomplishment. There is no set time for the beginning of the common school movement. The early Puritans made every effort to extend education to as many children as possible and levied taxes for this purpose. Similarly, as we have seen, the Dutch in New York used combinations of public and private support, and in Philadelphia very early public funds were used to finance charity schools for the poor. But by the time the country was moving toward an irrevocable conflict with England, a retrenchment in public financial support had occurred. There was less public financial support, not more.

In the cities, charity schools were important in the eventual step to common, public-supported schools; but rural schools were important to the movement, too. For decades rural communities used combinations of parental fees, church support, and public money. The move to full public funding was a smaller step than in urban areas. The Northwest Ordinances were a significant move along the road to public-supported schools for everyone in the newly opening western lands. The ordinances of 1785 and 1789 established the conditions for admission into statehood in the areas carved out of British treaty territory. In the surveyed lands in each township, sections were reserved for the support of education through sales or rent. The newly established rural communities now had a way to almost immediately start public schools.

The results were highly mixed, however, with embezzlement and the diversion of funds not uncommon, and most communities opted for the immediate windfall gain from sales over modest, long-term support from rent. The practice, nevertheless, was continued with all new states but Texas, Maine, and West Virginia subsequently receiving grants of land to support the establishment of schools. As late as 1850, California was granted by the federal government more than one section of land for the support of education. The practice was followed in other western states, and was an encouragement to establish public-supported common schools. In the immediate post-Revolution years, some individual communities primarily in the Northeast took the initiative to follow federal practice and made land grants available for public school support. The grants usually were taken out of public-held Indian lands.

Toward Systems of Public Education

One characteristic that marked the expansion of schooling in post-revolutionary America is that it took place in the context of forming comprehensive state and local educational systems. To be sure, these systems often were in embryonic form, incomplete and underfunded, fragile, and slow in forming, but by the 1850s and 1860s it was possible to speak of American systems of public education spread unevenly throughout the states.

In New York, for example, as early as 1784 the state legislature created a board of regents to oversee colleges and other schools, but the original intent was never fully realized. Fragmentation replaced what was to be a comprehensive scheme as oversight of educational institutions was spread among regents, the legislature, and local constituencies. Political and economic interests tended to side against the formation of a comprehensive, hierarchical administrative structure. New York is an example of what happened throughout the country. Very early we have the basic structure that characterizes American education today with collegiate level public education financially and administratively separate from lower levels that are governed administratively through a mix of state, county, and local entities (Kaestle, 1983; Tyack & Hansot, 1982).

A variety of initiatives were taken in localities throughout the mid-Atlantic and eastern seaboard to develop administrative structures and financial strategies to support a broadening of educational opportunity. In Connecticut, for example, land in its Western Reserve territory was sold and invested to create a permanent school fund. The interest was distributed for use by local schools, and there was enough income that by 1820 it was no longer necessary to levy a supplementary state property tax for school support. Similarly, in Massachusetts, "school societies" were authorized by the state to raise funds through local taxes and tuition, reinforcing a pattern found throughout much of the county: Elementary schooling was voluntarily financed through combinations of funding and controlled by local communities (Kaestle, 1983; Tyack & Hansot, 1982).

In most cases, school fees were charged, with the poor often exempt. New York City was the site of first attempt to establish an urban free school serving a broad-based population. Similar to New York, other states established provisions for public school support, but the results often were mixed or short term. For decades, Virginia attempted to establish a system of public-supported education along the lines of Jefferson's proposals, but failed. It was impossible to form supporting political coalitions. The 1816 constitution of Indiana explicitly mandated the legislature to establish a general, comprehensive system of free education open to all, but it took more than three decades to get started. States passed laws supporting public education only to repeal them shortly after when the full cost was realized, such as in the case of Illinois and New Jersey.

Under the Tenth Amendment of the federal Constitution, education is one of the powers reserved to the states, so individual states are free to go their own way regarding education. Public demand, tradition, and common practice are influencing factors shaping local schooling, and across individual communities substantial differences existed (Cremin, 1980). By the latter 1820s primarily across the northern part of the country, locally controlled schools were common, supported individually or in some localities through combinations of taxes and tuition, and sufficient in number to provide elementary education for most children. Skeleton administrative structures were in place. Variety existed in the extent, kind, and substance of schooling, but except for the very poor many children had access to some kind of schooling. By the late 1830s and early 1840s this pattern changed rapidly in support of full public funding.

Support and Opposition to Common Schools

Those advocating for public-supported common schools encountered four major centers of resistance. One was among those that provided for-pay educational services. For almost two centuries extending back into the early colonial times, children and youth throughout the country relied on local, fee-paying schools. This is the way most colonial children attained their education, and by the 1830s there was a vibrant but fragmented industry, largely unorganized, unregulated, and varying greatly in substance and quality. The South in particular relied heavily on fee-paying schools. Small schools that often consisted of a part-time teacher and a few pupils and charged fees increasingly played an essential role in rural America as frontier boundaries extended westward. Thousand acquired rudimental learning as these enterprises provided essential educational services that otherwise were not available.

The movement for free, public-supported education for all represented a fundamental break with the past and a threat to those earning their livelihood teaching others for a fee. They could be put out of business. There also was some question as to whether or not public-supported education could extend its reach into the crooks and crevices of American lives in the way enterprising entrepreneurs could. For a few pennies parents in the most inaccessible corners of American life could find someone to teach their child. Public schools could not easily do this and were relatively costly.

Another center of resistance was among the wealthy. They already paid the largest share of taxes by virtue of their wealth, and stubbornly resisted paying more, particularly for the education of children from the lower social economic and immigrant classes. The wealthy took issue with the idea of elevating the lower classes through education. Many that controlled the levers of power in communities were locked in a battle with laboring groups over wages and the conditions of work. The rapidly advancing economic transformation extracted a brutal price on workmen and families. Long working hours, unhealthy and crude working conditions, low wages, work stoppages and layoffs, and increasing dislocation caused by the competition of immigrant workers accepting lower wages and tolerating the very conditions "American" workers were organizing to combat, were the source of violent clashes. Wealthy planters, merchants, businessmen, and industrialists were now expected to support the education of the children of the very social classes with whom they were locked in battle. Wealthy industrialists in New England were reluctant to support common schools. Support in the West was lukewarm. The southern planters generally opposed public-supported education, and righteously justified the prevalent caste system of education. A common fear was that widely available education might facilitate bringing the laboring masses into political power. Echoes of the early Federalist position reverberated (Curti, 1959, pp. 194–200).

School reformers such as Horace Mann and Henry Barnard worked to counter resistance by supporting conservative goals: Common schools could in fact guard against social upheaval, they asserted. Social ills of poverty, crime, and intemperance could be eliminated; and free public education could increase wealth, help secure property, and prevent revolution. Republican institutions and financial capitalism could be safeguarded. Horace Mann reassured the public that no controversial issue would be taught. Noah Webster informed everyone that a spirit of national unity would be forged where unity was lacking. Reformers, however, kept conspicuously silent on the issue of slavery because it was an issue that would inevitably cause resistance regardless of the side taken. There was no neutral path (Curti, 1959, pp. 196–199; Kaestle, 1983, pp. 75–82).

Among the wealthy and powerful there developed a counterview deemed essential to support. A number of citizens among the wealthy reasoned if they did not act, they and all that they possessed could be swept away in a wave of social revolution. Educational opportunity, they reasoned, could no longer be solely in the hands of the privileged. They used their power with local Whig politicians, and their persuasive influence with Democrats to advocate among local and state legislative bodies for public school support. Among the more affluent, then, there was division. Some were against public support and warned of the danger of educating working-class children; others cautioned that this had to be done to ensure social harmony; eventually, they were the more successful as public support swung behind the common school. But the wealthy tended not to see the school as an instrument of social transformation like labor, but as a tool of social control. Children would be exposed to a common moral and political creed that would contribute to creating social and political cohesion, and at the same time, broader educational opportunity would help check poverty, crime, and social unrest and promote economic opportunity.

Religion and Education

A third center of resistance developed around questions of religion. This was a difficult but decisive issue. Morality and virtue were outcomes thought central to education, but how could instruction be given without grounding it in a particular religious teaching? Controversy followed once linking the teaching of morality and virtue with a specific religious denomination crossed the line. Community leaders and parents viewed with opposition or outright hostility proposals for public-supported common education without clarification of the place religious teaching had in schools. In communities with mixes of rival Protestant dominations there was fear that one would gain power and control over schools. And in communities with mixed concentrations of Protestant and Catholics already simmering conflict made the generation of support for public schools difficult to achieve.

Religious differences were embedded in ethnic, economic, and social class differences, and in many communities Protestants were engaged with Catholics in a low grade of warfare over questions of job competition, wages, street crime, and violence in addition to religious and cultural differences. Protestants questioned, "Why should their superior social and religious beliefs be subject to dilution by inferiors," especially since they provided the majority of tax support? And the same hostility and tension found on neighborhood streets confronted their children in schools. Common school advocates had to neutralize opposition. Horace Mann did this with a brilliance that earned him a place as the "Father of the Common School."

Enter Horace Mann

As a young man, Horace Mann studied law and was well read and educated according to the standards of the time. However, he rejected the strict Calvinistic beliefs of the Massachusetts, Congregationalist household he grew up in and later was attracted to Unitarianism and its heavy deist influence. He had a well-developed social consciousness, and as a member of the state legislature between 1827 and 1833, he supported laws limiting the sale of alcohol, establishing hospitals for the insane, and creating the Massachusetts Board of Education. He also was involved in the temperance movement.

After being trapped in a violent, bloody Boston ethnic riot between Protestant and Catholic, he decided to abandon law and accept a position as secretary of the Massachusetts Board of Education in 1837. It was his newfound belief that education offered the best chance for social reform that made him to decide to dedicate his life to education reform and the common school movement. Adults were set in their ways and could not be budged from their preconceived prejudices, he reasoned, but children were still malleable and could be shaped through education. Through his annual board reports, speaking engagements, and writing, he was a highly effective advocate (Curti, 1959).

How could morality and virtue be effectively taught without linking it with specific religious teachings? Mann affirmed that Christianity served as the foundational belief of the country, but also he contended that there were certain fundamental teachings independent of all denominational differences that formed the foundation of all Christian teaching. To Mann, these teachings are what school instruction can convey through nonsectarian use of the Bible without encroaching on specific denominational differences. Mann warned, however, deviation from the common moral teachings of the Bible could lead to public dissention and the lack of support for the common school. There were, Mann argued, four destructive alternatives to a nonsectarian, moral education that had to be guarded against.

First, all religious instruction could be excluded from the common school. While removing the source of conflict appeared to be a way to eliminate denominational differences, public support soon would be lost. Parents want morality and virtue to be taught in schools, and if it is not, the public soon becomes disaffected and looks for alternatives. School support cannot be maintained. Second, the law can prescribe a specific set of religious beliefs to be taught to all children, but this forces children to submit to beliefs possibly counter to their own religious upbringing. It violates the principle of freedom of religion. Third, the religious denomination that comprised the majority in a community could shape the religious teachings of the school. This obviously is discriminatory and would not be tolerated by those with other views. The simmering religious conflicts in society would be brought inside. Lastly, the government could withdraw from maintaining public education, but this returns to the condition where the amount of money a family had determines educational opportunity—a condition Mann considered unacceptable.

Mann also addressed in a similar way the political and ethnic conflicts that were fracturing communities. The only way to keep these virulent political discord from spilling into schools was to avoid all discussion of current political disputes and concentrate classroom instruction on the teaching of a common political creed. Students learned those articles of the republican creed that constituted the common foundation of political faith. "The combination of moral and political instruction," Joel Spring (1994, pp. 103–104) suggested, "meant that the student leaving the common school would share with fellow students a set of moral and political beliefs; the results would be the creation of a society with a consensus of political and moral values."

Of Whigs and Democrats

A fourth center of resistance to the common school ideal was political. The Whigs, an offshoot of the scuttled Federalists of Washington, Hamilton, and Adams, were locked in a protracted, mortal political struggle with the Jacksonian Democrats, a political mutation of the Jeffersonian Democrats of an earlier time. In the 1824 presidential election, the gruff, unpolished Andrew Jackson from Tennessee won the popular vote, only to be denied office by an apparent backroom deal between John Quincy Adams and Henry Clay to give electoral votes to Adams in return for an appointment as secretary of state. Whether true or not, Jackson had to wait another four years before claiming the presidency in an overwhelming victory. Needless to say, deep, festering animosity existed between the two parties. Each brought its political positions to the issue of education.

The Whigs believed in public education administered through a centralized system controlled by the state. They generally believed in the intervention of government to strengthen the institutional forms and infrastructural requirements for a smooth-working, free-market economy. They advanced government funding for the building of roads, canals, railroads, and, of course, schools. They were strong supporters of the common school movement because widely available education was perceived as a way to quell social unrest, instill values of morality and patriotism, and promote national prosperity. While Whigs talked in terms of looking out for the interests of the common man, they basically served the business class, however (Schlesinger, 1946).

The Jacksonian Democrats, in contrast, supported limited central government. They grew out of a vision of Jeffersonian Democracy that favored independent proprietors, farmers, and laboring men and expressed revulsion toward industrialism. The Jacksonian Democrats added anti-monopolistic and pro-labor sentiments, and they replaced as a counterweight arguments over property ownership with an emphasis on human rights. They talked of alienation, social justice, economic equality, the rights of the laboring classes, and the control of unbridled industrialism (Schlesinger, 1946). Schools were considered to be the domain of families and local communities, not the state. Democrats supported education, but they wanted it to be left in the hands of community citizens so that the state could not dictate how students were educated and what they learned. They also wanted to thwart any danger of public education falling into the hands of the moneyed interests to be used for their own ends. The Whigs slowly won the battle, however.

Neither party could control its constituencies. Both political parties supported the idea of public common schools, but they differed over the questions of how schools would be financed and controlled. This prevented progress from being made. Education became part of the battles between the two parties and within parties on a range of national issues, including immigration, worker rights, free soil, the federal banking system, the extension of national transportation systems, and, most contentious, slavery. The Whigs broke apart, fractured, and many defected to the new Republican Party, joined by disaffected Democrats to elect the upstart politician from Illinois, Abraham Lincoln, in 1860. The Democrats lost a major constituency, the labor vote. Labor sided with the drive for common school systems. The wealthy eventually split on the school issue. At the same time, in rural areas support for state-administered school systems was less forthcoming and citizens tended to side with the Democrats. Perhaps this is because rural areas had a long history of small, independent, relatively isolated community-run schools and few communities were willing to give up this independence.

The Economic Transformation

A major factor changing public attitudes toward financing schools was the increasing violence and social dislocation associated with the industrial transformation of the American economy. The nation was at the beginning stage of a long 100-year path to industrialization. The scientific revolution spawned by the Enlightenment set into motion in 18th-century England an industrial transformation that positioned the country to dominate world commerce. Belgium, France, and Germany followed. By the 1820s and 1830s the transformation was fully underway in the United States, and at the same time it created considerable social and economic dislocation.

The evolving economy radically transformed the lives of people. To be sure, more goods became available, but thousands of people engaged in local, agrarian, low-cash, and barter economies. Suddenly they were thrust into a market economy that required higher levels of income. More goods were available, but more goods were out of reach of many. To get goods, many individuals had to find wage employment, thus stimulating migration to production centers, creating job competition, and producing pockets of labor surplus. Even in rural communities, the economic foundation was shifting—an argument Whigs used to support government intervention in infrastructure development. A commercial transportation network was formed through which rural communities could market agriculture product and manufacturing areas could feed back into it with goods (Furnas, 1969; North, 1966; Ware, 1964).

Wage competition set worker against worker. Up until the War of 1812 with the British, growing domestic demand and export trade kept employment full and wages relatively high, but by the 1820s there was a expansion of manufacturing that placed increasing demands on more investment capital and labor. The economy grew in "fits and starts," boom periods with high employment interspersed with slack times, little work, scarce money, and increased depravity. It was common to speak of the "social crisis" at hand. The laboring classes responded in two ways. First, they resisted through organized action, which included political organization as well as strikes, and violence against owners and other workmen considered strikebreakers. A Workingmen's Party was at the head of this nascent movement to form unions. Second, they targeted immigrants.

Labor, the Workingmen's Party, and the Common School

By the late 1820s suffrage had been extended to virtually all male citizens by removing property ownership requirements for voting eligibility. Now common workingmen could vote, although females had to wait another 100 years before they were considered capable of exercising this fundamental right. Increasingly throughout the 1820s and into the 1830s, the Workingmen's Party formed with the avowed objective of achieving political power for the laboring classes. An immediate goal was to counter the influence and control of the wealthy through political action. Workingmen wanted a 10-hour working day, better working conditions, better pay, and a voice in labor issues. Most important, they wanted education opportunity for their children.

The political movement was primarily centered in the Northeast and concentrated in major urban areas throughout Pennsylvania, Delaware, Massachusetts, New York, and in Washington, D.C. Political action tended to be on the local level. Boston, New York, and Philadelphia were centers of particularly strong activity. The Workingmen's Party called for public funding for common schools. If their children were to have any chance in life, they reasoned, they must have an education at least on the level of the education that is available to more affluent children. "Knowledge is power," became their motto as they pressed the campaign for public financing. Education was considered a tool to achieve a "leveling" throughout society.

The Workingmen's Party wanted to use public-supported schools as a way to achieve social and economic independence and mobility. Charity schools were not sufficient because in the eyes of workingmen they only served to reinforce social class distinctions, and taught their children to be willing and obedient workers in an exploitative industrial system. They claimed the wealthy wanted to use charity schools to control the lower classes. The absence of educational opportunity consigned "the multitude to comparative ignorance, and [secured] the balance of knowledge on the side of the rich and the rulers," *The Working Man's Advocate* (March 6, 1830) claimed, for example, and it followed that "the monopoly of the rich should be broken up, and that the means of equal knowledge, (the only security for equal liberty) should be rendered, by legal provision, the common property of all classes" (Vassar, 1965, p. 174). Members became forceful and effective advocates for free, public-supported common schools.

As the Workingmen's Party turned their political effort to securing public support for free schooling for all, it became increasingly obvious, however, that the emphasis on empowerment and change put them at odds with other school reformers that stressed the use of public schools for the political purpose of bringing the working classes under control. The Workingmen's Party had a fundamentally different focus: The extension of education opportunity through public funding was seen as a means by which workers could protect themselves from economic and political exploitation, and achieve economic and political power. In today's terms, education was considered an instrument of social reconstruction, not control. To the Workingmen's Party, free education was one way for their children to break out of what they considered an evil social and economic system and gain the upward mobility that promised a better life. A sound education for their children would be the foundation on which other social and economic changes could be addressed by an educated laboring class with intellectual skills comparable to the affluent.

At the height of their political influence from 1827 to 1837, the Workingmen's Party put aside their difference with other school reformers, however, and joined forces to generate wide-spread agitation for public-supported, free common schools. They worked to get local communities to tax themselves to support common schools.

Immigrants and Working-Class Warfare

A major reaction by labor to sweeping industrial change and economic insecurity was the attack on immigrants. Employers used immigrant labor as a means to create an alternative labor supply outside of the growing labor movement that was willing to work for lower wages and under poor conditions. As the labor movement attempted to organize, employers used immigrants as strikebreakers to replace the locked out striking workers. Then too, immigrant labor contributed to a surplus labor pool that kept wages down.

In the interest of maintaining a rather large labor pool, brokers actively recruited for employers those workers primarily from the two largest sources of immigrant labor: Ireland and Germany. Young, potential workers were lured to the emerging industrial centers with transportation help and promises of a better life. Families came in the search for escape from a subsistence life with no future. In some cases, whole small communities were recruited and came in mass. Recruitment became so extensive in Germany that authorities resorted to passing laws forbidding the practice and jailing American recruiters, but immigrants kept coming.

Resistance by American workers became nasty. The Irish in particular were victims of degradation. They were the most convenient targets because they could be singled out by their Catholic faith. They also lived bunched up in the poorest, most squalid, depressed areas; had large families; and were relatively hopeless against the large odds that they faced. The Irish were easy to exploit because as a hated minority they had few avenues of recourse except for the Catholic Church. They clung together for support, and clung to their religion, and this fed suspicion and apprehension.

This was a time of intense social and civic conflict. Other immigrants experienced abuse, and northern abolitionist and free Blacks were targets of violence, but the Irish bore the brunt of abuse. Anti-Catholic demonstrations erupted in Boston in 1823, 1826, and 1829. The convent school in Charlestown, Massachusetts, was destroyed by fire in 1834. In 1840, Baltimore was burned to the ground. A group of thugs attacked the Irish section, and lit fires to force the residents out of their dwellings, but they were not very smart. They chose a windy day, and the fires got out of control, destroying the city. In 1844, a destructive, bloody struggle extended over a four-day period in Philadelphia. Authorities allowed the Catholic version of the Bible to be read in school along with the Protestant King James Version that William Tyndale played such a large part in assembling, and this set off a violent reaction. Two Catholic churches and 30 buildings were burned and lives were lost. It took the intervention of 3,000 troops to quell the violence. In New York City, the Protestant Association focused a continuing stream of abuse on the Irish, to be joined by the *New York Protestant* and its hate writings: The Irish were portrayed as drunken degenerates that engaged in all sorts of crime, including murder and the rape of daughters and wives. They were human "dirt." Throughout America, wherever Catholics lived or worked they experienced hostility, discrimination, and degradation (Dinnerstein et al., 1996; Takaki, 1990).

Protestant churches put aside their differences with other Protestant dominations and became key supporters of public-financed common schools because they realized that they could use public schools to promote their religious views. The introduction by Mann of the idea that public schools could adhere to a secular, nondenominational Christian morality smoothed the way for the political acceptance and support of the public financing of public schools for all. But once public schools were in operation, Protestants were able to capture control of community schools through the domination of school boards; and local school boards are the controlling power.

Protestants tended to hold the major positions of wealth and political influence in communities. This provided the advantage they used in elections to secure the controlling majority on school boards and other related political offices. They used their power to control policy and financing. To be sure, there were school boards with mixed political allegiances; some with labor representation, and some with Democratic dominance, but overall public schools throughout America in 19th and first half of the 20th century reflected a strong Protestant religious influence. Common schools were not common. Up until the social awakening of the civil rights movement of the 1950s and 1960s, it is not surprising that many Catholic parents continued to refer to public schools as "Protestant schools" (Kaestle, 1983; Spring, 1994) pp. 80–84).

William Seward and Catholic Schools

The conflict in New York City during the 1830s to 1850s over Protestant control had permanent national implications. The smoldering hostility between Protestants and Irish Catholics broke out into the open in New York City when the Catholics petitioned for a share of the public school fund to establish schools for Irish immigrant children. Up to this time, Protestants had control of public schools, including their anti-Catholic instruction. They discriminated against the Irish children and the schools generally fostered an anti-Catholic atmosphere. Large numbers of Irish children did not attend school of any kind because they were badly treated. Governor William Seward backed the petition with the reasoning that many Irish Catholic children did not attend school because of overt discrimination, but yet it was in the greater interest of society that all children have access to education. Otherwise, Catholic children, he cautioned, end up as adult illiterates that are a burden to society.

He denounced the discriminatory treatment of "foreigners." Faced with the unyielding resistance of the Public School Society, Seward proposed to the state legislature the inclusion of Catholic schools as part of the state school system while at the same time retaining existing charter agreements and religious affiliations. Catholics would administer their own schools supported with public funds. Steward's bold move caused a political uproar. He lost the following election, left the fracturing Whig Party, and joined the newly forming Republicans. He became Lincoln's secretary of state, adding the last chunk to the continental dimensions of the United States with the purchase of Alaska in 1867.

The Catholics could not reason with Protestants. The issue became so inflammatory that a riot ensued in 1842. The Protestants controlled the school funds, and would not support Catholic use of public money, but yet would not remove discriminatory practices from schools, curb hostility toward Irish Catholic children, or eliminate Protestant religious material. In the end after a long, contentious struggle with the Public School Society, the Catholic hierarchy resorted to the establishment of a separate, self-financed system of Catholic schools. Plenary councils held in 1852, 1866, and 1884 established the framework for the Catholic school system that we have today. Despite Horace Mann's urgings, common schools fundamentally reflected a Protestant religious ideology.

Overall patterns of financing and public perceptions started changing in the late 1820s and early 1830s so that eventually public funding primarily drove school expansion throughout the country. Public-financed schools replaced private, fee-charging schools, but this was not a smooth progression, and advance often was followed by retreat. The provision of free education for all children continued to be hotly debated. In Massachusetts, for example, there was a strong effort mounted in 1840 to abolish the board of education, only two years after it was established. In Pennsylvania a tax support system of common schools was created by the state legislature but it was voluntary with communities opting not to participate. These tended to be places where German immigrants and religious groups wanted to maintain their own schools. But by 1847, only 158 out of 1,225 districts were not participating. The provision of free schooling in communities also was made optional in Connecticut and this did not change until 1868. Rhode Island and Michigan continued to have mixed financing with tuition and public funds until the 1850s. Many communities in the South did not make public funding available until the 1870s (Kaestle, 1983). At the same time, it was in cities where the most steady progress was made. Overall, public school enrollment in cities shot up quickly, reaching 60% to 80% of eligible children by 1850. Despite pockets of resistance, the momentum for public schools carried over into the 1900s to bolster the development of the free, public school system that we have today.

McGuffey, Pestalozzi, and Instruction

Teaching in the antebellum period tended to reflect the conservative philosophy and practices of Noah Webster: strict, sometimes harsh discipline intended to promote obedience, conformity, and adherence to the dominant Calvinistic, Protestant moral code. Drill and memorization were the common teaching modalities. As the common school movement gained momentum, the basic pattern Webster set was extended through the work of William Holmes McGuffey. Following the lead of Webster, McGuffey embedded in a series of readers lessons on morality and virtue. While pupils learned to read and master vocabulary, and probe lessons on history, they also were exposed to teachings on morality, religion, nationalism, and social behavior. McGuffey conveyed basically a conservative political and social message; but McGuffey went a step beyond Webster. He presented a strong justification for the existing social order.

McGuffey supported the increasing concentration of wealth and social and ethnic class divisions as a condition ordained by God. He advanced four ideas to justify existing social and economic conditions. First, wealth is a sign of God's approval. God blesses the wealthy, and good fortune is a sign of inner salvation. The poor, however, are poor because this is an outward sign of His disapproval. In a society that was characterized by increasing difference in income distribution, McGuffey provided a justification for the accumulation of wealth and the domination of the wealthy over the less fortunate (Mosier, 1965).

Secondly, both the wealthy and poor have moral and social responsibilities. To be worthy of their blessed state, the fortunate have to use their wealth in constructive ways that justify their favored status. This means caring for the less blessed. At the same time, the poor have the responsibility to follow God's word: to be industrious and moral, to obey the rules of society, and to act favorably toward the more fortunate. Perhaps they, too, will be blessed one day. With the justification of poverty and the promise of a better life, McGuffey readers made poverty sound like an inevitable but possibly amendable condition of life.

Third, McGuffey's readers projected wealth into the public consciousness as a social and personal good. This is what people should strive for. And fourth, his readers reinforced long-held beliefs extending back into colonial times that lack of good fortune and poverty are primarily related to the individual's moral weakness. It is the individual that needs moral mending, not society. But reminiscent of the Puritan concept of collective guilt, the lack of virtue is extended to whole groups considered inherently degenerate and perhaps outright dangerous because of their station in life, and religious, ethnic, and cultural differences. They have innate moral defects, and for this reason they are less deserving. The poor Irish factory worker, Polish minor, slave, and destitute Amerindian are less moral and virtuous, and thus less deserving. They could be exploited with little guilt by the favored in the quest of wealth.

The number of copies sold reflects the profound impact McGuffey's readers had on the American population. Over 8 million copies sold between 1836 and the start of the Civil War. After the war and up to 1920, a staggering 1 million copies were sold (Mosier, 1965). Daily, children learned the primary function of government is the protection of property; popular political participation has to be approached with caution; the spread of women's suffrage is threatening; and the new age is corrupting and it is necessary to return to the Calvinist, Protestant moral code of the early Puritan religious leaders. The church and state are portrayed as the bedrock of social stability. Girls tend to be slighted in the readers, although they made up a large part of the common school enrollment. The issue of slavery is ignored, as are the issues of immigration and ethnicity (Mosier, 1965). The McGuffey readers significantly contributed to setting the tone for instruction in common schools.

There were counter voices. Those that did not agree with the use of schools as a mechanism of social control as represented through the work of Webster and McGuffey sought alternatives. One of the most plausible alternatives was represented through the work of the Swiss educator Johann Heinrich Pestalozzi (1746–1827). His work conveyed a child-centered vision of education based on love and respect, and reflecting Locke with instruction organized around the child's natural growth and rich learning experiences from the surrounding environment. Simple ideas, according to Pestalozzi, accumulate and build up over time into complex powers of reasoning and abstract thought. Abstract learning is combined with concrete experiences appropriate to the interests and maturation stage of the child; learning should be a happy experience, punishment should be avoided, and pressure on the child to learn beyond his or her natural pace is harmful. Trial and error, and the use of objects, activities, and observations mold learning. Education is a process of exposing the child to rich experience through which sense impressions are formed, stored in the mind, reformulated through additional experiences, and combined to create deeper meaning (Heafford, 1967).

Pestalozzi was born into a middle-class, Swiss-Italian family, but with the early death of his surgeon father hard times descended. The family struggled with poverty. Pestalozzi managed to finish Latin high school and enrolled in college at age 15, but never finished. A formative experience while a student was his exposure to Rousseau's *Emile* and the idea that education could be a tool of social change. He wrote a number of essays expressing his ideas on education. He believed that the right kind of teaching could produce a citizenry capable of addressing the ills of society, and by extension, instigate political change. These views led him to engage in political action that landed him briefly in prison.

Pestalozzi tried farming and eventually failed, but in the meantime used the teaching of his own children to develop some of the fundamental concepts that he would eventually apply to educational ventures through which he honed and refined his pedagogical principles. Always short of money, supporters and benefactors gave him money as well as political, and importantly, long-term financial support. Through his writings he gained international recognition. His work *Leonard and Gertrude* brought him international acclaim and was decisive in making known his educational ideas. During the last 30 years of his life, a flow of visitors came to Switzerland to view his educational ideas in practice. Unlike theorists such as Rousseau and Locke, Pestalozzi put his ideas into practice and showed dramatic result in contrast to contemporary school practices.

Americans became aware of Pestalozzi's work early. As his work became more widely known through his writings, American educators traveled to Switzerland to directly observe his methods in practice. They enthusiastically brought back their interpretations of his ideas. William Maclure, Marie Duclos Fretagot, William Phiquepal, and Joseph Neef, for example, introduced Pestalozzian methods to Philadelphia in 1809. Robert Owen incorporated the Swiss educator's views in his communal living experiment at New Harmony, Indiana, in 1826, with further applications extended to New York and other places primarily through the efforts of socialist dissenters' intent on making society more human and equalitarian. Horace Mann expounded on his visit to Prussian schools using Pestalozzian methods in his 1843 *Seventh Annual Report*. German immigrants settling primarily in the Midwest founded kindergartens patterned on the practices of Pestalozzi introduced through the work of Friedrich Froebel. Significant was the early work of Edward Sheldon of the Oswego (NY) Normal school. After the Civil War he expanded efforts so that Oswego became the leading national school for the preparation of teachers for what was termed the "New Education" based on Pestalozzian principles. Pestalozzian ideas combined with those of Johann Herbart and Froebel produced an American interpretation of educational reform that revolutionized elementary education (Cremin, 1961; Kaestle, 1983).

Women, Schools, and the Struggle for Equality

Women in antebellum America faced deep and persistent discrimination. The common school movement offered middle-class women a decisive wedge to open a crack in the discrimination barrier. Opportunity was advanced in three ways: middle-class women found socially acceptable employment as teachers; girls attended common schools in increasing numbers; and young women had an opening to higher education through teacher training. A strong argument was made that women were more suited as teachers than men, thus opening the way for their employment. In what became known as "republican motherhood," women were employed in common schools to shape the minds and morals of the little boys attending, youngsters who would grow up to be the middle-class bankers, merchants, surveyors, engineers, accountants, and farmers, and the spiritual, political, industrial, and commercial leaders of the New Nation.

This was a sacred duty, a divine mission. Horace Mann proclaimed "the Author of nature pre-adapted her, by constitution and faculty, and temperament, for this noble work" (Mann, 1845, p. 60). With his spellers and readers, Webster provided the tools to impart lessons of patriotism, nationalism, and morality to guide immature lives. The pure, exemplary behavior of women provided a model to live by, and the daily lessons of drill and recitations imparted basic skills to build an intellectual life. Personal and social good resulted, and the young boys were morally safe in the hands of virtuous women.

Women were thought to be naturally superior teachers. They had innate nurturing abilities. They knew how to take care of children; men did not. Women teachers also were thought to have inherently stronger moral character. They were models of virtue, whereas men were suspect. The claim was, "women were destined by God to be teachers of the young because they were more moral, patient, understanding, inventive, and nurturing than men" (Tyack & Hansot, 1982, p. 65).

There were two less exalted reasons. Women teachers also were attractive because they were thought to be easier to keep under control. They did what their superior asked, usually a man, did not chafe at restrictions, and were more malleable and conscientious. They were considered willing to accept subordinate lives. Perhaps one of the major reasons why school districts turned to female teachers, however, was cost. Women teachers worked for considerably less money than men. In times of economic upturn when labor costs were high, the trend was for local schools to hire more low-paid women. Men teachers were priced out of the market. Although the ratio of female-to-male wages varied greatly from town to town, generally, women teachers earned 40% to 50% or even 60% less than men. In the South, the wages of women teachers typically were even lower, 85% to 100% of those of men. This differential stayed relatively constant throughout the antebellum period (Kaestle, 1983; Perlmann & Margo, 2001).

The young age of female teachers presented a challenge. Boys often attended for part of the year after harvest time and before spring plowing and planting. Young female teachers were sometimes younger than the older boys, and in any case certainly less strong. It was difficult to keep pubescent boys under control. Typical practice was to use male teachers for part of the year. Generally, discipline problems also were "solved" by having a male overseer present. Females tended to teach the younger children, males taught the older boys, and almost all secondary school teachers were male. It was also a commonly accepted belief that female teachers did not have the intellectual ability to teach "higher" subjects. Nevertheless, by mid-century female teachers comprised between 50% and 70% of teachers, and in some locations, the figure was much higher. In Massachusetts, the percentage of female teachers increased from 56% in 1834 to 78% by 1860; in Connecticut the percentage was 71% in 1857. Figures, however, varied greatly according to location and time (Kaestle, 1983; Tyack & Hansot, 1990).

Teacher turnover was a major challenge. Many men initially held teaching jobs, but they tended to leave after a few years to find better-paying employment. Teaching was basically viewed as an intermediate step. Women teachers did not stay for long, either. Low pay and confining conditions of employment tended to contribute to women leaving after only a few years. The problem of teacher turnover was greater in rural areas where the pay was lower compared to urban locations, but nevertheless, relatively few young people stayed in teaching for long. Carle Kaestle (1883, p. 126) reported among the female teaching force in Michigan in 1860, that 77% were between the ages of 17 and 24; Joel Spring (1997, pp. 129–130) noted that in Pennsylvania in 1856 one third of teachers were under age 21, with many young teachers remaining only a single year. In 1859 in Connecticut, two thirds of the teachers were new. In his Eighth Annual Report (1844, p. 60), Horace Mann exalted in the fact that he was able to recruit 990 new female teachers, continuing a promising trend.

The young male could earn between 50% and 100% more working as a carpenter, carriage maker, blacksmith, lawyer assistant, surveyor, or accountant. For the young female, marriage was an attractive alternative, and married women were not allowed to remain teachers. Nevertheless, even a few years of teaching gave thousands of young women the opportunity to achieve a degree of independence and self-worth that they never would have been able to experience. To prepare to be a teacher they also had the opportunity to go to school beyond just a few elementary years.

With the common school movement, both girls and boys were educated together in the same classroom, following the same studies, in the same school. This was a significant development. By 1850, in New England, 81.4% of males and 75.7% of females aged 5 to 19 attended schools. The mid-Atlantic had the next highest attendance with 61.1% and 59.6%, respectively, with the south region experiencing the lowest attendance figures, 40.8% and 35%, respectively Nevertheless, these are remarkable overall attendance figures, and surprising figures for women in a nation continuing to struggle with the issue of gender discrimination (Tyack & Hansot, 1990, p. 51).

The Preparation of Female Teachers

Perhaps one of the most important outcomes of the common school movement for middle-class women was the opportunity for higher education (Kerber, 1980; Tyack & Hansot, 1990). Teachers had to be prepared, and this meant opening up ways for middle-class girls to pursue education. If women teachers were going to fulfill the role of "Republican Motherhood" and lead small boys along the path of civic and moral virtue, they had to be properly prepared. Initially it was difficult to find educated women to serve as teachers, particularly in the rural frontier regions. There were few formal ways to prepare teachers. The qualification to teach sometime meant only one year of schooling beyond the grade taught.

Emma Hart Willard is given credit for opening in 1819 the first formal school for the preparation of women teachers, the Troy Female Seminary. The young women were hired to be teachers as quickly as they completed studies. The founding of other seminaries followed, and all of them had a deep religious undertone. Teaching was a divine calling, and the moral nurturing of the soul of children was as important, if not more so, than the intellectual development of the mind (Curti, 1959).

One of the most widespread and important ways that young teachers engaged in professional development was the teacher institute. Initiated by Emma Willard and Henry Barnard in 1839, the idea quickly took hold and spread across the country. Teachers throughout a region met typically once or twice a year at a central location for two to four weeks to engage in a brief course on teaching theory and practice. They met with fellow teachers, found out the latest news, swapped ideas, learned of new materials, and absorbed the advice of more experienced teachers. The instructional sessions tended to be heavy on aspects of teaching for moral development. The emphasis was on creating conformity to moral standards rather than probing and debating issues of morality.

The need to prepare female teachers led to the establishment of normal schools, and opened the door to higher education for women. In some cases, "normal" departments were attached to academies. Most were tuition-free schools exclusively for women. The course of study was only for two years and focused on teacher education, nevertheless, it was "higher education." The normal school continued to be the major way middle-class women obtained advanced education up until the World War II period.

Many women attended even though they did not intend to teach. This was the best, indeed, probably one of the only means available for women of modest means to obtain advanced education beyond the elementary level. Many matriculated directly from elementary school. Those wanting to teach spent the first year reviewing what they covered in the elementary grades and what they would be expected later to teach. Additional subjects were covered the following year, giving the young woman the semblance of an education. The extension of educational opportunities to prepare teachers was part of the general evolution in changing attitudes about women.

Preparing the Educated Mother

The early education reformers advocating greater teaching opportunities for women also were among the strongest advocates for the wider extension of education to females in general. Emma Willard of Troy Seminary, Mary Lyon of Mount Holyoke Female Seminary, Catharine Beecher of the Hartford Female Seminary, and Zilpah Grant of the Ipswich Seminary, among early educational leaders argued that greater educational opportunity for women was needed not just to prepare school teachers, but because women required education to adequately fulfill their roles as mother and home keeper (Curti, 1959; Woody, 1974). The educated mother aided in the development of an educated son, was the message. Also, the management of the domestic household required an educated woman, and the educated woman was on a closer intellectual level to her husband. Education would create, in the words of David Tyack and Elisabeth Hansot (1990, p. 38), "the competent, devout, principled woman, a fit companion for her husband and skilled nurturer and teacher of her children."

Slowly, across communities, support developed for more educational opportunity for women. Primarily located in the Northeast, the support nevertheless was broad based. National education reform figures Horace Mann and Henry Barnard, for example, argued the education of females was the most effective weapon for correcting the wrongs of women, better than political agitation. As expected, labor reformer Fanny Wright invigorated the movement for women's education with her insistence on social justice. Others joined the movement because of the belief in the mission of women to advance God's kingdom on earth, and educated women could best do this. Still others saw commercial value in the education of women. Acceptance of girls' education occurred slowly, with more progress in small towns and rural areas than in cities (Tyack & Hansot, 1990; Woody, 1974). But as the movement advanced in small steps across the nation, there was something strikingly different. The educational drive went hand in hand with a political movement for women's rights.

As early as 1787 revolutionary leader Benjamin Rush proposed a model curriculum for women's education, and Quaker and Moravian women pioneered early efforts to provide educational opportunity primarily to girls from poor families. The provision of teacher training opportunity was an additional step along the road to educational equity, but all of these efforts, as important as they were to the breaking of discrimination barriers, conceived of educational opportunity for women as separate and on a different, if not less, intellectual level than education for men.

The drive for women's suffrage and the advancement in educational opportunity for women were linked. First, the education movement produced women leaders. Suffrage leaders, such as Susan B. Anthony for example, like so many other antebellum women achieved educational opportunity as a teacher. With the opening of education to women came an educated leadership. Second, the outlook of women changed with education. They were no longer willing to accept inferior status. "Educate and agitate" became a motto. Third, the drive by women to achieve civil and political equality was an extension of the success in education. If one was achieved, why could not the other? Some of the same women leaders in education played active, pivotal roles in the suffrage movement: Catharine Beecher, Margaret Fuller, Lucy Stone, Ellen Foster, and the indomitable Fanny Wright, among others. It is no surprise that the struggle for a political voice first found success in local school board elections. Women had gradually achieved local prominence as teachers and school principals. They could not indefinitely be denied a part in school affairs and not be allowed to vote for school board members (Woody, 1974).

Chapter Seven

Beyond the Common School:
The Academy and College

Boston's English Classical School established in 1821 is credited as the first public-supported secondary school in America. It was for boys primarily from affluent families. There were other roughly equivalent early schools, but they were private. Known as "English" schools, they increasingly challenged the grammar school with its classical curriculum because they offered a more practical and useful course of study. They were more responsive to the forces of industrialization sweeping the country. It was not until mid-century that the transition from private- to public-supported high schools started to parallel the drive for common schools, and it was not until the 1880s primarily in cities that public high schools became a significant number. By 1890, only 200,000 students attended public secondary schools in America; by 1910, this figure reached 1 million.

There were two basic reasons for the slow start. First, working-class parents tended not to support secondary education. In industrializing America, children went to work early, often at age 8 or 9 years. "Why should they support secondary schools," working-class parents reasoned, "when only the children of the wealthy will attend?" The same was true in agrarian areas, and the population was too widely scattered to form sizable class groupings. Second, there was stiff competition from private academies.

The Ascendancy of the Academy

In the antebellum period, the academy became the premier secondary school institution. For the middle-class boy (or girl, in some cases), an education could be obtained beyond the elementary grades. Academies were basically supported through fees, but other sources of funds were also available: endowments, gifts, state subsidies, lottery profits, and interest income from investments. Although the fees were relatively modest (in 1825, about $9 per term on the average in New York), families had to be moderately affluent for their children to attend. The academy was out of reach of the working class and the poor (Ravitch, 1974).

Comparatively few youth had available education beyond the rudimentary level, and many had no opportunity for schooling at any level, but for those who were able to attend an academy, multiple options opened. For some, the academy functioned as a "poor man's college," providing, as Benjamin Franklin suggested earlier, an "ornamental" education that would open an avenue to upward mobility. Through the study of literature, ethics, Greek, Latin, French, and philosophy a degree of social polish was obtained. For many, the academy offered a level of technical education that was crucial to economic development. Apprenticeship was a major institutional form through which technical skills are transmitted to the young, but as scientific knowledge and technical advancements became more important to work, an additional level of preparation was required that consisted of a combination of technical skill training and academic education. What we call today "engineering" was emerging in elementary form as a formal field of study, and its early presence was found in the academy. The academy contributed to the development of a skilled workforce to feed the advancing industrial transformation. The youth could study acoustics, algebra, calculus, and chemistry along with technical drawing, surveying, navigation, and hydraulics. For some the academies also prepared for admission to college, and provided many youth the elements of a liberal arts education.

The academy was particularly important as a rural educational institution. Academies as boarding schools were located in some of the larger rural communities. More affluent farmers sent their sons and daughters to obtain one or two years of education before returning to what was in the day an isolated farm life. The boys learned farm skills, such as the construction of improved equipment, metalworking, animal husbandry, and disease and pest control. Girls were sent to learn skills thought necessary for farm life: food preservation, health and nursing, childcare, and sewing, quilting, and mending. Girls were also given "polish" to equip them for potential upward mobility: music, language, art, and literature. The academy served a fundamental purpose for rural youth in that it was about the only institution that gave education beyond the very basic fundamentals.

The quality of elementary education often was so poor that parents sent their children to academies to complete remedial work or as an option to the town school. At the same time, in some academies the level of work was only at the elementary level. On the other hand, in some academies the quality of work was so high that students could be admitted to university at the junior level. It was also not uncommon for long-established grammar schools to convert to academies by adding practical subjects to achieve both the "ornamental" and the "practical" that Franklin advocated. In the early 1800s, academies dominated the secondary school level. By 1800, New York had 19 academies, Virginia 21, and Massachusetts 17. The number in Massachusetts jumped to 36 by 1820 and 68 by 1830, mirroring a national trend. Over 6,000 academies were spread around the country by 1850 (Nye, 1960, p. 162).

From the time of the founding of Franklin's school in Philadelphia in 1751 to its demise in the late 1800s, the private academy for roughly 120 years provided countless American youth an avenue to obtain education beyond the common school. It fed the agriculture, business, and commercial demands for a more scientific and technically educated labor force. In pure numbers, more technically skilled individuals were turned out by academies than by all of the four-year colleges combined. But by the 1870s the public-supported high school was pushing the academy into extinction. With "free" tax-supported high schools, increasingly parents opted to send their children to public high schools rather than fee-paying, private academies. In an ironic twist, the academy had demonstrated the desirability of secondary school level education and opened the way for public high schools.

The academies gave way to the public high school. Some academies were converted to state normal schools for teacher training. Most went out of business. Some, however, continue to this day. They tend to be "high end" private institutions catering to an elite clientele, such as Phillips-Exeter and Deerfield Academy, or in the form of day schools and military schools. They also have been regenerated in a different form, for example, the public-supported community college. The community colleges of today are very similar in purpose and function to the post-Revolution academy.

Making Money and Saving Souls: The Extension of Higher Education

The general momentum feeding the common school movement and the spread of academies also propelled the remarkable proliferation of colleges during the antebellum years. There was a general thirst for knowledge. Exciting new ideas were sweeping the country and people wanted education. Literary works, political tracks, and writings on art, history, geography, and science expanded intellectual horizons. The economic and industrial transformation underway demonstrated the value of knowledge. To feed popular demand, colleges were founded. Prior to the Revolution there were 9 colleges; in the two decades following the war 16 more were added, and by 1840 there were 78 permanent colleges and universities across the United Sates. The number of colleges increased to over 250 by 1860, and over 180 of these early colleges still survive. More early colleges, however, failed then succeeded. In the years between the turn of the century and the Civil War it is estimated that as many as 700 colleges were started. Early colleges were small and struggled with the lack of money. In 1839, only 11 schools had enrollments of more than 150 students, with the average enrollment less than half that number (Rudolph, 1962; Nye, 1960).

Popular demand drove this remarkable expansion, but also the possibility of wealth. Many of the new institutions were in the western frontier, and many were in places where rapid settlement appeared promising. Colleges attracted people, and investors saw the opportunity to purchase land and considerably increase its value by founding a college. Additional real estate expansion would follow. It was anticipated that the increase in land value in the surrounding area would yield an ample return on the original investment. Particularly desirable to investors were key road and river junctions that were promising sites for commercial development and transportation hubs. Sites opened by railroad routing were desirable.

The interests of investors, however, often clashed with educational interests. It took time to realize income from investments so there was reluctance to pour resources into a college that absorbed money and gave no immediate return. It was increases in land values that investors were after. Frederick Rudolph (1962, p. 47) noted, "Often when a college had a building, it had no students. If it had students, frequently it had no building. If it had either, then perhaps it had no money, perhaps no professors; if professors, then no president, if a president, then no professors." Colleges had to operate with sparse, uncertain, and insufficient revenue.

Religion, the Second Awakening, and Colleges

Religious-affiliated colleges had a higher probability of succeeding. Additional revenue could be generated through the church and endowments. Individual churches and missionary boards saw in the establishment of colleges the solidification of their religious presence. A source was established for the local preparation of clergy, church members had a place for religious instruction, and converts could be attracted by the presence of educational opportunity for their children.

The presence of one domination created rivalry leading to other dominations founding colleges. Eleven competing colleges were started before 1865 in Kentucky, 21 in Illinois before 1868, and 13 in Iowa before 1869. Not to be outdone by Protestants, eight French priests traversed across Indiana in 1842 to found what was to become Notre Dame. The Methodists and Baptists got a slow start. They believed that they did not have to formally prepare clergy or foster the education of laymen, but with the realization that the availability of colleges would enable them to tap into the pool of potential middle-class converts and lend more respectability to their beliefs, they changed course and became among the most aggressive founders of colleges. The Presbyterians outlasted everyone. By 1860 they established 25% of the colleges that survived on into the 20th century. Mainly the stream of Scotch-Irish Presbyterian immigrants flowing into the western frontier, and the support of a highly organized church hierarchy fueled Presbyterian enthusiasm. Eastern Congregationalists and Presbyterians combined efforts in 1843 to sponsor the Society for the Promoting of Collegiate and Theological Education in the West (Rudolph, 1962).

The expansion of religious-affiliated colleges was part of what is termed the "Second Great Awakening." The impact of the first Awakening in the mid-1700s was blunted in the years leading up to the Revolutionary War. Organized religion lost much of its status within the swirl of events surrounding the formation of the new nation. As noted in Part Two, there was a strong deist following, and sectarian influence was neutralized in the name of national unity. Prior to the war, religion dominated colleges. Presidents were religious figures and curricula were heavy with religious instruction. This changed in the years immediate to and after the Revolution. Colleges became more secular. Within the first 10 years after the turn of the century, however, a reaction set in and conditions dramatically changed. This was a revolt against deism, against the liberalism, tolerance, and rationalism of the Enlightenment; and against what was thought the general subversion of religious belief. Religious leaders were now appointed presidents of colleges, and even colleges with no denominational affiliation included a heavy concentration of religious instruction.

The majority of new colleges were religious, and they were, in the words of Russell Nye (1960, p. 180), "too often expected to produce devout church members, missionaries, or ministers—not young men interested in science, humanities, the arts, government, or the free pursuit of truth." David Potts (1988) reported that among Baptists, sectarianism tendencies increased as anti-Catholic sentiment and resistance to "surrendering" students to other Protestant dominations grew. There was an inward turning. The trend toward exclusiveness among religious colleges resulted in a weakening in the ability to attract students from the general population. Schools everywhere struggled with issues of enrollment levels and income. Some schools reduced entrance requirements. The very proliferation of inadequately funded institutions with a lack of qualified faculty, restricted curricula, and poorly prepared students resulted in mediocre quality at the best. Schools hard pressed for money took in all-comers regardless of qualifications, some as young as 13 (Nye, 1960; Rudolph, 1962).

Religion experienced prodigious growth, among Protestants mainly from re-energized followers and converts, and among Catholics from immigrant additions. The Catholics tended to be clustered in a few industrial cities, which resulted in high concentrations of believers that alarmed Protestants. The Catholic population increased so quickly that by 1850 it represented the largest single religious denomination in America. A relative new religious organization, the American Methodists, date from 1778, and by 1850 they were the largest of the Protestant churches, closely rivaled by the rapidly expanding Evangelical Baptists. These two dominations commanded the majority share of the new Protestant growth: Methodists primarily because they abandoned the Calvinist concept of predestination and proclaimed that all could achieve the possibility of salvation, and the Baptists because the fervent excitement of their brand of revivalism depended very little on an organized church hierarchy; all that was needed was a charismatic preacher with a willingness to tolerate harsh conditions in the hinterland to form bands of believers attracted by the promise of redemption (MacCulloch, 2009) Potts, 1988).

A striking difference between the First and Second Awakenings was that the latter was accompanied by the emergence of "American born" religious offspring. The southern African Methodist Episcopal Church and the American Methodists led the way, but by the early 1800s they were joined by the Seventh-Day Adventists, observers of the holy day of rest on Saturday and vegetarianism; the Christian Scientists who applied principles of Christian teaching to healing; and the Shakers who pooled their common property and lived in communes as they awaited the Second Coming. Their American founder, "Mother" Ann (Lee) believed that following the Second Coming there would be a reordering of the social order with women assuming power. As observers of celibacy, the last Shaker died in 1926. Other religious groups formed, but most did not last long.

More lasting, and most successful and most radical were the ideas of Joseph Smith, the gifted, semiliterate 22-year-old founder of the Church of Jesus Christ of Latter-Day Saints, also known as "Mormons." This church achieved worldwide appeal through its systematic approach to spreading its beliefs, its belief in posthumous baptism of ancestors, and its reverence for family and community. Even after fighting a war in the Mormon "homeland" of Utah with the United States government in 1857 over issues of sovereignty and polygamy, the religion survived to became America's fourth largest Christian domination (Johnson, 1997; MacCulloch, 2010). These and other religious expressions added to the rich spiritual inheritance coming out of the 19th-century Second Awakening that to this day largely define America's Protestant Christian heritage.

The Yale Report

The zeal to found colleges that reflected religious beliefs outstripped by far the ability of church groups to establish and maintain institutions of quality, and in the case of private investment ventures, institutional quality tended to be secondary to the want for profit. The lack of institutional quality was a deep, persistent, and widespread issue. Yale president Jeremiah Day took the matter in hand when he issued in 1828 a report on the behalf of the faculty setting forth the qualities of a high-status institution of higher education. Princeton soon added its support, and together the two institutions exerted considerable influence that defined for the next 50 years the character of higher education. Both institutions sent scores of graduates west and south to supply college presidents and staff. Other institutions, desiring to claim status, adhered as much as possible to the "Yale Plan," which soon was considered the yardstick by which to measure collegiate education. "The report echoed everywhere," Frederick Rudolph (1962, p. 135) observed. It helped to shift emphasis from an excessive religious orientation to the classical humanist tradition of the Enlightenment. But it locked American higher education into an academic perspective that was becoming outdated.

In his report, Day asserted that the "great object" of higher education is to equip the "furniture of the mind; expanding its powers, and storing it with knowledge." This would be accomplished through the disciplined study of the great works of the ancients within which resided the wisdom of the past, thus achieving a "balance of mental powers." The "instrument" of reasoning would be shaped by the study of math; "mental balance" would result from "bending the mind" in the direction of taste through the study of the classics. The study of the Greek and Roman classics constitute an essential part of a liberal education, the report affirmed, because they are "especially adapted to form the taste, and to discipline the mind, both in thought and diction, to the relish of what is elevated, chaste and simple." Through the report, the Yale faculty thought that it was laying the foundation of a superior education to fashion superior people. In the spirit of Erasmus, Yale was developing a refined leadership class. The new generation coming into prominence, they argued, had to have the polish that affirmed their high place in society (Bremner, 1970, pp. 494–502; Rudolph, 1962, pp. 130–135).

Running through all of the report was the implied application of faculty psychology. Extending as far back as Aristotelian ideas on how the mind works, reflected in the assertions of Locke, and advanced by both Thomas Jefferson and Benjamin Rush, the concept of faculty psychology was a powerful influence on shaping 19th-century teaching methods from the lower grades through college. It was believed that the mind was comprised of separate elements, or "faculties," that could be strengthened through rigorous exercise similar to the way that muscles are developed. Drill and rote memorization dominated instruction. When Day, president of Yale, referred to "discipline" and "furniture of the mind," he meant the exposure of students to the study of the ancient languages of Greek and Latin. They were considered the most useful subject for exercising the mental powers because they were difficult. It was thought that superior mental powers once developed were generalized to all applications. A superior mind meant a superior person.

Through a study of the ancients students also would develop a "cultured taste," and an understanding of the "divine truths" of revealed religion, and a comprehension of the source of modern literature. "It must be obvious to the most cursory observer," Day wrote, "that the classics afford materials to exercise talent of every degree, from the first opening of the youthful intellect to the period of its highest maturity. . . . Every faculty of the mind is employed; not only the memory, judgment, and reasoning powers, but the taste and fancy are occupied and improved" (Bremner, 1970, p. 501).

The report also addressed the provision of strong moral guidance as every college in America was expected to do. The Yale Report reinforced the idea that morality could best be promoted and preserved by keeping students cloistered in dorms located within a campus of surrounding classroom buildings. Students would have common living experiences under the beneficent eye of a faculty concerned for their welfare. In this way, a family-like structure could be maintained, and supervision approached what parents provided. Students would learn respect for others, common decency, and responsibility. Morality would be safeguarded. Dorms and residence halls within a campus architectural configuration became applied throughout America that exist to this day. From the beginning the model did not work as intended, but this did not deter supporters of the practice.

Also, as a way to protect students from immoral influences, founders tended to place campuses in fringe areas away from population centers in order to keep students relatively isolated from the temptations found in the backstreets and alleys of towns. To the delight of investors, however, areas surrounding campuses quickly built up, increasing property values but also bringing forbidden pleasures within reach of students.

Science and Engineering

Not everyone, however, agreed with the outcomes in the Yale Report. Schools following the Yale curriculum turned out "gentlemen" versed in the learning of ancient Greece and Rome; but were these individuals equipped with the technical and scientific tools necessary to build canals and railroads, carve out of the wilderness new towns, tame the vast plains, build factories, smelt iron ore, and penetrate deep into the earth after mineral wealth? The rational thinking of the Enlightenment opened the American mind in ways that went beyond classical literature and religious belief, and unleashed an industrial transformation. Science prior to the Revolution was prospering, and the following recovery after independence was accompanied with engineering applied to the remarkable technical progress that was transforming the country. Critics argued that the young were unprepared to tackle the challenges of a continent that was in the throngs of a profound industrial, scientific, and intellectual transformation (Furnas, 1969; Karier, 1967; Rudolph, 1962). A few colleges responded at first, later more.

Starting in 1806, Princeton admitted "science" students, but they received a certificate rather than a bachelor's degree because of the lack of a sufficient number of Greek and Latin courses. Union College substituted French for Greek. The University of Pennsylvanian in 1816 established a four-man "Faculty of Physical Sciences and Rural Economy." Starting in 1825, Miami University in Ohio offered an "English Scientific" course that included modern languages, applied mathematics, and political economy substituted for the ancient subjects. Like Princeton, students received a certificate rather than a BA degree. Columbia in 1830 and Wesleyan in 1831 introduced literary-scientific courses that were an alternative to classics. This was a modification that spread in the form of a parallel course of study that replaced the classical studies with more modern offerings or which diluted the classical program through substitutions.

The most enduring change was the elective pattern that continues to characterize American higher education. The idea was introduced at the University of Virginia by Thomas Jefferson and later became a central organizing element. His plan was adopted in 1824 and included eight "schools," each operating independently and capable of housing different departments: ancient languages, modern languages, mathematics, natural philosophy (science), natural history, anatomy and medicine, moral philosophy, and law. Students were free to elect studies in the school of choice and pursue a line of study. The university was not able to continue for long without modification. The scheme was too expensive. The attractiveness of the system was that it helped to undermine a classical curriculum locked in "superficiality and compulsion" and, in the words of Rudolph (1962, p. 127) "let loose an elective system of significant proportions."

The creation of the United States Military Academy at West Point in 1802 was a turning point. It was the first technical institute in America. Two decades later the last of the wealthy Hudson Valley Dutch Patroons, Stephen Van Rensselaer, founded in 1824 at Troy, New York, a premier technical school, Rensselaer Polytechnic Institute. Rensselaer was a forward-looking visionary. In the spirit of Benjamin Franklin, he wanted his institution to diffuse "a very useful kind of knowledge, with its application to the business of living." Studies were aimed at "the sons and daughters of farmers and mechanics." These were the individuals that would build the bridges, factories, steam engines, manufacturing systems, and technical innovation that America needed. Students engaged in "the application of experimental chemistry, philosophy and natural history, to agriculture, domestic economy, the arts and manufactures." All studies were infused with application—that is, the ability to use knowledge. The contrast with the Yale Report could not have been greater (Bennett, 1926, pp. 348–353).

Under the direction of two able leaders, Amos Eaton and B. Franklin Green, Rensselaer evolved into the first collegiate-level engineering school in America, granting a degree in 1831. Graduates of more traditional colleges also were attracted to the practical studies grounded in science and technology and enrolled for advanced work. Soon half of the enrollment comprised graduates of other schools, also granting Rensselaer the status of the first graduate school in America. Other institutions followed suit and copied what Rensselaer was doing. Among others, Union College established a Scientific Course in 1845. In connection with Yale College, Sheffield Scientific School started in 1847. Needless to say, there was a struggle within the faculty over this. Lawrence Scientific School at Harvard College opened in 1847, and Chandler Scientific School at Dartmouth College in 1852 (Bennett, 1926). Rensselaer, along with other institutions willing to adopt visionary changes, set into motion a strong challenge to the classical curriculum of the Yale Report and established the groundwork for the remarkable transformation of higher education following the Civil War.

The Dartmouth Case of 1819

A decisive decision by the United States Supreme Court in 1819 significantly impacted on the character of higher education in America. Dartmouth College was founded by Eleazar Wheelock primarily to educate American Indians, but it soon transformed into a college for White youth. When his son John attempted to take over running the school, Wheelock quickly clashed with the board of trustees over control. The issue soon became political with the state legislature bringing the institution effectively under its control. In a suit carried all the way to the Supreme Court, the verdict supported the trustees. At issue was the question whether Dartmouth College was a public or private corporation, and the finding that Dartmouth was private and independent from state control established the foundation for a parallel public and private system of higher education in America. Once the state issues a charter, the institution is considered private property subject to the established board but free from public control. Private colleges operate separate and independent from state-financed and -controlled colleges (Cremin, 1980).

The Dartmouth decision unleashed the spread of small, denominational colleges beyond the control of the state. But the decision also meant that states could not grow the collegiate educational system by taking over private institutions and converting them to public schools. It had to establish public institutions. The decision also made clear that the control of academic organizations rests in the constituted board and not the faculty. "Each new college," Frederick Rudolph (1962, p. 211) noted, "was now assured of its right to exist, if not of its right to survive in competition that the decision helped to unleash." Our extensive, extremely important parallel system of private and public institution of higher education owes its birth to the Dartmouth case. The legal framework was established for the remarkable spread of colleges during and beyond the antebellum period.

Chapter Eight
Education and the Oppressed, Exploited, and Conquered

The half dozen decades following independence were a time when society struggled with ways to accommodate and justify the treatment of women, the exploitation of immigrants and the laboring poor, and the brutal oppression of slaves and Amerindians. Those that were exploited were judged as inferior in intellect and character. This made it possible to exploit those who were considered less deserving beings without unduly disturbing perceptions of superior virtue, talent, and intelligence on the part of those exploiting. Jefferson's phrase "all men are created equal" certainly did not apply to the Irish worker toiling away in a factory or digging ditches, struggling to make a living at wages insufficient to maintain a family; and the inconsistency between ideals and reality was strikingly evident across the thousands of acres of fields where slaves in the hundreds of thousands toiled at backbreaking labor to clear the soil to plant and tend crops that brought wealth that they had no part in sharing. Or the inconsistency was evident in the long, forced march of the Creek Indians in the dead of winter as they were herded west across the Mississippi in order to vacate rich cotton-growing land so speculators could turn its sale into fortunes. Or the inconsistency was evident when thousands of the Mexicano inhabitants in the newly conquered southwest land taken from Mexico were forced south across the border to clear space for encroaching settlers even though they held American citizenship. The forces transforming America that brought wealth and change masked tensions that urgently required resolution. One major source of tension was that more than half of the population was not sharing in the promises of the Revolution. Gender, class, and ethnicity marked division lines.

During this time of remarkable national expansion schooling was an extremely important tool for extending opportunity, improving the lives of individuals, and addressing the social and economic welfare of the country. The future of the country was linked in large part with education. Many benefitted from its spread. But education can be used in both constructive and confining ways. It can be used as a partner of oppression and exploitation. In Chapter Eight, we turn our attention to three ethnic groups that continue to define us as a nation: African Americans, Amerindians, and citizens of the former southwest territory of Mexico, the Mexicano. We focus on their experience during nation building, and the uses and misuses of education.

Slavery: The Gathering Conflict

Post-revolutionary leaders tried to address the issue of slavery. They were partly successful, but not enough to bring the practice to an end without a climactic, wrenching conflict that tore the Union apart. The slave trade and importation of slaves was outlawed as of 1808. This restriction seemed to hold, with only about a thousand Africans smuggled in along the southern coastline over the next two decades. Domestic reproduction and relocation apparently made up for the end of the importation of human cargo. The indigenous Black population steadily grew, approaching the high birthrates among White citizens. There also developed a brisk business in kidnapping freed Blacks from the northern states and transporting them to the southern slave markets where they fetched high prices. Places like the coastal inlets of Rhode Island were prized hunting grounds because of the many coves to hide small craft before they made a getaway with the terrorized human cargo. But the New England shippers also continued to make fortunes off the slave trade. They no longer supplied the domestic market, but shifted to transporting slaves to Brazil and the Caribbean for European slavers, bringing commercial cargoes of rum, sugar, indigo, and other goods to the domestic American markets (Rappleye, 2007).

In the southern coastal states the demand for forced slave labor dropped during the opening decades of the new century. The tobacco lands were depleted, and agricultural production for all crops decreased as cultivation went elsewhere. The coastal states, especially Virginia, had an excess of unused slave labor and shifted into the business of supplying slaves to the opening western lands where sugar, and cotton production in particular, was rapidly expanding. The invention of the cotton gin by Eli Whitney made the growing of the short-fiber cotton characteristic of the South an extremely profitable enterprise. The tightly bound seed now could be easily extracted, and with the perfection of mechanical spinning and weaving the short fiber could be used by mills in the Northeast and in England. As suggested earlier, domestic use and exports soared, creating great fortunes north and south, and at the same time the fate of slavery was set: The centrality of slavery became entrenched and could not be displaced. There was no way to stop the practice. The fate of the southeastern Indians was also sealed since they were in the way of clearing land and creating expansive plantations. They had to be removed.

Ira Berlin (2010) estimated that between 1800 and 1860 up to 1 million Black people were "forcibly transported, into the American interior as part of slavery's expansion, redefining African American life" (p. 100). Families and communities that had been created in the American southern coastal region out of the diaspora of the Middle Passage were now torn apart and forced to rebuild their lives again under harsh, hard, uncaring conditions. The new inland expanses were full of swamps, bogs, uncleared brush, forest, stubborn soil, swarms of insects, dirt, disease, and uncertainty compounded by the stifling heat of summer and the cold of the winter. The driving harshness and brutality of overseers extracted a demanding human effort. Mortality rates soared and fertility rates plunged among those first laboring on the land. As holdings were established, consolidated, and expanded, the demand for eastern slaves increased so that by the time of the Civil War the interior southern regions were the most populated slave areas. They also were among the wealthiest, generating immense fortunes through a forced labor system that was one of the most profitable ever (Berlin, 2010; Kolchin, (1993).

The wage of slavery was tragedy. Families were broken up, men and women separated, children auctioned off, and husbands, wives, and children sent separately into a distance fate, never to be heard from again. Youth was a characteristic of the transported, and valued because of the potential long working lives ahead. By 1830, 45% of the slaves sold in the internal slave market were between the ages of 15 and 30. The older men and women stayed on the eastern seaboard. Childbearing-age women were desirable because they had reproductive capacity. Good-looking women were sought out and purchased as sex slaves, and some were put to work in brothels to earn income for the owner. Forced migration distorted the sex balance in the east and west and made the task of re-establishing family structures that held communities together all the more difficult. Marriage increasingly became to be viewed as a fragile bond, and as children got older they could quickly disappear into the slave economy. Berlin (2010) observed, "sales to the interior shattered approximately one slave marriage in five and separated one-third of children under fourteen from one or both of their parents. The preference of slaveholders both as sellers and buyers destabilized slave families, ensuring that husbands and wives would be separated and children would be taken from parents" (p. 110). Gradually, however, as inland plantation life stabilized and matured, families again were formed. On the other hand, Orlando Patterson (in Morgan, 2004, p. 108) argued that these were not families at all but rather "reproductive units" in the service of slave owners.

Captive people do not sit by and suffer abuse idly. Lost in a harsh, unfamiliar environment without recourse to family or familiar friends, individuals struggled to put some stability in their lives, reduce hardships, overcome difficulties of disease and poverty, thwart abuse and overwork, and construct new social communities. Several intermixed strategies were used. First, the slave population on the remote, rural plantations almost always outnumbered Whites. The Whites had the guns, but the slaves had the numbers and leverage. The Whites relied on slaves to work, and lost productivity during critical planting and harvesting times could be catastrophic if discontent and disruption could not be mediated. Many Whites realized that they had to engage in a degree of compromise with concessions that gave the slaves a minor measure of independence while preserving the authority of the master over the workforce. Slaves were able to extract concession that allowed them to accumulate small amounts of property on which to grow and market vegetables, and raise a few animals in order to sell produce, eggs, and meat and supplement their own diets. They secured the forging rights in forests and fields, cutting wood and collecting moss, berries, and other products of nature to use or sell. They also made footstools, spoons, bowls, chairs, quilts, and other handicraft products that they sold or traded. The bounty of hunting or fishing was consumed or sold. Gradually, as was the case along the eastern seaboard, a slave economy in the inland areas slowly emerged. This gave slaves a small margin to improve their diet, obtain better clothes, buy necessities otherwise not sufficiently provided by the master, and purchase a few luxuries to ease the burdens of life. It also gave them a small degree of control over their lives. Ironically, the ability to earn kept the slave on the land and plantation (Blassingame, 1972; Berlin, 2010).

Second, the practice of pay for "overwork" was advanced. The plantation owner, eager to expand production, paid for hours worked on Sundays, in evenings, and at times otherwise designated as free time for slaves. Once this concession was made, practice easily extended to hiring out slaves for wage employment during slack time to surrounding plantations and in towns to erect buildings, clear land, and fill in for labor shortages. Some slaves had specific skills in demand, such as wagon building or blacksmithing, and commanded good wages. The master kept part of the pay, but it was common practice for the slave to retain some of the earnings.

"Once slaveholders conceded the slave's ability to work independent and retain a portion of the product of their labor, there was no turning back" (Berlin, 2010, p. 124). What was given could not be taken away. Some slaves acquired a relatively high degree of status and independence, and had money, but typical practice was to contribute earning to a common pot benefitting the small, emerging community (Blassingame, 1972).

A reaction, however, soon developed. White workers complained bitterly that slave competition was depriving them of work and robbing them of wages and a livelihood. One Mississippi newspaper editor argued, "The [slaveholders'] policy of teaching Negros the various trades . . . tends to make the rich richer and the poor poorer, by bringing slaves labor into competition with white labor, and thus arraying capital against labor (for the negro is capital) and this will produce a spirit of antagonism between the rich and poor" (Takaki, 1990) p. 123). Across the South, legislation was introduced to keep slaveholders from using slaves for outside wage employment. Restrictions were difficult to enforce, and resentment grew with the White working class in conflict with the slaveholding class and their slaves.

A trading and communication network developed that fostered communities of interest, cemented family ties, established hierarchies of leadership, maintained cultural identity, and performed as the locus of courtship, marriage, and death rituals. Political, religious, and social alliances were formed. A sense of solidarity was nurtured (Blassingame, 1972). Some slave owners, however, fought any extension of independence, increased opportunity, or the development of solidarity on the part of the slave. Many slave-owning families lived in a state of continuing fear. Intermittent resistance and rebellion was accompanied by greater repression. The harsh treatment of slaves only increased the feeling of fear as each fed off the other. Some owners believed that the best way to guard against resistance and rebellion was to keep slaves in a repressed condition. Any hint of rebellion was quickly and harshly repressed. The lash was not spared.

Some slaves fought back. In a study of court records, John Blassingame (1972) concluded, "hundreds of slaves sued for their freedom, ran away from their masters, assaulted, robbed, poisoned and murdered whites, burned their master's dwellings, and committed suicide" (p. 107). To run away appears to be a prevalent option. John Hope Franklin and Loren Schweninger (Morgan, 2004) estimated as many as 50,000 slaves ran away on the average every year. A few runaways made their way to the northern states or to Canada, but this was the exception. Most stayed in the general area and most stayed away on the average for only a month. And most were caught. Both the family and the runaway were punished, but the runway apparently was willing to accept the consequences for even a relatively short time of freedom.

Social Regeneration and Schooling

On the surface the slave-labor system generated great wealth for some. There was wealth, particularly in the West South Central area, but it was not distributed throughout the region or among all elements of the population. The commercial exploitation of the land and people intensified during the antebellum years, primarily driven by cotton cultivation. Peter Kolchin (1993) observed that the economic growth rate of the South slightly outpaced the North in the 20 years between 1840 and 1860; but the backwardness of the southern society actually accelerated after

1830. The growth in monetary gain primarily was quantitative, not qualitative; more land in production but no improvement in the life of other than the rich. There was no strengthening of the social infrastructure, and there was little in the way of economic development other than the booming agriculture sector, and this was primarily in cotton. The New York Times correspondent Frederic Law Olmsted, traveling through the South in the 1850s, observed "a degraded land of poverty, illiteracy, ignorance, inefficiency, and lethargy in which slavery impeded economic development while eroding everyone's manners and morals" (Kolchin, 1993, p. 174). Others voiced similar observations. The South was trapped in an economic system that sucked out resources from everywhere else so they could be ploughed into the ever-expanding agriculture production of a few staple commodities for markets outside of the region.

Large parts of southern society were backward and underdeveloped. This applied to towns, roads, bridges, housing, medical services, people, and especially schools. Most southerners did not own slaves, and most lived on small farms with low cash earnings. The South lacked urbanization, and aside from a few ports through which to ship cotton, in 1860 New Orleans was the only southern city among the top 15 in the country. Importantly, the investment in education was lower than anywhere else in the United States. Ever since colonial times education for common people was limited, and it continued to be limited. School-attending pupils comprised 5.72% of the White population in 1840, compared with 18.41% in attendance throughout non-slaveholding states. The southern states had one third as many public schools, one fourth as many students, and one twentieth as many public libraries as the northern states. Compared to other sections of the country, the literacy rate was low. Retarded educational development placed real limits on social and economic development. The South was stuck in a repressive economic system that relied on slave labor and provided little future opportunity to the poorer White population, while the transformation necessary for altering the social and economic structure of the South lagged because of the lack of adequate capital and educated human resources (Kolchin, 1993; North, 1966).

Advocates of public education reform in the South made little headway compared to their counterparts in the North. It was not until after the Civil War that anything approaching a public-supported system of common schooling was put into place in southern states. There was resistance to the formation of centrally administered school systems, so the education of children was determined primarily by local arrangements. Like in the North and West, there was a mix of educational forms, and church-related schools played an important role, but a large proportion of White children did not go to any kind of school, and if they did, not for very long. In poor and isolated rural areas, field schools continued to be important. In states that had funds for the teaching of poor children, teachers could apply for tuition reimbursement for pauper children and this made enough children in attendance to open classes that also included poor farming and working-class children. In areas of higher population concentration, charity schools were provided for the poor. This was the major use of funding from public and philanthropic sources. There also was a smattering of fee-paying schools, and domination-sponsored schools were important (Kaestle, 1983).

What set the South off from other sections of the country was the prevalence of academies. These basically were secondary schools, and by 1850 the number in the South (2,700) outnumbered schools in both the New England (1,000) and the mid-Atlantic (2,100) regions. Apparently, upon completing the lower grades, the child in the South was more likely to continue on. Perhaps a money factor came into play. Poor children did not go to school, but middle-class children that could afford to start could also afford the academy years. The academies had a religious cast, and this was another characteristic of the South. "Virtually all academies, religious affiliated or not, stressed moral education, Bible study, and often some sort of catechism" (Kaestle, 1983, p. 193). Episcopalians (Anglicans), Presbyterians, Lutherans, Methodists, Quakers, Baptists, and Moravians among others were involved in running academies. They also extended their educational interest to the lower grades. Some affluent parents sent their children to academies, but the wealthy planter and professional classes tended as in the past to provide their children with private tutors (Kaestle, 1983).

Southern Blacks were denied education. As slaveholders came to fear subversion within the system by Blacks and from the outside by abolitionists, repression increased. Through education, slaves were exposed to the larger world of opportunity, could become discontent, and want freedom. Literate slaves could organize resistance among themselves. As the years wore on, stringent laws were passed forbidding under severe penalties teaching slaves to read. The decade of the 1830s was the most decisive one: Louisiana denied schooling by law to Blacks in 1830, Georgia and Virginia in 1831, Alabama in 1832, South Carolina in 1834, and North Carolina in 1835. At the same time, however, there is scattered evidence to indicate that a relative sizeable but unknown number of Blacks acquired the ability to read. In some cases, the master allowed or encouraged the teaching of promising individuals. Before the 1830s, some slave children were sent to school along with White children.

The major avenue through which initial literacy skills were learned was religion. For some denominations, the road to salvation was through the "Word," and knowledge of the Word was acquired through reading the Bible. White southerner J.B. O'Neill claimed, for instance, that in North Carolina "the best slaves in the state are those who can and do read the Scriptures" (Kaestle, 1983, p. 197). White itinerant preachers were used to bring the Word to slave churches, but the need outstripped the supply so carefully screened promising Blacks were prepared for pastoral duties. Sunday school and Bible study classes were held, and learning to read through catechism and scripture memorization was inevitably part of learning the Bible lessons. The Anglicans, Quakers, and Baptists played particularly active roles in bringing the Gospel to slaves, and by immersion in the Word, the ability to read. Literate slaves taught others.

But there were two sides to the involvement of the White religious hierarchy. As Kaestle (1983) suggested, the very emphasis on bringing Christianity to slaves was tacit recognition of Blacks as people, not just property. On the other hand, White religious groups tended to convey a message of acceptance and obedience, thus giving religious sanction to the practice and strengthening the hand of slave owners. But Blacks fundamentally rejected the idea of a pro-slavery Christianity. In the slave quarters a vigorous counterculture developed that "emphasized the immorality of slavery, the importance of black solidarity, and the value of various talents, including healing, preaching, conjuring, and reading." Over time, the slaves created their own religious institutions "within which whites had little, if any influence" (pp. 197–198).

White southerners spent an inordinate amount of intellectual energy in justifying slavery. The religious argument was probably the most appealing to the proslavery public. Southern biblical scholars and religious leaders spent an immense number of hours searching through both the Old and New Testaments to find passages that could be interpreted to justify bondage. Their conclusion: God sanctified slavery. Racial arguments also were used. Black Africans belong to a separate and inferior race and as such are not only more suited to hard labor in the southern climate but also biologically are subservient to Whites. A final group of arguments were more philosophical and revolved around the value of slavery to both the southern and northern economies, practical limits on getting rid of slavery, and the general good slavery was for the African brought to the New World. Southerners also tried to strengthen a conservative political coalition between southern agriculture and northern business interests but failed (Bartlett, 1967).

The South was trapped in a dilemma. It was supported by an economic system that retarded the development and growth of an alternative economic system that could more equitably distribute wealth, nourish other productive activities, and reduce reliance on slave labor and foster social and economic progress. The distribution and control of political power prevented change. Those in control of power were not willing to give it up or to change. At the same time, antebellum southerners lived in a state of contradiction. They professed to believe in freedom, liberty, and individual rights, but yet kept millions in the condition of bondage and degradation. The moral codes that they professed to live by were overshadowed by drive for wealth. They contorted religious beliefs in order to give sanctity to a hideous labor practice that was absent of any redeeming moral underpinnings. Deep down in the depths of their being, many southerners must have harbored the understanding that they, and the economic system that they vowed to defend, were unredeemable. Meanwhile, the beat in the tragic dance toward the horrific Civil War continued to increase in tempo.

To Clean the Land of Heathens

With independence, the challenge of addressing the Amerindian population now rested solely with the New Nation. Following victory, the treaty the British had made to set aside a large expanse beyond the eastern mountain fringe for the Native population was abrogated. Settlers moved in by the thousands in what was to become the Northwest Territory. The indigenous inhabitants were forced across the Mississippi onto reservations. With the unexpected Louisiana Purchase by Jefferson, the possibility of forcing all of the eastern Indians to west of the Mississippi became a reality. The farming frontier was inexorably closing in on tribal lands. Treaties made during the opening years of the century were simply overrun as tract after tract of Indian land was ceded, and each time boundary agreements were simply ignored. The encroaching settlers could not be stopped, and they could not be driven off land once it was occupied. A driving force was the fact that the money interests made huge fortunes through selling appropriated Indian land.

The political pressure to force tribes across the Mississippi onto unsettled land could not be overcome. Following the War of 1812, the government's policy toward the Indians sharpened, and by 1815 it was concluded that Native Americans could not be assimilated so they should be removed. The immense pressure of expansion into Indian land forced the government to act (Wilson, 1998).

The Civilization Act of 1819

Earlier, during his administration George Washington favored a policy of "civilizing" the Native population. War was expensive and destructive, he reasoned, so it was better to develop peaceful relations by encouraging local Native populations to settle and establish small farming communities. The government would help. Schools would teach practical skills of farming and building, prepare a technical class capable of supporting community needs, impart rudimentary reading, writing, and math skills, and build allegiance to the American form of government. The church would promote Christianity, teach a "white" value system, and reinforce subservience to ruling American authority. Trading posts would be established so the Native populations could become integrated into and dependent on a cash economy. This would stimulate business and commerce by opening new, extensive markets among the Amerindians. In 1795, a system of government-operated trading posts, referred to as "factories," was set up to provide an exchange of trade goods. Perhaps the most beneficial result, Washington believed, was that vast amounts of land now would be open by converting Native people from a hunter/gathering society that required extensive territory, to Indian communities that now only needed small amounts of acreage to engage in farming and commerce (Debo, 1970; Reyhner & Eder, 2004).

The policy of Washington attracted adherents and was given additional official federal government sanction with the passage of the 1819 Civilization Act. Through the act, missionaries were financed and sent primarily into southeastern tribal areas with a mandate to found churches and schools. Traders followed (Debo, 1970; Reyhner & Eder, 2004).

Thomas Jefferson supported Washington's policy in word, and stated he foresaw the assimilation of the Amerindians into a White, agricultural economy. But he also instituted appropriation of Indian land and removal, and under his administration the amount of land that Indian communities owned was severely reduced and most of the remaining indigenous populations in the Northeast were forced onto reservations. Additional Indian land was acquired in Tennessee, Georgia, Alabama, Mississippi, Arkansas, and Missouri. Over 200,000 square miles in total were taken (Wallace, 1999). Under President James Monroe, attention turned south. Whites wanted southern land for cotton growing. A duel policy was followed: Institute the Civilization Act while at the same time pursue removal. It was left to Andrew Jackson to complete the removal of all Indians east of the Mississippi.

The Civilization Act was only the first step, but there were two long-term consequences for Native people. First, a split that continues to exist to this day developed between "progressives," those wanting to assimilate, and the "traditionalists," the keepers of the Indian traditions and way of life. Those wanting to assimilate basically argued that the clearest path to survival was to become part of the White society. The major leaders of the progressives tended to be "mixed bloods," individuals of Indian and European ancestry that in some cases made up as much as

25% of the tribal membership. They used their capacity to work with Whites to broker agreement among tribal members. Often violent conflict erupted between the two Indian groups (Debo,1970; Remini, 2001). Once land was given up, it could never be reclaimed, the traditionalist warned, and the Whites would want more. But importantly, the intent of the Civilization Act violated the sacrosanct belief in the guardianship of tribal land for future generations.

The second consequence was catastrophic. The door was officially opened to White intervention in the Southeast and elsewhere. It did not matter whether or not the Indians conformed to the Civilization Act. It was irrelevant to the Whites if the Indians settled in communities or not. When the Whites wanted the land, they moved in and took it, and they used the Civilization Act as an opening wedge.

Andrew Jackson and Removal

Andrew Jackson, known among the Indians as "Long Knife" for his far-reaching, brutal ways, struck a major blow that resulted in the Native population being removed from the southeastern quartile of states. Jackson was hired by the federal government in 1816 to clean out the Native population from the Southeast. Similar to Black Americans, the cotton gin had devastating consequences. The Amerindians had to be cleared from the land to make way for cotton plantations. Jackson was the most likely person to do this. He was an aggressive, duplicitous, hardened slave trader, merchant, and land speculator who had no qualms about killing Indians. Jackson launched wars with the Cherokees, Chickasaws, Creeks, and Seminole, and on the side with the remaining Spanish in southeastern American. At one time or another he forced all of the Indian groups to capitulate to his demands. He extracted large concessions of land.

In 1819, he used the pretext of Indian raiders crossing from Spanish Florida into American territory to march into both west and east Florida, capturing Spanish holdings, and forcing them to capitulate and cede all of Florida and the Spanish lands along the Gulf coast to the United States. With the Adams-Onis treaty of 1821, the Spanish chapter in southeast America was closed. Jackson's actions were not authorized by Congress, but they willingly accepted his gift of conquest (Remini, 2001).

When Jackson ascended to the presidency in 1828, he completed southeastern Indian removal. He was able to get Congress to pass in 1830 the Indian Removal Act authorizing him to set aside lands west of the Mississippi in the Louisiana Purchase in exchange for Indian lands east of the river. Assistance would be given to help with removal and resettlement. Some tribes conformed; some balked. Among the five "Great Tribes" of the southeast, the Choctaws went to "Indian Territory" in what is today Oklahoma without being forced. The Creeks briefly resisted, relenting after being militarily mutilated. The men were shackled and the tribe was forced on to Oklahoma without weapons, household goods, food, or any means of livelihood. Considerable death among the Creeks was an outcome. The Chickasaws went peacefully. The Seminole put up a fight. The U.S. Army was forced to use bloodhounds to track and root them out of the swamps of Florida. Escaped Black slaves augmented the considerable fighting power of the Seminoles. Some were never caught, but as many as 40% of the Seminole population died in the struggle and the remainder were forced to march west to Oklahoma. The captured escaped slaves tended to be killed because it was thought that they could not be kept under control (Debo, 1970; LaFeber, 1989).

The Cherokees also put up a protracted struggle. In the western Appalachian Mountains of North Carolina, the federal troops were never able the extract a small tribal group. To this day, Cherokees reside in a reservation set aside, a reminder that some Indians did succeed in holding off the advance. In the flat lands of Georgia, state officials began evicting Cherokees that had settled down into towns. They did what the Whites wanted them to do with the Civilization Act of 1819, but to no avail. Unfortunately they lived in an area where gold in modest amounts was discovered. White militias forced them out. The Cherokees took a lawsuit all the way to the Supreme Count and received a favorable ruling, but Jackson refused to enforce the Court decision. A violent removal struggle ensued, and in a forced march in the dead of winter at least 4,000 of the estimated 12,000 captive Cherokees died from cold, hunger, sickness, exhaustion, and brutality. The "Trail of Tears," as removal is known, lives in the oral memories of many Native Americans (Debo, 1970; LeFeber, 1989; Remini, 2001).

Removal and Reconstitution

The Native Americans forced west arrived in "Indian Territory" under deplorable conditions. They were disposed of what they owned; they had no visible means of support; and families and tribal groups were depleted by the armed struggle and forced march, with their woes added to by disease, hunger, and sickness. In a remarkable feat of survival and reconstitution, they settled down, built villages and towns, and in rapid order transformed from a hunting/gathering culture into a small farming society. They also sold timber, minerals, and other resources of the land. They had no other option for survival. Maintaining a hunting/gathering culture simply was not an alternative. But the marginal quality of the reservation land meant that for many it was difficult to build anything but a substance life. The Sac-Fox, Kickapoo, Kaskaskia, Shawnees, Delawares, and Mingoes, among others, eventually were forced into Indian Territory with its shifting, constricting, and crowded boundaries west of the Mississippi.

Indians in the Plains States beyond Indian Territory did not escape the ravage of Whites as they moved west. In 1837, for example, a steamboat traveling up the Missouri River to Fort Union had a White passenger infected with smallpox. The stop was fatal to the Mandan tribe living along the river. Within two months, 1,569 of the 1,600 Mandan were dead. The Riccarees who moved into the vacated area enslaved the remaining 31 Mandan. By 1838 the smallpox epidemic spread outside of the former Mandan area, with 10 of every 12 Assiniboine killed by smallpox and 6,000 Blackfeet. The Whites had vaccinations, but they did not share the precaution against smallpox infection with the Indians (Flannery, 2001, p. 304).

Missionaries and Indians

Education played a major role in the reconstitution of Indian society, and missionaries had a large part. Prior to the Removal Act, missionary groups were successful in working with the Indians. By 1824, there were 32 schools in operation, and an additional 6 added in 1825, and yet another 14 by 1836. Supported through the Civilization Act, the Moravian and Presbyterians tended to work with the mixed blood elites; the Methodists and Baptists lived and taught among the common, usually full-blooded people and used Indian lay preachers. The Wesleyan Methodists found greater acceptance of Christian doctrine among Indians than others because they did not conform to the Calvinist doctrine of predestination, thus allowing for freewill and the potential for all to be saved. But generally, Indian groups resisted conversion. One major reason was Christianity "lacked the sense of balance and harmony between man and nature" which was a central belief among the Indians. And, in the view of Indians, there was no perceived moral superiority among the Whites (Reyhner & Eder, 2004, pp. 52–53).

The missionaries encountered resistance from those wanting to drive the indigenous populations away. They were accused of being too helpful. Opposition also was encountered from local liquor dealers. The missionaries tended to take the side of the Indians when they saw what they considered injustice, flagrant violation of the law, corruption, brutality, and abusive government policy. They also voiced opposition to the Removal Act; their observation was that the Indian people were already making considerable progress, negating any need for removal. Support of Indians meant that they were almost in a continuous state of conflict with the land-grabbers. In was not uncommon for missionaries to be forced to stop their work by Whites that wanted to encroach on Indian land. The missionaries also struggled against government policy that expected mission schools to support the removal of all eastern Indians.

Education in the Indian Territory

With western removal, the Indians started their own schools. Missionary help and government funds were important, but the initiative among the Native groups was instrumental. They saw formal schooling along lines of White children as essential to economic survival and to the perpetuation of their language and cultural heritage. Some concluded they had to adapt to a social and economic system along the lines of the encroaching Whites. From the first, the Indians established schools that taught in their own language. The missionaries soon learned that the most successful schools were the ones that gave instruction in the local language. Reading, arithmetic, and writing were taught. English was taught because it was realized that it was important in larger society, but also it was necessary to learn English "so that the white man could not cheat them" (Debo, 1970).

Taking a page from Webster, Indian children were taught about their culture and history in order to build a sense of identity and belonging. Farming and technical skills also were taught. By 1841 a national school system was established by the Cherokees under the direction of a superintendent with responsibility for 11 schools. In 1851, the Cherokees opened male and female seminaries to provide high school instruction. Among the Choctaw, in 1842 a system of tribal schools, including boarding and neighborhood schools, was set up under missionary boards. The Creeks, however, expelled all missionaries in 1836, saying, "We want a school, but we don't want any preaching, for we find that preaching breaks up all our old customs" (Reyhner & Eder, 2004).

A genius emerged from the Indian school effort—Sequoyah, a mixed-blood Cherokee who spoke no English and worked outside of missionary influence. A keen observer, he knew that the White man's language consisted of different marks. He isolated and assigned characters (marks) to 86 Cherokee syllables. To read and write in Cherokee was a matter of memorizing the characters, and in a short time Cherokees across the United States were communicating through writing with each other. Both the eastern and western tribal divisions, full blood and mixed, communicated in a network that provided a unity never before achieved. Some non-Indians did not like this, but the gift of writing that Sequoyah gave probably accounts in a large part for ability of the Cherokees to capture and retain a sense of solidarity and cultural identity to this day.

Removal marked acceleration in the downward trajectory of the Amerindians as a people. Forced into reservations with little in the way of traditional means of making a livelihood, they had to absorb "western" ways, but in so doing they gave up their way of life. They lost a great deal of control over their lives and the future. They suffered grinding poverty and high mortality rates. Repressed cultural traditions atrophied; it was difficult to keep traditions alive in the face of family struggle with poverty and community degeneration. No allowance was made for a growing population. Those struggling to make a living were crowded into yet smaller areas. Some retreated into the woods and isolated backcountry to lead solo lives. Young married couples had no place to go. Youth left to search for a way out of a future that had no future. Children away from home in boarding schools no longer fit into the community when they returned. When they left, they did not fit into the White communities either. "Mixed" marriages weakened family bonds.

Allotted land was systematically and progressively chipped away through "legal" and illegal means, so those that had already given up so much gave up more. They had little of value left. They had no power to resist. The long agony that was to go on for over another hundred years was reproduced throughout the United States as the original occupiers of the land were forced onto reservations. This was a dark, sad time for aboriginal Americans.

The Southwestern Conquest

The southwestern indigenous population appears to be of a different ethnic origin than the southeastern Indians. They also lived under 250 years of Spanish rule and have a distinct cultural identity to this day, but along with ethnic mixed Mestizos, Coyotes, Mulattos, and other variations including European Whites and Blacks, they suffered the same fate as Amerindians living in areas of the advancing Anglo, and later American rule. The incessant, westward movement of the Anglo population from the east into their land simply overwhelmed them.

Following the Mexican revolution and independence from Spain in 1821, Americans by scores moved into Texas, the large wedge of land that was an entry point to the immense southwest territory formerly held by Spain. The Mexican government initially encouraged emigration from the United States, perhaps in a bid to build a viable state that would anchor the entrance to its southwest territory. The policy was ill conceived and surely regretted. Settlers poured into Texas who had little allegiance to Mexico, and soon outnumbered the original population. All they had to do to become Mexican citizens was to convert to Catholicism and pledge allegiance to the new nation of Mexico, but they did not pay any attention to Mexican law. The settlers over the next three decades were a varied lot: traders, hunters, backwoodsmen; a rag-tag collection of vagabonds, fleeing criminals, adventurers, and slave hunters; poor dirt farmers seeking a better life, ranchers, some families, and speculators. Moses Austin acquired a large land grant in the most fertile region of Texas, passed on to his son Stephen F. Austin after his death six months later. Each of the original 300 settler families was given 177 acres of rich, cotton-growing land together with 13,000 acres of prairie pasture. Austin got 65,000 acres as a bonus. By 1830, Austin's colony had more than 5,000 settlers. Other settlements followed Austin's example. Eventually, 30,000 Whites and 2,000 slaves settled by 1835, surpassing the number of native Mexicans six to one. The Mexican government was weak, ineffective, and in an almost constant state of turmoil. The Anglos tended to look down with contempt on the darker-skin Mexicans. In 1835 after the Mexican government suppressed slaveholding and attempted to initiate tariffs, restrict immigration, and impose law and order, the Anglos rebelled (Gonzalez, 2000; Morgan, 2011; Morrison, 1965).

Following an initial defeat and slaughter of 187 by the Mexicans at the Alamo, and the massacre of 300 captives at the town of Goliad, Sam Houston, the hard-drinking former subordinate to Andrew Jackson, gained victory for the established provisional government at the Battle of San Jacinto. Houston, in a bold move during the heat of day at siesta time, attacked with his smaller force and scattered the napping Mexicans, catching Santa Anna, the Mexican president and general dallying with his mistress Jenny, one of a number he brought along. Santa Anna signed documents surrendering his army and granting independence, a complete victory by the Texans only seven weeks after the start of fighting. The Texan request to join the United States was delayed for a decade over the slavery issue, with annexation of the Republic of Texas finally in 1845 (Johnson, 1997; Morgan, 2011).

The annexation of Texas fed further expansion into Mexican territory. Presidents Monroe, Adams, and Jackson to Polk had their eyes set on former Spanish territory that would extend the boundaries of the United States to the Pacific. With a weak Mexican government, the large expanse was ripe for the picking. President James Polk made the move. His winning theme in the 1844 election was that it was America's "manifest destiny" to extend borders all the way across the continent to the Pacific, and he acted. Andrew Jackson tried to buy Texas from Mexico, but was refused. Sam Houston got Texas for him. Polk tried to buy California from Mexico, and also was refused, so he took it. But first, he settled questions over the northwest border with Britain by agreeing on the 49th parallel all the way to the Pacific. This freed him to turn full attention to the southern border and the rich land of California (Johnson, 1997; Morrison, 1965).

In the context of disagreements over debts owed Americans as a result of Mexican civil strife, Polk ordered General Zachary Taylor to occupy the south bank of the Rio Grande in Mexican territory in response to a Mexican skirmish. This was an act of war. Taylor fought decisive battles at Buena Vista and Monterey. Invasion and conquest was extended to Vera Cruz on the east coast, and to a march west across to Mexico City, where the conquering American General Winfield Scott received surrender. With signing of the Treaty of Guadalupe Hidalgo in 1848, and the subsequent Gadsden Purchase in 1853, the southern and western borders of the United States were established. Mexicans in the conquered territories were given citizenship.

Polk added more territory to the continental United States than any other president (Morgan, 2011). As war goes, the cost was high in lives but minimal in terms of what was gained: 1,721 killed in action; 11,550 killed mainly from disease. The United States gained immense mineral and agriculture wealth, the present-day states of Texas, New Mexico, California, and Nevada, and parts of Arizona, Utah, and Colorado, with the addition of some of the richest agricultural lands with the Gadsden Purchase. The underpinnings were established for 20th-century prosperity. The Mexicans lost many more lives, largely unaccounted for, and one half of its landmass. They lost considerable potential for greatness (Gonzalez, 2000).

The Americans absorbed territory that had over two centuries of Spanish colonial history. They over layered this with an Anglo governing structure, and a social, economic, and cultural context that mixed with but yet dominated the Spanish inheritance. As conquerors, they treated the indigenous population as inferior and subservient. The idea of manifest destiny created an attitude of superiority toward Mexicans. In the minds of White Americans, they were destined to rule over what they considered inferior peoples as evidenced by their darker skin, slighter build, way of life, and adherence to a lesser cultural inherence and the Catholic faith.

The attitude of racial and cultural superiority fed greed: the Americans took what they wanted. Thousands of small farmers, shopkeepers, and landowners were dispossessed of their homes, businesses, and farms, and by force driven into Mexico against their will. Entire former Mexican communities were uprooted and ejected. In Matagorda County, Texas, for example, every Mexican American was ordered to leave; in 1853 and 1855, the Mexican Americans were physically driven out of Austin, and most of the Mexican American population was forcibly removed from San Antonio by 1856 (Montejano, 1987). Those that remained were subjected to overt discrimination.

At the same time, Mexican Americans and Mexicans returning over the border to work provided most of the unskilled and semiskilled labor that built the Southwest. As Gonzales (2000, p. 47) observed, "at the time the territories were ceded the Mexican population in the acquired territory was around 116,000, but it increased steadily with the movement of hundreds of thousands back across the border as migrant labor. This meant that Mexican influence continued stronger than generally realized or acknowledged." Influence continues today for the same reason.

Mexican American children acquired some schooling through the Catholic Church and remnants of the institutions established by the Spanish. But when schooling was introduced by the conquering American power, it primarily was for Anglo children. English was mandated as a school subject as a way to eradicate Spanish in the newly conquered territory. When forced by public and legal pressure to extend educational opportunity to Mexican American children, the practice was to provide separate, but unequal schools (Spring, 1994).

In a real sense, the Mexican American war was a prelude to the Civil War just 15 years later. Young officers who later would face off in the lines at Manassas, in the trenches at Vicksburg, on the ridges at Lookout Mountain, or across the fields at Gettysburg got their baptism by fire in skirmishes with the Mexicans. Both Lee and Grant distinguished themselves by coolness under fire, and George McClellan, Thomas Davis, and Jefferson Davis, among others, took part. Texas adopted slavery, and the struggle over the admission to the union of the other states kept the slavery issues simmering, preventing any resolution to the conflict that broke out in a Civil War over the soul of the New Nation.

Part Three References

Bartlett, I.H. (1967). The American Mind in the Mid-Nineteenth Century. New York: Thomas Y. Cromwell Co.

Bennett, C.A. (1926). History of Manual and Industrial Education up to 18790. Peoria, IL: The Manual Arts Press.

Berlin, I. (2010). The Making of African Americans. Four Great Migrations. New York: Viking.

Berthoff, R.A. (1971). An Unsettled People. New York: Harper and Row Publishers.

Blassingame, J.W. (1972). New York: Oxford University Press.

Bremner, R.H. (1970). Children and Youth in America. A Documentary History. Vol. I: 1600-1865. Cambridge, MA: Harvard University Press.

Cremin, L.A. (1980). American Education. The National Experience 1783–1876. New York: Harper & Row Publishers.

Curti, M. (1959). Social Ideas of American Educators. Totowa, NJ: Littlefield, Adams & Co.

Curtis, S.J., & Boultwood, M.E.A. (1965). A Short History of Educational Ideas. London: University Tutorial Press.

Debo, A. (1970). A History of the Indians of the United States. Norman, OK: University of Oklahoma Press.

Dinnerstein, L., Nichols, R.L., & Reimers, D.M. (1996). Natives and Strangers. A Multicultural History of Americans. New York: Oxford University Press.

Flannery, T. (2001). The Eternal Frontier. New York: Grove Press.

Furnas, J.C. (1969). The Americans A Social History of the United States, 1587–1914. New York: Putnam's Sons.

Gonzalez, J. (2000). Harvest of Empire; a History of Latinos in America. New York: Penguin Books.

Heafford, M.R. (1967). Pestalozzi. London: Methune.

Johnson, P. (1997). A History of the American People. New York: HarperCollins Publishers.

Kaestle, C.E. (1973). The Evolution of the Urban School System. Cambridge, MA: Harvard University Press.

Kaestle, C.E. (1983). Pillars of the Republic. New York: Hill and Wang.

Karier, C.J. (1967). Man, Society, and Education. Glenview, IL: Scott, Foresman and Company.

Kerber, L.K. (1980). Women of the Republic. Intellect and Ideology in Revolutionary America. Chapel Hill: University of North Carolina Press.

Kokchin, Peter. (2003). American Slavery. New York: Hill and Wang.

LaFeber, W. (1989). The American Age. New York: W.W. Norton & Company.

MacCulloch, D. (2009). Christianity. New York: Penguin Books.

Mann, H. (1845). Eighth Annual Report. Boston: Dutton and Wentworth.

Montejano, D. (1987). Anglos and Mexicans in the Making of Texas, 1836–1986. Austin: University of Texas Press.

Morgan, E.S. (2004). The Genuine Article. New York: W.W. Norton & Company.

Morgan, R. (2002). Benjamin Franklin. New Haven, CT: Yale University Press.

Morgan, R. (2011). Lions of the West; Heroes and Villains of the Westward Expansion. Chapel Hill, NC: Algonquin Books.

Morrison, S.E. (1965). The Oxford History of the American People. New York: Oxford University Press.

North, Douglass, C. (1966). Growth and Win the American Past. Englewood Cliffs, NJ: Prentice-Hall, Inc.

Nye, R.B. (1960). The Cultural Life of the New Nation, 1776-1850. New York: Harpers & Row.

Perlmann, J., & Margo, R.A. (2001). Women's Work? American School Teachers, 1650–1920. Chicago: University of Chicago Press.

Phillips, K. (1999). The Cousins' Wars Religion, Politics & the Triumph of Anglo-America. New York: Basic Books.

Potts, David B. (1988). Baptist Colleges in the Development of American Society. New York: Garland Publishing, Inc.

Rappleye, C. (2006). Sons of Providence; the Brown Brothers, the Slave Trade, and the Revolution. New York: Simon & Schuster.

Ravitch, D. (1974). The Great School Wars New York City, 1805–1973. New York: Basic Books Publishers.

Reese, William J. (1995). The Origins of the American High School. New Haven, CT: Yale University Press.

Remini, R.V. (2001). Andrew Jackson and His Indian Wars. New York: Viking Penguin.

Reyhner, J., & Eder, J. (2004). American Indian Education. Norman, OK: University of Oklahoma Press.

Rudolph, F. (1962). The American College and University. New York: Vintage.

Schlesinger, Jr., A.M. (1946). The Age of Jackson. Boston: Brown and Company.

Spring, J. (1994). The American School, 1642–1993. New York: McGraw-Hill.

Takaki, R. (1990). Iron Cages; Race and Culture in 19th Century America. New York: Oxford University Press.

Tyack, D., & Hansot E. (1982). Managers of Virtue. Public School Leadership in American, 1820–1980. New York: Basic Books.

Tyack, D., & Hansot E. (1990). Learning Together; A History of Coeducation in American Schools. New York: Russell Sage Foundation.

Vassar, Rena L. (Ed.). (1965). Social History of American Education. Volume 1: Colonial Times to 1860. Chicago: Rand McNally & Company.

Wallace, A.F.C. (1999). Jefferson and the Indians. Cambridge, MA: The Belknap Press.

Ware, N. (1964). The Industrial Worker, 1840–1860. New York and Chicago: Quadrangle Books.

Wilson, J. (1998). The Earth Shall Weep; A History of Native Americans. New York: Atlantic Monthly Press.

Woody, T. (1974). A History of Women's Education in the United States. Volume II. New York: Octagon Books.

Part Four
Constructing the New Social Order

Introduction

All wars have tragic consequences. The Civil War was no exception with horrible destruction and slaughter that left whole communities crying for the dead, that indiscriminately churned out crippled and broken lives, that inflicted economic and social ruin that never could be fully overcome, and that created infectious, festering sores of resentment, loss, shame, blame, and alienation. A reluctantly united nation could never completely heal.

But wars also have unanticipated and sometimes little understood outcomes. This was the case following the Civil War. The United States experienced a remarkable social and industrial transformation. To be sure, the nation retained its agriculture economy as booming production fed the growing cities and fueled a vast overseas export market. The expanding rural economy also marked a population shift west as adventurous souls enticed by the promise of new, better lives went west to the opening agriculture lands. As the nation struggled to heal itself, it also moved swiftly into an urban-industrial age. In just steel and oil production alone, both engines of economic growth, the nation went from almost no production in 1860 to the dominating world producer by 1900. The productive energies built during the conflict between the states were unleashed: Manufacturing soared; road, railroad, and communication networks quickly spanned the continent; foreign and domestic markets opened; and new towns and cities emerged. The gross national product tripled between 1870 and the turn of the century. The nonagricultural workforce mushroomed by 300% in the 30 years following the war. The foundation was established for the economic superpower status of the 20th century (Johnson, 1997, pp. 511–516; LaFeber, 1989).

But the newly found confidence in the victorious northern states masked deep, protracted, political, economic, and social challenges. The population expanded at an unmanageable rate: 39 million in 1870, 63 million in 1890; and 92 million in 1910. Driving up population growth was the fact that infant mortality rates measurably dropped from 217.4 per 1,000 live births in 1850 to 120.1 in 1900. A large proportion of the population increase was from immigration. But now immigration was different. They came in massive numbers. Between the end of the Civil War and 1890 over 10 million arrived. By the end of the first decade of the new century, 1 million immigrants were arriving annually. They also came from different places and had different beliefs and cultural heritage. Initially most arrived from northwest Europe, but by 1885 the European immigration pattern had shifted south and east primarily because of severe economic times.

People were poverty-stricken and trying to find a better life. Most that came were uneducated and unskilled.

But significant to the inability to manage the new urban centers was internal migration. Huge numbers left rural areas in the search for jobs and a better life to become additions to a sprawling, disorderly, unhealthy, and dirty urban environment barely under control. Sixteen cities with a population of 50,000 and over marked the landscape in 1860; there were 109 in 1900 (Bureau of the Census, 1960; Johnson, 1997).

The poor in cities needed help. Slum living conditions were appalling. Cities had little organization and few social services. Streets were unpaved, spreading dust, dirt, and sickness in warm weather and mud in wet. There was no indoor plumbing, few sewer lines, and no garbage collection, so the human odorous rankness collected in streets. Horse transportation spread tons of droppings daily, to combine with the rotting piles of filth, to be pawed over and eaten by freely roaming pigs and dogs, in turn spreading their own filth. People did not have water in their dwellings and had to resort to an outside central source to fill buckets. Few bathed. In time, public baths became available in some cities to the poor for those wanting to occasionally bathe. The food supply was uneven and limited. There was no refrigeration, and the supply was seasonal, but often there was little money to buy food. Only the least expensive could be purchased, so food brought in from other than the local area rarely could be bought. It was too expensive except for the affluent (Furnas, 1969; Spain, 2001).

The housing supply was limited, and usually of poor quality. There was no heating, cooling, or indoor plumbing. Many people lived in crowded tenements, large multiple storied buildings hastily constructed to house the flood of rural migrants and arriving immigrants. Multiple families often lived together in one room. Ventilation was poor, sanitation conditions bad. In rapidly expanding industrial centers, the housing supply was so limited that "hall beds" were rented out primarily to the rural young women finding work among the looms, assembly lines, and sewing tables of factories. These were small spaces partitioned off in the corridors of tenement buildings with room for a chest and bed. Many of the poor, particularly newly arrived immigrants, lived next to the workplace in shacks and shanties. They lived among the dirt spilling over from the factory. The poor experienced what was called "the tyranny of distance." They had no way to move around. They had difficulty traveling to find the lowest cost food, better housing, or cleaner and safer communities. Medical services were out of the reach of the poor, and even if obtainable, crude.

John Higham (1970, p. 36) observed, "The sodden wretchedness of the slums settled more deeply into the heart of great cities every year." Infested water, liquid sewage freely running through streets, typhus, tuberculosis, hunger, and fire extracted a heavy toll of death. Life was relatively short. By 1900, a White female on the average lived to age 46 or 47; a male 43 or 44. These are figures for all segments of the White population, so it is reasonable to conclude that the affluent lived longer beyond the average, and the poor shorter lives. Black women on the average could expect to live to 36 or 37; males 33 to 34 (Furnas, 1969; Spain, 2001).

An unanticipated outcome of the Civil War was the social divisions that became more pronounced. Some became immensely rich, many poor. This was the age of the "robber barons."

Wealth became concentrated as capital and power were centralized; large companies swallowed small ones, and the number of low-wage industrial labors increased proportionally to skilled craftsmen displaced by mechanized production. In 1860, the average American was an independent rural farmer. By 1900 he was a wage-earning worker struggling against labor competition and corporate consolidation and control. Production technology was crude; work physically hard, and working days long—14 hours on the average. The productivity of workers soared, but wages remained low largely because of the large excess labor pool fed by immigration.

Rural farmers faced some of the same market conditions as urban workers. Large conglomerates formed that controlled market prices and transportation, squeezing profits out of the farmer's hand to put into their own pockets. Years of intermittent drought did not help the plight of the farmer. The American farmers lost ground so that by the closing years of the century their annual income was on the average less than that of a factory worker. A rural revolt ensued that resulted in the short-lived Populist Party. The social crusader Mary E. Lease best expressed rural discontent when she urged farmers to "raise less corn and more hell" (LaFeber, 1989; Johnson, 1997).

Farmers and urban workers faced the same problem. The newly found wealth of the country was an outcome of the stunning success of its productivity. Considerably more was produced on farm and in factory than could be consumed at home. Exports were the key to prosperity. But international markets were unpredictable and unstable. Relative prosperity was replaced by economic slump when export demand dropped. National demand followed international demand, so that in hard times there was a double slump. In 1873 there was a deep financial panic that lasted for five years, initiating a 23-year period of financial depression punctuated intermittently by periods of prosperous upturn. There were economic recessions in 1873 to 1877, 1886 and 1887, 1893 and 1897, and again in 1907. Of course, most of the affluent weathered "bust" times with the wealth accumulated during the "boom" times, but the laboring poor desperately struggled just to stay alive.

Social dissent grew. Strikes and riots gripped the nation. The 1880s became known as the decade of the "great upheaval." Walter LaFeber (1989, p. 152) reported in the period between 1881 and 1900, there were 24,000 labor strikes in the United States. The conflict between strikers, police, federal troops, and corporate agents were violent, bloody, and destructive. Workers almost always lost. Many workers joined the fledging union movement. Many others, indeed, thousands out of work simply roamed the country looking for jobs. There developed a large transitory labor force. These "knights of the road" hopped rides on freight trains, lived in barns and under bridges on the outskirt of towns, slept in alleys and parks, and begged or stole food. When work was found, some men with families sent money home, others just abandoned families, unable to face the disgrace of failure (LaFeber, 1989; Morrison, 1965).

The Focus of Part Four

It was inevitable that education underwent a transformation under the impact of the fluidity and extent of population change, of the increasing heterogeneity of the school population, of the puzzling forces of urbanization and industrialization that drove economic expansion but also created misery, need, and desperation. The vast concentrations of wealth altered economic and political power. Labor unrest threatened social and political revolt. The perception spread that society had to assimilate more effectively the mass of men upon whose sweat and expended lives the new social order was constructed (Baltzell, 1966). Schools respond to societal conditions. The whole idea of public education underwent a significant transformation (Cremin, 1961).

In Chapters Nine and Ten we examine this transformation. The intent is to link change in schools with change during this tumultuous period when society was engaged in a fundamental restructuring of the social order. Educational reformers reached back to ideas that Thomas Jefferson championed a century earlier and that Horace Mann used to foster the common school movement that everyone should have the opportunity to be educated. But no longer, reformers urged, could schools be solely used to create an intellectual elite. During the antebellum period the battle for public schools was won; now the concept of public schools had to be redefined, reformers urged. The purpose of schooling had to be radically altered to focus on all children of different classes, ethnicity, and religion. Little children had to be brought into school at an earlier age, instruction had to be tailored to fit different kinds of youth, multiple educational purposes had to be addressed, and education for vocation was a legitimate school outcome. The notion of education itself had to be broadly defined. Colleges and universities as well had to address the needs of the emerging industrial order.

Educational change came from two directions. At one level the social reformer and educator worked to address the most urgent conditions impacting on the lives of urban children, the subject of Chapter Nine. They used the kindergarten and lower grades of the common school to do this. They borrowed ideas from Rousseau on the education of children; they built a new psychology of learning based on concept of sense impressions advanced by Locke; and the experience of Pestalozzi supplied practical ways to restructure teaching. The work of Friedrich Froebel provided the framework for the education of little children. A social purpose was indelibly stamped on public schools: The physical needs of children were to be administered to, and links formed with home and community. The idea of nurturing conveyed the spirit of teaching.

Social reform groups placed kindergartens in slum communities across America. Edward Sheldon made Oswego the center of what was to become known as the "new education" based on an American interpretation of Pestalozzi's ideas. He attracted teachers from all over America seeking to become versed in new concepts of teaching. Francis Parker, formerly superintendent of the Quincy, Massachusetts, schools and later director of the Chicago Cook County Normal School, applied his innovative mind to develop the most creative approach to education in America by embracing manual activities, cooperative work and play, spontaneous activity, self-expression, and pleasure in learning (Parker, 1891). Other schools followed Parker's lead. John Dewey took Parker's ideas and through his work at the laboratory school at the University of Chicago and later at Teachers College, Columbia University, put theoretical form to the educational movement that was redefining common school teaching. Through his instrumental pragmatism he formulated a philosophy that linked schools with the reconstruction of society. School reform efforts were given voice.

A second center of change, the one examined in Chapter Ten, revolves around work in higher education to redefine the character of the American university, and the emergence of the high school. The classical curriculum tenaciously held on to its place as the source for the cultivation of an American elite, but now the complexity of industrial society with its need for specialized training, technical knowledge, and experts opened the way for a growing vocationalism. The study of chemistry and physics, mechanical drawing and strength of materials, and library science and journalism were expected to lead to jobs by a student population becoming more varied. Coeducation took hold as financially hard-pressed colleges removed restrictions on female enrollment in order to tap into an expanded source of revenue. Teacher training programs proliferated.

The changing character of higher education profoundly influenced the emerging public secondary school movement. Colleges required feeder programs to supply students. They needed more students, but they also needed students with the prerequisite knowledge to succeed in the science, math, technical, and professional courses now offered. But at the same time, more students with little expectation of continuing beyond secondary education were enrolling. These were the children of rural migrants, recent immigrants, industrial workers, or prosperous farmers that typically stayed in school a few years before entering the workforce. The needs of the two distinct populations were different, but both had to be addressed.

The focus of Chapter Eleven is on issues of ethnicity and education. Massive immigration presented complex problems. The challenge of integrating men and women into the economic and social structure was compounded by the emancipation of southern slaves. The outcome of the war forced the South to develop a different kind of economic system based on cheap labor to maintain agriculture production. Close to 4 million freed Blacks and large numbers of poor Whites were absorbed into an altered economic and social system that was not yet clearly defined. The failure of reconstruction and the lack of political will resulted by 1900 in the emasculation of the intent of the Thirteenth, Fourteenth, and Fifteenth Amendments to the Constitution as a system of segregation, exploitation, and judicially enforced inequality descended on the South. Violence against Blacks became commonplace, and Blacks and poor Whites were pitted against each other in a society that exploited both. Black citizens in an effort to control their own lives struggled to obtain educational opportunity.

The 1864 contract labor law that enabled the use of business agents to recruit laborer in Europe was applied to Asia. Now, Chinese, Filipino, and Japanese workers flooded into the West Coast port cities, and in urban centers across the nation by the thousands to provide cheap labor. They clashed with local labor. Counter to the high expectations they came with, they experienced discrimination, exploitation, and violence. Mexican workers similarly engaged in cultivating the fields of the southwest and Pacific coast farmlands encountered hostility from an Anglo population that wanted cheap labor but was not willing to give back fairness, respect, and appreciation. Finally, in Chapter Eleven, we examine the tragic consequences of policies to "assimilate" Amerindians. The nation could not yet conceive of fully assimilating citizens of different ethnic origin, of different religious beliefs, or of different skin tint into an already diverse population mixture that was becoming more mixed. At the same time, those populations were exploited. America in the post–Civil War years struggled to come to terms with its ethnic diversity. Schools, too, engaged in this struggle.

Chapter Nine
To Build a Better Society

A relatively unknown social scientist, Lester Frank Ward in his work *Dynamic Sociology*, argued that society could be remade through planned, organized, and purposeful action in which education played a major part. Education had to be dynamic and directed toward equipping the individual to live cooperatively and independently in a pluralistic, rapidly changing society. "The object of education is social improvement," said Ward. "Education is really needed for the purpose of making better citizens." Education should be employed for socially useful ends (Ward, 1968, p. 589).

With his work, Ward gave form to ideas that were formulating in the minds of social reformers like Jane Addams and Robert Woods of the settlement movement, leading kindergarten advocates like Sarah Cooper and Susan Blow, and Felix Adler of the Ethical and Cultural Society of New York who were concerned with the appalling moral and physical conditions of the working underclass. If education was to play a socially redemptive role, its perceived purpose had to change. The focus of the school had to change from academic training in order to create a cultured elite, to an institution that focused on individual and community regeneration. Education could be a tool of social reconstruction.

Inspired by religious moralism, crusading women by the hundreds following the war spread throughout the slum communities of American cities. They were primarily motivated by the belief that the more privileged have a moral responsibility to administer to the needs of the poor. These women tended to be the wives and daughters of the affluent working out their Christian responsibility to the less fortunate. They set up soup kitchens, sponsored clothing and shoe drives, maintained shelters for women, established public baths and playgrounds, organized sanitation leagues, founded settlement houses, ran kindergartens, and prodded schoolmen to put more functional programs in common schools. They experimented with lodging houses for homeless youth, reading rooms, informal religious services on street corners, and half-time and industrial schools.

What was different about the reformers following the war, however, was the enlistment of schools to join with them in the actual implementation of broader social reform efforts. To be sure, they directed their work to the slum streets of the cities, and to shelters and boarding houses for the poor, but at the same time they turned to kindergarten and elementary school classrooms to directly administer lessons on morality, to provide food and clothing, to assist the struggling and desperate, and to forge connections with slum mothers. They altered the purpose of public schooling. In so doing, reformers linked home and community with school.

Just as the purpose of schooling was rethought, the motivation behind social reform work underwent considerable change that moved education to the forefront of public concern. Much of the social work prior to the Civil War was conditioned by the long-held belief that individual moral failure is the cause of poverty. Individuals are poor primarily because they lack virtue. The accompanying need and squalor are the outward signs of moral degeneration, and both had to be addressed. But Ward helped to shift the emphasis from individual blame to social meliorism: Society itself had to be changed. It was still important to teach children of the lower classes lessons of morality and virtue, but the plight of the suffering poor is no longer solely attributed to personal failure. Political, economic, and social conditions are viewed as major contributing factors to the suffering and squalor of the slums rather than personal failure alone. It is society that creates slums, not the irresponsible behavior of sinners. It is the greed of the wealthy that contributed to inequality and poverty; and it is the lack of political will that tolerates poverty and suffering.

This fundamental shift in thinking was shaped and embedded in the evolving religious idea of the "Social Gospel." Daphne Spain (2001) observed that religion was taken out of the church and put onto the street. There was no such distinction as "deserving" and "undeserving" poor. All need help in overcoming the moral and economic erosion of urban and industrial life. Through voluntary associations, women worked to administer to the needs of the poor and achieve a vision of the "good society," one that took care of all of its people, was just and moral, checked the excesses of greed and wealth, combated the inefficiencies of government, and made cities wholesome and beautiful places to live.

This was a remarkable change in thinking and continues to influence American social thought in a profound way. The social and political views of "conservatives" and "liberals" today tend to align along the polar opposite views embodied in late 19th-century social reform. Is the underclass, as social conservatives suggest, primarily a product of their moral weakness and degenerate tendencies? If so, society must embark on the regeneration of the underclass through schools and penal and other institutions that shape individual morality and control deviate behavior. Or, as liberals contend is the underclass primarily an inevitable presence in a society that contributes to and tolerates moral failing, social inequity, poverty and exploitation, as the Social Gospel suggests? If so, society must reconstruct itself through the use of schools and other social institutions to promote the redeeming values of morality, equality, opportunity, and social justice. There is a public responsibility toward the poor because all are, indeed, "deserving."

The Social Gospel itself was an outcome of the social and economic dislocation accompanying the Civil War and its aftermath. The clergy were among those expressing the greatest alarm after the war. No longer, they warned, could reform efforts focus primarily on saving individual souls, but it was urgent that emphasis be redirected to the social and moral problems of American cities caused by rapid urbanization, industrialization, migration, and immigration. The cities themselves had to be saved, and in the words of Spain (2001, p. 63), the "movement applied Christian principles to the problems of daily life."

Individual salvation was linked to the salvation of society through constructive action "on issues such as such worker's rights, women's rights, temperance, race relations, immigration, public sanitation, and housing conditions." Advocates believed that "poverty had structural roots." Education was enlisted by followers of the Social Gospel in the crusade for social salvation.

Saving the Children:
The Kindergarten Movement

The first widespread founding of kindergartens was in the worst slum districts of the country. The children were among the most destitute: dirty, ragged, hungry, and sick. Known as free kindergartens, mission kindergartens, and charity schools, and supported through private contributions, they were "havens of benevolence." For children the kindergarten was a place where they could get a hot meal, a bath, and rudimentary health care. For some, the kindergarten was their only educational experience before starting work as child laborers (Peabody, 1882). Private groups took the initiative in founding kindergartens because public educators faced limited financial resources and were not interested in educating the very young of the poor. And they were as well immobilized by the inertia of tradition and bias.

As suggested in Part Three, German immigrants familiar with the work of Friedrich Froebel brought the first kindergartens to America. Froebel studied under the Swiss educator Johann Pestalozzi at the Yverdon Institute and brought ideas back to Germany to found a school for little children in 1837 at Blankenberg. Americans learned about the kindergarten from the fleeing German emigrants following the 1848 revolution and the successive immigrant waves that continued to flood into the nation's port cities well up into the 1850s. The immigrants attached kindergartens to the small, rural schools in German-American enclaves. In states like Pennsylvania, Missouri, Indiana, and Wisconsin, and in communities throughout the Midwest with heavy German populations, kindergartens were considered a necessary means to preserve elements of German culture that were fast slipping away. Little children could be exposed to German heritage early (Shapiro, 1983). Inspired by what they saw, interested Americans journeyed to Blankenberg to learn more about Froebel's play school. America quickly became familiar with the novelty of the kindergarten.

With the establishment of the American Froebel Union in 1867, Elizabeth Peabody is given credit for officially launching the kindergarten movement. Miss Peabody founded a successful fee-paying kindergarten in Boston for children of affluent parents. Reflecting growing nativism, other early efforts to launch private and public kindergartens for middle-class children, however, had less success. Affluent Anglo parents were reluctant to send their children to the "German school" (Shapiro, 1983).

A noted exception was the work of Susan Blow and William T. Harris, superintendent of St. Louis public schools. They opened the first public kindergarten in America in 1873. Earlier Harris conducted a survey among families of school children, and was shocked to find that poor children living in the slum factory and levee districts that went to school only attended on the average three years. They started first grade at age 7 and left at age 10 to work. The kindergarten enrolled children sooner, Harris concluded, adding additional years to an already short educational experience. He enlisted the help of Susan Blow, a part-time teacher experimenting with kindergarten instruction to initiate a trial effort in the St. Louis schools. Blow was acquainted with Froebel's work through her visit to Europe. Harris and Blow met resistance, but they had one decisive advantage: St. Louis was the center of a large Midwest German population that supported the work against opposition. Besides, the school district had money, with the booming commerce and industry, making St. Louis the second fastest growing city in the West. Success solidified the trial effort, with the school board making kindergarten instruction a formal part of the St. Louis school program (Shapiro, 1983; Vandewalker, 1913). Public school efforts in other parts of the country were less successful and continued to struggle.

The Social Crusaders

It was among social reformers in the urban centers working with slum children that the kindergarten found instrumental backing and early, wide success. Reformers were not constrained by issues of public support and ethnicity. Their work was largely financed through private wealth. In New York, Emily Huntington started a preschool program in 1876 and Felix Adler opened the Free Kindergarten of the Ethical and Cultural Society two years later for children of the unemployed. In Boston, Mrs. Quincy Adams Shaw financed and opened two kindergartens in 1877 for children of laboring men, then opened 14 more in 1878, and 12 more in 1879. Sarah Cooper in San Francisco capitalized upon the financial support from Jane Stanford, Phoebe Hearst, and Mrs. Charles Crocker to establish the Golden Gate Kindergarten Association and its extensive network of kindergartens throughout the Bay area. Through the work of the Chicago Free Kindergarten Association, 10 kindergartens were founded by 1884, drawing on the wealth of Mrs. George Amour and Mrs. W. A. Montgomery. Anna Hallowell in Philadelphia, Sarah Steward of Milwaukee, Grace Dodge in New York, and countless other women in cities and towns across the country blended private and public resources together to set into motion the drive for kindergartens. By 1890 there were 115 free kindergarten associations enrolling close to 15,000 children from poor, destitute families (MacKenzie, 1886; Shapiro, 1983).

Social reformers no doubt were motivated by the need and sadness that they saw around them. As one woman commented, the "motley throng of infantile misery and childish guilt . . . telling their simple stories of suffering, and loneliness, and temptation" touched them until their "hearts became sick." But reformers also were motivated by the fear of social dislocation. There was a pending political and social crisis if the "stupid and stolid" children of the underclass were left unattended. "Their bodies are becoming diseased by neglect, their minds brutalized by contact with indecent sights and sounds, and their souls, oh their poor souls, hardened by contact with lying and thieving, and swearing, and they are almost squeezed out of existence," was the lament of one alarmed citizen (Shapiro, 1983, p. 88). These children would grow up to haunt society as members of a dangerous class. They had to be trained. Reflecting the ideas of Rousseau, the kindergarten would provide a protective, caring environment that countered the corrosive influence of the slum street; an environment in which the little child could develop unhindered the moral characteristics thought essential for escaping the sloth of the slum (Brace, 1880; Shapiro, 1983; Wiggin, 1888).

Social reformers favored the kindergarten as a child-saving institution for several reasons. One, it reached children at an early age. Reformers reasoned since children went to work early, the kindergarten provided a few more years of educational contact in the crucial formative years when the child was still in a pliable state. Like fresh clay, little children could be molded before hardened by life. Moral, intellectual, and physical character could be shaped before the child entered the shop or mill. In addition, the kindergarten provided useful education for those destined to toil. It was the "best preparation for the arts and trades," Sarah Cooper asserted before the 1882 National Conference of Charities and Corrections (p. 134), "its gifts and occupations represent every kind of technical activity. The senses are sharpened, the hands are trained and body is made lithe and active." The muscles in particular could be shaped because they were in the "the pulpy consistency of early childhood." William T. Harris (1879) concurred when he told the National Education Association meeting "the child training for one year on Froebel's gifts and occupations will acquire a skilled use of his hands and a habit of measurement of the eye which will be his possession for life" (pp. 146–147).

Kindergarteners thought the exposure to simple counting, figuring, and measuring; the acquisition of vocabulary, and rudimentary reading and arithmetic skills; and the engagement in simple craft activities when coupled with the discipline of the group, moral training, and the training and exercise of immature muscles, all contributed to the ideal preparation for children soon entering into a young work life. William T. Harris conveyed the convection of others when he told the St. Louis Public School Board the kindergarten was "admirably adapted to the purpose of commencing the education of an industrial people" (Report of the Board of Directors, 1878, p. 220).

It did little good to train little fingers to be nimble or to sharpen perceptions unless there was some assurance of a positive commitment to work. The kindergarten taught manners and morals, and cultivated constructive attitudes and good work habits. Building character and strengthening morality would transform the slum child into a desirable worker, meaning one that was disciplined, hardworking, capable of following directions, cooperative, and respectful of authority. Though cooperative work and play, by living together, and by engaging in individual and group activities children learned a moral perspective and collective skills considered essential in an industrial society (Paddock, 1884; Brooks, 1887).

The instructional value of the kindergarten was considered a natural outcome of Froebel's system of "gifts and occupations." Froebel thought learning was an unfolding process dictated by the rhythms of human maturation and the innate urge of individuals to expand experience and knowledge. Sets of solid shapes in the form of the cube, and cylinder along with triangles, squares, rings, and sticks were presented to children to play with. They learned concepts of shape, size, and form, names of objects, simple measurement, ideas of proportion and balance, and worked together as they played with blocks. In the early age, the little children danced, sang, played number and word games, drew pictures, and worked with clay. Older children engaged in simple weaving activities, clay work, leather tooling, gardening, exploring, and reading through both individual and group activities. But all of this play was not just random activity. It had a purpose. It was to be both guided and progressive, the unfolding of experience and learning. Curtis and Boultwood (1965) best summed up Froebel's intent: "The teacher's task is to organize and guide the free and continuous development of the pupil through play—a gradual development of self-activity, never forced. He is to encourage the awakening senses, to help the pupil to find words to express his ideas and mental images, and to ensue the retention of such knowledge by play-way methods" (p. 379). This was a reflection of the ideas of Locke and Rousseau in different words.

Another reason why the reformer favored the kindergarten was because of care provided to needy, often-desperate children and their mothers. Children came to the kindergarten hungry and malnourished. They were fed a hot meal. They were sick. Medical help was given. Festering sores were cleaned and bandaged, skin diseases treated, and persistent and serious ailments attended to. Children came dirty, smelling from unwashed bodies and clothing. Lice was picked, and baths given. Clothing was laundered, but often it was so raggedy that it was replaced through the supply of donated clothing on hand. This was a time when there were no government services available for needy children and families. Slum kindergartens fulfilled a crucial social service role by providing for the physical in addition to the moral and educational needs of children.

The kindergarten also presented an opportunity to enter into the home and community life of the urban poor. Dedicated ladies combed the slum streets for potential kindergarteners, followed little waifs home, talked and visited with tenement mothers and invited the mother and child to the kindergarten. Hungry mothers were fed and illnesses tended to. Clothing, blankets, shoes, and warm coats for the winter were provided. Mothers were invited to share their problems with concerned reformers. They were invited to return and take part in lessons on nutrition, sanitation, and childcare, and to receive help as the kindergarten became a temporary place of refuge for the harassed, worried, and weary mother. Lessons on Christian morality were sandwiched in between. The kindergarten teachers in return visited the slum homes. They helped mothers on ways to keep the dwelling clean, to buy and prepare nutritious food, to improve sanitation, to tend to the sick, and to deal with problems of home and community. Soon the work was extended to forming neighborhood group meetings of mothers to address joint efforts to improve home and community life. "The kindergarten reaches directly into the home," Jacob Riis approvingly declared in *The Children of the Poor*. "No door is barred against her who comes in the children's name. In the truest and best sense she is a missionary to the poor" (Riis, 1892, p. 180).

This was socially redeeming work, the Social Gospel manifested in action. Kindergartens became a mainstay of settlement work, mission societies, community help groups, and all kinds of social and educational reform organizations. The scope of the early kindergarten reform work was not lost on educators. No longer could public schools ignore and isolate themselves from the living conditions surrounding the poor children of the underclass frequenting classrooms in increasing numbers.

Influence on Public Education

To be sure, public school educators such as William T. Harris, W.N. Hailmann of La Porte, Indiana, James McAlister of Philadelphia, and Edwin Sever of Boston played pivotal roles in the early kindergarten movement. The balance of influence, however, did not swing to public schools until after 1890, when the movement entered a new phase with public education assuming a strategic role. By this time reformers had gained a secure place for the kindergarten. In the 1880s, at least 400 private and public kindergartens had been established in 30 states. Twenty years later there were over 4,500, and the kindergarten was undeniably entrenched in American education (Smith, 1961). The influence of the kindergarten extended upward into the elementary grades.

The influence on public schools was substantial. The most visible impact was the provision of social services. City public schools located in poor sections began providing baths. Children arrived to face an assembly line of cleaning stations where they were deloused, soaped up in tubs of water, dipped and rinsed and dried, and supplied clean clothing while their dirty garments were laundered and mended. Schools employed nurses to take care of the sores and sicknesses of arriving children. Schools put in cafeteria facilities so hungry children could be fed. They put in playground activities, including sports and recess periods, so children from unwholesome crowded tenements could have a chance to exercise freely and breathe clean air. Schools taught manners, morals, cleanliness, and the simple act of getting along with each other in an environment that was more socially, economically, and ethnically diverse.

In city schools, teachers accommodated children speaking half-dozen or more different languages as they conducted day-to-day instruction. Schoolmen began to think beyond just day attendance and provide evening activities: courses in English for immigrants, civic classes, and practical instruction in hygiene, and recreational activities and health services. Some schools became neighborhood centers for coordinating social services and the work of "Americanizing" (Cremin, 1961; Vanderwalker, 1908).

The impact of the kindergarten was less visible but no less penetrating in altering conventional instructional ideas. Kindergarten advocates joined with others to challenge the rote methods of question and drill and the harsh discipline of the school. Public common schools reflected a moral perspective inherited from Calvinists' belief that the child was born corrupt and ignorant, that learning was a process of disciplining the will. Restraint and control characterized the classroom. The relative role of the teacher was to transfer society's moral and social beliefs to the child. But these views were less accepted in the post–Civil War educational and social environment. As suggested in Part Three, markedly different ideas were creeping into American education, and they were now filtered through the work of early kindergarten advocates based on the work of Friedrich Froebel's mentor Johann Pestalozzi. A new generation of educational thinkers and schoolmen no longer were constrained by past educational practices and religious beliefs.

An apostle of Pestalozzi, Edward Sheldon and his work at Oswego Normal School contributed to the spread of what soon became known as the "New Education." Trained teachers dispensed about the country new ideas on teaching and learning. A school district in the far west, or in an isolated rural midwestern community, or in the suburb of an eastern city could incorporate new ways of teaching and object lessons into instruction by hiring an Oswego-trained teacher or simply sending one of its own staff to the Upper New York school.

The individual who generated the most reform excitement was Francis Parker, superintendent of the Quincy, Massachusetts, schools from 1873 to 1880 and later director of the Chicago

Cook County Normal School. Parker was a bold, ingenious innovator. He openly took the ideas of others, such as Froebel and Pestalozzi, and, as he stated, put them to use feeding the "famished minds of children." The child must be at the center of teaching, said Parker. All instruction must have meaning to the child. Parker discarded the more traditional approach to schooling, eliminating the speller, reader, grammar and copybook, and instead built a program around current materials developed by teachers and stressed observation, discovery, and understanding. He wanted educational experiences that led to self-activity and cooperative work, and that were real and part of the child's world. "Real work is always interesting like real play . . . all school work should be real work," contended Parker: "We learn by doing" (Campbell, 1967; Cremin, 1961, pp. 129–134; Karier, 1967, p. 224).

Parker interrelated the subjects in what was to become known as "correlation." He wanted to merge manual, mental, and moral growth in the manner of Pestalozzi. As students worked in the school garden, made jelly, or built a weather vane, they learned how to measure, use fractions, spell new words, research facts, or study geography. In Parker's eyes, the school should be a "model home, a complete community an embryonic democracy," complete with garden, workshop, and laboratory (Parker, 1891). The purpose to schooling was to provide rich learning experiences drawn from the life of the child. What Parker implemented was a child-centered curriculum that contrasted sharply with the traditional subjects orientation, an orientation that is still prevalent today and probably best represented in the No Child Left Behind legislation.

When Parker moved to Chicago to assume the leadership of the Cook County Normal School, his work attracted the attention of John Dewey and his wife Evelyn. They sent their son and daughter to Parker's school and were impressed by what they saw and learned from Parker. In 1896, the Dewey's established their own experimental school in Chicago, the "Laboratory School" through which John could work out the theoretical implications of what he saw and experienced. Within a half dozen years, the school with John as director and Evelyn as principal, grew to be the most recognized experimental representation of the New Education. The educational work of Dewey was continued at Columbia University where he went in 1904. His writings dominated American educational thinking for a good part of the rest of the century.

Dewey acknowledged his debt to Parker, but he took the ideas of what was to become known as "Progressive Education" to a fuller, complete stage. He gave a theoretical structure too much of what Parker accomplished.

The educational landscape was shifting, and Dewey give it a strong push in the direction away from learning conceived as mastery of subject matter to greater emphasis on individual growth and development. Studies were conceived as child centered, as correlating abstract and concrete knowledge to create a conceptual whole, and as embracing concern for the problems of home and community that the child brings into the classroom. His work marks a transition from dependence on European formulations of educational thought to the emergence of an "American" philosophy of education and its accompanying indigenous applications.

Chapter Ten
Of Plow and Machine:
Education for the New Age

A second center of change revolved around the educational interests of businessmen, manufacturers, industrialists, and agriculturalists among those engaged in the productive activities of the nation. They wanted a diversity of college studies calibrated to the requirements of the changing economy. The complexity of industrial society generated the demand for educated individuals, but this did not mean the ability to conjugate Latin verbs or read the Odyssey in classical Greek, but rather it meant the requisite knowledge in math, science, technology, and technical skills that was fundamental for building specialized work skills. It meant courses in pharmaceutical chemistry, civil engineering, or architectural design, and it meant majors in biology, medicine, metallurgy, and animal husbandry. Work was becoming more specialized and subdivided into specialized fields and specific tasks. Much of work now required a combination of formal academic learning and technical and practical skills. In industry itself, foremen, engineers, and technicians increasingly were required to take on the creative functions of solving design and production problems, and introducing innovation and organization into the work structure. A new generation of educated supervisors, engineers, technicians, and managers was needed. There was no natural process, however, through which individuals engaged in work matriculated up into the ranks of skilled positions of responsibility and scientific and technical complexity. Some did not have the requisite academic skills, and some lacked the technical skills. Both needed to be formally learned. A new kind of formal schooling was required.

Private interests used their political influence and wealth to generate change. They acquired positions on college boards and challenged the domination of the classical studies; they supported and financed trade schools and technical institutes; they bankrolled progressive college leaders; and they individually founded colleges and universities, such as Cornell and Purdue, to advance the goals of a more relevant and functional education. Within a generation, higher education in America was transformed. Change took a number of forms.

First, attention was turned to attacking the domination of classical education. As discussed earlier, the first stirring of dissent and inroads in the classical curriculum were made prior to the Civil War. Led by Rensselaer Polytechnic Institute, engineering and scientific studies were established. Other schools followed (Rudolph, 1962). Following the Civil War, change quickened. Businessmen, manufacturers, and men of wealth provided founding and supporting grants to scores of public and private colleges to "promote education beneficial to the industrial interests" of the country (Nobel, 1977). Schools such as Johns Hopkins, Stanford, Northwestern, Cornell, and many others built institutions offering scientific, technical, and specialized and practical studies as they abandoned traditional views on the importance of a classical curriculum. Turning their attention away from the Yale Report of 1928, they offered a less prestigious but more functional program of studies. Cornell University under president Andrew D. White, for example, included a blend of both liberal and practical studies so that the "captains of the army of industry" could be prepared alongside the "rank and file." White concluded the machines of production needed both educated. Students engaged in vocational subjects, applied technology, applied science, basic research as well as the more "intellectual" subjects. Said White, "We shall fit the youth of our country for the professions, the farms, the mines, the maufactories, for the investigations of science, and for mastering all the practical questions of life. . . ." (Butts, 1939, p. 187).

By the 1870s and 1880s, the process of redefining the dimensions of higher education was well underway. Colleges across the country turned in increasing numbers to the idea that higher education could play a major social and economic development role. Expressing ideas similar to Robert Molesworth and the Commonwealth men more than a century and a half earlier, education could be used to enhance the worth of individuals by building on their inherent potential, while at the same time an educated workforce would join in propelling the social and economic development of the country forward. All would benefit from the increased prosperity. In today's terms, college education was considered a tool of human capital development. This was a profound change in thought. One disgruntled critic lamented that the changes in higher education constituted "the greatest educational crime of the century against American youth—depriving him of his classical heritage" (Rudolph, 1962, p. 295).

The "elective principle" was a major force driving change. Very early the University of Virginia tried to implement Thomas Jefferson's idea of offering student choices in a curriculum spread over eight "schools of study." Because of cost, the plan was never fully implemented, but it was highly influential. Other colleges began to offer students the option to choose "elective" courses given alongside but outside of the body of required classical studies. Science and engineering made their entrance in this way (Rudolph, 1962, pp. 110–135).

With renewed vigor following the Civil War, electives were turned to as a way to break the grip of classical studies on the college curriculum. The classics were not attacked directly, but rather by offering optional parallel sequences of courses the classics soon became reduced to one of a number of possible fields of study. Students could "elect" large parts of their program. It did not take long to enlarge offerings and identify official alternative "majors" and "minors." Classics lost its hold and atrophied. Interest and relevance replaced tradition and little used knowledge, and permitted students to engage in the remarkable expansion of knowledge that was transforming society. New subject departments were built, and studies were offered that formed crucial service links to the larger community. The dimensions of our university today go back to the elective principle.

Another powerful force of change was the influence of German universities. To be an educational leader of note, one had to go to Germany; the country was engaged in a remarkable political and industrial transformation with education at the center. The Industrial Revolution that grew out of Enlightenment thought enabled England to first dominate world production followed by Belgium and France. With greater political unity, Germany soon followed. After the Civil War the United States became fully engaged in an industrial transformation that thrust the country into the ranks of leading industrial powers. In the meantime, Germany had gained domination over its European rivals in fields such as metals and chemicals largely because of its university system. It used universities as centers of graduate research, generating knowledge used to drive the machines of production. Americans wanted to do the same. Over 2,000 Americans went overseas during the decade of the 1880s to learn from the Germans.

Americans brought back a realization of the essential research role of the university not in just science but in all fields of inquiry from history, economics, psychology, and theology, to food preservation, farming, metal casting, mechanical engineering, and textiles. This opened the way for the development of the multi-university, expanding into what were considered legitimate areas of study. The role of professors and students changed. Under the guidance of the research professor, "scientific" methods are used by teams of graduate students to uncover the knowledge hidden within the folds of specialized fields of inquiry. Our graduate schools continue along the same lines today.

The passage of the Morrill Federal Land Grant Act of 1862 was perhaps the most crucial development. It was inspired by the idea of using universities as tools of social and economic development. It gave a specific "American" complexion to higher education. The aspect of vocationalism was reinforced, with higher education providing the practical, scientific, and technical skills required by the advancing industrialism. The idea of "service" to the community was advanced.

The Morrill Act was born out of need, its supporters argued. Antebellum colleges were too sectarian, locked into a philosophy designed to cultivate a select elite, indifferent to the forces of change in America, and adverse to scientific, technical, and practical studies. Teaching and learning was based on what was considered by some as the faulty concept of faculty psychology. A half-century of national struggle to define agriculture education found support in the agrarian centers of the country. Farming states pushed for federal support of institutions of higher education that would advance agriculture and mechanical training. President Lincoln signed the bill leading to the founding of a major university in each state dedicated to the advancement of agriculture, industry, and commerce.

The act provided for the support of at least one college "where the leading object shall be, without excluding other scientific or classical studies, to teach such branches of learning as are related to agriculture and the mechanical arts" (Rudolph, 1962, p. 252). Because the definition of what the new land grant institution would offer was so loosely defined, individual colleges were characterized by an extraordinary variety of course offerings ranging from metal machining and woodworking to domestic science, dairy husbandry, corn farming, welding, mathematics, literature, chemistry, and economics. Some schools kept the traditional subjects and had language and classics departments. Most schools offered combinations of the more traditional programming mixed with the newer programming thrust. Traditionalists derided the new schools as "cow colleges." The common element that evolved throughout land grant colleges, however, was direct relevance to the productive enterprises of farm and factory, business and market (Cremin, 1961). The overriding theme was service to the wider community through a functional education relevant to present social and economic needs.

To provide support for land grant institutions, each state was given 30,000 acres of public land or its equivalent in land script for each senator and representative. Oklahoma, Texas, South Dakota, and Washington set up entirely new schools in competition with the existing state universities, and Wisconsin, Minnesota, North Carolina, and Missouri converted state schools into land grant endowed colleges. Michigan, Pennsylvania, Maryland, and Iowa created A & M (agriculture and mechanical) institutions. In six states private colleges were given the land grant to change the emphasis of studies, and in Oregon the Methodist College of Corvallis was reorganized as a land grant school. At Yale, the Sheffield Scientific School became the land grant institution. Yale could not yet take the step to substantially realign its mainline university. In New York and Indiana the money of private benefactors was combined with the land grant to found Cornell and Purdue (Rudolph, 1962, p. 253).

In 1890, Congress passed a second Morrill Act. The purpose was to fund "black" colleges. A key stipulation was that unless provision was made for separate and equal opportunity, no funds would go to states that denied college admission on the basis of race. Seventeen states set up land grant schools for Black students (Rudolph, 1962, pp. 253–540). In a remarkable variety of form and intent, every state eventually established a land grant school in what became the leading state universities in a national system of higher education that played a fundamental role in propelling the economic and social development of the country forward.

In a related development, privately endowed technical institutes also proliferated. These supplied the large group of trained, middle-level skilled technicians, foremen, and managers with proficient technical skills linked with enough formal theoretical training to implement the designs of engineers. They were essential cogs in the machine of production. The graduates knew how to build things, and at the same time they could work with the scientific and engineering knowledge that was playing an ever-larger role in industry. Privately backed technical schools such as Pratt, Rose, Case, Drexel, and Amour, to name some, turned out young men who could address the knowledge and skill requirements for specific industries. Some graduates went on to higher education, but most went directly into work and their practical training complemented the skills of the college graduates (Bennett, 1937).

By the late 1800s, three strands of influence were present that continued to define the character of American higher education to the present. One thread extends back to the classical humanism of the Enlightenment and through the English influence transferred to the colonies. The classical curriculum was the outcome. It manifests itself today in liberal arts studies, and core requirements in the arts, language, literature, and the humanities. The other thread is evident in science and engineering, specialized research and graduate education and is traced to German influence. Universities are considered a tool to advance and generate knowledge. The third thread of influence stems from the land grant movement and stamps the function of service on the university's mission. The scope of education is extended to a large segment of the population, as individuals are prepared in a variety of roles to serve the social and economic interests of the extended community.

The Form and Function of Secondary Education

In the rapidly evolving remade world, advocates of change contended students had to be prepared to matriculate into the expanding network of schools which equipped the young for work. Colleges, universities, and technical institutes, however, faced a number of real problems in recruiting students. There were not enough, and it was difficult to find students adequately prepared. Urban immigrant youth lacked language skills and money, and they usually had to go into work at an early age. Rural youth migrating to the urban centers with their parents often possessed technical skills learned on the farm, but they too, had to overcome barriers of poverty and the lack of prerequisite skills.

It was not unusual for higher education institutions to accept students that completed no more than elementary education. Colleges provided extensive remedial programs. They also offered pre-college preparatory programs. They did this because there were relatively few high schools in America, and most were private and most continued to offer a very limited curriculum heavy on "literary studies." And many were of marginal quality. Select private academies and prep schools tended to be a good source of relatively well-qualified students. But only the more affluent could attend, and wealthy parents did not always want their child to attend a "cow college," or spend time in engineering workshops where they got their hands and clothes dirty with grease and grime. In fact, Harvard divided its engineering program: Students took the theoretical and scientific courses on campus, and the practical work of forging, metal machining, and the fabrication of materials was given at "Boston Tech," the institution across the Charles River that transformed itself into what is known today as the Massachusetts Institute of Technology.

The potential pool of students was limited. Public-supported high schools increasingly became the focus of the possible: They could potentially provide a large student population shaped to fit the requirements of universities. First, however, their numbers had to be increased and their program of studies realigned (Bennett, 1937; Reese, 1995).

The expansion of public-supported high schools initially gained support in areas of the Midwest. Some parents in the larger towns saw the immediate value of extending educational opportunity for their children. Perhaps there was a lack of private opportunity. High schools, however, continued to struggled over the questions of who they should serve and why? Common practice was to extend a few years of elementary education so selected students could take college preparatory work. In many cases, the high school was merely a room in the elementary school set aside for older children; in some cases, the sixth, seventh and eighth grades were designated "secondary education." Students left public common schools at college age, but not necessarily with adequate preparation. Nevertheless, the practice spread with combined public primary–secondary schools.

The inevitable division into separate schools was just a short step, but not an easy one. In some communities, separate high schools were separated from elementary schools. As the practice expanded into other towns and into cities, however, resistance grew. William Reese (1995, p. 57) suggested, while resistance was from a minority of citizens, it was strong. Opposition to public-supported secondary schools fell along three lines.

First, as in the case of the common school movement, private schools were opposed to the spread of public high schools because they considered them a threat—which proved true. Later in the face of the public secondary school movement many fee-charging private schools floundered. Parents opted for "free" public schools rather than paying fees. With a few exceptions, private academies, the most common form of post-elementary education, were gone in large parts of the country by the first decade of the new century.

Second, opposition came from an unexpected quarter: working-class parents. Parents of modest means supported the common school movement, but not secondary schools because they believed that their children would not be able to take advantage of the opportunity because they had to work. Farm boys were needed in the fields, and city boys went early to the factories and shops. Child labor was common, and essential for many families.

In addition, as the battle for the shape of secondary studies got underway, many working parents could see little value in "traditional" studies designed to cultivate the niceties of the more privileged. Few of their children could be expected to advance from the elementary grades upwards through the secondary schools into higher social and economic levels. Why should the workingman, the argument went, "pay for the professional education of the lawyer's son, the minister's son? The community does not provide my son his forge or loom" (Curoe, 1926, p. 81). Elementary education, on the other hand, was considered by elements of the opposition as a means of uplifting the working class.

Rural opposition took a similar shape. Studies conceived as more appropriate for "rich children" were not attractive. The claim was made that only the more affluent would benefit from public-supported high schools. Even when the significance of the classical studies was reduced by what was called the "English" stream, and later by what was called "modern academic studies," some complained that math, science, art, literary and language studies only made farm boys unfit for physical labor. The pig farmer or the fruit grower saw little value in his son studying French, algebra, or extended English courses. He was expected to work on the farm at the conclusion of schooling. More "functional" studies had to be offered before the high school could garner greater support.

The extension of the high school was also opposed because of cost. Rural schools almost always were inferior to urban, and adding another institutional layer only stretched already limited resources. Opponents complained that separate high schools for a limited number of potential students were too heavy a tax burden for low-income, rural families. Then again, perhaps the most intractable rural problem was low population density and distance. Cohorts of more than a handful of a few qualified students were difficult to form in communities (Curti, 1959; Reese, 1995).

A third strand of argument similar to common school opposition was the resistance encountered by members of the more affluent. Why should they have to pay for the education of those paying little in taxes? Shouldn't those wanting more education pay for it? Others cast doubt on the wisdom of educating the poorer classes. A luminary no less than Charles W. Eliot of Harvard argued that although mass common education was a public good, financing secondary education was a different matter. "Our theory is republican, but our practices in several details are fast becoming communistic," he warned. Soon elements of the public would be expecting free soup from the state, shattering "republican pride, self-respect, and independence." While it is true that the nation was founded on the ideal of "equality of all men before the law," Eliot observed, this did not mean equality of social standing, possessions, or powers and capacities. Rather there were "irresistible natural forces which invariably cause the divisions of every complicated human society into different classes." Public-supported secondary schools were in violation of those natural forces, he contended (Reese, 1995, p. 74). At a fundamental level, the working poor were considered untrustworthy and less deserving, and more education could be dangerous.

Opposition was greatest in the South. The affluent White class had a long history going back to colonial times of not supporting public education other than charity schools for what were considered the lower classes. Pre–Civil War society was supported by slavery and the exploitation of poor Whites. After the war, the southern political leadership and the economic elite re-imposed their domination on both the Black and poor White populations, albeit in a different form as tenant farming while maintaining opposition to any kind of education that even hinted about changing the social order. The northern argument about the use of public common and high schools to promote broad social and economic reforms was flatly rejected. One southern writer claimed the idea that public schools were a mechanism of mobility was nothing more than a "cruel hoax." Voicing hints of Charles Eliot's argument, he noted it was a fact the "rich and the poor are mutually necessary to each other's well being," and even if educated, children of the poor would "be compelled to return to the habits and occupations of poverty" (Reese, 1995, p. 71). As for the education of Blacks, another writer noted Whites should not support free schools because of the tendency of education to "make some negroes idle and vicious" and in the case of others, "create undue competition" with Whites (Anderson, 1988, p. 96).

Although after the Civil War some attempts were made to establish public high schools in the South, private academies continued to be the institution of choice of the more affluent. There was little interest in abandoning them for free public high schools. The ability to send children to an academy was a sigh of status, an indication that there was enough wealth to spend on education. The private fee-paying academy also worked as a sorting mechanism, automatically isolating the upper classes from the lower. Lower-class children did not attend academies because their parents simply could not afford to pay school fees. Public-supported high schools were thought dangerous because they could break down long-standing class barriers.

Then again, there was little-felt urgency to address through education the pressures of industrialization that confronted northern school officials. After the war, the south continued to maintain a basically rural, agricultural economy based on the cheap labor of an underclass, and officials had little interest in extensive investment in human capital development, an attitude carried over from the antebellum period. Douglass North (1966) observed, "The failure to invest in education, to raise the level of skills of both its white and its former slave population continued long after the Civil War period, undoubtedly contributing to the miseries (compounded by the era of Reconstruction) that characterized the South for the rest of the nineteenth and into the twentieth century" (p. 95).

Overall, the concept of a public high school serving the needs of community youth was slow catching on across the nation. The efforts at remaking studies to embrace the newer subjects had appeal, but still the assumption in the minds of many was that the high school was an institution primarily focused on preparing the few to matriculate up into higher education. It is true that colleges and universities wanted feeder schools, and general support for this new layer of public education was germinating, but few youth completed high school. By 1890, only a little over 200,000 students attended public high schools in a nation of over 63 million, less than 1% of the total population. Up until 1900, to attend a public high school was a rare event (Krug, 1964).

Despite the relatively few youth of the nation attending, the Kalamazoo case of 1874, nevertheless, brought the question of the character of public high schools to the front and laid the groundwork for the expansion of free public high schools. Overcoming initial local opposition, school promoters in the Michigan village of Kalamazoo built a consolidated "union" school with public funds, housing graded classes from the elementary level up to and though the "higher school." Opposition continued as the higher school itself became more popular, and expenses mounted. A suit was filed and eventually taken to the Michigan Supreme Court. In *Charles E. Stuart and Others v. School District No. 1 of the Village of Kalamazoo and Others*, the court ruled in favor of the school district.

This was a momentous decision, giving legal legitimacy to the use of public money to found high schools. Other school districts started separate high schools, securing a place in a hierarchy of schools from the lowest grades up through university supported with public funds. It was left to educators in the 20th century to flesh out all of the elements in what was to become a loosely articulated "system" of public education that today traces its beginning back almost to 150 years.

Education and into Work

Colleges and universities were one focus of change. They put pressure downward to help shape feeder programs in the lower grades that prepared students to matriculate into the increasingly diverse programs characterizing higher education. Another source of pressure on secondary education came from a very different source, and debate was no less contentious: What to do with the slowly growing population of urban youth that was entering high schools but had no intention of completing? And few would continue beyond secondary education even if they completed, but they sought out some kind of preparation for work in the search for upward mobility, even if it was only for a few years before entering the shop or factory.

Those working to extend secondary education also faced immense pressure from local businessmen, builders, and operators of small manufacturing establishments, job shop owners, and agriculture firms among other users of trained workers who promoted vocational education. They wanted public schools to train boys in work skills that were immediately useful in local communities. Initially attempts were made to place vocational subjects in both the upper grades of common school and in the high school (Bennett, 1937). Both were rejected.

There were three similar opposing arguments. Placing vocationally related instruction in public schools would limit the eventual job options of students. As one critic commented, vocational training "would take from the poor child his only chance of obtaining the knowledge necessary to the enjoyment of the higher privileges and honors of citizenship, and would condemn him to serve forever among the hewers of wood and the drawers of water" (Clarke, 1885–1892, pp. 925–929). Second, the primary function of schooling is to immerse students in the study of the intellectual products of the race, for they were the key by which to unlock the "treasures of all human learning." The inclusion of practical subjects in any form only took valuable time away from the more important fundamental subjects, and posed the threat of retarding intellectual development. And third, vocational education was resisted on the ground that it was not "general education" and did not contribute to the education programs of all students, regardless of station in life or probable occupational destiny. Emerson E. White lent his weight to the opposition as onetime Ohio State superintendent of schools and president of Purdue University: "The primary and imperative duty of the public school is to provide training and to teach knowledge of a general application and utility. It recognizes no class distinction, social or industrial, but provides a general education for all classes of youth." (Bureau of Education, 1881, p.8). Educators were not yet ready to accept a differentiated system of studies in secondary schools, at least one that included training for work.

The Vogue of Manual Training

Calvin Woodward was an individual who believed that he had the answer to the ongoing struggle over the substance of high school instruction: "Put the whole boy in school," he said. He meant to provide both mental and manual instruction (Woodward, 1906).

Woodward was dean of the newly formed School of Engineering at Washington University, St. Louis. He thought that he found a potent innovation in what he termed "manual training." Students completed a sequence of predetermined hand tool exercises using wood and metal. The work was difficult, nonutilitarian, and completed to exact, accurate specifications. Combined with the manual exercises was instruction in the modern studies: science, math, literature, and language along with technical drawing. Before engineering audiences Woodward stressed the college preparatory value of manual training. Students were immersed in "technical" work while at the same time they acquired skills in the academic subjects fundamental to college-level engineering. Before education audiences Woodward emphasized the more "general value" of manual training. While recognizing that the "grand result" of manual training was increased interest on the part of students in industrial occupations, he assured educators the program would turn out "better lawyers, more skillful physicians, and more useful citizens." He was fond of citing the related occupational placements of former manual training students: druggists, lawyers, bookkeepers, accountants, engineers and foremen, salesmen and agents, manufacturers, teachers and merchants among a wide assortment of occupations. Woodard was adamant that manual training was not trade training. It would help strengthen "all the boys who are growing up to manhood" (Krug, 1964, pp. 23–26; Woodward, 1906).

His ideas caught the attention of those struggling with how to include more practical and functional studies in the secondary school. John Philbrick, the influential superintendent of schools for the state of Massachusetts, for example, supported manual training "as an additional instrumentality to meet the wants of individuals not previously well provided for." He added, it "puts the high school studies in the foreground, while hand-work is made supplementary" (Philbrick, 1885, pp. 83–85). The immediate popularity manual training achieved, in fact, was Woodward's argument that he had achieved a true educational synthesis. In his scheme, the modern studies of the high school made up about one half of the instructional time, and shop work, technical drawing, and related content material the other half.

There was a steady stream of visitors to St. Louis to see firsthand Woodward's school in action. Visitors carried away course outlines, syllabi, and visions of starting similar schools along with the encouraging words of Woodward. He crossed the country extolling the value of manual training as general education for all students. Many immediately used his ideas. The movement quickly spread from town to town and coast to coast, and manual training became the most talked about education innovation of the decade. All kinds of practical and technical programs were referred to as "manual training" even though they had little similarity with Woodward's work. Early reform work in the lower grades such as Francis Parker's program in Quincy, Massachusetts, the "new education" of W. N. Hailmann, and the introduction of sloyd, arts and crafts, and drawing in the kindergarten and primary school were considered complementary components of manual training. Woodward later complained that his initial concept of manual training was reinterpreted beyond recognition (Coats, 1923; Herschbach, 2009).

Woodward cunningly played the traditionalists at their own game. He insisted that the series of rote, rather meaningless and difficult tool exercises was intellectual training. They strengthen the "executive faculty" of the mind, just as the study of Greek or geometry strengthened other faculties. "Manual exercises are intellectual exercises," said Woodward. "Certain intellectual faculties, such as observation and judgment in inductive reasoning, cannot be properly trained except through the instrumentality of the hand" (Woodward, 1889, p. 92). He received crucial support from Nicholas Butler, president of Columbia University, who similarly argued that the executive faculty of the mind had to be developed as well as the receptive—that is, the ability to put thought into action. Manual training did this, Butler claimed, reinforcing Woodward (Butler, 1883, pp. 215–237).

Woodward's claim bordered on the insulting for some. He was equating the filing of metal and the chiseling of wood with the study of the great works of the past. Nevertheless, the movement for practical studies could not be stopped even though Woodward linked curriculum change with the concept of faculty psychology that was fast fading in importance.

Three fundamentally important outcomes of manual training influenced the secondary school movement. First, despite the decline of manual training after the turn of the century, Woodward's early work was instrumental. He succeeded in driving a wedge into the traditional school curriculum, which was stubbornly resistant to change. In so doing, he opened the way for the introduction of various practical subjects into the school curriculum for both men and women.

Second, he helped to bring about in the high school the fusion of technical studies with the academic. This ultimately resulted in the establishment of the comprehensive high school as the hallmark of American secondary education. Third, the acknowledgment of the importance of technical studies resulted in the establishment of what was termed the "technical high school," "mechanic arts school," or "polytechnic high school," terms designating specialized secondary institutions formed out of the manual training movement. We continue to have similarly specialized schools today (Bennett, 1937).

Educating Together: Girls in the High School

The increasing involvement of females in education both as teachers and students brought the issue of social bias forcefully to the fore. As previously recounted, social reform groups led by women played a remarkable role after the Civil War among those mired in the poverty and squalor of the urban slums. Child-saving organizations, charity associations, social settlements, women's societies, kitchen garden clubs, and education reform groups of all kinds worked to alleviate social ills of the new industrial order. They enlisted the aid of education in cleansing, moralizing, and humanizing society. Their work with the kindergarten movement was remarkable. Changes were initiated that ultimately worked their way up into the elementary grades of public schools, fundamentally changing the way that we think about educating children.

Now, women were becoming more active in secondary schools. They entered the ranks of secondary school teachers and students. Resistance was encountered, but nevertheless, significant inroads were made. By 1900, women constituted 50% of high school teachers. The social and education reform work in the postwar years demonstrated that women had ability, and they could get things done by mobilizing public support for change. No longer could the antebellum arguments be used that women were less capable than men, and while intelligent, it was a different sort of intelligence that rendered them less suited for activities best left to men. In the postwar years, these arguments were reduced to disgruntled mumblings. Women teachers also were attractive to secondary school officials for the same reason that they staffed common schools: They worked for considerably less pay than men teachers (Perlmann & Margo, 2001; Tyack & Hansot, 1990).

Opponents of any role for women in secondary education turned to different arguments. High schools were becoming feminized through the influence of the large numbers of women teachers and girl students, was the complaint. There was a nurtured "sissy tinge" that was a danger to the masculinity of boy students. The lament was that society itself would suffer, as there was an overall decline in masculinity. The issue came to the fore because coeducation classes had become the norm. Generally, school enrollments were small, even in urban areas, so schoolmen relied on female enrollments to maintain "reasonable" class sizes and high enough overall enrollments to keep high schools open. In most cases, girls made up the majority of attending students; and girls stayed in school longer with significantly higher completion rates. But boys also were put to shame in coeducation classes; girls consistently outperformed boys. It did not take long for coeducation classes to be termed an "evil," threatening the very cohesion of the nation. Masculinity was under siege (Tyack & Hansot, 1990, p. 148).

Critics argued for separate classes. They couched arguments in terms of what was in the best interests of girls. They switched from contending females lacked mental ability to the contention that coeducation classes had damaging physiological effects. Renowned authorities no less than Edward H. Clarke, a specialist at Harvard Medical School in nervous disorders, and G. Stanley

Hall, psychologist and president of Clark University, affirmed that while it was true that girls outcompeted boys, in so doing they paid a high price. Clarke and Hall claimed that hard study and academic competition with boys was destructive to the development of female reproductive potential. There was a limit to the capacity of the body, and when "blood was channeled to the brain, it was not available for the development of the reproductive organs," said Clarke. A girl had a finite supply of energy, and if was "drained away from the creation of the reproductive organs in order to feed an overactive brain, her basic physiological development and future health were at stake." Too intense concentration on academic studies could result in "monstrous brains and puny bodies," the loss of health, and even sterility. Using the "objectivity" of science, both contended there were biologically defined education and social roles, and the differences should be maintained, not fused (Tyack & Hansot, 1990, pp. 149–152). Females required a different, less taxing course of study in the high school, or better yet, a school separate from boys.

Another argument used by critics fed the nativists' and racists' impulses gestating within the nation's psychie. The girls attending high school primarily were from prosperous Anglo families, and by overburdening their brains the country was committing "racial suicide." They would reproduce, if at all, at a lower rate than the immigrants pouring into the seaport cities from southern Europe, the laboring classes working in the mines, factories and fields, the poor slum dwellers, and the criminal classes and the Mexicans, Asians and freed Blacks. Too rigorous of an education was an impediment to the "natural" place of the Anglo girl as a wife and mother (Tyack & Hansot, 1990, pp. 146–153).

Overcoming Resistance for Change

The place of females in public schools could not be denied, however. They attended in larger numbers, but opposition continued to fester in the background well into the first decades of the new century. One major source countering opposition were the organizations for women's rights, suffrage advocates and community reform groups. Members engaged key social and educational reform roles. They were instrumental in helping to reshape postwar public common schools, first through the kindergarten and then on up into the elementary grades. Efforts were turned to the secondary level. The women's campaign in high schools was linked with other social reform movements late in the century: temperance, child labor, marriage laws, divorce laws, property laws, playgrounds and public baths, civil service reform, industrial conditions, public hygiene, along with others. This gave school advocates strong allies and linked the issue of women's rights in high schools to other national issues of social justice, equity, and reconstruction. Women's rights advocates argued that to restrict secondary schooling for girls was to restrict their opportunity to shape their own lives. Girls continued to join public high school coeducation classes (Cremin, 1961; Reese, 1995; Tyack & Hansot, 1990; Woody, 1974).

Large high schools tended to be on the fringe of the argument. They were not faced with the necessity of coeducational classes because overall school enrollments were large enough to support separate classes for boys and girls. In some large high schools, there were even separate entrances for boys and girls. All-girl schools also were especially common in the South up until the 1880s. Both took what appeared on the surface to be the same subject, but this did not always mean both had an identical education. Claiming female frailty, girls were offered less rigorous instruction. Female "normal high schools" were designed to prepare girls to be common school teachers, but the course offerings tended to be restricted, lacking the full academic range found in schools for boys. Women were at a disadvantage in pursuing college education.

The early public high school tended to be a middle-class, Protestant institution, and for this reason there was not the fear among parents that was found in the early common school that their girls would be exposed to "undesirable" associations with boys of a lower station in life. There were few sons of Catholic Italian immigrants, or dirt-poor rural migrants, or Mexican laborers, or illiterate meat-packing workers attending the early high school. Of course this changed by the turn of the century (Tyack & Hansot, 1990, p. 145).

Middle-class boys of high school age did not attend in large numbers or dropped out for the pragmatic reason that they did not need more education to get a "good" job. Staying in school for any length of time meant considerable foregone earning. For girls this was not true. Fewer employment opportunities were available for middle-class girls.

Home Economics: For the Good of Girl and Home

The debate over women and schooling caused a rethinking of what was the best course of studies for girls in the high school. With minor differences, girls and boys in full coeducational schools took the same courses included in the "modern studies": chemistry, physics, physiology, algebra, geometry, Latin, Greek, French, German, rhetoric, English literature, and history, among other subjects. Girls from middle-class families tended to be the mainstay of high schools, and the studies were alleged to equip them for the life roles of teachers, wives, and mothers. Some, however, questioned the relevance of the high school studies for girls. How was the study of German or geometry going to help the girl oversee the kitchen or take care of little children better? This questioning became especially frequent after 1890 when the composition of public high school attendance started changing as well as increasing dramatically. Did daughters of the rural farmer or immigrant factory worker need to learn ancient Greek? How was the girl from a working-class family eventually destined for the spinning mill going to profit from the study of Shakespeare or algebra?

There was a shift in expectations: Some believed that a "terminal" education was wanted that would equip the girl with "practical" skills relevant to her position in life. One of the earliest changes was the inclusion of "normal departments" in coeducational high schools designed to prepare girls as primary teachers. This was followed by the addition of special business and commercial courses. An unknown percentage of girls enrolled in manual training, but this appears to be a variation far removed from Woodward's ideas, linked by name but not substance. Great variation existed, but manual training programs for girls tended to be organized around the "household arts," including food, cooking, clothing, laundering, sanitation, and home management. Home economics made an appearance. Science in the form of chemistry, physics, and biology were considered a strong foundation for home economics. The attempt was to raise the level to an academic study of home, health, nutrition, and intelligent consumption. The terms "domestic science," "home science," "household economics," and "domestic arts" were used as titles of public high school programs for girls. There also were available public and private variations of cooking and housekeeping schools (Report of Special Committee of Lake Placid Conferece, 1901, pp. 1–24; Tyack & Hansot, 1990).

By the turn of the century, "home economics" became the widely accepted term as the organizing framework for high school studies specifically designed for girls. Its use was solidified by a group of women that met together in a series of meetings from 1899 to 1908 at what became known as the "Lake Placid Conference." Their efforts were directed at defining the term "home economics," identifying what it meant in practical education terms at the different grade levels; addressing teacher preparation; and preparing college-level leadership. The women of the conference advocated for college-level home economic positions, such as that held by Marion Talbot, dean of women and professor of "sanitary science" at the University of Chicago, and Virginia Meredith of the Minnesota agriculture school. This would solidify the professional standing of the field. They also reasoned that in order to nurture the spread of home economics in the high school, teachers had to be prepared. But this first required defining what was meant by the term. One of the more lasting outcomes of the Lake Placid Conference was the formulation of a comprehensive outline of home economics from first grade through secondary school that functioned as a preliminary baseline for the field. The education of both rural and urban girls was addressed.

Rural girls were portrayed as one of two types. The "aim" of one type is to marry in order to "get away from the humdrum existence of the home nest, to save herself from the pity of her neighbors and the disgrace of spinsterdom." This uneducated girl is fated to become a "household drudge," it was alleged, "a woman prematurely aged, a worker of the hands only, rearing children who are in no sense an improvement on herself." The other type has a no less dismal future. She also wants to escape from the confines of the rural home, and is "consumed with an insatiable longing to live a different life from the one which confronts her, to extricate herself from the terrible monotony of the life for which she knows no panacea." She goes to an urban industrial center to join "the great army of untrained, unskilled bread winners, exchanging the sweet country air for the air of store or factory, in many cases falling into a lower moral atmosphere," resulting in "a worse fate than that in store for her married country sister." The obvious answer is more education, but not an education of one or two "superficial years" of music, art and elocution that only makes her more discontent with home, but an education that "puts her in harmony" with home life: home economics. Such an education would prove to be "a blessing rather than a bane to their homes" (Thomas, 1901, pp. 51–52).

Working-class urban girls struggled. There were girls mainly of foreign parentage "thickly intermixed" with girls of "American stock," but they lacked an understanding and desire for "something better," and had a "more stoical indifference to deprivations, and none of the pride and sensitiveness of their American neighbors." There were girls of the urban poor, many "culled from the country and small towns"; there were juvenile delinquents, "youthful sinners against the law"; there were girls that were "victims of their environment," struggling to cope with squalid surroundings; and girls with "inherent tendencies for evil," and girls with "unbalanced temperaments, perverted appetites and lack of control." It was argued that these girls too could be reached through the medium of home economics (Thomas, 1901, 51–52).

For both the country and urban girl, the subject helped generate a sense of responsibility, form good character, enlighten her about the "scientific management" of the home, and instill the understanding that she was primarily responsible as wife, mother, or sister for the "existing conditions and atmosphere of the home; that on her rests the decision of the problems as to whether the home shall be the place wherein each member shall reach his or her highest physical, intellectual and spiritual development" (Thomas, 1901, p. 52). These lofty aims—probably unachievable aims, but aims, nevertheless—appealed to the crusading women and their belief in the redemptive value of home economics.

Formerly most girls attending public high schools were middle class as previously suggested, but the work of the Lake Placid Conference reflected a significant shift in public awareness. A new student population was entering the high school, a few at first, then many as the new century moved to the end of its first decade; these were the male and female offspring of the urban working class, the poor migrants and immigrants, and rural youth that formerly would not have attended school. Perhaps because of the close links with women's rights organizations, suffrage advocates and urban reform groups, the 1899 to 1908 Proceedings of the Lake Placid Conference reflect a deep awareness of the reconstruction of the social and economic order underway. A new America was in the making, differing significantly from the past in manners and morals, ways of making a living, income and class distribution, demographics, ethnicity, politics, and education. The interface of home and society was of major concern. The home is the "organic" unit of society, home economics advocates tirelessly proclaimed, and it warrants study.

Two major concepts were advanced through the work of the conference. The idea of correlation was fundamental to the education work of the reformers dedicated to the regeneration of school life. The idea of correlation, advanced by Pestalozzi a century earlier and promoted by Francis Parker, brings together knowledge in the way it is actually used, providing the learner a fuller and deeper understanding of knowledge and its use, an understanding, moreover, rooted in surrounding activities of everyday life. The work of social reformers mainly focused on the elementary grades. The members of the conference now extended the idea of correlation to the high school level, and in this way joined with others in advancing a concept of learning that seriously challenged the hold of faculty psychology and its mental discipline emphasis on the minds of late 19th-century educators.

Members of the conference envisioned a high school that was opened to new ways of thinking about instruction and what students learned. Subjects such as metal machining, drawing, engineering, chicken farming, or cooking and sewing did not have to be justified on the basis of mental discipline, as Calvin Woodward was attempting to do with manual training; their place in the school's program of studies was because of their intrinsic value to young people in the preparation for learning and life.

The destruction of the idea that all students profit from the mental discipline inherent in a few difficult classical studies was necessary to the opening of high school instruction to the highly diversified population flowing into the schools. As conference members emphasized, home economics was as useful to the discontented farm girl as it was to the urban youthful sinner, the victim of the environment, the middle-class girl aspiring to go to college, or the girl of foreign parentage. In abbreviated form, they recognized that a differentiated curriculum was needed, one that shifted the emphasis of studies from mental disciple to functional and useful knowledge targeted to different student populations. This was an enormous shift in thinking. It was the foundational idea of comprehensive high school studies after the turn of the century. It was an idea that the Committee of Ten in the 1890s, however, struggled with but could not fully accept.

The Committee of Ten

In an effort to plot a path through the increasingly complex and rapidly changing high school and college landscape, the National Educational Associated appointed in 1892 a committee of prominent education leaders to examine the question of college admission requirements. There were so many differences in the quality and kinds of studies of individual high schools and colleges that there was no uniform way of making admission decisions. Chaired by Harvard University president Charles Eliot, the committee issued its report in 1894. The findings went beyond admission questions. The report had national implications on the standardization of high school curricula. It promised to be the blueprint for the curricular construction of the modern high school of the next century. This did not happen. The report was out of date on the day that it was issued. The major point of failure was over the question of whether the high school should provide a common education for all students, or should it provide specific and differentiated studies appropriate to the backgrounds and future employment and social destinations of students. The report came out for a common high school education for all students in the name of preserving a "democratic" system of education; but it used the concept of "common" in an unusual way.

What was defined as a "common" education was not common to all students. The committee recognized that there were differences among students, so they formulated four "tracks" defining different high school courses of study. The four tracks were organized in a descending order of status and difficulty. Committee members, however, continued to conceive the public high school primarily as a college preparatory institution. All four tracks were assumed to prepare for college admission. This is what was common. To counter the criticism that non-college bound students were not served, the committee asserted that all high school students, even those with no aspirations of continuing on, could profit from studies in one of the tracks (Kliebard, 1986).

Despite claims that all four tracks were equal in value for college admission, the Classical track was prestigious because it required both Latin and Greek and was valued for educating an elite. The Latin-Scientific track accommodated in part the question of status, and it also accommodated the need to build skills in math and science for advanced studies in college engineering and science programs. The Modern Language track offered neither Latin nor Greek. The study of Latin could be elected as an option in the English track that probably served as a "catch-all" for students. The committee itself noted that the last two tracks, Modern Languages and English, were "distinctly inferior to the other two" because they lacked a study of Latin and Greek. Excluding the defining character of each track, the bulk of the remainder of studies in all four tracks was similar. The committee did observe that in the inferior English track, instruction in bookkeeping and commercial arithmetic were permitted as options for algebra, and instruction in the useful arts or trades might be substituted for science. Manual training and home economics were not considered (Kliebard, 1986; Krug, 1964; Report of the Committee of Ten, 1893).

The report provoked debate. Critics contended that it was seriously out of step with the times. The work of the committee was a moderate departure from traditional studies inherited from the antebellum period. The scheme of high school instruction outlined was justified on the grounds that most high school graduates were from families of the well to do. The committee had to accommodate this group. Different studies for non-college bound students would amount to a system of class education, committee members claimed. There would be no opportunity for the sons or daughters of the poor to pursue college education. But the committee ignored the fact that the poor would be unlikely to go to college regardless of the kind of high school program. A program of studies that was more functional would at least attract more boys and girls from the farms and fields and the urban factories and shops, and keep them in school and give them practical skills that could be used.

The committee was trapped in its own beliefs. Members believed in the idea of mental discipline, and they could not imagine a high school program that did not aim at social and cultural betterment. They clung tightly to the humanist ideal of a liberal education for all. They were insensitive to the economic and social changes around them. They could not conceive of the virtues of an education cast in practical terms for the sons and daughters of the working class. And they seemed oblivious to the substantial demographic changes that were filtering throughout society, oblivious to the great numbers of immigrants, the freed Blacks, the Asians, and Mexicans that were attempting to extricate themselves from want, seeking to build homes and communities, and edging slowly into the nation's schools.

Chapter Eleven
Education, the Uprooted, the Despised, and the Dispossessed

Except for Native Americans, America is a land of immigrants. All of us trace our ethnic heritage to somewhere else. Some came by choice, some came out of desperation or hope, and others were forced. Immigrants built America, its good and its bad. But there was nothing easy about immigration. New arrivals tended to confront periods of tolerance mixed with times of intense hostility. And they encountered hard economic times. Mood swings in the American psyche tended to correspond with the fickle gyrations in the economy. During good times immigrants are wanted, indeed recruited, to man the machines of production, dig wealth from the ground, excavate canals and railroad beds, drain swamps, and plant and toil in the fields. Their labor was fundamental to the creation of wealth for others. During bad times they confronted abuse. Americans uneasy about economic hardship, corruption, crime, rural blight, and urban squalor tend to blame the new arrivals for the breakdown in the social order. Employers play ethnic group against ethnic group, and established workers against new arrivals to beat down the wages of each, generating deep animosity. Politicians generated hate as they arouse middle-class opposition in response to shifting political alignments as immigrants organized to vote. Their entry into politics disturbed many formerly secure as they saw their influence diluted and slipping away. Others reacted to the personal and cultural traits brought: "different" food, clothing, political beliefs, and religion—particularly religion (Handlin, 1951; Higham, 1970; Kraut, 1982).

The display of negative attitudes directed to immigrants varied by ethnicity and time. Those who fared less well were those most different from Anglo-Saxon ethnicity. They were conspicuously defined by "habits of life," culture, and ethnicity. They could not hide from their skin color, eye shape, language, social practices, place of origin, or religious beliefs. Assimilation was difficult, if even an option.

Some feared the increasing polarization of American society. In time, it would tear the nation apart. The obvious gulf between the suddenly growing Catholic populations and American Protestants was threatening. The desperation in the slums, the crime, the immorality, the poverty, and the dirt and disorder were, to some, evidence of the poisonous influence of immigrants. Open conflict was provoked by labor unrest. The conflict between Whites and Asians became so brutal and widespread that immigration restrictions were put into place. In the South, a wave of terror descended as Blacks were forced back into a system of exploitive labor and prevented from becoming a part of mainstream America.

Across the country a mood of quiet unease descended, punctuated by outbreaks that shattered the facade of harmony. Prosperity created feelings of goodwill, the excitement and promise of the opening western lands generated hope, and the prodigious productive powers of the country bode well for future prosperity, but there were deep fracture lines that exposed national anxiety. How could a fractured and disorderly society resolve its own disorder?

One response was the increased influence of the nativist movement. The know-nothings of the 1850s fed an anti-Catholic nativism in the 1870 and 1880s that gained in political scope and influence in the postwar years. The nation was becoming "mongrelized," nativist argued, and they urged the creation of a more homogeneous society by closing off all immigration and keeping "America for the American born." Nativists joined in denouncing immigrants as the source of corrupting ideas, of labor and political unrest, and of the degeneration of moral and social standards. The nativists' movement never coalesced into a national political party, but comprised a loose, scattered network of local groups often allied with hate groups such as the Order of the American Union, the Patriotic Order of Sons of America, and the American Progressive Association. In 1887, the American Protective Association was established to check Catholicism in the United States. In the South the Ku Klux Klan, the Red Shirts, and the Knights of the White Camelia threatened, burned, maimed, shot, and killed their way across the conflicted South. Anxiety, fear, and terror were spread among immigrants, particularly in the South among Blacks, Catholics, and Jews. By the end of the century, nativists were a strong political force, not because of their numbers but because of their widespread presence in hamlets, towns, and cities all across America. Their political influence always outweighed their numbers. By the first two decades of the new century the goal of restricted immigration was achieved in part, to cumulate in 1921 and 1924 with the triumph of shutting off all immigration (Kolchin, 1993; Higham, 1970).

Americans who were also alarmed by social disorder but chose to believe that the road to social salvation was through the redeeming influence of the Social Gospel struck an opposite note. These were the reformers who worked in the poor city districts recruiting little children to the kindergarten, visiting the slum homes of immigrants and the underclass, starting settlement houses and community clubs, and pressing for satiation laws, the establishment of public baths, paved streets, and playgrounds. Individual morality had to be addressed and crime checked, but these individuals saw poverty and dislocation rooted in social, economic, and political conditions as primary underlying causes of human misery and conflict. Society itself had to be redeemed (Spain, 2001). And, rather than intimidation, violence, isolation, and exclusion, the belief was "Americanization" and assimilation were the way to create a more harmonious, fair, and prosperous society (Higham,1970). Schools could play a big part in fostering social regeneration, as reformers set about reshaping American education (Cremin, 1961).

Yet another response, and the one examined in this chapter, was the effort of the excluded groups themselves to overcome the discrimination and violence they encountered, find support and security among themselves, and navigate the difficult road that edged them into the economic and political mainstream. They worked at hard, often dangerous and unhealthy jobs, tolerated abuse and low wages, and accepted their status as underclass motivated by the promise of a better life for their children. They took unknown risks, and spread across the country seeking a better life. They formed self-help groups, community clubs, and mutual assistance organizations; they founded newspapers and their own banking and lending systems. When possible, they bought land, opened shops and stores, had fruit stands, peddled pots and pans, and became independent craftsmen in order to keep out of wage labor employment that invariably keep them poor (Higham, 1970; Kraut, 1982). They believed strongly in the power of education, and public schools for many provided a way that they could not otherwise afford for their children to edge their way into the economic mainstream. But they met resistance, and had to fight and overcome barriers of exclusion. Although strictly not immigrants, the search of Blacks and Native Indians to find a place within the human mosaic of America will also be examined in Chapter Eleven. In many ways their experiences were similar to the arriving immigrants. First, we briefly look at the dimensions of European emigration.

The Huddled Masses: European Emigration

Immigration from Europe was massive, and this was what frightened nativists. Once politically organized they could overwhelm Protestant, Anglo voters and gain control of town councils, local bond issues, tax rates, and schooling. They could control the money resources of government. This was already happening with older immigrant groups. The Irish were on the verge of completely controlling Boston politics. In Illinois, the German immigrant John Peter Altgeld won election by promising the large number of German and Irish voters that he would protect their interests. Political fear was compounded by the fact that the majority of immigrants were either Catholic or Jewish, so that by the turn of the century Protestants no longer represented the majority religion in America (Baltzell, 1966; Kraut, 1982).

Italians were the largest emigrant group as peasants primarily from southern Italy left thousands at a time, many to join small communities formed by members who had gone ahead to the United States. The Italians settled in the large eastern cities, but many fanned out across the country to join construction crews and mining camps, to start truck farms, to establish fruit and vegetable businesses, and some went as far as the west coast to establish prosperous fruit orchards and vineyards. The California wine industry got its start (Kraut, 1982).

The Jewish population was the second largest immigrant group, and like the Italians they spread throughout the country, primarily to urban areas. However, by far the largest number, perhaps as high as 75%, stayed on the east coast, mainly in New York City, New Jersey, Pennsylvania, and New England. Most came because they were impoverished, and they made up over half of all of the Russian emigrants, and perhaps as high as 80% to 90% of the arriving Polish and a large share of the Romanian. They were fleeing poverty, but also a resurging Pan-Slavism and its brutal pogroms drove them to leave. Many were killed, forced from communities and driven into destitution. They came to American in the search for security.

The highly diverse third largest group comprised Slavic immigrants. They are only considered together as a group because of a common but distant ethnic origin: Poles, Czechs, Russians, Ukrainians, Slovaks, Bulgarians, Serbs, Slovenians, Croatians, and Montenegrins came with their very diverse cultural backgrounds. As many as 4 million Slavs came. They tended to be more educated and prosperous, but perhaps as many as 60% to 80% returned home to buy property with savings earned in America. Temporary emigration to American was seen as a way to acquire economic security at home (Dinnerstein et al., 1996).

Greeks and Hungarians came, many like the Slavs to accumulate savings to invest upon returning home, but many changed their minds, many never intended to return, and many never made it back. And Lithuanians, Portuguese, Armenians, and French Canadians came in large numbers to work in mines and factories, and to start farms. Middle Easterners came from Syria, Lebanon, Yemen, Iraq, and Arab Palestine. Dutch came and tended to settle in farm communities. Welsh and Scandinavians came, among others. The Scandinavians tended to settle in northern areas such as Minnesota and Wisconsin that are similar to their home climate.

Some of the new arrivals settled in ethnic enclaves, but many spread across the nation. Single men came to earn. Families pooled their money to send sons who then send money back home, saving their families from destitution. Families came but often after sending a family member ahead first to ease the way. Labor agents recruited in Europe and helped new arrivals locate. Combined, immigrants contributed in thousands of ways to the expanding industrial system, many only finding work in dirty, hard, low-paying jobs.

The new immigrants appeared different. They were primarily from religious groups other than Protestant: Serb Orthodox in an unknown number, 125,000 Lebanese Maronites, 50,000 Melkites, 100,000 Greek Orthodox, 25,000 Moslems, and millions of Roman Catholics among scores of lesser religious assemblages. This caused tension among Protestant groups and fed an already growing nativism. They did not like what they considered was the occurring religious dilution. Immigrants also became embroiled in violent, bloody conflicts with capital, and they fought back. Immigrants assumed leadership positions and made up the bulk of membership of the growing labor movement, with conflicts between unions and capital fracturing social stability. Immigrants, often poor and destitute, were accused of being the major contributors to increases in crime and violence and the general dislocation taking place in urban centers. Then again, as suggested, immigrants worked for less, increased competition for jobs, and put others out of work. Employers exploited the excess labor pool.

Immigration from Europe reached its peak in 1907 when 1,285,000 entered. By this time, resistance to immigration was growing. Fear of the accumulating population of immigrants from Southern and Eastern Europe in ever-greater numbers was based on the perception that their presence was damaging to America. It may be true that immigrants were good for the rich employing class because it gave them a full labor pool to exploit, and the middle professional class was indifferent, but the accusation was that for the large working class in America immigration was a disaster. Immigrants were at the center of labor violence. The standard of living and wages were lowered, the "pigsty mode of living" among immigrants was ruining cities, social standards were down, and morality was destroyed by drunken brawls, crime, and the "course peasant philosophy of sex" carried to America. But perhaps the greatest fear was that immigrants sought help among city political bosses. They changed the political calculus (Hofstadter, 1955).

Immigrants increasingly relied on public education. Some groups, such as Italian or Jewish immigrants, were initially fearful of or isolated from public schools. But as the new century progressed the work of school reformers became more urgent. After the turn of the century, social reform advocates, those promoting health and hygiene in schools, backers of vocational training, and professional educators struggled to surround public schools with a new purpose: to bring immigrant and working-class children into the cultural, social, and economic mainstream by "Americanizing" children, providing education for work, and formulating programs to address moral, social, and physical needs. Immigrant children moved into schools in increasing numbers to change the ethnic complexion of schools and of American society.

Reconstruction: Freemen and Education

With the end of the Civil War and enactment of the Thirteenth Amendment, slavery was abolished in the United States. Thus began the long 100-year journey to fully realize what this meant. Newly freed slaves attempted to make a new life in a hostile environment controlled by those that formerly held them in bondage. The White southern leadership lost the war, but they were intent on controlling the peace in order to keep White southern society "white." This is a "white man's country" was the almost unanimous resolve, as Blacks were kept separated and in a condition of subservience through locally applied, sporadic violence. To gain complete dominance, White southerners knew that all they had to do was to wait until northerners tired of Reconstruction. The presence of federal troops could not be kept indefinitely—and wait they did.

Southern Blacks did not wait to get away as far as possible from slavery dependence and demonstrate the power of their new relationship. They refused to work under the control of former masters; they migrated locally and formed new, extended communities; and they moved from the country into towns. To be free was linked with the ability to read and write. In a remarkable display of purpose, Black communities all across the South embarked on a literacy crusade. Soliciting support from the Freeman's Bureau and northern philanthropic groups, Black communities combined their own limited resources to found schools. Adults and children attended together, night classes were opened, and lessons were given on Sundays. These largely private efforts were merged with newly established public common schools for both Blacks and poor Whites supported by the state (Kolchin, 1993).

The few high schools that were founded for Black youth were almost exclusively located in urban areas. But after 1880, there were no public funds available for support, and what little money that was available was spent on White schools (Anderson, 1988). But secondary education throughout the South was not generally supported for "common people."

Initially, northern missionary teachers staffed common schools, joined by Black teachers that acquired the opportunity for some education prior to the war. Some educated northern Blacks traveled south to help. As more Black teachers were prepared in "freed people's schools," they replaced Whites. Newly founded normal schools started training Black teachers, so that by 1870 there were 20 such institutions turning out thousands of young, educated teachers. These schools were the symbol of an independent, free people. But Black schools throughout the South faced difficult problems. One was the lack of money. All schools, Black and White, experienced dwindling public resources as urgent needs elsewhere drained away already scarce school funds; but Black school funding dramatically dwindled at a greater rate. The Black community itself was driven deeper into poverty as it became locked into an exploitive labor system of sharecropping. There was little money to support private schools to compensate for the loss of public resources (Anderson, 1988; Kolchin, 1993).

White resistance was the most troubling problem. Northern teachers were warned to leave or else face violence. They were harassed, followed, beaten up, and even shot. Black educators received similar treatment, with vigilante groups waylaying Black teachers and beating and killing them. Black school leaders experienced the most intimidation with the effort by Whites to subvert the education of Black children. Black schools were burned. Nevertheless, hundreds of thousands of Black children attended schools. Similar arguments made against the education of other ethnic groups were applied to the education of Black children. If too educated, Blacks would not want to work in the fields, and they were likely to join the ranks of social agitators. Perhaps more threatening, an emerging literate Black class would shortly outnumber the large illiterate poor White underclass (Anderson, 1988).

All southern Whites, however, did not oppose the education of Blacks, but they wanted a different kind. The split appears to be between the landowning class struggling to reestablish domination over of a ruined agriculture economy, and the newer generation of businessmen and industrialists that saw advantage in providing an education preparing young Black men to work at jobs in the reconstruction of the "new" southern economy. They were not interested in widely expanding educational opportunity, but they wanted to redirect limited Black education along lines that would more fully serve the social and economic interests of the White power classes, while retaining ethnic separation (Anderson, 1988). This is the theme Booker T. Washington would later successfully exploit.

In the immediate postwar years among northern reformers there was the strong belief that it was essential to develop a leadership class among educated Blacks. The Freemen's Bureau, administered under the War Department, northern philanthropic groups such as the Peabody Fund and the Slater Fund, mission societies, churches, and inspired individuals bent their efforts toward identifying promising Blacks, north and south, and securing higher education opportunity. In the North, for example, the child prodigy (Willy) W. E. B. DuBois was singled out for mentoring by his White teachers and school officials in his New Barrington, Massachusetts integrated school. He was encouraged to go on to higher education and financial aid was acquired, but not enough for him to complete his doctorate at Humboldt University in Berlin, the most prodigious university in the world where he studied for three years, but enough to support his return to the United States where he earned the Ph.D at a lesser university, Harvard (Lewis, 1993). In the South, private efforts supported the founding of schools such as Fisk University in Nashville, Howard, Morehouse and Morgan College, Atlanta University, and more; many churches sponsored small schools such as Saint Augustine in North Carolina and the Arkansas Baptists College (Anderson, 1988). Higher education was almost exclusively a private effort. One exception was the establishment of nine Black Land Grant institutions in the 1870s and 1880s, followed with another seven by 1915.

These higher education efforts were crucial. An educated leadership class was prepared that in Black communities across the South contributed to social and economic development. Importantly, a small nucleus of leaders was formed to advance the struggle for social and economic justice. The total output from Black higher education institutions, however, was small. In 1900, there was close to 4,000 Black students attending colleges and professional schools, with 400 annual graduates. These were added to the 3,000 existing graduates in a population of 10 million Blacks (Anderson, 1988).

By the mid-1880s the optimism that a Black, educated leadership class along with White leaders could work together to form a new South of cooperation and harmony no longer existed. This was an unreal expectation. The wounds of the Civil War were too deep to heal. Hope yielded disappointment; enthusiasm gave way to bitterness. Victory freed slaves from direct owner-control, but it also freed former masters from any sense of responsibility and exposed Blacks to virulent violence. When northern Whites and federal troops withdrew following the end of Reconstruction, Blacks were stripped of protective shielding and left exposed to fend for themselves.

This was a time of shame. The efforts of Blacks to advance their own welfare were ruthlessly suppressed. In the spring of 1866, for example, 46 Blacks were taken from their homes in Memphis and lynched. Indiscriminate killing continued throughout the South. Blacks that showed initiative or signs of leadership, that refused to observe the lines of White authority, that objected to the abrogation of civil rights laws, that refused to work on the land, that organized resistance, or that aspired to affluence were in danger. For a Black to attempt to better his condition was to invite violence from his poor White neighbors. To be sure, there were pockets where discrimination and violence were less, but an array of "Jim Crow" laws implemented throughout the South disenfranchised Blacks, violated their human rights, and forced them into a permanent state of subservience. Enforcement of Black Codes was brutal. In one Florida county in 1871, 163 blacks were murdered, 300 in parishes outside of New Orleans. From the 1880s on over a 20-year period up to one Black citizen was lynched on the average every three days in the South. No one was held accountable. All-White juries would not convict for crimes against Blacks by Whites (Boyer & Morais, 1955; Morgan, 1975; Woodward, 1966).

To the southern ruling class it was essential to force the former slave back onto the land and keep him there. The basis of his wealth was destroyed in the war: farm equipment, animals, buildings, the productivity of the fields, and the very machine of production—the slaves toiling under a forced labor system. The prewar plantation system was a highly productive enterprise with high monetary returns, and the large returns enabled the southern landowner to compete with low prices in world markets. Now all that was left was the land. To regain an economic footing, it was essential to reinstate a low-cost production system. Former plantation workers represented the potential labor force if they could be forced back onto the land.

This was done in several ways. Violence and intimidation was one. Resistance to quality educational opportunity for both Blacks and poor Whites was another. What made the economy of the "New South" different was that both Blacks and poor Whites were forced into low-cost labor. The uneducated were stuck in low-income employment. And another way to force Blacks back into low-income employment was to deny them any possibility of becoming independent landowners. It was next to impossible for Blacks who wanted to establish their own farms to get loans or credit of any kind. Title deeds and surveys were difficult to get, and Blacks faced legal restrictions on buying land. To escape wage labor, many former slaves entered into rental and sharecropping arrangements. This gave some semblance of independence, but it was largely an illusion. True, they were no longer dependent plantation hands, but they were locked into a system of peonage debt, and it was difficult to find a way out from it; all of the cards were stacked against them.

Typically the arrangement was to share part of the crop between the landowner and the farmer working the land. The amount the Black farmer received was as little as one sixth or one eighth of the crop at the low end, and up to a fifty/fifty split at the high end depending upon how good the farmer was at bargaining or how desperate the landowner was for labor. But farmers and their families had to eat until crops came in, and they borrowed from landowners or merchants at usurious rates. Common practice also was to require the sharecropper to purchase seed, farm tools and equipment, food, clothing, household implements, indeed, just about everything the family needed from the landlord's store at inflated prices. The landlord also bought the farmer's share of the crop at prices he set, gaining good profits for himself on the open market, but the farmer received little in return. Peonage laws were enforced that required the indebted farmer to work for the landowner until the debt was paid off, which it rarely was. The indebted farmer was tied to the land, and at the same time the landowner no longer had responsibility to feed, cloth, or nurse the sick, or to supply farm animals and equipment or to oversee work. And he still owned the land. To the freed slave, he may live in a shack, but it no longer was in the slave quarters, and he had the security of a family and the independence to make some decisions.

To ensure that Blacks stayed on the land, vagrancy and apprenticeship laws were enacted. There were strict rules. Blacks were not allowed to go into towns, and in places where they were allowed they were restricted to well-defined sections. An individual straying was quickly arrested and sentenced to work for a White employer for a specified time. It was not consequential that in times of heavy labor needs, such as planting and harvesting times, the arrest rate was high, and at times of low labor needs, low. Youth found wandering around that could not show any evidence of employment were arrested and assigned to serve an "apprenticeship," which generally meant working for subsistence in the fields for a White owner. Additional restrictions were instituted through laws that prevented local Blacks from leaving the state. Guards were posted at road, water, and railroad crossings (Morgan, 1975; Woodward, 1966).

Some Black farmers succeeded in acquiring land but they continued to struggle to get "fair" prices for their crops. The percentage of Black farming families that owned land was around 2% in 1870, with an increase to 21% by 1890, and leveling to 24% by 1910. In the upper South, ownership was at 44% in 1910 (Anderson, 1988). These families could eke out a modest living and had considerably more independence on their own holdings (Kolchin, 1993). At the same time, Blacks with craft skills enjoyed a relatively high level of income and independence.

Their skills were needed to reconstruct the South. In the prewar South, plantation owners trained Blacks to do the technical work that was required (making bricks, building wagons, constructing buildings, forging farm tools, and treating sick animals), and these same individuals constituted a large part of the technical workforce after the war (Report of the Committee of the Senate, 1885).

By the turn of the century, desperate poverty was replaced for some by a growing security based on more education and improved economic conditions. There was a small leadership class. The literacy rate among the former slave population increased from 5% in 1860 to 30% in 1880, and to 70% in 1910, a remarkable gain given the unrelenting resistance encountered (Anderson, 1988). Black communities across the South and elsewhere built confidence, and the educational and economic conditions that empowered them to begin the long struggle to fully realize the promise of freedom, dignity, and opportunity that the nation had given to them in the Thirteenth, Fourteenth, and Fifteenth Amendments to the Constitution—a promise that was almost immediately abridged. As the new days of the new century turned, former slaves set out to make their own history.

Asian Immigration and Education

The Asian immigrants came singly and in threes and fours, often from the same towns; they came in small groups, and in large mobs crammed in stinking ships; a few came with wives, but most were single men escaping poverty, looking for a better future, with high expectations and a willingness to work. Discontentment at home drove them to dream, to take risks, and to reach across the Pacific to the new land of promise. Similar to Europeans, families pooled money to send a son with the expectation that the money sent back home would enable them to survive. In some cases, whole villages contributed. Some borrowed money for passage from relatives or friends. Common practice for many others was to enter into a binding contract with a labor recruiter to repay the passage cost from wages. They were bound to a specific workplace by peonage debt. Most of these arrangements were exploitive.

As the arriving immigrants stepped out onto the docks of port cities, they were tired, confused, ignorant of the ways of the land and frightened, but full of hope. Immigrants came from all over the Pacific and Asian region, but most came from China, Japan, and the Philippines. Most experienced nasty, ugly overt discrimination and abuse. They had little legal protection. Almost half eventually returned home. Those that stayed persevered, and engaged in the slow climb along the ladder of social and economic mobility. Their children, and their children's children went to schools, worked in the factories and farms, research labs and shops, and packing plants; they fought in the wars of the nation, and became engineers, doctors, lawyers, auto mechanics, shopkeepers, farmers, investors, and builders. Some were failures, but overall, American citizens of Asian ethnicity make up the most educated segment of the population; they have the highest mean income level, and lowest incarceration and poverty rates. Their children achieve in school at the highest level. The Asians in America illustrate the essential importance of education. The initial denial of educational opportunity was intended to keep the young in a position of social and economic inferiority; their ascendency is a triumph of countering discrimination and personal persistence, but it also is an affirmation of the power of educational opportunity.

Asians immigrating east to America faced the dual hardship of establishing a stable life in the new land as well as combating the institutional discrimination embedded in the legal codes. The early American post-revolutionary leaders wanted to keep the county "white." Benjamin Franklin, for example, observed that the "tawny" Blacks and Asians should be excluded from America in favor of increasing the "lovely White," and Thomas Jefferson proclaimed that he hoped the new nation would become a "sanctuary" and a home established for Europeans and their White progeny. Revolutionary leaders puzzled over what to do with the existing non-White population.

The political "solution" was enacted in the form of the Naturalization Act of 1790, and appeared to offer future certainty. It would keep the "tawny" from establishing a foothold. The act stipulated that for those not born in the country, only individuals of Caucasian ethnicity could become citizens through naturalization: So much for equality among men. This meant that Asians and other non-Europeans coming to America were left in a state of vulnerability. They could not vote and legal protections did not apply. The testimony of a non-citizen Asian, for example, could not be used as evidence in court. If a crime was committed against an Asian by a White there was no legal recourse. Also, in many states non-citizen Asians and others were prohibited from owning land. The result was that an Asian worker was stuck for life in low-wage employment with little prospect of achieving economic independence. As a further impediment, the Cable Act passed in 1922 stipulated that any American woman marrying an "alien ineligible to citizenship" automatically lost her citizenship. The Naturalization Act of 1790 remained law until 1952 (Takaki, 1989, pp. 14–16).

The Heathen Chinese

Americans basically wanted Chinese to come and work but not stay and settle down. To guard against the possibility of Asian offspring born in the United States acquiring the right of citizenship by birth, Chinese women were discouraged or not allowed to accompany men. With no women there would be no families, and with no families there would be no future for building permanent homes and communities. The Chinese man would come and work, and perhaps return home with enough saved to invest in a wife and a good life, but more likely he would stay, laboring at wages too low to save, and eventually bent and broken from his labors, passing on unnoticed except for the physical results of his sweat and toil that he left behind as an unattributed monument to his life. He was wanted to build roads and bridges, excavate rail tunnels, dig drainage ditches and irrigation canals, and clear land and plant, but he was not wanted to stay and become part of the richness of America that he, too, could pass on to those of his blood.

The first Chinese men were recruited and brought to Hawaii in the 1830s and 1840s to clear land and bring into production sugar plantations. With the discovery of gold in 1849 and California statehood, enterprising Anglos turned to China as a source of critically needed labor. At the time, excluding Indian and Mestizos, only about 15,000 individuals of European origin populated the state. With the gold rush, more Europeans quickly poured in, but they wanted to mine for gold, not grow food, build roads, construct bridges, cut timber, or drive wagons. Chinese laborers filled the gaps, and they were cheap, had no legal rights, could be abused, did the dirty work, and could be easily replaced. The demand for Chinese labor became so great that in 1864 the Burlingame Treaty was adopted to provide for unrestricted immigration of Chinese men. Employers argued for this because they wanted to create a surplus of labor to meet the booming labor demand, but also to increase competition with White workers and keep wages down. And unlike the Italians, Slavs, Greeks, or Poles, the Chinese were a politically proscribed population and thus not a threat because they were not "allowed to become part of her body politic." They would be, Ronald Tikaki (1989) suggested, "in effect a unique, transnational industrial reserve army of migrant laborers forced to be foreign forever" (p. 99).

The Chinese worked at every kind of job common to unskilled laborers. Some merchants and businessmen also came, but they were considerably fewer in number. Generally, the Chinese laborers tended to work in gangs and completed work quickly and efficiently. They outperformed Whites at a lower cost to employers. Thousands cleared swamplands for farming, and planted and harvested crops. Skilled farmers in China, they taught their overlords how to extract rich field and orchard crops from the land. They became dominant in agriculture. Thousands were used to complete the western California leg of the transcontinental railroad, however at a sad cost of hundreds of lives and subjection to cheating, abuse, and outright fraud. The labor saving on the railroad from Chinese workers was $5.5 million, an enormous amount by today's standard. Builders saw the advantage of using Chinese labor. Soon Chinese labor was used in manufacturing.

The Chinese themselves wanted to engage in mining, but met stiff resistance from Whites. American White miners demanded from the state action to exclude "foreign miners," and the politicians responded with a monthly $3.00 tax on "foreigners" unqualified to become citizens. This was clearly aimed at Chinese: They could not become citizens even if they wanted. More taxes came. Each arriving passenger not eligible to become a citizen faced a charge of $50. With some exceptions, an 1862 law "to protect Free White Labor against competition with Chinese Coolie Labor, and to discourage the Immigration of the Chinese to the State of California" levied a $2.50 per month fee on noncitizen Chinese. These legislative actions were in response to a growing movement to exclude all Chinese from the American shores. Whereas employers were instrumental in getting the Burlingame Treaty enacted, White organized labor and nativists now mounted an ongoing successful counteroffensive to shackle the threat of Chinese competition (Takaki, 1989, pp. 80–82; 1990, pp. 215–249).

Resistance to Chinese workers stemmed from several causes. One of the most primary was that Chinese laborers were moving into mining in increasing large numbers. They were excluded by White violence from potentially the richest gold sources and worked the downstream placer claims with more modest results. But they acquired money beyond what they could earn in uncertain day labor. They moved down to the valleys, towns, and coastal lands and they used the newly saved resources to rent or lease stores and shops, and to engage in farming, often sharecropping. They made arrangements to have brides sent over, and formed families. With children, they acquired land. By the late 1860s, 24,000 Chinese were in the gold fields, each day sifting from river sands a few dollars worth of gold, with the alarmed Whites ever watchful.

The big strikes worked by the Whites were running out, but collectively the Chinese gold flake by gold flake were amassing a considerable amount of money. This was disconcerting to some Whites.

Easy gold became difficult to find, and independent miners could not work the quartz deposits requiring heavy investment in machinery and equipment. Besides, mine owners preferred to use lower cost Chinese labor. White miners moved down out of the mountains and into the expanding industrial areas. Chinese followed Whites, and both competed for the same jobs. Competition became violent. Employers realized that they could gain considerably more profit and ensure less worker rebellion through Chinese labor. In 1860, for example, 2,719 Chinese lived in San Francisco, with 1,500 industrial workers employed. A decade later, 12,022 Chinese resided in San Francisco, and industrial production expanded to 12,000 employees. Chinese workers took advantage of this expansion. They comprised nearly half of the working force (Kraut, 1982; Takaki, 1989).

It was not only on the west coast, but also across the country that employers realized the value of Chinese labor. In 1870, Chinese agriculture workers were shipped across the country by train to the Mississippi delta area to replace striking Black and White farm workers. Blacks and poor Whites were forced into tenant farming, and together in a show of unity they refused to grow the cotton crop. Similarly, in 1870, Chinese workers were brought in from the west coast to break a strike in the North Adams, Massachusetts, shoe industry. The strike was broken. Within three months it was clear the Chinese workers produced more shoes than the White workers at less cost. White workers were forced back at a 10% wage reduction. Over 300 Chinese workers were brought to Belleville, New Jersey, to replace rebelling Irish workers, and 190 were transported to Beaver Falls, Pennsylvania, to break a strike, among other locations across the nation. The transcontinental rail system made it possible for employers to use a new tool against organized labor: Chinese workers. The same railroads that made it possible to bring Chinese workers east, however, made it possible to bring White workers west where they quickly became engaged in ugly conflict with Chinese competition. For example, by the end of the 1870s there were two White workers and one Chinese worker competing in San Francisco for every one job. In the same year, scores of Chinese were beaten and killed in a spree of violence across California (Takaki, 1989, pp. 80–99; 1990, pp. 215–249).

What to do about the Chinese? "I do not believe they are going to remain here for long enough to become good citizens," Charles Crocker, one of the main officials of the Central Pacific railroad and a wealthy beneficiary of cheap Chinese labor told a Senate committee, "and I would not admit them to citizenship." The federal decision was more definite: The Page Law passed by Congress in 1875 forbade the entry of Chinese, Japanese, and "Mongolian" contract labor. With the Chinese Exclusion Act of 1882, legislative intent was more narrowly focused. With some exceptions, for 10 years it was unlawful for Chinese workers to enter the United States, residing Chinese had to register, and naturalized citizenship was denied. Subsequent renewals effectively sealed off immigration until after World War II. The Chinese population in the United States dropped from 105,465 in 1880 to 89,863 in 1900 to 61,639 in 1920 (Takaki, 1989, p. 111).

Another source of conflict between Chinese and White workers was women. In the West, women were scarce, and the population of women relative to men was small. Few women wanted to become part of the rough, crude life that characterized the pioneering days of the West. Miners and adventurers brought few women with them. A booming prostitution industry emerged. A lucky miner might spend huge amounts of his new wealth on drunken splurges and dallies with favorite prostitutes. Some "houses of ill repute" became famous, but life could be dangerous. Irate, drunken miners got into fights over favorite prostitutes, killing each other and the prostitute. Chinese men lacked Chinese women, so they turned to frequenting the same houses of prostitution as the White men. Deep antagonism developed. Blood flowed, and the violence and killing got so out of hand that political officials got involved. Provisions were made for the importation of Chinese women prostitutes. Most were not "professional," but lured to America with false promises of a wonderful new life waiting. They were held under conditions of debt peonage. One woman gives an account that she was sold by her father as a 6-year-old and taken to America where she was held captive. As a 12-year-old she was forced into prostitution. Common practice was to release a young woman after four or five years when she had "worked off her debt," but usually there was little in the way of a promising future waiting. Brutality, beating, disease, and drugs took a toll (Takaki, 1989, 1990).

Ronald Takaki (1989, p. 41) observed that most Chinese women entering California before 1875 were listed as prostitutes; but the figures are misleading. Chinese men able to save money used the "prostitute" gap in the law to arrange for the transportation of brides, often from their home villages. They also worked through other loopholes and around corners of the law to increase the number of wives brought to America. In 1852, of the 11,794 Chinese in California, only 7 were women. In 1870 the ratio was not so lopsided, but nevertheless it was severely out of balance: 4,566 females in a total Chinese population of 63,199, or a count of 1 female for every 14 males. But as more women arrived, families were established. Thus began the drive for upward mobility as land was purchased and farms and businesses started in the name of children who were American citizens by the right of birth. Communities formed.

The Struggle for Schooling

By the 1880s schooling became an issue. A pattern developed that also characterized the treatment of other ethnic groups experiencing discrimination. First, there was little effort to extend educational opportunity to Chinese American children. In fact, schooling is denied. In San Francisco, for example, the school board in 1884 refused the request of parents to enroll their child in the public school. Citing the "law of self-preservation," the board justified its refusal on the ground that it was protecting "American" children from the "invasion of Mongolian barbarism." If little White children were forced to go to school with Chinese children they would be infected by the morally inferior, degenerate and deviate propensities inherent in the genetic makeup of "coolie" children. Mixing children in school was a threat to racial purity. One California politician warned, "Were the Chinese to amalgamate at all with our people, it would be the lowest, most vile and degraded of our race, and the result of that amalgamation would be a hybrid of the most despicable, a mongrel of the most detestable that has ever affected the earth." Reinforcing the argument of ethnic inferiority, two years later the state legislature prohibited the licensing of marriage between a White person and a "negro, mulatto, or Mongolian" (Takaki, 1989, pp. 101–102).

A second way school integration was opposed is through the use of separate facilities. The Chinese parents went to court on behalf of their children. The California courts ruled favorably, stating that Chinese children could not be denied school attendance. The California state legislature responded by revising the school code to provide for the establishment of separate schools, with the additional provision that when separate schools were available Chinese or Mongolian children were not allowed to attend schools for White children. The San Francisco School Board immediately started a separate school for Chinese children. Other towns with populations of Chinese children followed suit. Through legal and political means, the parents in San Francisco eventually broke down the ridged policy of segregation, and their children attended the regular city high school (Spring, 2008, p. 163). But resistance to full integration for Asian children continued in California and other places through the establishment of attendance districts based on ethnic housing patterns.

Yet a third form of resistance to full integration was through secondary segregation. This is the practice of segregating students within a school based on language, ethnicity, achievement, special services, or other ways to separate. Social class, income levels, and ethnicity tend to characterize membership in special classes that often are offered separated and isolated from the "regular" school program. This is the most common form of school segregation today.

From the Land of the Rising Sun: The Japanese

Like the Chinese, Japanese workers were first brought to Hawaii to labor in the agriculture fields clearing land, planting, and harvesting tropical crops, primarily sugar. And like the Chinese, they encountered a more compatible work environment compared with the hostility and exploitation experienced on the mainland. Filipinos, Koreans, and Portuguese along with Japanese and Chinese made up the bulk of the population and workforce. Few local Polynesians were included. White Europeans were a small minority among a mixture of various skin hues. Unlike the mainland, intermarriages were fairly common. Unlike the mainland, wives were brought, so communities developed. Later when the United States annexed Hawaii following a coup, individuals moved to the mainland.

The Japanese came to the west coast largely to fill the space in the labor force vacated by the Chinese. By 1880, Chinese workers in California made up 86% of the agricultural force in Sacramento County, 65% in Yuba, 67% in Solano, 55% in Santa Clara, among other high concentrations laboring on the rich lands. Now they were leaving and not being replaced. Many left the rural farms and migrated to the cities as the Chinese population urbanized. Some went home to China, but with the Exclusion Act of 1882 there was no longer a supply of cheap, imported Chinese farm labor to maintain or continue the expansion of agricultural production. With the introduction of refrigerated railroad cars, food demand soared as shippers attempted to supply the needy east. Japanese workers were attracted to the U.S. mainland by the relative high wages.

Between 1885 and 1924, 180,000 immigrated to the mainland, mostly young men to toil in the fields (Takaki, 1989).

The strong Japanese central government wanted to avoid many of the issues faced by the Chinese, so it extracted concessions. First, the Japanese government monitored and approved all emigrants to ensure that they were literate, healthy, and not indigent. Uncontrolled emigration was not allowed. Second, in an attempt to avoid problems of prostitution, drunkenness, and debauchery, and to generate community stability, women were allowed to come under a "Gentlemen's Agreement." By 1920, Japanese women represented close to 40% of immigrants. Men and women went with the purpose in mind of earning enough to bankroll a better life in Japan, but once in America, most did not return (Takaki, 1989, pp. 42–53).

The Japanese formed families, and like the Chinese they met resistance when attempting to enroll their children in school. The question of the denial of Asian children the right to attend school was settled with the legal cases brought by the Chinese, but community school officials turned to the practice of segregated schools. The San Francisco Board of Education, for example, established a separate school for Chinese, Japanese, and Korean children in 1906 with the argument that it was relieving overcrowding and congestion. Its real motivation was made clear with the statement that it also was avoiding the placement of White students in a situation "where their youthful impressions may be affected by association with pupils of the 'Mongolian' race" (Spring, 2008, p. 164). Japanese parents boycotted the school, and the Japanese ambassador got involved, taking the complaint of overt discrimination to President Theodore Roosevelt. He intervened to ease the situation.

The Japanese were more successful than other Asian groups in achieving early economic security because of their strong sense of group survival. They formed associations for collective assistance, and readily adopted western business practices that aided success. Unable to borrow money from Anglo banks, they formed rotating credit associations. Ten people, for example, would annually contribute over a 10-year period to a common economic "pot" used to accumulate capital. Members would have drawing rights to finance capital investments in small businesses and land purchased through the citizens rights of their children. They also leased land and made tenant-farming arrangements. Farming corporations were formed, often with a White middleman as the legal front, or corporations were formed with the assets placed in the name of their Nisei children. Community associations countered "legal" discrimination, intimidation, boycotts, and organized threats and restrictions placed on Japanese growers. As the Japanese expanded into packing and shipping, and fruit stand and store operators, White apprehension grew. Vertical integration developed, linking independent growers to distributors and in turn to ethnic retailers, creating alarm among Whites that formerly controlled markets (O'Brien & Fugitsa, 1991). But by the 1930s, the Japanese in America had established a relatively high level of economic security, if not political. They were living on borrowed time, however. In one of the most repugnant land grabs in American history, everything was taken away from them. They were put into concentration camps for the duration of World War II.

Escape to a Better Life: The Koreans

Koreans came after 1903, but in much smaller numbers and for only a short time. The Japanese imperial government gained control of Korea, eventually assigning it the status of "protectorate." Oppression was harsh and widespread, and young men attempted to escape persecution by fleeing. In addition, widespread drought inflicted poverty and starvation. Some fled through China, working their way down to coastal towns to take ships to a new future. One immigrant later recounted, "We left Korea because we were too poor," and another concurred: "We had nothing to eat. There was absolutely no way we could survive." The Japanese government also opened Korean emigration to Hawaii for a short time, probably to counter unrest. Using Japanese-issued passports, both young men and women joined the flow of migrants to work in the fields of Hawaii. Some managed to cross over to the mainland. By 1905, however, the Japanese government cut off all emigration. Some continued to find ways to leave, but over a 15-year period the total number of Koreans migrating to America was small: around 8,000. Two groups today characterize the Korean American population in the United States. A relatively small number of families trace their origin to the early 1900s; second, larger numbers arrived after 1965 when immigration opened.

The migrating Korean population tended to be from urban areas, educated, with 70% literate, and represented a mix of experiences: students, teachers, policemen, clerks, laborers, miners, and servants. Most were young. Women came. Of the 6,685 entering between 1903 and 1906, 10% were women; over the next 15 years an additional 1,066 came. Men brought their wives and families if they could find a way. By 1920, women constituted 21% of the Korean adult population in the United States. Over 40% of the Korean immigrants were Christian. Missionaries encouraged Koreans to emigrate (Takiki, 1989, pp. 53–57).

Ducking Under the Citizenship Barrier: The Filipino

In an imperialistic splurge, the United States took the Philippians along with other possessions from the Spanish in the aftermath of the 1898 Spanish-American war. Following annexation, Filipino migrants went by the thousands to work in Hawaii, and later in the 1920s to the mainland. As citizens of an American "possession," they could easily duck under the citizenship barrier. The threat of cutting off Mexican labor with immigration restrictions caused California planters to seek cheap labor in the Philippines. An unlimited supply of workers was available. The Philippines were under Spanish rule for 400 years, so the population was well immersed in Western culture, unlike other Asians. Over 90% were Catholic. The Americans established schools, so that by the time young people started coming to the mainland in the 1920s they were experienced with American teachers and instruction. The majority emigrating, however, was from poor, partly educated farming families, and they mainly found low-skill, low-paying jobs. Most were young, and typically fewer women came. In 1930, only roughly 7% of the 45,202 Filipinos were women; the figure was higher for Hawaii: 10,486, or 16.6% of the 63,052 individuals. Many of the men on the mainland were migratory farm laborers. Even though they engaged mainly in low-paid, uncertain work, it was better than at home. There was always future promise. One recent immigrant commented that at home "he found himself sinking down into the toilet." The one or two dollars a day that he earned seemed much better than the 15 cents a day he could make at home (Takaki, 1989, pp. 57–62).

While most signed contracts with labor agents for a limited time with the expectation of returning home after three or four years, few went back permanently. As Spanish-speaking citizens, Filipino men on the mainland had a reasonable possibility to merge into the southwest population that itself was the product of a long period of Spanish influence in America.

Of Sikhs and Mexicans

Land developers and planters also tried recruiting workers from India, but the period of immigration was short: two years from 1907 to 1909. Immigration officials put insurmountable restrictions in place, followed by outright prohibition by Congress eight years later. In total, about 6,400 came, primarily to southern California to work the land. Most were Sikhs recruited from the Punjab and they encountered the same restrictions other non-European immigrants experienced. Partly because of religious and cultural views, and partly because of restrictions, less than 1% of the arrivals were women. The Sikhs worked in clearing and making habitable what today is the Imperial Valley, the domain and play area of the rich, as well as a rich farming area. The men tended to come in small groups from the same families or villages, sharing responsibilities and resources. Some left and went home, but many stayed and married into local Mexican families, creating a small mixed ethnic group that continues to reside in southern California.

Up to 76% of the Punjabi men acquired Mexican wives. The Alien Land Act of 1913 prohibited land ownership by noncitizen Sikhs because they were not White, but they could acquire land through Mexican wives. The children tended to become Catholic through their mothers and integrate into the Spanish culture (Takaki, 1989, 2008).

An Eye to the South: The Return of the Latino

With the American conquest of the Southwest in the 1840s, thousands of Mexicans were driven across the border as Anglos took over their property. Sixty years later they returned in large numbers, attracted by the possibility of jobs and recruited by labor contractors increasingly turning to Mexican workers to fill the void left by the lack of Asian labor. The Chinese were no longer coming, excluded by law. The Japanese also fought exclusion, and through community associations bought land, and started farms, stores and shops to engage in their own enterprises. But shortly they stopped coming. The Immigration Act of 1924 excluded all Asians. One farm producer lamented, "We have no Chinamen; we have no Japs. The Hindu is worthless; the Filipino is nothing, and the white man will not do the work" (Takaki, 2008, p. 297). The National Origins Act also restricted immigration from Southern and Eastern Europe, but left immigrants from the Western Hemisphere free to come. Mexicans comprised potentially a huge labor pool, and they flocked to "El Norte," looking for security, and desperate to escape violence, poverty, and widespread starvation. Mexico was in the throngs of very hard times and economic conditions were bad. Revolutionary outbreaks made life dangerous. Criminal activity was rampant. Large landowners also bought large tracks of fertile land, forcing the small farmers off and into conditions of wage labor and tenant cultivation. It was easy to get from the interior to El Norte. By 1895, the Mexican International Railroad had finished an extended line from the Mexican heartland to the Texan border 900 miles north. And it was easy to get into the United States: One just walked across the unguarded border (Takaki, 2008).

Most Mexicans that came were uneducated, rural immigrants. They worked the farmlands along the border area from Texas, New Mexico, and Arizona to California. Many more labored as migrant workers, moving as field work was needed and crops ripened from southern to central and northern California and up through Oregon and into Washington. Some worked in the Midwest, moving as far north as Illinois, Wisconsin, and Michigan. In the Southwest alone, the Mexican population grew from 375,000 to 1,160,000 in the short span from 1900 to 1930. In California, by 1920 Mexicans made up three fourths of the farm workers. Women came and labored alongside men, and families formed with the intent of securing permanent residency. The birthrate was high relative to Whites. Mexican mothers averaged nine or ten children; White mothers three. At the rate of nine children, a Mexican mother would have 729 great-grandchildren to the White's 27. These children were United States citizens by birth. Most adult immigrant Mexicans, however, were not legally admitted (Takaki, 2008, pp. 303–305).

Mexicans worked in agriculture, but in time employment expanded to low skill labor and blue-collar work. They built roads, worked on the railroads, excavated, worked in food processing plants, labored on construction sites, washed restaurant dishes, staffed hotels, and collected trash. Women worked as domestics, labored in fields and canneries, and increasingly worked in industry. The Mexicans urbanized. Farm work was seasonal, and in between the men and women migrated to urban centers to find work. If successful, they stayed. Manufacturers wanted Mexicans because they were "good" workers. They also engaged in all kinds of unskilled, dirty jobs that others did not want to do. The Mexican labor is preferred "to other classes of labor," one employer observed. "It is more humble and you get more for your money" (Takaki, 2008, pp. 295–300).

In the urban centers and rural towns Mexicans settled down and created what was termed "the barrio," a collection of shacks and run-down houses located in slum areas where they lived in relative isolation from the larger Anglo population. They built communities in an attempt to reconstruct life like they had in their home villages. Newcomers could find a place to stay and find information on jobs. They helped one another. Soon there were small grocery stores and bakeries with Mexican goods, shops where Mexican clothing and household items could be purchased, community-meeting places, and of course, makeshift churches where the Mexican version of Catholicism was practiced. They were tightly bound together by their common poverty, hope, and need for one another. But their very isolation and self-reliance fed suspicion and misunderstanding among Anglos. Mexicans in America became the target of discrimination. They were kept apart from Anglo society.

There were unwritten but clearly understood restrictions. There were only certain places in town where Mexicans were allowed to go, shop, or eat. In some stores, shopping by Mexicans was limited to certain hours, such as Saturday mornings; food was available at some restaurants, but as carryout picked up at the back door. They were not allowed in certain bars and theaters. A young Mexican male quickly found himself in mortal danger if accused of getting "friendly" with a "white" girl. Mexicans were expected not to loiter and to return to the barrio on "their side" of town at sunset. In the morning as their parents went off to work their children walked to a segregated school (Takaki, 2008).

Tension increased. The large number of Mexicans coming north generated nativist alarm. It was threatening, causing a dramatic shift in ethnic composition, was the claim. White racial purity was under siege. One contemporary claimed that the region should become the home of millions of Whites but was in danger of becoming "the dumping ground for human hordes of poverty stricken peon Indians of Mexico." *The New York Times* in a 1930 article argued for immigration restriction, stating, "It is folly to pretend that the more recently arrived Mexicans, who are largely of Indian blood, can be absorbed and incorporated into the American race." Underlying much of the alarm was the issue of labor competition. As in the case of Asian, Irish, and Eastern European workers, Anglo workers claimed that wages were driven down and jobs taken away by Mexicans willing to work for less. To Whites, the threat became real as Mexicans left the sugar beet fields and peach orchards and took jobs on railroads and construction sites, and in warehouses and manufacturing plants. By the late 1920s, the labor market became flooded as unemployment went up. As the Great Depression hit, blame for White unemployment was directed to Mexicans. There was a demand for repatriation. Hungry, out of work Mexicans were offered the "bargain" of temporary relief in return for shipment back to Mexico. Herded into boxcars like animals, tens of thousands were transported to their "homeland." Even those reluctant to leave were rounded up and sent. About 400,000 Mexicans overall were repatriated, including children born in the United States holding citizenship (Takaki, 2008, pp. 305–307). The immigration stream from the south was cut off, to flow later in our time.

Navigating the Education Path

Schooling was an issue. Mexicans who remained after the American conquest of the southland and west struggled to achieve educational opportunity for their children. Even those that were formerly among the elite faced difficulties as their wealth and means of livelihood progressively eroded and they were pushed down into the laboring class. Laws and tax codes were enacted that made them prey to the new Anglo order. Few could hold on to the wealth and land that they had. For their children, a major recourse was Catholic or nonsectarian private schools. If parents could organize the resources, they established bilingual private schools so their children could continue to be exposed to the Mexican culture and Spanish language. At the same time, they learned English. Their children also were free of the anti-Mexican bias curriculum promoted through public schools. The alternative was bilingual education offered through Catholic schools. Barriers in both cases were laws by communities that made it a criminal offense to offer instruction in any language but English. This was an attempt by Anglo educational officials to eradicate Spanish influence in the conquered territory.

With the dramatic increase in Mexican children of immigrants following the turn of the century, an attempt was made to work with public school officials to open access and eliminate discriminatory behavior. As in the case of other ethnic groups, the initial response was to discourage or deny schooling; the Whites did not want Mexican children attending school with their children. They would be an unwholesome, corrupting influence, was the charge. Mexicans were portrayed as inferior to Whites and the two should not mix. One concerned mother expressed agreement that the Mexican child should have the right to some education, "but still let him know he is not as good as a white man. God did not intend him to be; He would have made them white if He had." Another parent expressed the often-voiced concern for daughters. "Why don't we let the Mexicans come to the white school? Because the damned greaser is not fit to sit aside of a white girl," was the angry opinion (Takaki, 2008, p. 303).

But there also was a practical argument made that was repeated over and over with other immigrant groups. The Mexican was needed to work in the fields. Education would ruin the upcoming generation. They would no longer be willing to labor at low wages weeding, picking prunes, cultivating broccoli, or washing dishes. There was agreement that some education was reasonable to "Americanize" the child, but schooling above the lower grades was not desirable. It would make the child unsuited for drudgework. One Texan educator best expressed the sentiment of Whites when he noted, "You have doubtless heard that ignorance is bliss; it seems that it is so when one has to transplant onions. If a man has very much sense or education either, he is not going to stick to this kind of work. So you see it is up to the white population to keep the Mexican on his knees in an onion patch" (Takaki, 2008, pp. 303–305). It is not surprising that little attempt was made to encourage Mexican children to go to public schools. School attendance laws were routinely ignored.

Parents fought exclusion. The expected reaction of White community leaders was the establishment of separate, segregated schools. Segregated schools for Mexican children were justified on the basis of language use: Mexican children needed special instruction because they spoke Spanish. In the school for Mexican children they learn to be good Americans and good workers. Joel Spring (2008, pp. 180–185) recounted, Mexican American children were subjected to deculturalization programs designed to strip away Spanish Mexican values and cultural inheritance, replace Spanish language with English, and lock the young into low paid labor. Instructional programs were anemic. The student did not learn much. The low status of Mexican Americans was affirmed. Curricula were characterized by anti-Mexican bias. Parents fought segregated schooling.

In the late 1920s the League of United Latin American Citizens (LULAC) was formed in an attempt to increase the political power of American citizens of "Latin" heritage. Comprised primarily of middle-class Mexican Americans, the organization attempted to walk the line between preserving its cultural heritage and language and adhering to the traditions of the United States. It held a vision of a multicultural and multilingual America, and opposed segregated schooling. Its main argument was that discrimination and segregated schooling were impediments to building a unified society. The LULAC challenged segregation in the courts.

The first challenge was against the Charlotte, Texas, Independent School District in 1928. A child was placed in a "Mexican" elementary school based on her probable ethnic origin with the argument that this was necessary for language purposes. The parents contested the placement. The state court ruled that the local school did not have the right to segregate Mexican children, but at the same time the argument of the school district that placement decisions were based on the need of special instruction in English was not dismissed. However, when it turned out that the child was fluent in English, the case fell apart and she was admitted to a "white" school. In a similar case in 1931, the state court ruled that segregation based on ethnicity was unconstitutional, but at the same time the Del Rio, Texas, school board was justified making placements based on instructional needs. These two decisions made it possible for school districts to assign all Mexican American students to separate schools based on the assertion that they required special instruction because they spoke Spanish.

The struggle to eliminate segregated schooling continued after the interlude of World War II. State court cases in California and Texas were precedent setting, forerunners to the nationally important 1954 Supreme Court ruling in *Brown v. the Board Education of Topeka*. In *Mendez et al. v. Westminster School District of Orange County*, a California district judge ruled in 1946 that segregated schooling for Mexican children is illegal. Separated Spanish-speaking students, he noted, are retarded in learning English because of the lack of exposure. In other words, the argument for segregation based on the need of "special instruction" is invalid. In a second case, *Delgado v. Bastrop Independent School District*, the Texas court ruled in 1948 that local schools lacked the legal right to segregate children of Mexican heritage in separate schools. Separate instruction could be given to some students who needed help with English, but it had to be given in the first grade and in an integrated school (Spring, 2008). With these two ruling, the Mexican American community contributed to the momentum of the civil rights movement of the 1950s and 1960s to achieve the full implementation of the educational rights of all children across America.

Surrender and Submission: The Native American Population

With forced relocation to reservations, the remaining Amerindian populations in America were battered into submission. The pattern of conflict with encroaching Whites, resistance and battle, forced surrender, and removal and confinement to a reservation repeated itself following the Civil War throughout the upper Plains States, along the hills and mountains of the Rockies, over the Continental Divide and up and down the Pacific coast. When a lone, emaciated Modoc warrior slowly picked his way out from among the thick, wooded tangles and lava beds surrounding Mount Lassen in northern California to surrender to the U.S. Army in 1897, the Indian wars were over. The Modoc war was the last official Indian war. By the turn of the century the American Indians ceased to be a significant force in American history. With few exceptions, they were confined to reservations. In the meantime, Amerindians continued to struggle for individual as well as cultural survival.

The southwest Amerindians suffered from a bad decision: They sided with the Confederacy in the Civil War. They received little sympathy or support from the federal government in the struggle against encroaching White settlers. The already diminished acreage that they had on "Indian lands" was reduced more. The northern Plaines Indians engaged with the U.S. Army in a separate struggle to preserve traditional hunting grounds, protect their cultural heritage, and maintain independence as a free people. The northern Plaines Indians relied on the vast open country as the hunting grounds for their primary source of food, the buffalo. Whites were already destroying migration trails and reducing herds. The invention of barbed wire led to the practice of fencing off large sections of formerly open land. Local railroad lines began linking towns, cutting through formerly remote areas. The completion of the transcontinental railroad in 1869 meant disaster. Hunters came by the thousands and transportation routes opened the way to markets. Buffalo were killed by the hundreds of thousands; 60 million exterminated in a few decades. The tongues were packed and pickled in brine-filled barrels and shipped east along with the hides, most destined by boat down the Mississippi to European markets, the rest on by rail to American cities. Pickled tongue was considered a delicacy, the hides made leather goods and the removed fur felt. A felt fashion craze was launched.

Great swaths of the plains were killing fields, littered by piles of rotting buffalo carcasses and perfumed by stench for miles. The conflicts between the U.S. Army and Indians were violent, wide ranging and brutal, and as the death of George Custer at the Little Big Horn in 1876 showed the Indians were not always on the losing side. It was not the U.S. Army that forced the Plaines Indians to capitulate and settle in reservations, but starvation. Their primary food supply was gone (Debo, 1970).

The Fate of the West Coast Amerindians

By the time of Columbus, the west coast was probably the most heavily populated region north of Mexico with an estimated 700,000 Indians in California alone. There was abundant fish and game: deer, trout, salmon, rabbits, foxes, gophers, quail, ducks, and geese. Berries and roots flourished and the inhabitants learned how to blanch the bitter tannic acid from the endless supply of acorns from the prolific oak forest to make bread and gruel. Life was relatively easy in the mild, temperate climate. Further north up the Oregon coast where the forests turn to Douglas fir, spruce, and pine, the diet of acorn gruel gave way to salmon that swarmed up the many rivers, forming a mass from bank to bank, easily caught, dried and smoked, supplying the main food source for the year. All this changed. The Spanish occupation took a disastrous toll. By the time the United States took the territory from Mexico, the Native population had been reduced to less than 200,000. But the transfer of possession to the United States was followed by more carnage. Only an estimated 30,000 American Indians were left in California by the turn of the century. In other words, 170,000 were wiped out (Wilson, 1998).

The influx of gold seekers after the discovery in 1829 at Sutter Fort was at the root of the final catastrophe. Roughly 4,000 Whites settled in the coastal west by 1845, increasing to 15,000 on the eve of the gold rush. By late 1850 after gold was discovered, the number swelled to 92,000; and by 1860, soared to 380,000. A leading cause of Indian death from the time Drake made landfall off of San Francisco on was from disease sailors brought. The Catholic priests and Spanish settlers brought more death by disease. The Spanish governor of California, for example, reported in 1818 that of 64,000 baptized Indians, 41,000 died, apparently of disease. Slavery also contributed to the death of Indians. More than 10,000 Californian Indians lived in conditions of Anglo servitude following the victory over Mexico (Wilson, 1998). Their life of hard labor was not long.

The greatest loss of Indian lives after American occupation was through outright murder. James Wilson (1998, p. 228) observed, "more Indians probably died as a result of deliberate, cold-blooded genocide in California than anywhere else in North America." Marauding Whites believed they had the right to kill Indians on sight: men, women, children, and babies. No survivors: All they came across were killed. Common practice was to organize "sport" hunting parties to track down and kill Indians the way hunters today kill deer or quail. "Scalping" parties were formed with prize money given. A peaceful, defenseless tribe, the Digger Indians, for example, was completely wiped out by roving gangs bent on killing Indians for no obvious reason. The atrocities were unspeakable and could fill volumes. There was no way to enforce law and order and human decency in such a vast, sparsely populated area with the few federal and local law personnel, even if the will existed. Also, the west coastal Indians, with few exceptions, did not learn fast enough to band together in defensive numbers. They were easily picked off in small groups. The so-called "Indian wars" were primarily puny skirmishes.

Why such horrible, unspeakable atrocities? Why the slaughter of thousands? "Why," as one San Francisco paper shamefully queried in 1881, such "murderous outrages committed on aboriginal inhabitants of California?" From the distance of history it is difficult to see into the minds of the self-appointed Indian killers. James Wilson (1998, p. 234) suggested that the wholesale slaughter of Indians is rooted in 19th-century belief in White racial supremacy. Slavery may have been legally abandoned, but the idea of the biological superiority of the "Anglo-Saxon race" continued. This is the belief that drove the hatred of the nativist, the belief that was in the mind of the arsonist that lit the match to burn down schools for Black children. This was the justification for tailing the immigrant Italian worker on his way home after a 16-hour work day and beating him senseless in a side alley, or restricting Mexican citizens to separate sections of towns or not letting Chinese children go to school. Outrages, reinforced by Darwin's work, were propelled by the theory that different "races" were created at different times on the evolutionary path and varied in intellectual ability. Thus some were destined to remain inferior, unequal, exploitable, and expendable. Of course, an equal plausible cause was gross human moral depravity.

The remaining Indians on the western plains were forced onto reservations to join others in a pattern of reservations spread across the United States. Some like the Iroquois and Pueblos managed to hold onto a portion of their original tribal lands, but others, many others, such as the Cherokee and Choctaw, were forced from their ancestral homes and onto a completely alien landscape away from their sacred mountains and meadows, out of reach of the tribal burial grounds, and devoid of the forest, streams and mountains, and game that sustained them spiritually and physically. They had to adapt to a new land and a new way of life. They were expected to learn to farm, but the fertility of the new land that they were forced onto usually was too poor to support the kinds of European farming methods they were taught to apply. Some Indian groups were left relatively undisturbed by the reservation system, but this was an exception. The Navahos scattered over the vast southwest desert, for example, were too remote for Whites to bother with and the land was of little interest with the abundance of large fertile stretches easily taken elsewhere. Some tribes suffered more than others. The Sioux and Cheyenne lost their life of wild independence and could no longer travel for miles and days over the undulating plains. In their eyes, they were cooped up and constrained in what amounted to a large outside jail. The thinking of the American government was that confining Amerindians on reservations was the best way to control them. For the Amerindians, the reservation in all of its constricted aspects became the center of their tribal government, their schools, their cultural institutions, and their limited economic activity (Debo, 1970).

Making Amerindians into Whites

Everything soon changed. There was renewed interest in changing Amerindians into "white people," even among the "friends" of Indians. If the Indians learned to think and live like White people, the reasoning went, then they were in a stronger position to resist the inroads into their allotted reservation lands by frontier settlers and land-grabbing speculators. Moreover, the best long-term protection for Indians was for them to learn to live like and among Whites. Secretary of the Interior Carl Schurz, for example, observed the only two alternatives for Indians were extermination or civilization. "Civilizing" could be done through schools (Adams, 1995; Debo, 1970; Reyhner & Eder, 2004).

The Civilization Act of 1819 was intended to encourage Indians to settle down into farming communities and adopt Anglo ways. They would convert to Christianity; schools would teach them reading and writing, farming and trade skills. Eventually they would acquire European attitudes toward work and learn to become patriotic Americans. Trading posts would integrate them into a cash economy. It did not work. The Civilization Act did not achieve its aims primarily because the Native Americans themselves took control of reservation schools and bent them to the purpose of reinforcing tribal solidarity. Schools were used as one means of perpetuating tribal survival.

Now, however, many Whites were saying education had to be taken out of the hands of Indians and put to use for deculturalizing children—that is "Americanizing" them by removing them from tribal oversight. The federal government geared up its efforts to assimilate Amerindians into the general population. The first government boarding school for Indian children was open at Carlisle, Pennsylvania, in 1879, and others followed. Soon a pattern developed. Reservation elementary schools became feeder programs for the off-reservation schools that continued with elementary education. At the same time, mission and private schools continued operating on reservations under government financing and control. But there was a difference. Tribal influence over education was taken away as the federal government assumed control of all schools for Indian children receiving government support. By 1900, this included almost 20,000 of the close to 25,000 Indian children enrolled in boarding schools (Reyner & Eder, 2004, p. 153). The justification was that under tribal administration, Indian schools discriminated. Contrary to the government policy of deculturalization, tribal leaders did not want White and Black students participating in educational programs crafted for Indian children to build tribal allegiance and maintain cultural identity. Besides, they were paying a good part of the bill out of tribal funds. These were their schools, and they wanted to use them to reflect the best interests of the tribe.

Secretary Schurz acted quickly to solidify federal control. In 1880 he required all instruction in public or private Indian schools receiving federal money be taught in English. Local language use in schools was forbidden. This was contrary to the several decades of experience by missionary teachers that the most successful instructional programs incorporated a combination of local dialects and English. Schurz was interested in assimilation, not Indian achievement. The administration of schools was taken out of the hands of Indians and put under the Office of Indian Affairs in the Interior Department. Many of the schools used McGuffey readers, immersing Indian children in stories of morality, patriotism, and nationalism as seen through White eyes. The Indian children studied U.S. history where they learned of the exploits of the brave, noble, and gallant White men defending their homes, wives, and children from the murdering, vile, beastly savages: their parents, grandfathers, and forefathers. Indian children learned God ordained their low station in White society, and their responsibility was to obey, work hard, live a moral life, and respect those that were superior by virtue of their higher station (and this did not mean Indians). Summer teacher institutes were conducted across the country for teachers and staff of Indian schools. The focus was on assimilating Indian children into White society. Schools administered under the Indian Bureau were "created to 'civilize' Native children, to eradicate Native identities, languages, and cultures" (Lomawaima & McCarty, 2006, p. 1). "Cultural genocide was substituted for policies of removal and actual genocide" (Reyhner & Eder, 2004, p. 107).

What were the schools like? Schools on reservations typically went up to the third grade. Instruction tended to be very remedial and highly limited: familiarization with the alphabet, knowledge of simple English words, and knowledge of counting and simple addition and subtraction. Children were left with a smattering of English and counting and arithmetic skills based on an abstract system counter to the way Indians used knots in ropes or strings woven into a blanket to record stories, time, and quantities. Students in off-reservation boarding schools continued elementary education. They continued English language training, had history lessons, were instructed in what was expected of an American citizen, and learned discipline and obedience. The students farmed, raised food for their meals, cooked, were taught how to eat with fork, spoon and knife, learned sewing, woodworking, simple metal work and other vocational skills. Sports were big. Students sang, learning "American" songs. Some schools instituted a system of "outing" placements. Primarily Indian boys were placed with White families to directly learn farming methods. This was a good experience for some, but the practice also deteriorated into a way for farmers to get inexpensive labor. Demand grew as Indian child labor was exploited.

The boarding schools were run like military camps. Strict rules were harshly enforced. Students marched to and from the parade ground and to and between classes. Bells or whistles gave signals to stand up and sit down. Students had to eat in a certain way. Ridged schedules were kept, and punishment followed tardiness. Uniforms were worn, hair cut, and boots polished. Only English could be used, and punishment followed even a whispered Indian word. The students were kept under close watch (Adams, 1995).

Life in reservation schools was not easy. The Indian commissioner noted in 1882, "Children who shiver in rooms ceiled with canvas, who dodge the muddy drops trickling throughout worn-out dirt roofs, who are crowded in ill-ventilated dormitories, who recite in a single school-room, three classes at a time, and who have no suitable sitting rooms or bathrooms, are not likely to be attracted or make rapid advancement in education and civilization" (Adams, 1995, p. 112).

To be sure, there were dedicated men and women who devoted their lives to working with and for the Native Indians. Many worked within the federal bureaucracy. Carlisle superintendent Richard Pratt, for example, believed Indians were equal to Whites, but lost his position over conflicts with bureaucratic interests. Grand Canyon explorer John Wesley Powell also stressed that Indians had to be addressed as equals. Elaine Eastman, wife of Sioux Charles Eastman, Katherine Drexel, and Helen Hunt Jackson, among many others fought against the debasement of American Indians. Hunt hoped her book *A Century of Dishonor* would do for Amerindians what *Uncle Tom's Cabin* did for advancing the cause of Blacks. In individual schools across the nation, enlightened teachers worked to insert more meaningful instruction into programs, treat with kindness and compassion homesick and confused children, temper harsh treatment, and acknowledge the value of Indian ways (Lomawaima & McCarty, 2006; Reyner & Eder, 2004).

A breath of reform came with the appointment by President Grover Cleveland of William N. Hailmann to the position of superintendent of Indian schools. As suggested earlier, Hailmann was active in the "New Education" movement based on the ideas of Johann Pestalozzi and Friedrich Froebel. He tried to put kindergarten methods that the crusading social reformers applied to programs for urban slum children into Indian schools. He also supplied schools with books for "pleasure reading," changed bathtubs to showers, supplied individual towels, and provided more milk to children. He reinserted native language use in schools, and criticized the militaristic way schools were run as "unintelligent warfare against the Indian idiom." Soon, officials were talking about "object lessons" and "child-centered" instruction, but these changes did not last. Hailmann lost his position in a political shuffle when William McKinley took office (Reyner & Eder, 2004).

On the basis on any kind of measurement government involvement with Indian education was appalling. First, officials and staff lacked understanding of Indian culture, and they did not want to understand. They refused to acknowledge that to get Indians to change, they had to first understand the beliefs Indians held, their codes of behavior, and what they held important and sacred. Second, there was a lack of respect. Indians were treated as inferior and as objects of exploitation. But to gain respect, one has to show respect. In the Indians' view, Whites were not to be trusted, took from the Indians what they could, and only brought misery, sorrow, destruction, and death. The ways of the Whites despoiled the land. The God that they seemed to believe in apparently gave them no moral guidance. Why should they want to accept the Anglo way of life?

Third, the instruction that their children encountered appeared irrelevant. Their children were taught farming methods that did not apply to the rocky dirt, sandy soil, or sun-parched clay of reservation landscapes, or that required farming equipment or animals that they did not possess and never would. Their children were taught printing, but there was no paper or printing presses on reservations; they were taught shoemaking, but Indians wore moccasins made by women; they were taught building practices that had little application to the adobe, bush, or hide dwellings constructed. The history taught was demeaning and insulting, math too abstract, and English language training incomplete. Indian children learned words and phrases, but not enough to speak "properly" or to write in sentences and paragraphs.

And fourth, the norm was poor quality instruction. It was difficult to find qualified teachers willing to work on remote, isolated locations. Teachers were challenged by the fact the children knew no English and they had no understanding of the Indian language. On reservations, some teachers merely sat in the classroom while children were left to play outside. At the same time, it must have been an extremely difficult experience for the teacher far away and isolated from her family and friends, and isolated by deep ethnic and cultural differences from the very people whose children she is attempting to teach. The young women recruited primarily from the Midwest and West on the average did not stay for more than a year. Some less (Child, 1998; Reyner & Eder, 2004).

Finally, the "assault on cultural identity" was disturbing to Indians (Adams, 1995). The schools attempted to strip away all outward signs of tribal identity and at the same time adapt Indian children to "white ways." There was little understanding of the trauma created in boarding schools by forcing Indian boys to cut their hair and shed tribal clothing. Girls could no longer use the colorful blankets specially woven for them by grandparents, and they had to wear prescribed dress absent of any individual meaning. "White clothing" also was resented simply because it was uncomfortable. Boots were stiff and uncomfortable, and woolen underwear and clothing unbearably itchy. All government boarding schools harshly enforced policies forbidding the speaking of tribal languages. "Beatings, swats from rulers, having one's mouth washed with soap or lye, or being locked in the school jail were not uncommon punishments" (Child, 1998, p. 28). Perhaps most resented, the assault on identity was extended through new names. The girl Sah-gah-ge-way-gah-bow-e-quay, for example, became Sarah Bowie. But this destroyed lines of lineage that could no longer be traced back into time. The boy or girl was separated from family history. In practical terms, this became an impediment to proving kinship lines in lawsuits over property rights (Adams, 1995).

The most appalling condition was corruption. The administration and operation of Indian schools was part of the political spoils system. From top to bottom, appointments were based on connections and political favors. By 1900, the overall expense of the system of Indian schools was about twice the cost of running local schools elsewhere. Not all of this money went to maintaining the system of Indian schools. An unknown amount went into unidentified pockets. But the result was that money allocated to support Indian pupils was siphoned off. In some boarding schools, warm clothing, blankets, and heat were not provided in winter; food rations where short; supplies of teaching materials, books, and equipment were limited; activities were curtailed, building repair shoddy, and maintenance lacking.

Sickness and death were endemic. Some children were so homesick that they became physically ill. And conditions in boarding schools bred disease. The girls and boys lived in overcrowded rooms, unventilated and not always clean; poor diet contributed, as did exposure to European diseases. Medical care was irregular at best. Some recruiters, intent on meeting student quotas enrolled sick children. Tuberculosis swept through student dorms. Measles, smallpox, and influenza killed. Cases of trachoma were particularly prevalent among Indians. Sick, infectious students were not separated from the healthy.

Hundreds of Amerindian young people died at boarding schools, and cemeteries were a prominent feature of Indian schools. "School officials rarely maintained open communication with families even when poor health or contagious disease threatened the lives of children. . . . By failing to provide a safe, healthy environment, in which the students could live and learn, and by failings to maintain an honest and timely dialogue with parents, boarding school officials alienated those American Indians families who most wanted their children to be educated" (Child, 1998, pp. 67–68).

Allotment: Taking the Best of What Is Left

The movement by Whites onto Indian land could not be stopped. The political pressure could not be ignored. The lure of riches from Indian property bred corruption. The U.S. government embarked on a destructive policy to the long-term integrity of Indian people, lands, and culture: allotment. Indian lands set aside by treaty would no longer be held in trust by the tribe. Each Indian family was allotted a prescribed number of acres secured by fee titles. This opened the way to dispossess the Amerindians of most of their land. Many of the same "friends" of the Indians advocating for government takeover of Indian education argued for allotment in the mistaken belief that it would ease Indians more fully into White society. They saw the elimination of tribal lands as positive. "As long as Indians live in villages they will retain many of their old and injurious habits," an Indian agent of the Sioux tribal reservation in South Dakota wrote in his annual report in 1877. "I trust that before another year is ended they will generally be located upon individual land or farms. From that date will begin their real and permanent progress" (Debo, 1970, p. 299). But allotment was really a systematic way backed by government and court to take remaining Indian land from them.

The "breaking up" of Indian land started before the Civil War and continued. The dispossessing of tribes of their land was done in several official and unofficial ways. Armed gangs of White men invaded, indiscriminately killed the men, women, and children and simply took the land. In some cases, Indians were "encouraged" to sell their land. Falsified titles and deeds were used to possess land, and as Angie Debo recounts, individual Indians were bribed, beaten, pistol-whipped and jailed to force them to sign deeds. In some cases, tribes "leased surplus land" to Whites, but in reality it was permanently lost. The Kansas attorney Martin J. Bentley engaged in a practice followed in the Southwest. He took a group of Kickapoo across the border to Mexico where falsified deeds were obtained for prices ranging from $330 to $1,500 for each section. He returned across the border and subsequently sold the parcels for $49,970, $39,000, and $28,300. Since the transaction was completed in Mexico it was largely out of sight and resistant to American law. The Kickapoo were "encouraged" to stay in Mexico (Debo, 1970, pp. 316–331).

Considerable political pressure was put on Congress to officially sanction taking remaining land from Indians. An attempt at getting legislation passed was made in 1879, 1880, 1885, and 1886. Finally, the Dawes Act was passed in 1887, named for its sponsor Senator Henry Dawes of Massachusetts. Except for the exempt Five Civilized Tribes, the Osages and some of the northern Sioux tribes, the president was authorized to allot all Indian land in the United States to individuals. The typical standard share was 160 acres to each household head, and less for single men and children. The excess land was auctioned off to Whites. In many cases, the Indians were forced off of the best pieces of land and reallocated to holdings of poor quality

(Debo, 1970, 299–315). But this policy did not allow for population growth among reservation Indians. Dawes was completely convinced that a new day was dawning for the Amerindians: They would be released from the domination of tribal rule. He could not conceive that the only thing Natives were released from was the limited authority over the shrinking amount of land that they had. Now they had virtually no control. Tribes had the collective strength to resist the onslaught on their lands; but individuals simply did not have the means to resist. A federal government decision to treat Indian land issue in state and local courts rather than at the federal level only made an already corrupt system more corrupt. State and local judges "rewarded" their supporters with the wealth of Indian lands. Individuals had no experience in land transactions and no money to support legal help. Along with the practice of guardianships, the best of what was left from 300 years of European occupation was taken.

Remaining wealth was taken from Indian lands through the guardian system. The Amerindians had always contested their categorization by the United States government as "domestic dependents." They insisted that they were sovereign nations occupied by a foreign conquering power. This was not just an exercise in semantics. The classification as domestic dependents gave the U.S. government far-reaching power over the lives of Amerindians. This power was exercised in the case of removal and land allocation. Treaty obligations simply were ignored.

Some places allocated to Native Indians on reservations proved to have valuable natural resources: fertile soil, timber, rivers and lakes, and mineral deposits. How could this be taken? Land-grabbers used guardianships. Because of the status of domestic dependents "guardians" were court appointed to exercise control over Indians judged incapable of conducting their own affairs. This practice turned into judicially sanctioned thievery. It was not difficult to get courts to declare Indians incompetent to administer their affairs.

The easiest way was in the case of orphans, but as Debo (1968, 1970) documented, "orphans'" were "created" at an alarming rate, and this attracted public attention. The practice was widened to encompass adults. Soon any Indian family on land with valuable resources was at risk of having their legal heir declared "incompetent." Some of the most egregious cases were in Oklahoma where oil was found on Indian land in what turned out to be the richest field in the United States. In one case, squabbling potential guardians could not resolve among themselves who would get control over the rich flow of oil bubbling from the ground. The judge resolved the conflict by appointing eight guardians and an additional eight attorneys authorized to extract fees from the estate. In the same area, an additional 30 adult full-blood Indians were declared "incompetent." Greed trumped morality. A guardianship gave the executors control over allotments, government payments, sales from inherited land, income from resources, and custody of all income (Debo, 1970, pp. 316–331).

By the turn of the century even the most ardent advocates of assimilation knew this was not occurring. The policy was a failure, and it caused immense distress among reservation Indians. The Indians were destroyed as a people. Through "legal" means Amerindians on reservation land throughout the United States were dispossessed of their cultural heritage and physical resources. A proud people were reduced to a state of dependency and poverty. Some Indians, unable to cope with poverty and moral degradation, simply withdrew to remote areas to disappear among the wooded hills and thick timber; others with no resources to sustain a livelihood squatted on the holding of relatives or friends, or sought help from church groups, or found work as day laborers among ranchers. "A whole generation born too late to receive allotments was growing up in illiteracy and squalor," Debo (1970) observed, "with no land and no tribal relations" (p. 329). As the old century turned to a new one, the Amerindian struggle continued as the very resources essential for continuing their way of life as a people were systematically stripped away. Most of value was taken in the name of emancipating Indian families from their tribal cultural heritage.

References for Part Four

Anderson, J.D. (1988). The Education of Blacks in the South, 1860–1935. Chapel Hill: The University of North Carolina Press.

Barnard, C. (1881). New Roads to a Trade. *The Century Magazine*, December, 285–288.

Baltzell, E.D. (1966). New York: Vintage Books.

Bennett, C.A. (1937). History of Manual and Industrial Education, 1870 to 1917. Peoria, IL: The Manual Arts Press.

Berthoff, R. (1971). An Unsettled People Social Order and Disorder in American History. New York: Harper & Row, Publishers.

Boyer, R.O., & Morais, H.M. (1955). Labor's Untold Story. New York: United Electrical, Radio and Machine Workers of America.

Brace, L. (1880). The Dangerous Classes of New York and Twenty Years Among Them. New York: Wynkoop and Hallenbeck.

Bureau of Education. (1881). Circular of Information, No. 2-1881. Washington, DC: U.S. Government Printing Office.

Bureau of Education. (1897). Report of the U.S. Commissioner of Education for the Year 1896–97, Vol. II. Washington, DC: U.S. Government Printing Office.

Bureau of the Census. (1958). Historical Statistics of the United States, Colonial Times to 1957. Washington, DC: U.S. Government Printing Office.

Butler, N.B. (1883). Manual Training. Proceedings and Addresses of the American Institute of Instruction. Saratoga Springs, NY.

Butts, R.F. (1939). The College Charts Its Course. New York: McGraw Hill.

Campbell, J.K. (1967). Colonel Francis Wayland Parker: The Children's Crusader. New York: Teachers College, Columbia University.

Child, B.J. (1998). Boarding School Lessons, American Indian Families, 1900-1940. Lincoln: University of Nebraska Press.

Clarke, I.E. (1885–1892). Art and Industry. Education in the Industrial and Fine Arts in the United States. Bureau of Education (4 vols., Part I and II). Washington, DC: U.S. Government Printing Office.

Coats, C.P. (1923). History of the Manual Training School of Washington University. Bureau of Education, Bulletin No. 3. Washington, DC: U.S. Government Printing Office.

Cooper, S.B. (1982). The Kindergarten as Child Saving Work (pp. 131–134). Proceedings of the National Conference of Charities and Corrections. Madison, WI.

Cremin, L.A. (1961). The Transformation of the School. New York: Alfred A. Knopf.

Curoe, Philip. (1926). Educational Attitudes and Policies of Organized Labor in the United States. New York: Bureau of Publications, Teachers College, Colombia University.

Curti, M. (1959). The Social Ideas of American Educators. Totowa, NJ: Littlefield, Adams & Co.

Curtis, S.J., & Boultwood, M.E.A. (1965). A Short History of Educational Ideas. London: University Tutorial Press.

Davidson, T. (1884). Teaching the Mechanical Arts. *The Form*, 383–391.

Debo, A. (1968). And Still the Waters Run. Princeton, NJ: Princeton University Press.

Debo, A. (1970). A History of Indians of the United States. Norman: University of Oklahoma Press.

Dinnerstein, L., Nichols, R.L., & Reimers, D.M. (1996). Natives and Strangers, a Multicultural History of Americans. New York: Oxford University Press.

Drescher, S. (2009) Abolition: A History of Slavery and Antislavery. Cambridge, MA: University Press.

Dworkin, M.S. (1959). Dewey on Education. New York: Teachers College Press.

Furnas, J.C. (1969). The Americans: A Social History of the United States, 1587–1914. New York: Putman's Sons.

Gonzalez, J. (2000). A History of Latinos in America: Harvest of Empire. New York: Penguin Books.

Handlin, O. (1951). The Uprooted. New York: Grosset & Dunlap.

Harris, W.T. (1886). Industrial Education in the Common Schools. *Education, VI* (June).

Harris, W.T. (1889). The Psychology of Manual Training. Bureau of Education, Circular of Information, No. 2-1889. Washington, DC: U.S. Government Printing Office.

Harris, W.T. (1979). The Relations of Kindergarten to the School. Proceedings of the National Education Association. Philadelphia.

Herschbach, D.R. (2009). Technology Education Foundations and Perspectives. Homewood, IL: American Technical Publishers.

Higham, J. (1970). Strangers in the Land Patterns of American Nativism, 1860–1925. New York: Anteneum.

Hofstadter, R. (1955). The Age of Reform. New York: Vintage Books.

Johnson, P. (1997). A History of the American People. New York: Harper.

Karier, C. (1967). Man, Society and Education. Glenview, IL: Scott, Foresman & Co.

Kliebard, H.M. (1986)). The Struggle for the American Curriculum, 1893–1958. New York: Routledge.

Kolchin, P. (1993). American Slavery, 1619-1877. New York: Hill and Wang.

Kraut, A.M. (1982). The Huddled Masses: The Immigrant in American Society, 1880–1921. Arlington Heights, IL: Harland Davidson, Inc.

Krug, E.A. (1964). The Shaping of the American High School. New York: Harper & Row, Publishers.

LaFeber. W. (1989). The American Age. New York: W.W. Norton Co.

Lewis, D.L. (1993). W.E.B. DuBois. New York: Henry Holt and Company.

Lomawaima, K.T., & McCarty, T.L. (2006). "To Remain an Indian," Lessons in Democracy from a Century of Native American Education. New York: Teachers College.

MacKenzie, C. (1886). Free Kindergartens (pp. 48–53). Proceedings of the National Conference of Charities and Correction. St. Paul, MN.

Morgan, E.S. (1975). American Slavery American Freedom. New York: Norton.

Nobel, D.F. (1977). America by Design: Science, Technology, and the Rise of Corporate Capitalism. New York: Knopf.

North, D.C. (1966). Growth and Welfare in the American Past. Englewood Cliffs, NJ: Prentice-Hall, Inc.

O'Brien, D.J., & Fugitsa, S.S. (1991). The Japanese American Experience. Bloomington: Indiana University Press.

Paddock, S.S. (1884). Industrial and Technological Training (pp. 210–212). Proceedings of the National Conference of Charities and Corrections. St. Louis, MO.

Parker, F.W. (1891). Notes on Talks on Teaching at the Martha's Vineyard Summer Institute. New York: Kellogg.

Peabody, E. (1882). The Origin and Growth of the Kindergarten. *Education, 5*(May), 5-7-27.

Perlmann, J., & Margo, R.A. (2001). Women's Work? American School Teachers, 1650–1920. Chicago: The University of Chicago Press.

Philbrick, J.D. (1885). City School Systems in the United States. Bureau of Education, Circulars of Information, No. 1-1885. Washington, DC: U.S. Government Printing Office.

Reese, W.J. (1995). The Origins of the American High School. New Haven: Yale University Press.

Report of Special Committee of Lake Placid Conference. (1901). Home Economics in Elementary and Secondary Schools (pp. 51–57). Proceeding of the Third Annual Conference on Home Economic, Lake Placid, NY.

Report of the Board of Directors (1978). Twenty-Third Annual Report of the St. Louis Public Schools for the year 1877. St. Louis: John J. Paly and Co.

Report of the Committee of Ten on Secondary Schools. (1893). Bureau of Education Bulletin No. 205. Washington, DC: U.S. Printings Office.

Report of the Committee of the Senate Upon the Relationship Between Labor and Capital (4 vols). (1885). Washington, DC: U.S. Government Printing Office.

Reyner, J., & Eder, J. (2004). American Indian Education. Norman: University of Oklahoma Press.

Riis, J.A. (1892). The Children of the Poor. New York: Scribers and Sons.

Rudolph, F. (1962). The American College and University. New York: Vintage.

Shapiro, M.S. (1983). Child's Garden; the Kindergarten Movement from Froebel to Dewey. University Park: The Pennsylvania State University Press.

Smith, T.L. (1961). Progressivism in American Education, 1886–1900. *Harvard Educational Review, 32*(Spring), 168–190.

Spain, D. (2001). How Women Saved the City. Minneapolis: University of Minnesota Press.

Spring, J. (2008). The American School from the Puritans to No Child Left Behind (7th ed.). New York: McGraw Hill.

Takaki, R. (1989). Strangers from a Different Shore. New York: Penguin Book.

Takaki, R. (1990). Iron Cages; Race and Culture in 19th Century America. New York: Oxford Press.

Takaki, R. (2008). A Different Mirror: A History of Multicultural America (1st rev ed.). New York: Bay Back Books.

Thomas, A. (1901). Household Arts in Country Schools; How to Teach Them (pp. 51–57). Proceeding of the Third Annual Conference on Home Economic, Lake Placid, NY.

Tyack, D., & Hansot, E. (1982). Managers of Virtue. New York: Basic Books.

Tyack, D., & Hansot, E. (1990). Learning Together: A History of Coeducation in America. New York: Russell Sage Foundation.

Vandewalker, N.C. (1908). The Kindergarten in American Education. New York: The Macmillan Co.

Wilson, J. (1998). The Earth Shall Weep. New York: Atlantic Monthly Press.

Woodward, C.M. (1882). The Function of an American Manual Training School. Proceedings and Addresses of the National Educational Association. Saratoga Springs, NY.

Woodward, C.M. (1885). Manual Training in General Education, *Education, IV*(July), 615.

Woodward, C.M. (1889). Relation of Manual Training to Body and Mind. Proceedings and Addresses of the Department of Superintendence, National Educational Association. Washington, DC.

Woodward, C.M. (1906). The Manual Training School. Boston: D.C. Heath and Co.

Woodward, C.V. (1966). Reunion & Reaction. Boston: Little, Brown and Company.

Woody, T. (1974). A History of Women's Education in the United States, Vol. II. New York: Octagon Books.

Part Five

Toward a More Perfect Society

Introduction

The nation entered the 20th century with confidence. A new industrial order was in the making that generated enormous national wealth. It is true that its distribution was lop-sided, with staggering differences in income distribution, but the general level of prosperity increased to the point where the relative affluence generated an expanding middle class and even those at the lower end of the economic scale could dare to look to a possible future of modest promise, even if remote. To be sure, thousands of people in cities, towns, and hamlets across America struggled daily with the wretchedness of poverty and squalor, and many labored in hard, dirty, uncertain jobs with long hours and little pay. Others could not find work, victims of the vicissitudes of the market. In 1900, over 6.5 million workers could not find a job (Allen, 1952, p. 49). For many wages were low. Because of the glut of labor primarily from heavy immigration, employers could keep wages of the unskilled barely above the poverty level. But at the same time, immense wealth was generated.

The gruff loner, John Pierpont Morgan, for example, created the most powerful banking house in the world, and with his absorption of the steel empire of Andrew Carnegie created the United States Steel Corporation, the largest corporation ever seen by the world. A shy, determined man from Ohio, convinced that it was God's destiny for him to earn money, became the wealthiest individual in the world, creating Standard Oil and vertically integrating the oil industry and controlling freight rates to put competitors out of business. John D. Rockefeller soon extended his holdings to monopolize all kinds of mining and land resources. There were millionaires by the score representing "new" money that was generated through financial manipulation, large capital investments, control of markets, and ever-growing monopolistic conglomerates. Capturing the control of banking, real estate, railroads, transportation hubs, oil and mineral resources, timber, and great swaths of land produced great wealth for a few (Holbrook, 1985).

Wealth was also created through agriculture. Cyrus McCormick massed a fortune manufacturing farm machinery, but also helped to create fortunes in the Plains for those that could make heavy capital investments in large planting and harvesting machinery and use seasonal mass labor. Trains and refrigerated freight cars brought meat from ranches in Texas to the packing houses in Chicago and on to the markets in the east; and fruit and vegetables were shipped from the west coast to eastern tables In the far west, Hugh Glenn accumulated 50,000 acres of prime wheat-growing land in the Sacramento Valley, harvested over 1 million bushels of wheat a year, employed more than a 1,000 men, and reaped a fortune through overseas shipments.

A monopolistic growers cooperative was formed in southern California to control planting, harvesting, marketing, and pricing of lush citrus. The organization of other farm groups followed to control markets for specific products. At the same time, Mexican field workers labored for pennies a day (Furnas, 1969). All across the country in cities, farms, and ranches great wealth was generated for some.

The expanding cities created jobs, industrial production absorbed hundreds of thousands of workers, agriculture production was on the rebound, and the sparsely settled western lands filled up around clusters of economic activity. Science made advancements almost everywhere, fueling economic growth and improving life. The land-grant colleges, business, and engineering schools proved their worth by funneling scores of highly trained men and women into local and regional economies. The sores of social strife and individual want were covered, however, with a balm of complacency and smugness as Americans contemplated a bright future (Allen, 1952; Berthoff, 1971; Hofstadter, 1955, Johnson, 1997).

The Loss of Complacency

As the new century progressed America lost much of its complacency. The country was jolted out of complacency by an orgy of political corruption, by civic incompetence and indifference, and by the massive piling up of corporate and individual wealth that contrasted sharply with the squalor of the city and poverty of the farm. The brutality accompanying labor unrest shocked the nation. The working conditions of many challenged the very concept of capitalism. Muckraking journalists, such as Jacob Riis, *How the Other Half Lives*, Robert Hunter, *Poverty*, and John Spargo, *The Bitter Cry of the Children*, told tales of woe that penetrated deeply into the American soul. The economic recession of 1907 further edged complacency aside. People became fearful of an uncertain future. Something had to be done. It was obvious to many that the dream of relative economic security and cultural homogeneity and harmony was pushed further into the future (Allen, 1952; Boyer & Morais, 1971; Johnson, 1997).

There were disturbing conditions that troubled the nation. Seven eighths of the country's wealth was in the hands of the upper one eighth of the population, with the remaining one eighth of wealth divided among the remaining seven eighths of the population. The average annual income of the middle class was $1,500; for the poor it was $150, which meant that nearly half of the population was living on the edge of poverty (Berthoff, 1971, p. 340). Women made less than men, with less than a dollar for a 10-hour day not uncommon. Children earned $2 or $3 a week. Following the Civil War, wage increases were averaging around 4% per year, but after the turn of the century this stopped and there was a decline in buying power. Workers could not keep up with real increases in the cost of living. Up until 1914, real hourly wages basically remained stationary. Productive capacity increased five times between the turn of the century and 1914, but workers did not share in the increase in wealth (Hofstadter, 1955, pp. 169–170). Berthoff (1971) noted poverty was primarily concentrated in cities, and as rural inhabitants flocked to cities to find better opportunity, poorly paid farm hands were transformed into poorly paid machine tenders (p. 315).

Labor, Capital, and Conflict

The bitter conflict between labor and capital destroyed complacency. Its raw violence spread alarm throughout the nation. The conflict took on a new dimension because of the media attention given to conflict after conflict. Local incidents became national news: the strike of silk workers in Patterson, rubber workers in Akron, shirt makers in New York City, loggers in the Northwest, field workers in California, and miners in Michigan, Idaho, and Colorado brought ugliness to the eyes of the American public. There was violence on both sides, but capital usually had the upper hand with hired guns to murder and terrorize.

A new wash was painted over the conflict between labor and capital with the 1907 trial of "Big Bill" Haywood. In Caldwell, Idaho, the state's former governor Frank Steunenberg was killed in 1905 on a winter night, "sent to eternity" by a bomb rigged to go off as he returned from a walk through the new snowfall and opened his garden gate. Steunenberg was at the front of the brutal six-year resistance by Idaho mine owners to the efforts of miners to organize, and was hated by miners. The bombing appeared to be retaliation for the heavy-handed tactics of the owners and deaths of miners in their suppressed efforts to secure better working conditions and wages. The trial of accused labor leader Haywood became national drama, with issues taken all the way to the Supreme Court (Lukas, 1997).

No one could stay neutral. The country's most famous defense lawyer, Clarence Darrow, was enlisted to aid Haywood; Theodore Roosevelt voiced his disdain for Haywood and unionism; William Howard Taft and Socialist leader Eugene Debs added a political shading to the trial; the young actress Ethel Barrymore and the baseball great Walter Johnson attended the Idaho trial. In New York City, 40,000 garment workers marched in a demonstration of support for Haywood.

He was acquitted, but the result of the 1907 trial went far beyond Haywood: The trial exposed the violence labor used. The trial also exposed the great amount of secret money used to bankroll antilabor activity, the collusion between law officers and owners, the under-the-table payoffs, the buying of politicians to keep in their pockets, and the extent of the use of thugs, spies, and hired gunmen was fully exposed. Capital conducted all-out war on labor. Capital now stood stark naked before the public, shorn of its cloak of morality, exposed in its full greed, and absent of any feelings of humanity (Lukas, 1997). It was difficult for corporate America to continue to justify the wealth accumulated from the efforts of thousands that lived in grinding poverty, kept down by those that controlled the levers of power (Boyer & Morais, 1971; Lukas, 1997).

Throughout the 1880s and 1890s capital always maintained the moral high ground and conditional public support by maintaining that it was protecting individual rights and the welfare of the nation by thwarting the organized violence of labor groups infused with subversive communistic and anarchist doctrine and bent on destroying individual liberty (Boyer & Morais, 1971 Hofstadter, 1955). Things changed. After the carnage associated with labor conflict of the early 1900s, capital could no longer easily garner public support. To be sure, labor engaged in violence, and the miners in particular were experts with dynamite as the murder of Frank Steunenberg demonstrated. These were men and women trying to survive in a time of great greed, a time when the odds were stacked against them, and a time when public awareness had yet to be awakened.

Congress eventually acted. The Commission on Industrial Relations was authorized and following Woodrow Wilson's election put into operation. They came out hard against capital: State governments are dominated in order to use the law for corporate ends; workers are prevented from organizing by aggressive action; the wealthy squander their riches while the workers who are essential for the generation of wealth are kept in poverty; and wealth has become concentrated to an alarming degree. But perhaps more alarming, the commission stressed, was the control of the thoughts of Americans. Corporate monopolies "controlled the ownership of influence." One outcome was the formulation of safety and working regulations, including child labor laws (Allen, 1952; Boyer & Morais, 1955, pp. 185–186).

Public complacency was largely shredded by a new thrust in journalism, as Allen (1952, p. 88) noted, "toward the deliberate, unsentimental, searching, factual reporting of what was actually going on in American business and American politics." The swing in public awareness was initiated early, building up until it spilled over into public action. Robert Hunter, in his 1904 book *Poverty*, vividly recounted the plight of the hungry, filthy, and poorly housed, as many as 20 million, unseen strangers to others as they trudged on tired legs through the dark, two hours before sunrise to take their place alongside the humming machines of production, to emerge after dark, to struggle home, to eat meager fare and to sleep in a crowded room on makeshift beds and sofas, having earned barely enough to stay alive.

Manufacturing technology was crude and dangerous. Men increasingly worked to the pace of the machine as mechanization took hold. Work was hard, and for factory workers the working life usually was over by the age of 40. Low-level labor was replaced like so many interchangeable parts. There existed virtually no safety standards, with the rate of maimed or killed high among all workers. Safety was only an afterthought. There were no health standards. Factories were dirty, unsafe, and toxic places to work. By 1913, industrial fatalities on the average totaled 35,000 a year (Boyer & Morais, 1955, p. 184). There were no child labor laws, with the child going to work as soon as he or she was physically able. Children suffered sobering high rates of accidents and mortality, particularly in late afternoon and evening after six or eight hours of exhausting work. They were tired. Children became "the prey of the great cutting knives, or of the jaws of the tin-stamping machine" (Allen, 1952, p. 50). The seriously injured child had no future, and there was no workman's compensation, so the maimed worker had no way to pay for medical care or support life as a cripple. There was no job security, and pensions were the rare exception.

Ida Tarbell launched a series of articles in *McClure's* magazine exposing the predatory practices of Standard Oil as it built its monopoly on the destruction of others. Lincoln Steffen published articles exposing municipal corruption in St. Louis in the same magazine. Others exposed rampant corruption at all levels of government all across the country. Journalists took up the cause of exposing the seamier side of the great industrial and social transformation that was producing immense wealth but at the same time eating people up and spitting them out like unwanted pulp discarded on a pile of rubbish.

The picture was not pretty. America was shocked out of its complacency. "Thus began the revolt of the American conscience," Allen (1952, p. 89) suggested, "which was to be the dominant phenomenon in American affairs until about 1915 when it was submerged in the oncoming tides of World War I, and which finally petered out about 1920 – leavings behind it, however, influences and patterns of thinking that were to continue to this day." Education was swept up in the revolt of conscience. This is a time Lawrence Cremin (1961) identified when the schools of America underwent a remarkable transformation over a three-decade period—the subject of Part Five.

The Focus of Part Five

Following the turn of the century there were complex, intertwining currents of change. Politically and socially, this period spawned what is termed the "Progressive Era," the time roughly defined by the turn of the century and World War I. What is termed "progressive education" is linked to the larger progressive political movement. Reformers were alarmed by the destructive powers centered in the urban centers. Faith was placed in the capacity of public schools to work toward a more just and harmonious as well as a more efficient society. Social disintegration had to be checked. "Democracy has to be born anew every generation, and education is its midwife," the American philosopher John Dewey reminded the public (1916, p. 410).

Progressives and Reform

The condition of the poor, especially in squalid slums of the disorderly industrial cities, alarmed the progressives. The social fabric was being torn apart by the lack of morality, the challenge to religious beliefs, crime, abandoned children, labor unrest, and ethnic strife and dirt and disease that spread through the crowded tenements and beyond and into every community. Most perplexing was that the mass of exploited immigrants supported the political bosses that were corrupting the very idea of democracy. Political machines threatened the very idea of civic virtue (Hofstadter, 1955).

Progressives set their political sights on curbing corruption, breaking the grip of political machines, tempering the influence of big money, reforming civic government and addressing the problems of everyday life attending the squalor and discord of the city. The spirit of the Social Gospel motivated them. To be sure, many puzzled over why the "new" immigrants from southern and eastern Europe could not quickly lift themselves out of conditions of poverty and want, and assumed that it was because of conditions of innate mental and moral deficiencies. But the commanding explanation, progressives reasoned, was found in the urban environment itself and the industrial machine and manipulative financial system that overwhelmed the social order. To change individual lives, society had to be reformed (Berthoff, 1971). Progressives considered schools a major instrument to do this. In the 1880s and 1890s reformers worked around the edges of public education to bring about change, but with the turn of the century schools became central to the effort of civic, social, and economic reconstruction.

The Social Efficiency Movement

The progressive element in education coexisted and worked in tandem with the strong national movement to achieve greater social efficiency. It was the extension of the general efficiency movement to the running of schools. A major argument of efficiency proponents was that if society could be made productive enough issues of poverty and want would disappear. There would be enough wealth to go around, even though some would have more than others. Production changes that generated greater output with less resource use were making this possible. These were the changes that generated enormous wealth for a John Rockefeller or a Henry Ford. But at the same time the production system became more complex.

The field of business management grew in scope and importance in response to the evolving complexities in the corporate world. Engineering made remarkable advances through better materials, research and development, refined machine design, and the use of scientific knowledge, but the coordination of the production task itself became more complex. Business managers and engineers found what they were looking for in the ideas of a young engineer, Frederick W. Taylor. He had been experimenting since the 1880s and 1890s with the use of time and motion studies to achieve greater productivity. By the turn of the century he was ready to take his ideas nationwide, with presentations to professional engineering groups and universities. He demonstrated a way to increase production and to lower costs through internal controls and oversight by management. Management took control of the work process that was now relinquished by the worker. Soon business schools, such as the ones at Harvard and Dartmouth, organized formal courses of "scientific management" following Taylor's methods. The efficiency movement was poised to sweep through the country. By 1910 everyone was talking about improving social efficiency.

Raymond Callahan (1962) observed that the influence of business and industrial values so saturated American society that it was relatively easy for the efficiency movement to take root. Soon churches, dance halls, department stores, small shops, breweries, farms, garment factories, the army and navy, law offices—and schools—took up the cause of promoting greater efficiency. Efficiency saturated the bloodstream of American life. Little was overlooked.

If Progressives wanted to make America more just and humane, advocates of social efficiency wanted to construct a society that was smooth running, free of conflict, and one that addressed human capital development. Tyack and Hansot (1982) noted education was considered "a major form of human engineering" (p.107). Progressives and efficiency advocates were sometimes in opposition, but combined they expressed a guarded optimism about the ability to reconstruct America and its future, and contributed to the construction of an institutional framework that continues to characterize public education today. In time, efficiency became the stronger force for change, absorbing under the mantle of social efficiency much of what progressives were trying to accomplish.

The focus in Chapter Twelve is on major ideas that influenced the reconstruction of public schools. The discussion centers on key figures and the philosophical and psychological concepts they brought to bear on two decades of national discourse. These individuals are roughly grouped under "progressives" and "social efficiency advocates," although their ideas cannot always be so neatly categorized. Chapter Thirteen is an account of the development of the high school. Following the turn of the century, elementary schools continued to undergo changes inspired by the work of the reformers of the 1880s and 1890s. At the same time, national focus shifted to the high school, an educational institution that assumed greater importance in the effort to address the social and economic ills becoming so visible.

The focus of the discussion is shifted in Chapter Fourteen to the decades of the 1920s and 1930s. This is a time when the dimensions of American public education were fleshed out. It also is a time when the nation struggled to maintain its cultural, social, and economic equilibrium. The high school found its place, and the structure of American public education was defined for the next century. Efficiency triumphed.

Chapter Twelve
Reconstructing the Meaning of Education

By the end of the century currents of educational change barely evident in the early 1800s became a swirling eddy, creating crosscurrents of beliefs and practices that challenged public schools. The staggering social and economic transformation driving change tested the time-honored assumption that the major function of education was to prepare a leadership class through a classical education steeped in literary studies. The concept of mental discipline based on faculty psychology fell apart, unable to support the preeminence of a curriculum structured around the liberal arts. It could no longer be argued that faculty psychology was a valid concept of how learning takes place. Classical studies lost its psychological foundation. The last significant expression of the preeminence of classical studies through the Committee of Ten in 1893 provoked national debate that by the conclusion of the first decade of the new century put an end to the concept of mental discipline as a viable formulation of learning.

There were four major clusters of ideas that vied to replace classical perceptions of education. One cluster can be loosely grouped under the term *social amelioration*, the ideas of those individuals that want to use school as a tool to create the good society, one that is more just, equal, and harmonious, and a society free of want and conflict. Inspired by the Social Gospel, this cluster of ideas emerged out of the work of social reformers and kindergarten supporters of the 1880s and 1890s, and was carried over into the new century (Spaine, 2001). There is a strong belief in the power of education as a tool of social reconstruction.

Closely allied is a cluster of beliefs that is related to the work of the *developmentalists*, individuals who study the natural order of development in the child and its implications for education. Much of their thinking was informed by the experimental work increasingly taking place in the emerging field of child study. Both of these two clusters of ideas overlap, and both trace their pedagogical roots to the work of the Enlightenment thinker Locke, and to Rousseau, Pestalozzi, and Froebel. John Dewey was the leading figure in synthesizing these two clusters of ideas after the turn of the century.

A third cluster of ideas relates to *scientific curriculum making,* which uses the tools of mathematics, measurement, and precise standards to make educational decisions. Practitioners also draw from the experimental work taking place in psychology and human development. They support the belief that a more orderly, efficient, and predictable society can emerge out of what is a chaotic, uncertain environment wasteful of human potential. Science can help achieve this end.

Scientific curriculum-making fed into and augmented the cluster of ideas surrounding the doctrine of *social efficiency*. This is the belief that society can best be reformed not only through better-run schools, but also by molding students to predetermined social characteristics, attitudes, skills, and knowledge useful for taking a productive place in society. Social behavior and work behavior are both enhanced. Both views tend to see schools as a tool of social control (Kliebard, 1987).

None of these clusters of ideas were applied in pure form to school reform, and they were mixed—that is, practitioners taking and using what was of value to them; and theorists appropriated parts of each other's ideas. There was no one reform movement in the United States after the turn of the century, but rather a fragmented, multiple-faceted movement that eventually coalesced around key concepts sometimes in conflict to construct the framework of 20th-century American education. For purposes of discussion in this chapter the four clusters of formative ideas are grouped under the two headings: progressive education and social efficiency.

Society and the Child: Progressive Education

The progressives were a loosely organized group of social reformers with no national political organization to work through. They fed off the earlier work of Lester Frank Ward in *Dynamic Sociology* that shifted public thinking away from *Social Darwinism* and its emphasis on the survival of the fittest to the idea that collective intelligent human action could shape society for the good of all. They were primarily united by conviction, and advanced social reform through settlement houses, sanitation leagues, church groups, organizations to rescue wayward women, community improvement groups and schools, among others. Jane Addams worked with immigrants at Hull House in Chicago, the Pratt family established soup kitchens in Baltimore to feed the needy, and Emily Griffith in Denver started the Opportunity School for poor children.

Herbart Kliebard (1987) observed, that progressive educators viewed schools as a "critical mediating institution between the family and a puzzling and impersonal social order, an institution through which the norms and ways of surviving in the new industrial society would be conveyed" (p. 1). Progressives in education wanted to make five basic changes to public education.

1. They wanted to extend the breadth of education opportunity to embrace all social classes, and especially children of the underclass, the poor, and immigrants. Progressives feared these children would grow up to be criminals, indigents, and social agitators unless they experienced early the beneficial influence of education. Immigrant children in the eyes of reformers had be attracted and kept in school because there was no other good way to teach them to conform to "American" social norms. Outreach programs into slum neighborhoods were only partly successful.

2. In order to attract and hold students "of the rank and file" school studies had to be radically reformed. This meant *what* was taught to students as well as *how it was taught* had to be changed. Irrelevant subjects, harsh instructional practices, and abusive treatment drove lower class children away from formal schooling. Individual difference in learning had to be recognized and accommodated. The early work of Francis Parker, kindergarten reformers, and New Education advocates, covered in Part Four, as well as the work of John Dewey and others provided direction, and progressives turned to promoting widespread curriculum change.

3. Schools had to accommodate the social, emotional, and physical needs of children as well as the intellectual needs. This meant continuing to promote the inclusion of baths, school nurses, cafeterias, playing fields, and assembly halls in schools. It meant having school clubs, dances, and recreational activities; and it meant reflecting a fuller understanding of human maturation and the psychology of the child. The child development movement provided direction for this.

4. Reformers wanted schools to focus on vocation. Few would go on to higher education, indeed, complete high school, so schools had to concentrate on preparing the large number of students matriculating into schools to live a full, constructive, productive life and this included preparation for jobs.

5. Importantly progressives wanted to embrace community. This meant not only teaching students about family and community life and good government, but also meant extending the reach of schools directly into communities.

Lawrence Cremin (1961, p. x) noted that the character of progressive education was pluralistic and frequently contradictory, and as a movement it "meant different things to different people." But the very diversity of beliefs made it a dynamic movement that in a remarkably short time stamped its identity on American education. John Dewey was among the most influential individuals.

John Dewey, Society, and the Child

John Dewey was a commanding intellectual figure. He gained an international reputation as the leading philosopher of pragmatism, and through his writings on education acquired a place at the center of progressive education. Dewey was a social reconstructionist—that is, he believed in the use of schools as a tool to reconstruct society in contrast to the more conventional use as an instrument of social control and preservation of the status quo. Dewey also placed the developing child at the center of instruction, thus appealing to those who wanted a more child-centered rather than content-centered curriculum. This linked him to the child development movement. But Dewey also wanted to make the school more socially centered.

Pragmatism and Dewey

Pragmatism is a uniquely American philosophy. The initial overt formulation of pragmatism is found in the work of Charles S. Peirce. He held that the meaning of any idea is best found in the practical consequences following from its use. He argued concepts are experimentally verifiable, and meaning is changeable and can be expressed as probabilities rather than absolutes.

William James and John Dewey took Pierce's work a step further. James formulated pragmatism as a method through which the theoretical as well as the practical consequences of a concept could be tested. Dewey elaborated the most complete view of pragmatism. He constructed an approach he called "instrumentalism" for experimentally testing a concept relative to a specific problem Using the "scientific" technique of hypothesis, checking, reformulation, and rechecking, Dewey thought man could ferret out experimentally "truth" and meaning. Social problems thus could be attacked on a rational and scientific but yet humane and individualistic basis. Rejecting metaphysical absolutes, utopias, and religious "truths," he stressed the possibility of a harmonious, pluralistic society constructed out of social consensus built from reflective, intelligent thought. As society itself changed, ideas, beliefs, values, and social institutions, however, also change in response to the changing material circumstances of life. Meaning is constructed out of life experiences, Dewey asserted. It is up to humans to adopt forms of social institutions, ideas, and values that are best found useful at a particular historical time (Grob & Beck, 1963; Karier, 1967).

Dewey wanted education to develop young men and women sensitive to social issues with the inclination and capacity to act on them. "Dewey's good society," Clarence Karier (1967) observed, "was a pluralistic society, encompassing a maximum amount of freedom, where reasonable men were deeply involved in using intelligence to create a more humane society" (p. 144). His ideas were attractive at a time when America was attempting to counter some of the ugliness in society and struggling to redefine itself. He became inextricably linked with the progressive education movement.

As a quiet, shy, modest youth from rural Vermont, in his last year at the University of Vermont he excelled in philosophy, and after teaching a few years in Vermont and Pennsylvania went on to complete his graduate studies at the new university of Johns Hopkins in Baltimore. He came under the influence of the philosophy of Hegel through his mentor George Morris, became immersed in Kant through his work on Hegel, was introduced to the experimental psychology of G. Stanley Hall, and followed the logic of Charles S. Peirce and the early formulations of pragmatism. He went to the University of Michigan in 1885, and to the University of Chicago in 1894 where he made a name as chair of the department of philosophy, psychology, and pedagogy.

Dewey, Society, and the Child

In Chicago, Dewey and his wife, Alice, looked for a school to enroll their children and were immediately attracted to the Cook County Normal School run by Francis Parker. As suggested in Part Four, Dewey was profoundly influenced by what he learned from Parker. Within a year the Deweys founded the Laboratory School at the University of Chicago. It was an experimental school that gave him the opportunity to more completely work out his educational theories and their social implications. To a degree generally unrecognized, Dewey reformulated much of what he learned from Parker to established the theoretical underpinnings of progressive education in his greatest works on education: *School and Society* (1898), *Democracy and Education* (1916), and *Experience and Education* (1938). By the time he moved to Columbia University in 1904 he had achieved wide recognition. Through a long career that extended up until his death in 1952, John Dewey was at the center of a rich, intellectual climate in America. After moving to Columbia University, increasingly he turned his attention to education, and became a leading voice that educators listened to as they engaged in the reconstruction of American schools after the turn of the century.

Dewey presented three core ideas that formed the substance of his education work. First, the relationship between schools and society had to be strengthened and maintained. While Parker wanted to make schooling child centered, Dewey also wanted to make schooling more socially centered. Dewey was deeply concerned by the fact that while industrialism held the promise of materially and morally improving society for the good of all, it was fast becoming a tool of abuse. The brutal, ongoing conflict with labor, spreading poverty, unrest and crime, and unhealthy and grueling work conditions demonstrated this. Uncontrolled and unchecked, industrialism unfortunately tended to promote class division, the exploitation of many for the private gain of a few, appalling living and working conditions, and servile and drudging work. The intellectual, moral, and aesthetic value in work was lost (Dewey, 1917, pp. 222–225). At an earlier time, Dewey contended, the church, home, and farm were stabilizing influences on individuals and society, but with urbanization and industrialization and the breaking down of social cohesion public schools were the only social institution with the potential to cut across class and ethnic and religious lines, to bring the children of all Americans together. Modern urban industrial society was destroying all sense of community, common identity, and common goals.

Dewey thought that students could learn what a model industrial society could be through reliving its problems, and manipulating its material, technique, and knowledge. In this way, students could be equipped to shape society for the good of all. "When the school introduces and trains each child of society into membership within such a little community, saturating him with the spirit of service and providing him with the instruments of effective self-direction," Dewey contended, "we shall have the deepest and best guarantee of a larger society which is worthy, lovey and harmonious" (1959, p. 49).

Echoing Parker, the fundamental point Dewey attempted to impress upon the educational world was "education could prepare the young for future social life only when the school itself was a cooperative society on a small scale," and in an industrial society this meant that the school had to become more industrial, and an "embryonic community life active with types of occupations that reflect life of the larger society, and permeated throughout with the spirit of art, history, and science."

For Dewey the exposure of children to occupations was essential, but he used the idea of "occupations" in a specific way. He did not mean vocational training. Occupations were the activities reproduced in miniature that were "fundamental to life as a whole, and thus enable the child, on one side, to become gradually acquainted with the structure, materials, and modes of operation of the larger community; while on the other it enables him individually to express himself through these lines of conduct, and thus attain control over his own powers" (Dewey, 1896, p. 418).

A second core idea was the character of instruction. Dewey used teaching methods to reinforce the relationship between society, experience, and knowledge. Content and method were fused. Meaning came out of experience. Reflecting his pragmatic bent, Dewey opposed the teaching of abstract ideas unless linked with the opportunity to engage in the actual conditions out of which meaning and understanding are developed. This involved the use of occupations through which to correlate the teaching of academic and concrete knowledge in the context of having students work on activities that relate to their immediate social environment.

Students participated as a group in activities such as gardening, cooking, printing, textile work, and construction. Students published a school newspaper, baked bread, ran a school store, planted a garden, and built a model house. These were rich in learning experiences alive with the opportunity to extract meaning and demonstrate the social uses of knowledge. These experiences are the content of instruction. Students start to understand how knowledge is alive,

Dewey thought, and how knowledge is used, and as well as how it is linked to the past and simpler forms of communal life.

Dewey's third fundamental core idea was the formulation of a psychology of learning that placed student experiences at the center of learning. William James and Edward Thorndike among others were advancing the use of empirical research to study human psychology. Dewey thought this was useful, but he took his theorizing in another direction. Dewey was attracted to the ideas grounded in the work of Locke, Rousseau, Pestalozzi, Froebel, and others that mental growth was a process through which sense impressions from the world surrounding the child were received, analyzed, compared, and combined to generate meaning. Dewey thought learning occurred as a result of the reorganization of the individual's intellectual and psychological structures through interaction with the environment. To Dewey, this meant the child had to be exposed to a full range of human experiences in order to gain a meaningful understanding of knowledge and its relationship to reality, and to build powers of reasoning and abstract thinking.

As suggested, for Dewey, activities provided a medium for the activation of learning. Children, Dewey contended, have a natural impulse to communicate, construct, investigate, and experiment, and activities from the world of the child provide the best means of bringing this impulse into an interplay with ideas and knowledge to create meaning. Activities are interesting, hold the attention of the child, and provide a means of stimulating the imagination; they expose the child to the materials and processes in his immediate surrounding world; and, finally, they provide a variety of subject matter necessary for the correlation of a broad range of knowledge and information.

Experiments with cooking, for example, exposed the child to the physics of heat and steam, the chemistry of foods, and the arithmetic of measurements. Construction in the shop led to an understanding of simple tool processes, intimately acquainted students with the smelting process of metals, the biology of living trees, the social effects of machinery, and the history of industrialism. The child gains an impression of the importance of invention by building a cotton gin, and learns to work cooperatively by constructing a shed. As the child draws on paper, or as he dabbles with mud and clay, he fulfills the urge to express and create (Dewey, 1916, pp. 194–206; Dworkin, 1959, pp. 76–88; Mayhew & Edwards, 1966, pp. 40–41).

Dewey was at the center of formulating what eventually became known as "interaction/developmental psychology." The child learns best through the interaction with his environment and the meaning he constructs and reconstructs through experience. Whiffs of Locke can be detected as well as traces of pragmatism. At the same time, the experiences included in the curriculum correspond to the various maturation stages of the child so he is exposed to learning that is not only interesting but appropriate to a given development stage. Understanding of the child was placed at the center of curriculum work (Kliebard, 1987).

Concepts of interaction/developmental psychology were applied in various permutations to feed different strands of thinking. The Swiss psychologists, Jean Piaget, for example, conducted experimental work on development tasks of children; Maria Montessori established a play school for children "to liberate" them from ridged, outmoded pedagogy; and Marietta Johnson, a former teacher from Minnesota, started the Organic School in Fairhope on Mobile

Bay that put into practice the idea that formal studies follow from activities and occupations. Few fully accepted and applied Dewey's ideas in total, but educators all over the county used "bits and pieces" of the progressive mantra to guide changes they thought made instruction more sensitive to how children learn. Elements of interaction/developmental psychology continue to be represented in what today is referred to a "cognitive psychology."

The Herbartians and Instruction

Dewey's ideas found support among the Herbartians. Americans interested in reforming elementary education popularized the work of German philosopher Johann Friedrich Herbart (1776–1841). Herbart studied under the Swiss educator Pestalozzi, but he wanted to formulate a more complete theoretical framework depicting how learning takes place. His ideas appealed to Americans and they selectively interpreted and reinterpreted key concepts, adding their own contributions. The McMurry brothers, Frank and Charles, at Illinois State Normal University, and Charles DeGarmo, president of Swarthmore College, were leading advocates and played a major role in the formation of the Herbartian Society.

The Herbartians were zealots (Krug, 1964, p. 100), and the sheer intensity of their reform efforts attracted national attention. Their ideas sparked debate, with two major doctrines introduced: interest and correlation. Student interest was considered the primary motivating force and direction-setter for determining what to teach. Correlation was the means through which instruction could best be organized. The work of the Herbartians also contributed to discrediting the doctrine of mental discipline with a new conception of learning.

Herbart supported the Pestalozzian idea that learning takes place through sense impressions, thus in American eyes placing him in the school of interaction/developmental psychology alongside Dewey. Herbart thought that the mind is a *tabula rasa* (blank slate) at birth that is filled with meaning as the young encounter successive experiences. The acquisition of knowledge, and emotional and intellectual impressions take place through a process of what he termed building up "apperception." New sense impressions are absorbed into the mass of understanding already in the mind to create new understanding. It follows that the best learning environment is many-sided and filled with rich experiences. Learning, however, cannot be haphazard but must be carefully planned and carried out so that students can absorb impressions from the greater world in an orderly way that facilitates absorption into the existing apperceptive mass (Curtis & Boultwood, 1965, pp. 355–368). For his American disciples, this can be achieved in several ways.

Learning best occurs when new ideas are presented in the context of already familiar ideas. Impressions with no contextual grounding are not readily absorbed. Correlation is the predominant way of controlling the presentation of learning experiences to provide contextual grounding . Correlation applies to relating elements in the various courses in the program to each other, as well as relating the content within each course (Kliebard, 1987 Krug, 1964). How can correlation best be approached?

One of the most enduring contributions of the American Herbartians is the lesson plan. They believed that the lesson plan provided the teacher with the means of correlating instruction in a way that ensured the assimilation of new ideas to old. Five steps were elaborated: First, "Preparation" involves student revision of old knowledge to make sure the relation to new knowledge can be understood. The context of learning is clarified. Second, "Presentation" entails the teacher presenting new facts, knowledge, and experiences. "Association" engages the student in comparing and contrasting the old learning with the new. Fourth, "Generalization" involves the recapitulation or review of what is learned and making conclusions about its wider significance. The "Application, " the fifty step. presents the opportunity of demonstrating learning by using the new skill or knowledge in different ways to solve problems (Curtis & Boultwood, 1965, p. 361).

Lesson plans in modified form are widely used today. The advanced planning helps to ensure a smooth and cogent lesson. But even in their day, teachers tended to fall back on a predefined, somewhat ridged, linear, and hierarchically organized plan counter to the spirit of learning as a highly individualistic, open, interesting, imaginative, and creative process of gaining insight and meaning. Lesson plans relate well to lockstep, group instruction, but not to more individualistic and open schemes that have students working at their own pace on different activities. Codification loses flexibility. Also, today lesson plans tend to be used more as a management tool to help administrators to gauge whether or not teachers are following predetermined curricula.

G. Stanley Hall and Child Psychology

The educational influence of Granville Stanley Hall spans both sides of the turn of the century. This was a time when psychological concepts of teaching and learning came to the fore. Hall contended he was an experimentalist, so in the minds of some his work fit nicely with that of individuals like Edward L. Thorndike who were attempting to build a more "scientific" educational foundation. Advocates for social efficiency considered him one of theirs. Hall also was a developmentalist, and his work in child behavior helped to put the word "development" in the rapidly evolving branch of interaction/developmental psychology. Progressives also identified with Hall. He loosely affiliated with the Herbartians and Parker and Dewey, but Hall was highly unorthodox in his behavior and thinking so he tended to promote dissention in a period characterized by dissent.

After being highly influential, Hall's primitivistic conception of the stages of human development lost favor. John Dewey, for example, was initially influenced by Hall, but later moved away from his ideas. Reflecting the influence of Darwin, Hall concluded that the development of the human race mirrored evolutionary development, so that the child was considered to be at the primitive, savage evolutionary stage. He was fond of quoting "ontogeny, the development of the individual organism, recapitulates phylogeny, the evolution of the race." He thought curricula were best structured so that subject matter corresponded to each of the stages.

The "culture-epochs theory" applied to curricula thus gave educators a way to select and organize instruction. Studies for little children revolved around the time of primitive man, for older children the Native Indians, and so on to "modern" man. This idea generated an immediate challenge among those that rejected the assertion that the biological nature of the child reflected the primitive past. Hall's ideas were counter to what biology and anthropology were finding. But at the same time, as an alternative educators were motivated to look to the cultural environment rather than the anthropological past as a curriculum influence.

Hall also brooked dissent through what can only be termed fascist ideas: individualism was socially damaging and had to give way to totalitarian, collective ideals; the best education is that which makes obedient servants to the state; and instruction in school should aim at indoctrination. Diversity should not be tolerated. Schooling for girls should be separate from boys; the laggards and dullards should be kept out of school. By giving help to the poor, sick, and defective, Hall contended, the "wholesome" natural selection process through which the race is improved is disrupted. And he extolled the virtues of aggressiveness, virility, and patriotism (Cremin, 1961; Karier, 1967; Kliebard, 1986).

The work of Hall, nevertheless, continues to have lasting influence. He was founder of the American Psychological Association, cofounder of educational psychology and the child study movement, which evolved into the field of child psychology, and he almost single-handed destroyed the creditability of the *Report* of the Committee of Ten and thus opened the way for the development of the comprehensive high school. His work in child development considerably helped to shift teaching focus to the student. His study of adolescent psychology produced lasting results.

Hall and the Committee of Ten

Kliebard (1987 p. 13) suggested Hall was the most powerful critic of the work of the Committee of Ten. The struggle over the conclusions of the committee went on for almost two decades after the turn of the century because the stakes were so high. Rejection of the *Report* meant rejection of several hundred years of educational domination by the classicists, invalidating the doctrine of mental discipline, relegating time-honored subjects to lower status, and radically altering the composition of faculties. It meant the eventual loss of jobs, which happened. In 1900, Latin and Greek teachers outnumbered the combined number of all other teachers in secondary schools. By 1920, Greek teachers had almost disappeared from school halls and only a handful of straggling Latin teachers remained.

Hall's arguments were based on his perception of the characteristics of the future school population. They were not going to be from the upper classes. Three "extraordinary fallacies," Hall observed, blinded the committee's judgment. First was the mistaken belief that all students should study the same thing in the same way for the same amount of time regardless of the background and probable destination of the student. This simply was not true, said Hall. Eventually the public high school would be faced with the "great army of incapables, shading down to those who should be in schools for the dullards or subnormal children." How was a curriculum designed for college preparatory purposes going to address this fact? The high school enrollment in the future will become so varied that a curriculum of common studies for all is not workable (Hall, 1904, p. 510).

Second, even when taught well, all subjects are not of equal value for all students. Hall pointed out mental discipline advocates believe that it is the form of the subject that is important because it embodies the disciplinary value of instruction, such as endless memorization of ancient Greek verbs. Hall argued that content was most important; and it had to be specialized and varied. This is what the aspiring engineer, accountant, mechanic, beet farmer, clerk, or surveyor needed. And the third fallacy was the doctrine that fitting for college was the same as fitting for life. The two were different, said Hall. The *Report* was only a way for the Committee to enforce college domination on the high school curriculum (1904, p. 511).

His arguments were overpowering. Charles Eliot, chair of the Committee of Ten and president of Harvard, attempted to refute Hall. His major argument was the observation that the committee already considered: the resistance of parents and the difficulty of creating a differentiated curriculum that sorted students into different fields of study. How could this be done equitably or even in practical terms? Any sorting into different fields of study automatically limited future social and occupational options of students. The American public, argued Elliot (1905), does not want "its children sorted before their teens into clerks, watchmakers, lithographers, telegraph operators, masons, teamsters, farm laborers, and so forth, and treated differently in their schools according to those prophecies of their appropriate life careers. Who are to make these prophecies?" (pp. 330–301). A single curriculum concentrating on college preparation was better. But his argument that the Committee of Ten provided the best option could not gain traction.

The clash between Hall and Eliot put in stark terms the challenge advocates of a more differentiated curriculum had to address before they could fully advance the case for school reform. Any time a course of differentiated studies is followed by individual student groups there has to be a functional and equitable way to sort that is acceptable to student and parent alike. At the turn of the century this did not exist. It was assumed that all students studied the same thing at the same time in the same way, but education reformers from Parker and Dewey to Herbart, Hall, and Thorndike brought into focus individual differences that were essential to address. Increasingly, it was no longer possible to ignore home backgrounds, aspirations, interests, and achievement differences. But how could students be sorted? At the time there was no good answer.

Hall, Development Tasks, and Adolescence

His work with adolescent psychology probably is what Hall is most remembered for. By the turn of the century considerable interest was developing in the possible dimensions of the differentiated instructional program of the high school, but Hall observed there was little effort to understand the psychology of adolescence. Educators focused on the kind of subject matter to include, but gave almost no attention to the nature, needs, and interests of high school students. Teachings methods lacked an understanding of adolescence and overlooked completely in instruction the moral values essential for bringing up adolescents.

Hall recognized what he termed distinct development stages, each with distinct development tasks to be attained. These were defined periods of human development, such as childhood and adolescence, that indicated not only appropriate content but also teaching strategies. Hall thought that high school studies could be best defined through knowledge of the requisite development tasks appropriate for adolescence. He was close to Herbart's doctrine of interest. The idea of development tasks was widely adopted and has remained in the intellectual toolkit of educators for the last hundred years.

Hall achieved national recognition as the leading authority on adolescent psychology with his publication *Adolescence* in 1904, a fifteen-hundred-page work. Not all was praise. A leading educator, Charles Judd, for example, observed that there was "so much mythology" in Hall's book that it was not surprising that educators could not follow what he presented (Krug, 1964, p. 121).

Nevertheless, Hall was treading on ground that few dared to follow: conditions of adolescent sexuality. A major contribution was sensitizing teachers to what can be a period of trauma in the lives of youth. Adolescents experience a period of great psychological stress, Hall counseled. They must come to terms with their own sexuality, form a coherent value structure, find an identity among peers, and discern their relationship to the adult world. How can high school teachers best cope with inevitable problems that arise from this stress?

He formulated a practical answer that had a profound impact on high school studies: sublimation. School experiences had to be included that provided ways to enable the sexual energy of youth to be channeled into constructive, acceptable forms of behavior. This was to be a primarily unconscious process, Hall counseled (Curti, 1959). One major way, for example, was through sports. All of the pent-up sexual energy of youth is simply dissipated. Clubs, bake sales, art contests, band, school government, cross-country running, theater groups—these and other activities provided constructive ways to give expression to the restless energy of youth while at the same time helping them form constructive relationship with peers. Educators used Hall's ideas to call for a radical reformulation of high school studies.

What was Hall's legacy? Hall gave great importance to physical health, and his shadow is evident on the playing fields, running tracks, courts, and bleachers spread throughout American schools. He provided a psychological reason to have sports, clubs, assemblies, and other activities in schools. He did important pioneering work in the field of child psychology. The idea of development stages continues to be important. And almost alone among educators he brought out in the open the importance of sex as a factor of human behavior and discussed it in frank terms.

Social Efficiency in Education

In 1901, Edward A. Ross, a sociologist, brought out his book, *Social Control*, in which he expanded on the conditioning of individual behavior to conform to the group. This was essential for the stability of society, Ross argued, and schools were the best institutions for producing in children the essential kinds of behaviors and beliefs consistent with the requirements for society's welfare. In the new age, asserted Ross, education replaced religion "as the method of indirect social restraint." The idea of the school as an agent of social control dovetailed nicely with the concept of social efficiency. An efficient society was a society that had the means to exert control over its citizens. Educators quickly fell into line with what Ross was saying. Schools could produce responsible citizens by focusing on the selection and shaping of individuals along socially constructive lines.

The efficiency movement caused, in the words of Cremin (1961), a fundamental "transformation of the school" from an institution formerly employed primarily to cultivate intellectual ability to one focused on mass education designed to fit individuals into productive social and economic roles. Joel Spring (2008) observed social efficiency in education meant three things: (1) sorting students according to their probable life destinies, (2) providing the experiences to develop appropriate social skills, and (3) developing the skills and knowledge students require to become productive adults. A fourth can also be added—applying appropriate tools to classroom and school management.

All social and educational movements need intellectual arguments to support their actions. Ross gave educators a sociological argument to support radical, transforming changes.

The emerging field of psychology also provided powerful arguments, and educators could immediately identify with them because they applied directly to teaching and learning. Among the most important work in educational psychology was that of Edward L. Thorndike. He gave school reformers intellectual tools that they could use to support the idea of social efficiency.

Conditioning and Control: Thorndike

Edward Lee Thorndike was a brilliant student of William James at Harvard. As a professor at Teachers College, Columbia University, Thorndike with his graduate students embarked on numerous experimental studies that earned him a place as the "Father of Educational Psychology." His output was prodigious: 50 books and 450 monographs and articles over his academic lifetime. He used the quantifying methods of the physical and natural sciences and applied them to fact-finding, and to statistical and experimental work in education. He was an evolutionist, believing in the supremacy of genetic inheritance, but at the same time like the pragmatists William James, his mentor, and John Dewey he believed in the capacity of society to improve itself. His work extended to problems of heredity, eugenics, learning processes, and individual differences in addition to mental tests, educational measurement, child study, adult learning, scientific management, and educational administration among many other interests. Thousands of graduate students worked under him, and hundreds of thousands of educational practitioners were exposed to his ideas. He had immense influence throughout his 50-year career (Curti, 1959; Karier, 1967).

His 1901 paper with Robert Woodward on the transfer of training quickly thrust him into the national spotlight. They experimentally tested the assumption that the learning of one subject, such as ancient Greek or Latin, had a positive effect on the subsequent learning of other knowledge because of the general intellectual improvement achieved. The argument of the classicists was that through the study of Greek and Latin and other such "difficult" subjects, mental ability was strengthened. It was alleged the power of the newly developed intellectual ability was transferred to the learning of other subjects, facilitating better overall learning and enhancing "general intelligence." This did not occur, Thorndike and Woodward found. Ability in one subject is specific to that subject and does not have transfer value except as there are "identical elements," that is, learning that can be used in a direct way: the learning of Latin was good for lawyers, but not for plumbers. Thorndike and Woodward added yet another element in the growing body of dissent that eventually destroyed the idea of mental discipline.

This work was significant; it opened the way for providing multiple courses of study in the school. Learning was valued for its specific content, and not for some alleged general value in improving mental ability. The classicist's argument for the premiere place of Greek, Latin, and other "superior" subjects in the school curriculum was directly undercut. To advocates of social efficiency, a subject had to prove its utilitarian value, and the alleged idea of mental disciplinary value was found lacking. Advocates of social efficiency pressed for a differentiated curriculum with specific courses to address the career goals of students and more directly address employer demand.

Thorndike's work on learning theory aided the advocates of social efficiency in additional ways. Thorndike and his graduate students embarked on formulating concepts that would evolve into what was later termed "behavioral psychology." Probably inspired by the work of the Russian physiologist Pavlov in training dogs to respond to the stimulus of bell ringing, Thorndike undertook studies related to human conditioning and developed a theory he termed "connectionism." According to Thorndike, stimulus/response (S-R) bonds are formed from the application of a specific stimulus strengthened by positive reinforcement. He formulated the "law of exercise" to explain the effect of repetitions on the strengthening of neurobiological connections (S-R bonds), and the "law of effect" to establish the value of rewards and punishment on the reinforcement of behavior. In this way, he gave educators a mechanistic approach to instruction that included establishing behavioral objectives, structuring appropriate teaching strategies, and measuring outcomes. By manipulating the instructional inputs to establish S-R bonds, desired outcomes could be realized. In other words, instruction could be used to shape student behavior in the direction of desirable, predetermined ends. Social efficiency advocates were delighted.

Educators could quantify outcomes to judge the effectiveness of instruction and gauge the ability of students. It was just a short step to quantify data on student performance and turn it into measures of student mental ability. The concept of IQ was formulated to use as a sorting device among students.

The establishment of a justification for sorting students was aided by Thorndike's social beliefs. As an avowed evolutionist, he believed that heredity is the determining factor in the intellectual and social behavior of humans. There are innate and inherited qualities that condition the ability to learn. According to Thorndike, these qualities vary by social class and ethnicity, but they are invariant. They remain fundamentally fixed throughout life. The rich were rich because they were more intelligent and moral, and ethnic differences in intelligence conformed to a relative placement on the genetic scale. "Racial differences," he declared, "are not mere myths" (Thorndike, 1911, p. 40).

Whites obviously are on the top. He did not believe in equal educational opportunity. The gifted at the top should be given priority, and in fact, it is dangerous to think that the lack of ability could be overcome through education. He opposed the idea of universal public education and compulsory school and attendance laws. He believed education should be distributed so "those who can use it best have the most of it" (Curti, 1959, p. 485).

His impact on the shaping of American schools was considerable. He gave educators a justification for the differentiation of school subjects and the sorting of students, and with his major role in the testing movement and service on national committees to formulate testing instruments, gave them the tools they needed. Educators applied the doctrine of behavioral psychology as the major way to shape studies to achieve what were considered outcomes of efficiency; he introduced school administrators to efficient ways to manage schools, and he played a role in the scientific management movement in both business and education. He exposed hundreds of thousands of school practitioners to ideas on how to teach students that persist to the present. "Thorndike, perhaps more than any other single individual, helped standardize, and structure American education in the twentieth century" (Karier, 1967, p. 176).

At the same time, Thorndike projected the values of his own White middle-class background and he had a hard time seeing beyond them; he gave the politicians, business people, and power brokers what they wanted to hear: Status in life, wealth, intelligence, morality, and genes were positively correlated. And his views on the genetic heredity of class and ethnicity, his disdain for the underclass, his distaste of immigrants and opposition to immigration, and his embrace of eugenics made him a partner to some of the worse ugliness in America. "One must question to what extent his social opinions are truly related, scientifically, to his experimental work, and to what extent they are determined by his own unconscious participation in the prejudices of our own time" (Curti, 1959, p. 498).

Efficiency, Teaching, and the Administration of Schools

Twentieth-century education was shaped by the concept of social efficiency, and nowhere is this more evident than in the organization and management of schools. By the turn of the century there was a new generation of educators that faced the challenge of absorbing great numbers of children into already crowded schools. Many of these children were from the working class, and many were immigrants recently off the boats bringing thousands to the port cities, but both groups of children came to school poor, dirty, and unfamiliar with the middle-class ways of teachers. These were a motley group that not only had to be taught but managed. School administrators turned to the practices of business to build systems of hierarchically managed schools. They also borrowed ideas of measurement and management from Thorndike and others.

Raymond Callahan (1962), in *Education and the Cult of Efficiency*, detailed the building of school systems patterned on the corporate model. The board of education mirrors the corporate board of directors; the superintendent of schools is analogous to the CEO of a corporation with various attending, centralized, lower-level officers; individual school principals and local school officers are similar to division heads and managers; school counselors and others perform local unit functions; the teachers are the workers and the students the product. Such organizing schemes, however, tend to support top-heavy bureaucratic structures that focus primarily on maintaining control and standardization; that tend to lack innovative capacity; and that shun creativity and individual initiative outside of the organizational framework. The driving force behind bureaucratic inertia tends to be the preservation of the status quo and the protection of power relationships and jobs.

David Tyack and Elisabeth Hansot (1982) pointed out that educational administrators of the time did not consciously set out to be servants of the corporate model, but rather they were "emulators of the most successful models of the age-businessmen" (p. 114). Schoolmen had little experience in managing ever-enlarging school systems that involved the expenditure of large sums of public money. They turned to the best source of experience that they could find.

School administration was professionalized, with colleges offering courses and degrees in educational administration. Aspiring administrators were exposed to ideas of social efficiency, of management, and the work of Frederick Taylor; and they learned to use tools of measurement: tests, rating scales, and surveys to gauge the efficiency of school organization and classroom practice. By the end of the first decade, educators were constructing tests to measure student progress ranging from handwriting and arithmetic to language use. Rating scales were constructed to gauge the "efficiency" of teachers and administrators. Teachers were judged on such factors as intellectual capacity, voice, self-control, understanding of children, neatness of room, moral influence, and growth of pupils in subject matter. Administrators were rated on such factors as capacity for leadership, sense of justice, cooperativeness and loyalty, care of the school environment (light, heat, ventilation), and so on to the management of play and athletics and helpfulness to teachers in discipline. Typically the results were quantified to produce "scientific findings." "Student efficiency scores" were based on surveys eliciting responses to such items as "Do you read a newspaper?" "Do you have a regular schedule for study?" "Do you read at least one book a month?" and "Do you always use clean language?" Rating scales were even developed to gauge the efficiency of the school janitor (Callahan, 1962).

It did not take long for efficiency measures to be converted into costs. Superintendent Frank Spaulding of the Newton, Massachusetts, schools led the efforts to put education on a cost-analysis basis. By using "measures of quality," Spaulding asserted, comparisons can be made not only between schools but also between the different subjects taught. And quality was the basis of determining school effectiveness. But Spaulding skipped over the fact that what he meant by "quality" was actually cost effectiveness.

To determine quality Spaulding relied on two factors. First, the relative unit cost of instruction is calculated by determining such related factors as number of students per class, number of classes taught, numbers of students completing, and teacher salary. The yield is the unit cost of teaching one student, for one class period for each kind of subject in the school. To this, Spaulding figured what he referred to as the cost of one "student recitation." He found, for example, 23.5 student recitations could be given in French to 5.9 in Greek for the same cost. French classes were obviously a better educational investment, and of course in Spaulding's eye, better value, and thus represented greater quality and efficiency. He took the next logical step of increasing class sizes and the number of classes per day taught by each teacher to yield greater value. "His scientific determination of *educational value* turned out to be a determination of *dollar value*" (Callahan, 1962, p. 73). Nevertheless, educators over the country hailed his brilliance as they applied a similar calculus to programming decisions.

Franklin Bobbitt, instructor in educational administration at the University of Chicago, pushed Spaulding's ideas on efficiency in a different direction. He promoted the use of standards to measure efficiency of classroom instruction. Industry used production standards, and it was only reasonable that standards be applied to measure expected instructional results. For example, it was possible to set up a standard for students to add at a rate of 65 combinations per minute, at an accuracy of 94%. Scales were established to not only record the extent to which students in each class attained the standards, but also the time that it took. Teachers were rated accordingly (Callahan, 1962, pp. 79–83). Bobbitt had lasting impact on American education as witnessed by the No Child Left Behind legislation and Core Standards movement.

Human Capital, Meritocracy, and Social Efficiency

Elements of school change promoted by the efficiency movement also appealed to progressives because they, too, were motivated by the idea of building school programs that more closely addressed the interests of a varied student population, that had direct application to the lives of youth, and that were functional. The ideas of developmental tasks, of maturation, and recognizing human differences were part of the progressive educators beliefs. But there were important differences with the advocates of social efficiency. There developed among efficiency advocates a strong conviction that the fundamental purpose of public education is its contribution to the development of human capital. Repeating what Robert Molesworth and the Commonwealth Men stressed in the 1730s, the arguments Benjamin Franklin made to support the founding of academies, and the insights of vocational educators when they challenged the classical curriculum, efficiency advocates called for a refocusing of the purpose of American education to concentrate on "life needs." They were convinced the emerging industrial society in America required a new kind of schooling that promotes social welfare and economic advancement through the development of human capital. In the next two decades, the high school was shaped to this end, and human capital development became a controlling objective of public education at all levels up to the present.

A companion of the idea of human capital development is meritocracy. Efficiency advocates argued that by using the test instruments developed by Thorndike and others a more equitable society resulted. This is the vision of a society that is "scientifically" managed, with social sorting accomplished through "objective" measures of human intellectual capacity, and with trust placed in the hands of the most capable. In schools a cadre of professional administrators take charge in the sorting and management of future human resources. Rather than family wealth or poverty, position in society, or family connections, student programming is based on "merit," that is, test results and academic progress. Merit is manifested through the apparent match of individual characteristics and ability with occupational requirements.

Both the ideas of human capital development and meritocracy are fundamental to the larger umbrella concept of social efficiency. Both progressives and those more inclined toward control functions of education spoke in terms of social efficiency. Both a Dewey or a Thorndike were struggling with managing the dimensions of a disruptive society grappling with the little understood forces of urbanization and industrialization, and both looked to schools as a means of stabilizing the conflicted social and economic environment. Both spoke of reform, but progressives tended to use the language of social and economic justice, maximizing human opportunity and rehabilitating democracy; efficiency advocates tended to speak in terms of social control, budgets, limits on individual potential, and conformity to the norms of the group. Both, nevertheless, drew heavily from the reconstruction and control aspects of efficiency, even if indirectly, so that in the eyes of less discriminating educators the two positions appeared to be part of the same parcel of education for social efficiency. A combined assault was mounted on more academic subject content in favor of promoting social purposes of education.

In the two decades after the turn of the century, social efficiency manifested itself through formal systems to prepare and certify teachers. School administrators were formally trained, and became part of the hierarchical system of school management. And there was a proliferation of different kinds of courses preparing students in vocational, technical, scientific, business, and agricultural fields. A "counseling and guidance" function was added to schools. Students were tested, sorted, and trained for placement in jobs "appropriate" to their probable "life destiny." Concerted efforts were made to bring children of immigrants and the underclass into the fold of public education. The junior high was added to the school mix to catch students that might continue for a few years beyond elementary grades but would not go on to the high school. Arguments over the purpose and structure of secondary education were brought to a conclusion with the formation of the comprehensive high school. These changes are the subject of Chapter Thirteen.

Chapter Thirteen
The Transition: Formation of the High School

The social efficiency movement reflects the late 19th- and early 20th-century interests of businessmen, manufacturers, and industrialists to make education more functional. It is seen in the challenge to the classical curriculum; the achievement of the Land Grand Act; in college majors and minors in agriculture, business and engineering; in manual training; and in the debates over the function and purpose of high schools. After the turn of the century, its clearest manifestation is in the vocational education movement to put more technical, scientific, business, and agriculture subjects in schools. Nonvocational subjects such as history also took on new character with emphasis on the development of good citizens. High school studies took on a functional cast.

The high school became the focus of change not only because of the increase in the sheer number of attending pupils, but also because the character of the high school population itself was rapidly changing. The increases in enrollment alone commanded national attention. There were around 200,000 high school students enrolled in 1890, with more than a doubling by 1900 to over 500,000, and a doubling again to over 1,000,000 by 1910 (Krug, 1964, p. 169). These were hard economic times, but more children of the working class were filling high school classrooms. Perhaps parents stuck in poverty thought that this was the best way out for their children. Urbanization also made schools available to more young people; schools were within physical reach. The increase continued, so by 1920 there was a doubling of enrollments again to over 2,000,000 students and more than a doubling again by 1930 to 4,399,422 students. High school enrollment in 1920 comprised 28% of the youth population (age 14 to 17), and by 1930, 47%. An annual average of 7,000 new classrooms a year was required in the years from 1920 to 1930 (Krug, 1972, p. 42).

The issue of providing subject realignment to address the growing high school population became a dominant concern. The report of the Committee of Ten assumed high schools prepared most attendees to go on to college, when in fact few students in the swelling high school population would ever continue on to higher education, even if they completed. The significant increase in high school enrollment signaled a fundamental shift in purpose from an institution serving an elite population to one providing mass education functional in character. Hall detected this change early.

The classicists knew they were fighting a losing battle. For example, Charles Eliot, chair of the Committee of Ten and president of Harvard, reversed his position four years after his debate with Hall. Probably in reaction to the efficiency movement, he declared in 1908 that he now favored the sorting of children in the elementary school years into their "probable destinies." He acknowledge that manual training had been a step in the right direction, but he urged the establishment of trade schools to prepare youth of the future working class for "a life of skilled manual labor." He advocated, however, keeping intact the classical curriculum for those students "destined" to go on to college. Eliot was fighting a rear guard battle to preserve what he could of the humanist perspective. A partial loaf was better than none (Kliebard, 1987, p. 123).

The Vocational Education Movement

The question of "real vocational education" was thrust into public view with the formulation by Governor William L. Douglass in 1905 of the Massachusetts Commission on Industrial and Technical Education. Manual training was no longer considered a viable option for workforce preparation. Calvin Woodward had linked manual training to the concept of mental discipline rooted in faculty psychology, but Thorndike, Hall, Dewey, and others were rapidly dismantling the concept. The newer generation of youth needed "real" vocational education, businessmen and educators agreed. The commission comprised of nine representatives from manufacturing, agriculture, education, and labor had two objectives: (1) investigate the trained labor needs of the Commonwealth, and (2) suggest ways of implementing work preparation programs in state schools. It was significant to the work of the commission that Susan M. Kingsbury, a sociologist, was a consultant. She turned the *Report of the Commission* into a document of national interest (Bennett, 1937; *Report*, 1906).

Five major themes were presented in the *Report*. First, the villain behind child labor and early school leaving was the school itself because it did not offer subjects of a practical character. Children leave school to work because of the dissatisfaction with offerings. They see little value in them. Second, industry no longer wants child labor, and thrives better with an educated workforce. By Kingsbury's estimate, there were 25,000 youth age 14 to 16 in Massachusetts laboring in low-skilled, low-paying jobs from which there was no escape. They were locked for life into a disadvantaged labor market position by their lack of education. Third, men and women of the laboring poor, those in "intimate contact with the harder side of life," want the opportunity of work preparation in schools for their children. Earlier and greater efficiency as wage earners can be developed, self-reliance and self-respect fostered, and "steadier habits of industry and frugality can be promoted," said Kingsbury. Fourth, more technically skilled workmen are needed in Massachusetts. Skilled labor shortages result in the deterioration of product quality, reduced productivity, and the inability to compete in markets. Fifth, and importantly, preparation for work should be integrated into public schools. The elementary school curriculum should be modified to include instruction in "productive industry, agriculture, and the mechanical and domestic arts." A significant change was recommended at the secondary level. A system of separate and independent industrial schools should be developed and administered apart from the "regular" public schools (*Report*, 1906).

The Douglass Commission worked fast. A special permanent Commission on Industrial Education was established in 1909 to put form to the recommendations, and the administrative structure of the state was reorganized. David Snedden from Columbia University was appointed commissioner along with two assistant commissioners: Clarence Kingsley for general education and Charles Prosser for vocational education. The three went about developing a comprehensive system of vocational schools in Massachusetts parallel to "academic" schools.

The Douglass Commission was a propelling force behind the national vocational education movement. For example, inspired by the findings, James Parton Haney, director of art and manual training in the New York City schools, and Charles Richards, professor of manual training at Teachers College, Columbia University, founded the National Society for the Promotion of Industrial Education (NSPIE). Its avowed purpose was to secure state and federal funding for industrial education. Extra funding, according to Haney and Richards, was essential to counter critics of workforce preparation programs who argued that vocational education did not belong in public-supported schools. The academic purpose of schooling would be tainted. But the argument that probably was most influential was cost. Vocational and science subjects are among the most costly to support. Class sizes are restricted and equipment and maintenance costs high. The strategy of the NSPIE was to secure public state and federal financial support to offset high potential local costs. Critics would be neutralized.

The NSPIE was political and effective. It cast its net wide to generate nationwide support. It secured Theodore Roosevelt's hearty approval. The officers and board members included representatives from leading corporations and labor unions; representatives from the Carnegie Foundation, the National Association of Manufacturers and the settlement movement; Andrew Carnegie approvingly gave his support. The venerable Calvin Woodard was a member. David Snedden played a major leadership role within the NSPIE and managed to color the organization's activities with his own philosophy of social efficiency.

The NSPIE was effective. By 1910, twenty-nine states passed legislation to aid or empower local communities to establish industrial education programs. In the same year, the National Educational Association came out in support of industrial education. The American Federation of Labor joined in support. Taylorism and the efficiency craze also reach a peak in 1910. More efficient workers could be produced was the theme spread about the country. The movement to put "real vocational" in public schools was strongly underway and could not be stopped.

Laggards, Immigrants, and the Junior High School

The junior high school was one early outcome of the vocation education movement. Educators were alarmed by what they considered an increasing number of "laggards" attending public schools. These were students who formerly would not have attended school, but now they were coming in larger numbers but encountered discouragement and failure. They could not keep up with the pace of lockstep instruction that required all students to follow and complete the same material in the same time. There were great differences in backgrounds, language use, and in exposure to the written material and home enrichment, not to mention poverty and living conditions. The concept of grouping students for instructional purposes was not practiced except by those teachers aware of the methods of the "New Education" carried over from the turn of the century.

Leonard Ayers documented in his 1909 study, *Laggards in Our Schools*, the high rate of retardation and failure in schools, affirming what teachers and parents already knew. The tendency among city schools was to keep all students enrolled until the fifth grade, carry one half of the remaining to eighth grade, and promote a tenth of the remaining to high school. The rate for repeating grades was high. Schools were filled with overage, "retarded" students. Ayres estimated 33% of all pupils were laggards. Any notion of efficiency was thwarted.

The worry was that the children dropping out of school were the very ones that educators wanted to stay. Without the benefits of schooling, they would become the incorrigibles, the criminals, and the social dissenters of society. But surprising, nationally there was little differences in attendance rates among White children of native parents and White children of immigrants. David Tyack, however, suggested this is probably due to minimal schooling for Whites in the South (1974, p. 242).

Achievement levels varied among immigrant groups. A 1909 a Senate study found among pupils two years or more behind grade level, South Italian and Polish were the most retarded: 63.6% and 58.1% of the respective students. These were pupils from non-English-speaking families; and not surprising for all nationalities from families who spoke English the "retardation" rate was lower. Age of arrival was important. Children immigrating before age 6 had a retardation rate of 43.5%, in contrast to a retardation rate of 91.8% among children arriving after age 10 or over. Poverty correlated highly with school failure (Tyack, 1974, pp. 242–248).

Some immigrant groups resisted sending their children to school because it conflicted with long-held family values. Adherence to family authority, loyalty, hard work, and ethnic identity were thought more important than "book learnings" that only opened the mind to strange ideas and unrealistic aspirations. In school, immigrants often learned that they were "different." Some immigrant children were incorrigible, indifferent to instruction, crude in speech and behavior, and a source of constant irritation. Discipline was resisted. At the same time many immigrant children grasped learning as way to inclusion and upward mobility (Tyack, 1974).

How could children be attracted, managed, and retained in school? To educators, this was a fundamental challenge that had to be attended to in order to bring children under the beneficial influence and control of the school. Once in school, they had to be kept there. Susan Kingsbury of the Douglass Commission provided direction. More "practical work" could be put into the lower grades. Other educators picked up on this suggestion. Arts and crafts, drawing, Sloyd (a Swedish system of tool instruction popularized in the kindergarten), and "shop" in the form of manual arts and industrial arts became popular. Domestic arts programs were expanded for girls.

The elementary school program was modified in the sixth through eighth grades to include programs that were not only of more interest to immigrant pupils but addressed job training. Charles Prosser of the NSPIE suggested, for example, putting in the seventh and eighth grades "preparatory" courses in commercial and household arts for girls and practical arts for boys. Citing the influential Douglass report, Charles De Garmo went a step further: the design of a "junior industrial high school" for students prone to earlier dropout. Others suggested pre-apprenticeship or industrial work could be provided in a general intermediate school encompassing the seventh, eighth, and ninth grades.

By 1910, individual schools began including a "dual" academic/vocational program in grades 5 to 8, and at the same time the idea of a separate junior high school quickly gained national attention. By 1912, in Los Angeles there were five of these three-year intermediate schools with three courses of study: general, commercial and elementary industrial. Soon the new three-year school spread across the country (Krug, 1964).

The junior high school was separate from both the elementary and high school, and it was largely considered a terminal program for students that otherwise dropped out early. The practical subjects were thought to have more appeal as well as value for potential jobs. It was also concluded that since immigrants lacked high intelligence, "manual work" was more suitable. Educators pointed out to immigrant parents that if their children did not drop out in the elementary grades and stayed for a few more years in school they would have considerably more earning power in the labor market. To counter the need expressed by parents that their children had to go to work early to help support family needs, schools started providing cooperative work experience programs. A student spent half a day in school studies, and the other half in a paying job placement.

The junior high school provided general education and skill training, and the job placement gave work experience and pay. Susan Kingsbury's concern was addressed that five sixths of all public school pupils never progressed beyond the seventh or eighth grades and lacked any kind of vocational preparation. Critics, nevertheless, continued to argue the vocationalization of the junior high school seriously eroded other social objectives. For this age group there was a need to emphasize "common" subjects (Krug, 1964, pp. 329–335).

David Snedden and Vocational Education

Educators pressing for the inclusion of vocational education in the high school encountered two issues: first, how to efficiently sort students into specialized programs; and second, determining the relationship of vocational education to the broader spectrum of other school studies. To what extent, for example, should vocational students engage in the study of history and music, or biology and geometry similar to nonvocational students, and should this work be pursued independently or with nonvocational students? As we saw in Part Three, Horace Mann, Henry Barnard, and other early common school reformers advanced the case for public-financed education on the grounds that in pluralistic America there had to be a way to provide common educational experiences. Earlier Noah Webster made a similar case, and Frank Ward in *Dynamic Sociology* did the same. How can an education common to all Americans be provided but at the same time still provide specialized vocational preparation?

David Snedden of Columbia University thought he had an answer and took the job to reconstruct the Massachusetts school system. Initially he had solid support from the business community and the Commission on Industrial Education. With Charles Prosser, his former student at Columbia as his assistant commissioner for vocational education, and Clarence Kingsley, an exceptional math teacher out of the New York City schools as his assistant commissioner for academics, they went about quickly dismantling the Massachusetts school system put into place by Horace Mann and replaced it with a dual system of vocational and academic education.

Snedden did not want vocational studies diluted with the academic, and thus less relevant and efficient. At the same time, there had to be common educational experiences. For Snedden, this could be accomplished through a common school for all up to the sixth grade. Beyond the sixth grade the dual system was best. Vocational education could be carried out in very specialized schools. In his view, quality vocational education had to be job specific and had three components: the general, technical, and practical. What was meant by "general" studies was narrowly conceived: "achievements of modern sanitation," the "history of metal working," and readings in "industrial cooperation," among many topics focused on industry, technology, and work. Studies such as math, science, and art had to be "intimately related with concrete practice." Snedden alleged he was reflecting Dewey's ideas related to the use of occupations (Snedden, 1910). But Snedden was way off the mark. Dewey considered the use of occupation as a means of enhancing learning, with little, if any skill training value.

Vocational studies focused on specific jobs: chicken farming, apple growing, streetcar and locomotive driving, tailoring, and metal machining among hundreds of other occupations. Training in each occupational cluster was provided in separate schools, ideally located near production facilities where students engaged in gaining practical experience through on-the-job placements (Snedden, 1910, pp. 37–41). The number grew from six state-aided vocational schools in 1908 to forty by 1912 and eighty-seven by 1916 when the dual system of separate academic and vocational schools was abandoned and Snedden was dismissed (Drost, 1967).

Snedden lost his job for two major reasons. He was successful, perhaps too successful. He was a very good administrator. Businessmen and taxpayers however learned quickly that the European dual system of vocational education that Snedden adopted with early student selection and differentiated studies was costly. The small, specialized schools with limited enrollment were expensive to establish and maintain. But also citizens highly objected to the way Snedden went about separating and selecting students for specialized training in the name of efficiency. His method and rationale was at the heart of public disenchantment.

According to Snedden, 2% to 4% of a given student cohort had the intellectual capacity to pursue work in the "traditional" academic studies leading to college. He was in basic agreement with Thorndike who put the figure at 4%. But even in the case of the bright, poor boy, Snedden thought it best that he not attempt an academic education because of the slim possibility of getting financial aid to pursue advanced studies. About 80% of a student population should pursue vocational education, Snedden urged, because it was the best fit with their abilities. These were sons and daughters of the "rank and file" that needed skill training and the development of their "cultural and social resources" to make them "good citizens."

Probably what was most unacceptable to the public, however, is how Snedden selected among the privileged and the rank and file. He preselected students by what he termed "case types" based on the parent's social and economic class, income level, occupational level, where they live, and although not overtly stated, ethnicity. Each case type related to a cluster of jobs. Students were assigned to a specific job category within a particular case type.

Snedden implemented a costly, static system of vocational education in Massachusetts. There was little room for social and economic mobility. The young stayed in jobs similar to their parents. His ideas reflected the class and ethnic distinctions Americans held at this time.

In this view, to improve society was to improve efficiency in the selection and preparation of individuals to take specific positions on the job scale. It also involved preparing individuals to accept their ordained position in life and exercise responsible citizenship. The rank and file student, Snedden assured the education public, if given "real vocational training" and education for "cultural and social resource," will be a "good citizen," well adapted and happy in his "life role" (1910). The rejection of Snedden's work and his dismissal were significant in two ways. First, Americans learned that they did not want the European kind of vocational preparation that separated students out early to follow highly specific job training. Vocational education, however, continued to be offered in the comprehensive high school up until the 1980s. Second, the scope of vocational education was limited and general. It was not possible to offer a comprehensive range of highly specific job preparation courses in a single school.

Federal Support: The Smith-Hughes Act

By the beginning of the second decade of the new century, industrial and vocational activities were the primary source of practical work in high schools. But programming was piecemeal and fragmented. Snedden's loosing struggle in Massachusetts to gain public acceptance caused educators to look elsewhere to promote the cause of vocational education. The considerable state momentum already underway was pressed forward to the national level in an effort to secure financial support. The NSPIE was the driving force in the eventual passage of the Smith-Hughes Act in 1917 to fund local vocational education. Supporting arguments were crafted in broad terms to appeal to a wide swath of constituencies.

Repeating an argument Susan Kingsbury made, first and foremost, federally funded vocational education can help to strengthen the economic competiveness of American industry, the educational public was told. Germany in particular was challenging the world economy through better production methods and better products. This challenge had to be met through a better-trained workforce. On the domestic front, individual communities and states are better economically positioned with a trained workforce.

A second argument aligned with the strengthening nativist movement. "American" boys and girls had to be protected from the increased workforce competition of immigrant children. It was alleged they brought skills from the "old country" and thus were better equipped and had a competitive labor market advantage. In addition, immigrant youth were willing to work for lower wages, which put American boys and girls at a competitive disadvantage unless they had superior work preparation.

An opposite argument was that immigrant children came to America unsuited to work in an industrial economy. They either had inappropriate attitudes or lacked skills. The escape from poverty required skill development through vocational education. It was also imperative to keep the immigrant and children of the underclass in school so they can be exposed to beneficial influences of education. Practical work did this.

Labor leaders were told it was to their advantage to join the movement for vocational education or else they would have no say in shaping the character of school programming. Manufacturers were told vocational education was the key to progress; agriculture interests were told there was common ground with urban school reformers; and home economic supporters were told their support was critical. A major argument that turned the tide for federal financial supports was the link to the war effort. Vocational education was vital to national defense. Skilled manpower was needed to build the machines of war (Fisher, 1967).

Together David Snedden and Charles Processor drafted a bill for the Commission on National Aid to Vocational Education, established by the U.S. Congress. It became in 1917 the National Vocation Education Act, better known as the "Smith-Hughes Act." The act did not blaze new trails. It confirmed much of what was going on about the country and removed the issue of cost. Federal funds were allotted to public school vocational programs of less than college grade in agriculture, home economics, and trades and industry. Later, support for business education and nursing was added. Federal funds picked up part of the cost of vocational subjects, and state or local communities absorbed the cost of any "general education" connected with the vocational program. Funding for schooling above the secondary level was not allowed because the intent was to prepare the "rank and file," not the "captains of industry."

The Smith-Hughes Act standardized vocational education along certain lines, and committed the movement to a craft-orientated instructional program. It also helped to generate the public perception that vocational education was primarily for lower ability students. Also a split among vocational education proponents was brought out in the open. David Snedden was elected president of the National Society for Vocational Education, the renamed NSPIE. He tried to impose his unacceptable idea of a dual system of vocational and academic schools on the movement. He lost the struggle with supporters of the idea of a comprehensive high school incorporating academic as well as practical studies. A system of vocational studies less "efficient" then Snedden wanted has been the mainstay of work preparation in the American high schools.

Shaping the High School

All the currents of early 20th-century educational change came together in the work of the Commission on the Reorganization of Secondary Education (CRSE). The progressives got some of the elements of change that they wanted, and the efficiency proponents realized some of their objectives. The commission was the offshoot of committees established by the National Education Association to address the perplexing questions of the articulation of high school subjects. Almost single handedly, chairman Clarence Kingsley, Snedden's former associate commissioner for academic studies, produced through the CRSE a document titled "Cardinal Principles of Education" that established the framework for the American high school to the present. It was an innovative document, and attested to his sharp mind and flexibility in thought. In the 1918 final report the CRSE came out in support of the idea of a comprehensive high school with a differentiated program of studies.

The idea of a differentiated high school program still caused uneasiness among teachers in what were considered the more traditional academic fields: The boy studying agriculture or the girl focusing on business subjects had little interest in Latin or algebra. The inclusion of the newer, more practical but less academic courses meant that mainline subjects such as foreign language, English, and history faced declining relative enrollments as more students elected to pursue what was becoming an array of mostly vocational course options. The battle three decades earlier over the place of the classics still continued but in a considerably reduced form: Was the purpose of the high school to prepare an elite for college, or to prepare the young for life? The proponents of efficiency and vocational studies had little doubt about life studies, but in all of the more conventional high school subjects, professionals engaged in reassessing the function of their respective subjects. National committees were set up, and out of this effort developed the National Education Association's Commission on the Reorganization of Secondary Education (CRSE), established in 1913 (Drost, 1967).

Kingsley had to guard against zealous supporters of a dual system of vocational and academic schools, and at the same time he recognized that both fields of studies had to be represented in secondary education. He also recognized both the interests of the social efficiency advocates and progressives had to be accommodated. And through a number of subject-matter committees reporting to the CRSE, a wide representation of views was obtained. As the ongoing work of each of the subject-matter committees became known and reports issued, vigorous debate followed, much of it acrimonious. The modern language people, for example, battled with defenders of classics; and mathematics educators argued over the apparent degenerative state of high school instruction. Others argued over the concept of correlation and its potential effect on watering down academic subjects. The overall argument was made that in order to retain a place in the school's program of studies, a subject had to show immediate worth (Krug, 1964, pp. 339–340).

Among all of the fury unleashed, the 26-person committee was able to issue in 1918 its final report, largely written by Kingsley: the *Cardinal Principles of Secondary Education*. Given the times, this was a remarkable document. It was a clean break from education in the past. First, the report identified seven explicit outcomes for all of public elementary, secondary, and higher education: "Health, Command of fundamental processes, Worthy home-membership, Vocation, Citizenship, Worthy use of leisure, and Ethical character" (CRSE, 1918, pp. 9–11). Through its report, CRSE offered an expanded vision of American education that focused primarily on life activities, reflecting a strong social efficiency thrust. American education was to be relevant to youth and functional.

Second, in a feat that was simple in its intellectual brilliance, Kingsley offered a conceptual framework for the organization of American high schools around "specialization" and "unification." Specialization meant that schools offered courses of study appropriate to the student's interests and abilities. Agriculture and art were placed on the same footing as Latin and literature. If a subject field demonstrated a contribution to one of the seven outcomes, was of interest to students, and was appropriate to the particular age group, it was a candidate for inclusion in the high school course of studies. Of course, there were limits to how many different course offerings could be included in the four-year high school. Generally, instructional programs tended to fall along the lines of the Smith-Hughes Act with concentration in agriculture, home economics, trade and industry, nursing, and business education. There was a smattering of "general education" courses such as civics and health, and there was an academic concentration for students slated to continue on to higher education. And differentiation also applied to courses within a field of study; math, for example was offered at different levels, ranging from courses for low-ability students to those considered the brightest.

The early work on the "scientific" sorting of students by individuals such as Frank Parsons and Meyer Bloomfield, and Hugo Munsterberg and Edward Thorndike among others, made it possible to even think about offering a highly differentiated curriculum in a single, comprehensive high school. Using the measuring instruments in the fast-developing field of counseling and guidance, the educational public was told students could be "objectively" sorted and placed in fields of study appropriate to their interests and abilities. But if students were spread among different course offerings that fundamentally reflected income, social class, and ethnic differences, how could the long-held ideal of the common public school of bringing the children of all of society together in one institution be realized? The student engaged in pig farming on a local farm plot, for example, was somewhat removed from the classroom of the college-bound student studying French; the girl in home economics, the immigrant boy in remedial English, and the math student had little contact with the student studying modern literature or geometry. Children of the very poor and immigrants needed special help to encourage them to stay in school and they were more than likely to be in separate classes. The curriculum concentration determined in large part the relationships developed among students. Through differentiation, the purpose of using schools to build social cohesion was hampered. The solution: unification.

Unification was the idea that students of all income levels and social classes could be brought together through school activities designed to build "common ideas, common ideals, and common modes of thoughts feelings, and action that made for cooperation, social cohesion, and social solidarity"(CRSE, 1918, p. 23). This was, in the words of Krug (1964), "good, old-fashioned doctrine going back to at least as far as Horace Mann" (p. 391). But instead of trying to bring unity through common studies, it was recognized that at the high school level it was not realistic to have all students engage in a common, unifying curriculum. Kingsley's solution was to wrap high school studies in a layer of physical and social activities that brought all students together: sports, student government, assemblies, and clubs. High schools had been doing this, but now they had a clear reason. Hall also provided a psychological justification with his work on adolescence and sublimation. American high school programming has been characterized for 100 years by two centers of influence: specialization and unification.

Of Efficiency and Sorting

The passage of the 1917 Smith-Hughes Act effectively wedded secondary education to the concept of social efficiency, the idea that calls for the teaching of specific knowledge, skills, and attitudes to preselected students for predetermined goals. The student is shaped to well-defined specifications so as to become more useful to society both occupationally and in terms of social responsibility. First, youth are "selected" to follow specific educational "tracks" according to what is judged their probable occupational destiny. Next, specific, specialized preparation is given. This is accompanied with school activities and subjects designed to promote personal development and social, civic, and vocational objectives. The aim is to "create the socially efficient individual, a person possessed of vocational efficiency, physical efficiency, efficiency in civic responsibility, and social relations, and in the kind of personal culture appropriate to him"

(Drost, 1967, p. 185). The concept of social efficiency applies to the preparation of doctors and lawyers as well as masons, goat farmers, nurses, accountants, and machinists. An assumed but not often spoken expected outcome is that the sons and daughters of the laboring immigrant—the miner, the Black sharecropper, the Chinese tailor, or the Mexican field worker—occupy the lowest rungs on the occupational ladder.

The application of the idea of social efficiency requires a way to select students for their "probable" life destinies, and thus the course of school studies. This is where David Snedden got into trouble. Educators struggled with selection. A single course of studies for all students does not require selection. But as previously discussed, any time students follow differentiated studies there has to be an acceptable, reasonable egalitarian and workable way to separate them. How can this selection be done? In the past, selection was based largely on such factors as social class, ethnicity, gender, and wealth. In the social and political environment following the turn of the century such overt discriminatory ways of deciding educational futures had to be tempered with what at least appeared to be unbiased "objectivity."

Others addressed the problem of student differentiation. In Boston, Mrs. Quincy Adams Shaw, instrumental in founding early kindergartens, gave support to the Vocational Bureau established in 1908. Through the bureau, teachers were trained to serve as vocational counselors in local elementary and secondary schools. The work of the bureau soon extended to experimenting with testing instruments to use in guidance. In 1910, the bureau sponsored the First National Conference on Vocational Guidance in Boston concurrently with the meeting of the National Society for the Promotion of Industrial Education. The NSPIE provided financing and literally captured the leadership of the vocational guidance movement. For all practical purposes, the two organizations became one when in 1913 at the Grand Rapids convention of the NSPIE Charles Processer took the leading role in forming the National Vocational Guidance Association (Krug, 1964).

Frank Parson and Meyer Bloomfield of the Vocational Bureau supported the use of the quantifying tools of psychology to sort students. Hugo Munsterberg, a Harvard psychologist, extended testing methodology and Edward Thorndike worked out the statistical manipulation and testing instruments used by school administrators to effectively manage large numbers of students. The vocational guidance movement had a fundamental and instrumental relationship with the comprehensive school to the extent that it supplied the methodology and the professional cadre essential for differentiating students and assigning them to specific education programs.

Munsterberg provided the core concept. He formulated ways of "scientific matching" individual interests and abilities with apparent job requirements. Adopting his work, schools matched students with the course requirements of different fields of study. Robert Yerkes and Henry Goddard advanced Munsterberg's work and developed in 1917 scales to sort army recruits as war preparation advanced. Testing and sorting was on its way to becoming a way of life in America.

Two basic types of testing instruments were developed: interest inventories and aptitude measures. The interest inventory is designed to match the students' life interests with profiles of the like interests of individuals in specific occupations. Where there is a match, then "obviously" this is a field the student should pursue. The measured interests were used to "counsel" students into specific instructional programs. But it also was obvious that individual interests were not enough. How about ability?

A given student may have an interest in animals, for example, but interest alone does not support the choice of becoming a veterinarian. Math, science, and medical knowledge are essential. Can the individual master this knowledge? Any efficient sorting scheme has to address ability. The issue of ability is complex, however, and it was difficult to work out ways to define and measure ability. An imaginary construct of "intelligent quotient" (IQ) was invented. It is hypothesized that a single ability underlies all cognitive activity. It is alleged testers can measure complex human behaviors, aggregate them together, and calculate a single score indicating an individual's intellectual worth, the IQ. Perhaps the concept of IQ is a carryover from the idea of mental discipline and belief in the development of a single factor of "general intelligence." Scaling and factor analysis methods make it possible to relate an IQ score with occupational potential (Gould, 1981). By combining ability (IQ scores) and interest measures, school counselors now had a potent tool to "objectively" direct students into specific studies. The impact on schooling was immediate and lasting.

Educators finally had tools to sort the increasing numbers of working class, immigrant, and migrant poor children filtering into schools in ever-larger numbers to join with middle-class children. Programming was put on a "scientific basis." Selection was allegedly made on the basis of merit, that is, the intellectual ability one has. What remained was to refine and extend the use of testing instruments. The use of testing played out over the course of the 1920s as educators faced an ever more diverse and growing student population.

Chapter Fourteen
Interlude

This chapter covers the interlude between the Great War and the Second World War, a time up to the Great Depression in 1929 when the nation achieved an unprecedented level of industrial development, agriculture mechanized at a dizzy rate, science and technology produced undreamed of innovation, people continued to move to the city, and ever-larger amounts of wealth were aggregated in a few hands. At the same time the general level of prosperity generated a growing middle class anxious to move up in life. More people lived better. They had better paying and more secure jobs. The automobile gave liberating mobility; people communicated by telephone, listened to a new device called the "radio," played the phonograph, and went to the movies. Some families had electric washing machines. Electric irons came to the aid of women. Ready-made clothing could be purchased. There were more prepared foods and canned goods on the market shelves. The food supply was more secure and varied. Selected plant breeding improved crops and animal production, and refrigerated boxcars delivered food products to remote corners of the nation. Cities were electrified; and cities had waterworks and sewer systems.

But great rural parts of the country remained dependent on kerosene lamps and wood-burning stoves. More than half of the country did not have indoor plumbing. The water supply was from the backyard well or nearby stream. Many toiled to scrape out a barely substance level of living. A national road system was not yet developed, and paved streets in small towns were a rarity. Modern medicine was in its toddling stage. Antibiotics were unavailable so what are today considered relative simple medical issues took a terrible human toll. Colds and the flu killed; minor scratches became deadly, uncontrollable infections; and measles, scarlet fever, diphtheria, and the whooping cough snuffed out infant lives.

The growing economy had soft spots. Agricultural production was uneven. Overproduction resulted in catastrophic price drops for farmers and at the same time marginal land put into production in good times turned into eroded wasteland during times of drought. The Dust Bowl of the late 1920s and early 1930s destroyed millions of acres of formerly fertile land, killed crops and cattle, and drove thousands into abject poverty. The great migration of "Okies" to California commenced (Starr, 1996). Machines in places where agriculture flourished replaced thousands. In the South, fewer Blacks were needed to work the land, setting into motion a large internal migration to the nations' northern industrial heartland. Ira Berlin (2010) documented an average outflow from the time of America's entry into WWI to the stock market collapse in 1929 of 15,000 Blacks a month, primarily from the rich belt of fertile soil cutting across northern South Carolina, Georgia, and Alabama to Mississippi, and downwards and upward along both sides of the broad river (p. 152). Edward Ellis (1996, p. 410) puts the figure at 500,000 between 1916 and 1920 alone.

Industrial production was more even, but there still were soft spots so that job security for many was lacking. There was a general, uneven economic slowdown after the war, with a sharp depression in 1920-1921. Throughout the decade production fluctuated with internal and export demand. Wages shot up in 1923 because of a labor shortage, but dropped again in a pattern repeated throughout the decade. Technology also replaced workers, and child labor dropped markedly. By the end of the 1920s, the gyrations in the economy generated great uncertainty, and finally the great collapse of the stock market on October 16, 1929, plunged the whole nation into an economic depression deeper than anything experienced since the great national depression of the early 1870s following the Civil War. Half of the nation's wealth evaporated overnight. It brought deep poverty and suffering and destroyed lives.

Immigrants, Blacks, and Exclusion

By the early 1920s the nativist movement reached its peak. The crusaders for "100 percent American" achieved their objective: exclusion of "foreigners." In the decades leading up to the Great War, progressives such as Jane Addams and John Dewey argued for creating "unity" among all citizens, including the most recent to our shores, and they emphasized the richness of the cosmopolitan character of the country generated through immigration. Schools "Americanized" and brought immigrant children into the fold of society. By 1920, however, the spirit of unity was largely gone. Immigrants wanted to retain their own identity, and minority Europeans founded their own nationalistic organizations, each as John Higham (1970) observed, "asserting its own defiant group consciousness." They distrusted the idea of "Americanization" and the harmonious fusion of national identities. Higham quoted an Italian editor saying, "Americanization is an ugly word" (p. 254).

At the same time, after the war newly enacted state employment and licensing laws discriminated against aliens. Many jobs were made off limits. The growing movement to restrict immigration took on increasing racist tones. Following the war there was a wave of Jewish persecution in central and eastern Europe. Over 119,000 men, women, and children in the fiscal year 1920-21 alone fled to the safety of America to be met with a backlash of anti-Semitism. Immigration restriction proponents warned America faced a flood of "inassimilable" and "abnormally twisted" Jews, "un-American and often dangerous in their habits" (Higham, 1970, p. 309). Other ethnic groups were bashed: If immigration continued at its present rate the country would become "hopelessly bogged down in the mire of mongrelization." Alarmists warned 52,000 were coming monthly by the beginning of 1921. The Greeks, Italians, Slavs, and Hungarians threatened to submerge the old Nordic stock in a genetic swamp that sapped the virility of the nation and destroyed social progress (Higham, 1970, pp. 108–111).

The playing field was left open to nativists. Immigrant groups withdrew and progressives did not have enough players. The rise of Bolshevism, the Russian Revolution, and the Red Scare strengthened the hand of nativists. Foreign influence was dangerous to the interests of America, was the theme. The Espionage Act of 1917 and Sedition Act of 1918 gave government almost unlimited power to ferret out subversives dangerous to national defense, and helped to build an atmosphere of distrust toward immigrants. The gates were closed to immigration with the

passage in 1921 of a law to restrict entry through a quota system. The subsequent
Act in 1924 virtually restricted all immigration with a few exceptions. American n
cepted the "huddled masses."

The resurgence of the Ku Klux Klan contributed to the distrust of "foreign elements."
der William J. Simmons the reenergized Invisible Knights of the Ku Klux Klan reemerged in
1915 to surpass by far in number and scope its previous hate and terror activities of intimation,
destruction, and death. Simmons linked romantic visions of white-robed horsemen galloping
through the night to rescue the white purity of the nation with evangelical piety. He was a spell-
binding speaker, and with the addition of two professional fundraisers collecting and keeping
$8 of every $10 in membership dues raised, by the mid-1920s the Klan's membership, restricted
to White Protestants, reached 4,500,000. The Klan was a moneymaker. Its role expanded.

The reenergized Klan relocated the center of its activities to the northern industrial heartland, the upper and lower plains and the west. The Klan exerted considerable political influence, and state governments in Indiana, Ohio, California, Texas, Oklahoma, Arkansas, and
Oregon were dominated. Through its national office, now in Indiana, they had the money and
political power to elect mayors, members of state legislatures, governors, and congressmen.
A national campaign was directed primarily against immigrants, Jews and Catholics—especially
Catholics—in the small towns and manufacturing centers and rural farms and villages spread
over the upper and lower mid-west and west. The Klan thus helped to extend the hate monger-
ing in cities by nativist groups throughout rural America (Higham, 1970).

Never long dormant, violence broke out against Americans of African heritage, but its
center shifted. As suggested earlier, agriculture mechanization drove hundreds and thousands
of Blacks north and west in search of jobs. With war preparation, labor demand mushroomed,
with some industries sending recruitment agents south to scour the fields and farms for Black
workers. The machines of production worked full time to fill war needs. Whites and Blacks
earned "big" money, but with the armistice on November 11, 1918, war production sharply
dropped and paychecks stopped coming. Whites and Blacks now competed in the labor market for the same industrial jobs, and Blacks worked for less. Edward Ellis (1996) observed that
White workers resented Blacks and "White employers used them as pawns in a power struggle
with unions" (p. 412). Violence spread but his time it was located in Chicago, East St. Louis,
Topeka, Omaha, Minneapolis, and scores of small cities and towns across the northern, midwestern, and western areas of the country.

Edward Ayers (1993) points to another factor influencing ethnic violence. In settled communities with a history of Blacks and Whites living together individuals learned to accommodate one another without resorting to violence. But with the mass migration out of the South
to northern and western communities that never before experienced ethnic mixing with a Black
population, there often was a violent reaction to the presence of uninvited "intruders" upset-
ting the formerly settled community dynamics. And as more Blacks came, tensions increased,
overflowing into violence. The hate and fear of foreigners generated by nativists and turned into
violence by the Klan easily transferred to migrating Blacks. Horrible inhuman travesties played
out: brutal whippings, Blacks driven out of communities by hastily organized vigilantes, the jailing for no legal cause, the burning of homes, beatings, and killings. Lynching reemerged in all

also grated on Whites. "Black ma
d, especially when blacks prospered
rs, 1993, p. 210). Ira Katznelson (2013)
e that the Black "did not aspire to social equality" with the White.
ching was the most extreme way the White South used to protect and
ny (pp. 140–141).

omen and the Social Revolution

Women got the vote in 1920, but political equality at the ballot box was not considered to displace their role as guardians of morality. Only "lewd" women drank or smoked in public. Short hair was frowned on, the sign of a hussy; face power was used, but anything more was *prima facie* evidence of suspicious behavior. The orthodox clearance for skirts and dresses was six inches above the ground. Bathing suits consist of a loose outer covering over a tightly knitted undergarment worn with long stockings. There was no discussion of the "birds and bees" at home. Girls from "respectable" families were supposed to have no sexual temptations, avoiding even a simple goodnight kiss until the "right man" came along. It was illegal to provide women birth control advice. It was understood, however, that boys sometimes succumbed to temptation, but not with "good girls," and transgressions could be forgiven. At the same time, daughters from certain immigrant groups, referred as "chippies," were considered "easy" and a source of sexual experience for young men (Allen, 1931; Morrison, 1965). All of this changed as the 1920s progressed.

As the decade advanced, acceptable skirt and dress length went up to nine inches above the ground and then to a "shocking" 12 inches. Women wore their hair short, and wore dresses of "thin" material. Shockingly, some even wore short or sleeveless dresses and blouses. Parent's agenized over the three evils: cars, drink, and cigarettes. Young men and women escaped parental supervision through the independence of the car. Parents imagined the unimaginable. Prohibition made drinking illegal, but also made drinking more popular, more daring, and more widespread among the young intent on challenging the adult world. Even (probably especially) the sons and daughters of the "better classes" engaged in getting "blotto." And even "nice girls" defiantly smoked openly. Hipflasks and joy riding were in. To the discomfort of adults the young listened to "passionate crooning" and danced in a gyrating embrace with "bodies glued together cheek to cheek." "Petting parties" became an indoor sport (Allen, 1931). Parents began to understand that their world was not the world of their offspring or of tomorrow; and they had nightmares over what could, or did or did not happen.

A social revolution was underway and it could not be stopped. It was initiated partly by the growing independence of American women. The war also changed morals and manners, codes of behavior, and attitudes about life and fostered the questioning of the beliefs of an older generation that got that country into a world war. The young wanted to fashion their own lives. Science and technology spoke the language of a new kind of life, and the formable industrial machine offered promise of a more affluent life. Prohibition spawned social disobedience: The automobile, the radio, phonograph and movie; the fashion and the confessional and sex magazines; Freud and libido and the "flapper" pointed to a different kind of life. The divorce rate continued to climb; more married middle-class women, often over the resistance of husbands, took jobs. The birth rate also decreased. Many men also rallied over what they thought were social injustices, and both men and women supported "liberating tendencies" (Allen, 1931, p. 193; Carroll & Noble, 1988).

But many others attempted to cling to the ways of their parents, and there was plenty of "old-fashioned" thinking about morals and manners, and sex and fidelity. It was not easy to overthrow behavioral and moral codes when there was no substitution that was not wrapped in confusion and distress. Allen (1931) observed the social revolution "had been born in disillusionment, and beneath all the bravado of its exponents and the talk about entering upon a new era the disillusionment persisted. If the decade was ill mannered, it was also unhappy. With the old order of things had gone a set of values which had given richness and meaning to life and substitute values were not easily found" (p. 109).

Reaction and Accommodation: Schooling in the 1920s

Schools not only had to cope with massive increases in enrollment, but they were on the front lines of the social revolution. They had to accommodate change that was not understood. It was the young people in the classrooms and halls of schools that were testing the morals and manners under assault, that challenged authority and that struggled to find equilibrium in a society that was out of kilter. G. Stanley Hall counseled schoolmen to accommodate and find outlets for the great forces of emotion and drive that were surging through the veins of adolescents. Dawning on educators was a deeper understanding of what he meant.

The schools also had to struggle with the ethnic warfare that continued to cause great riffs in society. And schools had to struggle with the uneven distribution of wealth that created some school districts that were generously endowed, others that managed to get along, and still others that could barely operate. Disparities in attendance and academic achievement reflected disparities in social standing and wealth. Large percentages of the youth population still had no interest in schooling, did not attend, dropped out early, or had no local school available. In parts of the country, such as in the South and rural America, educational opportunity was seriously curtailed or did not exist. The advent of the Great Depression at the end of the decade touched all schools. Education was urgently enlisted to help reassemble a broken society.

Schools coped with change in a number of ways. As the 1920s progressed, educators increasingly turned to the new tools of administration and testing even though the idea of scientific management was no longer in vogue. They standardized routine systems of management, built detailed record-keeping systems, applied testing to sort and classify students, modified curricula, put in student services, and countered pluralism through the homogenizing influence of school assemblies, clubs, sports, and participation in school government. Tyack (1974) observed that administrators thought they knew what the new school recipe required. Schooling "was too 'bookish,' ridged, and undiversified, ill-adapted to the great variety of students flooding the upper grades of elementary schools and the secondary schools, and poorly serving the needs of the economy for specialized manpower" (p. 180). "Cultural studies" were defended with great difficulty in favor of more practical work. Vocational education with federal funding made deep inroads in courses of studies. Classroom instruction was slanted to teach youth to maintain a level of constructive behavior. Schools provided counseling help to troubled youth. Schools opened a service function, consulting and working with parents and community leaders to address the immediate problems of the young (Krug, 1972; Tyack, 1974).

Concurrent with enrollment increases were increases of "backward" students, individuals a decade earlier Lenard Ayres termed "laggards." Now they were recognized as children with learning difficulties, and emotional and behavioral problems, and some with physical disabilities. They attended school in larger numbers. One reason for the general increase in school attendance was child labor was no longer needed. States began to enforce child labor and compulsory attendance laws. Technology advanced to the point where many repetitive, low-level jobs were engineered out of the production. Men, and particularly children, were phased out and replaced by mechanization. The young could not find jobs, or they could not legally work after the elementary grades so they continued on into the high school where some experienced a lack of success and often became troublesome. Those recognized as needing help were singled out to participate in what became known as "special education."

The practice of special classes quickly caught on. Joel Spring (2008) recorded the increase of special education students in Baltimore schools, for example, from 56 in 1920, to a jarring 1,179 by 1925. A pattern was developed that continues to this day: Testing and antidotal information is used to assign students to "special classes"; the special education teacher is given smaller classes, typically 18 students in contrast to the 30 or more in "regular" classes; modified studies reduced in difficulty are included; "life skills" studies are provided; and students with particular conditions are helped by specially trained teachers. As the decade progressed, however, special classes increasingly were used to deal with "problem pupils." These individuals tended to be unmanageable boys difficult to handle. To the objection and discomfort of vocational teachers, low-achieving and difficult-to-handle students were increasingly assigned to prevocational and vocational education classes. The Duluth, Minnesota, public schools went as far as to created a special department to offer basket-weaving and rugmaking as main activities for what were considered low-ability students (Krug, 1972, p. 112).

Testing, Sorting, and Exclusion

Testing gave educators a tool they could use to "objectively" sort students in the new comprehensive high school with its differentiated studies. Programming efficiency was the expected outcome. But testing also served American educators and the public another purpose. Testing was a tool used to confirm the existing social class and ethnic stratification in America based on "scientific" findings. Edward Thorndike expressed a popular opinion when he observed intelligence, wealth, and morality were inextricably linked. He restated what Americans had been saying for over three centuries when he affirmed ethnicity was linked with intelligence. And in his eyes and others it was the Nordics who were the most intelligent. They had better genes.

All through the 1800s Americans tried different ways to "scientifically" support a social class system that was heavy at the bottom with large numbers of the underclass: rural and urban laborerss, immigrants, slaves, and non-Europeans. And Americans needed a way to justify enslaving Blacks, brutalizing immigrant workers, restricting schooling for non-European children, and killing off Native Americans. Faculty psychology provided an early tool. It was a way to show intellectual differences in human characteristics linked with ethnicity. Cranial capacity was the place to look. If the mind is made up of different faculties similar to muscles that can be exercised, it only seemed logical that the greater the size of the faculties the greater is the potential for developing different capabilities. Craniometry, the measurement of the capacity of the mind, was launched in the early 1800s.

The skull sizes of different ethnic groups were used to affirm relative intelligence. One method was to measure and compare the foreheads of different ethnic groups. The frontal lobe is where the intellectual capacity of the individual was thought to reside. Protruding foreheads meant greater intelligence. This did not turn out well for "researchers," however. Whites did not show any "superiority," and among one sample, Blacks showed a higher preponderance of protruding foreheads (Gould, 1981).

Total cranial capacity was next measured by filling skull samples with mustard seeds, emptying them out on a scale or measuring cone and comparing the total volume or weight of the samples. This method was abandoned when it was pointed out that mustard seeds could be tamped down to yield greater measurement for a given volume size. Lead shot was next used, but was largely abandoned when "inclusive results" were found. Among proponents of White superiority initial experiments showed promise, but subsequent examination showed that body size and gender were not taken into consideration. For example, in a sample of South American Indians that showed the least intellectual potential, the skulls were entirely of small statue females. In contrast, Nordic samples tended to be heavy on large males. More controlled studies showed too much variation to make any conclusions (Gould, 1981). Some continued to try.

Gould, in the *Mismeasure of Man* (1981), reported on the work of Samuel George Morton, a distinguished Philadelphia scientists and physician who assembled a collection of more than 600 skulls. He ranked them according to characteristics, including average brain size. The care and extent of his work catapulted him into the ranks of leading craniometry scientists. His results confirmed what Americans thought they already knew: "whites on top, Indians in the middle, and blacks on the bottom; and, among whites Teutons and Anglo-Saxons on top, Jews in the middle, and Hindus on the bottom" (pp. 53–54). Gould examined Morton's original data from the mid-1840s and concluded his "summaries are a patchwork of fudging and finagling in the clear interest of controlling a priori convictions. Yet–and this is the most intriguing aspect of the case–I find no evidence of conscious fraud; indeed, had Morton been a conscious fudger, he would not have published his data so openly" (p. 54). Morton believed what he wanted to believe regardless of what the data showed.

Others turned to an examination of limb lengths in the belief that the "more advanced" ethnicities, such as northern European Whites, are more physiologically advanced as evidenced by shorter limb length. Darwin's influence is clear. It was suggested some ethnicities are more advanced and more intelligent because they are further along the evolutionary trail and more distant from their primate cousins. No significant results could be found. Next came physiognomy. Facial characteristics were considered a guide to intelligence, morality, and other characteristics that set humans apart: Eyes set close together indicated a weak mind; a round face meant a happy person; "Mongolian" characteristics were linked with moral degeneracy; a thin upper lip, large ears, and enormous jaw were indicators of criminality, and so on. Books and charts became available by the score so an individual could spot potential violent criminal behavior, size up a potential employee, or judge a suitor of his daughter. Of course the "typical" facial characteristics of Anglo-Americans tended to be associated with the most positive alleged attributes. "Professionals" went into business advising clients. The absurdity of such shallow thinking became so obvious that only diehards clung to the possibility of assessing human characteristics through facial features.

Alfred Binet and IQ as a Measure of Worth

By the early 1900s Americans found what they were searching for: a way to measure "scientifically" inherited, innate intellectual capacity. The Frenchman Alfred Binet conducted studies on skull capacity, but by 1904 he no longer believed craniometry had any validity and turned to building a test to measure mental ability. By 1908 he perfected a test Americans liked. Edward E. Thorndike, H. H. Goddard, Lewis E. Terman, and others immediately saw the potentiality of differentiating individuals and groups of individuals by "mental age." Test items are used to reflect different levels of mental age corresponding to the level of difficulty of corresponding test items. That is, the "average" 6-year-old typically completes certain items reflecting a given level of difficulty, the 7-year-old up to a higher level, and so on. Binet was primarily interested in developing a *diagnostic* tool to early identify students with potential learning difficulties. Students with a recorded mental age less than the chronological age were candidates for special help. But Americans made a different use of his ideas.

Dividing mental age by the chronological age and multiplying by 100, researchers calculated an intelligent quotient (IQ) that was alleged to represent inborn, innate, and unchangeable mental ability—that is, the hereditary intellectual endowment of an individual that cannot be changed. Test makers went a step further. Averages in mental ability could be calculated for entire ethnic groups. The IQ was used to sort students into different areas of study as reflected in the curriculum model Clarence Kingsley and the Commission on the Reorganization of Secondary Education established, thus accomplishing an efficient allocation of human resources. The results, however, were taken further to draw distinct lines of differences in the innate IQ levels of ethnic groups, achieving what the craniometrists could not accomplish. Americans now had a "scientific" way to establish human worth based on genetic inheritance. "Science" confirmed Morton's bigotry.

Binet voiced objections to the way his measurement tool was used and the accompanying rationale. First, he objected to the notion that intelligence is inborn and cannot be changed. While it is true that there is variation among individuals, all individuals also are capable of improving achievement with proper teaching, Binet stressed, even though some do not achieve at the corresponding age level. Second, the purpose of his measurement tool is not to rank individuals according to intellectual worth, but to identify poorly performing individuals. Third, human intellectual performance is due to many factors beyond just what can be measured by a single kind of test instrument. And fourth, the purpose of his scale is to measure in order to help and improve, not to label, sort, and limit. Mental testing should not be built on a theory of limits, but rather should be an instrument for enhancing and expanding potential while recognizing the richness and diversity of human characteristics and the limits of measurement. Children should be helped, not labeled, and he went on to develop different instructional interventions designed to increase attention span, improve speed, and enhance retention (Gould, 1981, pp. 146–158).

Gould elegantly summed up the use made of Binet's pioneering work in measurement:

"American psychologists perverted Binet's intention and invented the hereditarian theory of IQ. They reified Binet's scores and took them as measures of an entity called intelligence. They assumed that intelligence was largely inherited, and developed a series of specious arguments confusing cultural differences with innate properties. They believed that inherited IQ scores marked people and groups for an inevitable station in life. And they assumed that averaged differences between groups were largely the products of heredity, despite manifest and profound variation in quality of life" (p. 157).

The Test Makers and Ethnic Superiority

Test making in America made a huge quantitative leap in the war years. A number of individuals such as Robert Yerkes, head of the U.S. Army psychology unit, and Henry Herbert Goddard of the Vineland Institute in New Jersey saw immediate value in the concept of IQ for sorting army recruits. Among the great mass of raw army recruits, how could the potential captains, sergeants, truck drivers, and clerks be sorted out from among potential frontline troops? IQ tests could do this, with the less intelligent obviously destined for the trenches. A team was formed in early 1917. In a remarkably short time two IQ tests were assembled, an Alpha test for literates and a Beta test for illiterates. Extensive demographic data was collected related to age, place of birth, ethnicity, education, and so on. The tests were administered to almost 1.75 million recruits. (Note: In psychometric terms this is a gigantic sample.) A serious error in judgment quickly became obvious, however. There were not enough test booklets for illiterate recruits; they took the Alpha test designed for literates. In addition, the testing conditions were not uniform but sloppy, further invalidating the results (Gould, 1981). But the large sample size was pointed to as a validation of the findings. When the data were analyzed, the summarized and reported conclusions were shocking: They supported what the nativists and others were saying about the dilution of the American genetic pool.

Most shocking was the average mental age of the population: The data pointed to an average adult intelligence of a 13-year-old, just above the 8- to 12-year-old range that was considered in an adult to be on the edge of moronic. Sloppy testing conditions and the wrong use of test booklets were not taken into consideration. And most raw recruits had not completed high school, and others were newly immigrant arrivals. Recruits not completing a test for any reason were scored zero. Nevertheless, the finding is what the public absorbed even though it was of dubious validity.

A second set of findings analyzed by Carl Brigham was related to specific ethnic groups. The findings indicated that individuals of Nordic ethnicity had the highest IQ, followed by Alpine, Mediterranean, and Negro in descending order. Conclusions were drawn: The average man in many countries is a moron as measured by IQ; the darker-skinned people of southern Europe and the Slavs of Eastern Europe are less intelligent than the white-skinned northern Europeans. The Black man is at the bottom of the intelligence scale with an average mental age of 10.41 years, joined by recently arrived Jewish immigrant youth also low on the scale (Gould, 1981, pp. 192–195, 255).

Goddard speculated feebleminded indicated inherited, arrested human development, and was most present in lower income and minority groups, especially recent immigrants from eastern and southern Europe. It was among this large and expanding group through unrestricted immigration that the moral degenerate, criminal, pauper, and prostitute came (Kevles & Hood, 1992, p. 7). The army test results showed the number to be alarmingly large.

What was not compiled and reported is revealing as well as damning. The aggregated scores of African heritage individuals living in some northeastern states were higher than the cumulative aggregated scores of Whites living in some of the southern states. The reason is clear when the correlation between state expenditure for education and scores is considered. Southern states provided little education opportunity for Blacks and Whites in comparison to northern states where both groups scored higher (Gould, 1981, p. 219). This finding totally undercut the assertion that raw, innate, and invariant heredity mental ability is measured. Whatever is measured by the IQ test is conditioned by education, among other environmental factors. It is simply not plausible to think that Whites and Blacks with better genes chose to live in the North, and individuals with a lesser genetic endowment ended up living in the South.

The finding also presented a potential explosive political problem for the test makers. Nordic supremacists would not stand for such a finding. The whole idea of measuring mental ability and the testing movement itself was threatened. Yerkes, Goddard, Brigham, and other test makers had to fight against similar findings that invalidated the idea of fixed, inherited IQ, and that certain ethnic groups were endowed with more intelligence than others. Individuals of immigrant groups assigned to the lower ends of the mental range, for example, had improved IQ scores above their group that strongly correlated with years living in the United States. Did familiarity with the ways of America, better education, or adaptation to conditions account for the gain in the supposedly innate IQ? Similarly, test takers from a non-English-speaking heritage were at a distinct disadvantage on the Alpha or Beta versions of the test, and while the data showed this disadvantage correlated with years living in the United States, the finding was dismissed (Gould, 1981, pp. 220–221). The viability of the IQ construct cannot be questioned without also throwing out the idea of separating individuals based on inherited mental differences. If mental ability can be improved, why not provide remediation, as Binet suggested, instead of sorting and limiting?

The test makers nevertheless went ahead and proclaimed test results were "objective" measures of human ability achieved through "scientific" means. America was receptive. The nativists immediately found support for the drive to limit all immigration. The Ku Klux Klan could terrorize, knowing that it was doing its part in countering corrupting "foreign" and inferior domestic genetic influences; and segregationists justified Jim Crow laws, separate schools, and limited education opportunity with the knowledge that they were preventing the intermingling and possible spread of inferior genes. Poverty and want was explained: The poor were poor because they lacked intelligence; the inherited genes were bad, and this could not be easily changed. Social and ethnic stratification could be explained because it was based on inherited intellectual differences.

Mental testing gave America the means to explain inequality, social and economic discrimination, the exploitation of others, exclusion, and success and failure. And the role of the school is to sort, select, segregate, restrict, and train. Resources should be directed to the gifted, the upper-class Whites because they have the intellectual capacity for advanced work. Since intelligence is a genetically inherited trait, schooling can make little difference in the intellectual development of the less endowed.

Schools were significantly impacted. The war was over in 1918 and there were millions of unused test booklets. They were given to schools for pennies, and educators embarked on a binge of widespread testing. The use of testing was solidified. Patterned on the work of Binet, specific test instruments were made for testing American schoolchildren. The most influential was the Stanford-Binet, constructed by Lewis Terman, a professor at Stanford University. It became the model for almost all subsequent IQ tests developed to the present. Terman took Binet's scales and revised them, increasing the number of test items and extending the range of categories. He also worked out standard deviations separating each chronological age level. The mental ability of children in all grades could be measured and sorting accomplished. But like Binet's work, this was an individually administered test. Once group-administered tests were developed, the testing movement in schools became unstoppable. Terman constructed the National Intelligence Test for elementary schoolchildren. In 1920 alone, 500,000 copies were sold. Others followed suit. School testing became a multimillion-dollar enterprise (Lemann, 1999).

Edward Thorndike constructed an intelligence test for college-age students, and Yale University developed its own instrument. Carl Brigham was the most successful. An associate of Yerkes, after the completion of the army testing, he moved on to Princeton where in 1923 he developed the Scholastic Aptitude Test (SAT). It was a modification of the army test in revised and upgraded form. In 1926 the SAT took its place as the premier college examination in America. Over 8,000 high school students were administered the test and the scores reported to colleges. Lemann (1999) noted the SAT has changed "remarkably little over the years" (p. 31). And it continues to embody within its theoretical constructs all of the flawed assumptions about innate ability, genetic inheritance, measured IQ, and mentally imbedded ethnic differences.

Eugenics: Rescuing Racial Purity

Among the most enthusiastic supporters of intelligence testing were the defenders of racial purity, the American advocates of eugenics. The late European discovery of the unnoticed work of Gregor Mendel on genetics coupled with Darwinian theory stimulated the study of genetics. The statistician Francis Galton provided analytical tools to study human inheritance, and he is credited with launching the eugenics movement in England. By the first decade of the 1900s, eugenics got underway in America. In simple terms, eugenicists claim by selective breeding from the best, and restricting breeding among the worst, genetic improvement can be realized.

Specialists in agriculture were immediately attracted and put selective breeding concepts into practice. Cows that gave more milk, hogs that grew faster, corn that had higher yields, and peaches resistant to blight soon made their presence on farms. Why not similarly improve humankind? Eugenicists preached by restricting the multiplication of the unfit, and protecting and encouraging reproduction of the genetic purity of the more gifted, the viability of the American genetic pool would be preserved. Eugenicists were bothered by the fact that the birth rate among the more affluent White population was dropping and among "lesser" elements of the population rapidly increasing. The feebleminded would take over. "Racial suicide" was being committed. The solution was to restrict immigration, which was finally accomplished fully in 1923, and keep the more "inferior racial stock"—the central and eastern Europeans, Blacks, Asians, American Indians, and mentally lacking—from breeding with the Anglo-Saxon stock. The solution to human improvement was viewed as essentially biological, not economic, social, or educational.

By the 1920s, a total of 26 states enacted miscegenation laws forbidding marriage among racial groups with the threat of imprisonment. More odious, the same states enacted sterilization laws that empower state agencies to identify potential "defectives," and to test and sterilize children in order to prevent future breeding and thus contribute to the dilution of the genetic pool. Interestingly, it appears that the sterilization of children was directed primarily to poor Whites. By the early months of 1929, California had performed more sterilizations than all of the other states combined. The most plausible explanation is the large and overwhelming influx of poor Whites fleeing the ravages of the Dust Bowl. California even took the extreme measure of posting armed guards at the highways leading into the state to keep the "Okies" from entering—a clear violation of law (Starr, 1996).

Thousands of young children, the exact numbers are lost to history, grew up, went to school, took fulfilling jobs, and got married. But they never understood why they did not have children. As children they were institutionalized temporarily in some kind of state agency because struggling families could not care for them. Some were orphaned, but most were just poor. Along with their families they escaped from poverty, and now with their spouses were living productive lives. Some sought medical help, and discovered the reason they could not have children: state-sanctioned sterilization. They, along with thousands of others, were denied the richness of a full family life because of a perverse belief in genetic determinism.

Nature, Nurture, or Both?

Critics attacked the foundation of testing. The idea of IQ and the testing movement is based on a polygenic view of mankind. Prior to Darwin, ethnic ranking was primarily based on monogenism, the belief in a single source of origination as conveyed in the biblical story of Adam and Eve. Racial and ethnic differences are considered the outcome of the fall from Grace, with some falling faster and further than others (Gould, 1981).

By the time of the formulation of IQ, polygenism dominated as the way to explain genetic differences. As suggested earlier, it is believed humans differ because some are further along on the evolutionary trail than others. In other words, there are multiple sources of human origin, and those originating earlier are more genetically developed. Some ethnicities are degenerate or simple-minded because genetically they are less developed than others. Education cannot change this. Critics contested this view. Today, DNA sampling has destroyed the idea of poly-genism. There is a remarkable lack of genetic diversity among humans, and all of us come from one source: Africa (Cavalli-Sforza, 2000; Olson, 2002).

The testing movement soon generated contentious debate in the form of the nature or nurture argument. Old arguments were brought back to life. Is IQ an inherited, innate human characteristic that defines individual differences between ethnic groups? Or is IQ changeable, conditioned by environmental factors If intelligence is malleable then differences in achievement can be moderated through education. Schools thus have a responsibility to provide the richness of programming required for boosting the intellectual development of all students. If testing is used, it is to diagnose learning problems, as Binet advocated, not to sort and limit. Individual differences are recognized, and special help is given when needed. More resources are directed to those lagging behind, not less. And a variety of human characteristics are recognized to be cultivated that go beyond the limited factors measured through test instruments purportedly used to measure human intellectual worth.

Those believing in nature as the source of intellectual development contend the best schools can do for most students is to emphasize nonacademic goals designed to make good, moral and productive citizens. There should be little emphasis on subject mastery. At the same time, school resources should be used where they produce the best results: solid academic education for those with superior genetic inheritance

The idea of IQ stands or falls on the contention that it is unchangeable. Despite data showing IQ scores change, the test makers ignored this. Critics did not. Researchers in child development in the 1930s conducted studies in the orphanages and homes for mentally challenged children and found that with individual, sustained interventions over a period of time, intellectual performance measured through IQ tests improved. IQ scores changed. In repeated studies, for example, institutionalized little tots with IQ scores in the 30s and classed as feebleminded, when placed in nurturing environments showed remarkable advancements to an IQ range of 90 and above, with some score gains in the 115 IQ range. In other studies adopted children with birth mothers classed as "dull normal" to "feebleminded" soon acquired IQ scores approximating the range of children from homes of "brighter" mothers. Increasingly, social welfare workers, social scientists, biologists, writers, and members of minority groups thought to be "inferior" spoke out against the idea of social sorting on the basis of a relatively small number of test questions (Kevles, 1995). Walter Lippman, for example, a respected intellectual and journalist writing in the *New Republic* observed there was no more validity in IQ tests than there was in "a hundred other fads, vitamins and glands and amateur psychoanalysis and correspondence courses in will power." The basic flaw, he concluded, was the belief that there was a construct of intelligence that "could be unambiguously measured" (Kelves, 1995, p. 129).

In a reversal that rocked the testing movement, Carl Brigham, now the official tester for the College Board, after reviewing national testing in the 1930s, said that he was wrong, and that his ideas and those of others on IQ and the measurement of individual and ethnic group mental ability were without a supporting scientific foundation (Kevles, 1995; Leman, 1999). Later he also cautioned that any organization owning "the rights to a particular test would inevitably become more interested in promoting it than in honestly researching its effectiveness" (Lemann,

1999, p. 40). Others pointed out that it was next to impossible to identify a genetic basis to differences within homogeneous groups, and equally impossible to identify racially-specific mental or behavioral traits based on ethnicity. This was "Nordic nonsense." There was a growing tide opinion on the part of psychologists, anthropologists, and geneticists that what were being considered genetically inherited ethic differences in human intelligence were, in fact, grounded in social and cultural differences. Kevles (1995) observed the studies in the 1930s "revealed that environment could either accentuate or reduce apparent genetic differences. And they strongly suggested that what I.Q. tests measure was some combination of nurture and nature" (p. 138).

Today the common belief is that both nature and nurture come in to play to influence human behavior. To be sure, there are birth differences among individuals, but what is the ratio? We do not know. But we do know that measured IQ is changeable, and that it is extremely limited in defining the richness of human behavior. Today test makers speak less of IQ and more of "aptitude," but the flawed assumptions that tests are based on have not gone away. Why continue to use such flawed instrumentation? One reason is that there are not good alternatives to social sorting based on income, class, and ethnic lines that have a "scientific" facade that the public accepts. Another is convenience. It is an easy way to sort people. Probably the most commanding reason is what Brigham warned about: There exists this huge, multimillion-dollar testing industry with vested interests that has few incentives to find alternatives.

The Education of Black Children

The national discussion surrounding social efficiency and testing impacted ideas concerning the education of Black children. As recounted in Part Four, by the turn of the century Black communities had made some progress in the struggle to expand educational opportunity in the face of strong resistance. The elimination or cutting of school funding for Black children, brutality and violence, and the enforcement of Jim Crow laws coupled with the absence of political power presented almost insurmountable obstacles to Black communities in the quest for education (Woodward, 1957).

The idea of social efficiency helped open a path. The case was made that an educated Black labor force can significantly contribute to the economic revitalization of the New South. Northern philanthropist William H. Baldwin, for example, made this argument: "The potential economic value of the Negro population properly educated is infinite and incalculable." The young require training both in work and "socializing" skills. The trained Black worker will labor at lower wages, Baldwin observed, "than the American white man or any foreign race which has yet come to our shores" (Anderson, 1988, p. 82). Baldwin and others were opening the way to provide education for Black youth in the name of building a more efficient local workforce. Booker T. Washington moved into this opening.

Industrial Education and Booker T. Washington

The son of a former slave and a student under General Samuel Chapman Armstrong at Hampton Institute in Virginia, the smart, wily, and astute Washington concluded White America was not going to admit Blacks into social and economic membership unless it was on the basis of lower status and a perceived, nonthreatening benefit to Whites. In a speech before the Atlanta Exposition in 1895, Washington offered a compromise solution to social and economic tensions in the South. He told the White audience of attending businessmen and industrialists they had a potential labor force among them that was undervalued because it lacked training in the necessary skills needed for the reconstruction of the southern economy. At the same time, Blacks understood their place in White society. Assuring the audience he said, "In all things that are purely social we can be as separate as the fingers, yet one as the hand in all things essential to mutual progress." He was the "Great Accommodator" his critics snidely remarked, that made Whites comfortable: Blacks would accept second-class participation in society in return for the opportunity to demonstrate their economic value through participation in the labor force. Schools of limited scope could prepare the young for the workforce. White society would value Blacks once they fully realized their worth, Washington argued, and a change in social attitude and acceptance would follow (Curti, 1959). Why use immigrant labor? Taking advantage of the growing nativist movement, he spent the next two decades building on this theme.

Washington was highly successful in attracting "white" money to support Tuskegee Normal and Industrial Institute that he directed and other Black industrial schools that were soon founded. He did not challenge the social and economic position of Whites in society and he made them feel comfortable. Both the philanthropic Peabody and Slater funds contributed. The railroad magnate Collis Huntington gave money, and so did Andrew Carnegie, H. H. Rogers of Standard Oil, and businessman Robert Ogden, among many others. John D. Rockefeller established the General Education Board and funneled over $180 million into private educational ventures primarily along the lines of what became known as the Hampton-Tuskegee model. President McKinley visited Tuskegee and Theodor Roosevelt invited Washington to the White House. Washington became recognized among White supporters as the national voice of African Americans. He zealously guarded this position and the money attached to it (Anderson, 1988; Lewis, 1993).

Washington continued to argue for industrial training rather than academic instruction for Black students. He scorned the teaching of Latin, French, or literature because it just made Black youth "unfit for laboring." To fend off criticism within the Black community, he stressed the training of teachers; some "academic" creditability was thus attained. But schools patterned after Washington's vision basically provided instruction in agriculture and domestic work, in craft fields such as masonry and carpentry, and in "moral and work habits." He established a model of segregated industrial training that persisted up into the 1950s and 1960s.

Washington was challenged by young Black intellectuals that refused to accept second-class status and agitated for social and economic justice. Among the most outstanding was W.E.B. DuBois, a graduate of Fisk and Harvard where he was the first African American to earn a doctorate. Part Four briefly mentioned that DuBois grew up in Great Barrington, Massachusetts. He attended an integrated school, and was recognized early as a child prodigy. Encouraged by his White teachers and in particular by high school principal Frank Hosmer, he excelled. He was helped to locate money to continue on to higher education where his brilliance as a writer and an intellectual matured. In 1910 he accepted a position with the fledging National Association for the Advancement of Colored People (NAACP). Started two years earlier by White philanthropists, DuBois contributed secondary influence in the initial stage as the NAACP struggled to find its identity. Asserting leadership, DuBois quickly propelled the organization forward into national focus through the *Crisis*, a publication for the membership that he edited and largely wrote. The *Crisis* became the intellectual voice of African Americans, membership mushroomed, and the NAACP secured a permanent place on the national stage (Lewis, 1993, pp. 386–407).

DuBois challenged Washington's vision of education for Blacks. Washington was wrong, DuBois contended, because Whites would never accept Blacks unless forced to on equal terms. Education was crucial, and taking a page from Thomas Jefferson, DuBois wanted to extend educational opportunity as widely as possible within Black communities. He wanted to give students the best academic education possible. Next, in a process of "creaming," the most advanced students are identified and continue on to a higher level, and so on until the most able make up what Du Bois termed "the talented tenth." It is "exceptional men," Du Bois observed, that will save the African American community. They will "guide the Mass away from the contamination and death of the Worst, in their own and other races." And the best among the Blacks will compete with the best of the Whites on equal terms. Washington was wrong, he chided, because Blacks with an inferior education will always be socially inferior (DuBois, 1903).

As his thoughts matured, DuBois added another dimension to his ideas on education. The Black diaspora lacks an identity, he observed. Blacks the world over need to reclaim their historical and cultural heritage. He joined in promoting the idea of a Pan-African Congress meeting regularly with a fixed central office to advance the cause of people of African heritage. They would reestablish an identity as a people (Lewis, 1993). A final piece in his vision of Black education was to facilitate an understanding of the rich social and cultural heritage Blacks unknowingly carry with them. He was not against integration, but he did not want integration with White society at the expense of Black identity becoming lost. To be sure, all should work together to create a harmonious society, DuBois stressed, but cultural identities need to be celebrated, not diluted, fused, or lost.

Both positions on education were carried into the 1920s as Black communities worked to extend educational opportunity for their children. In southern states the pattern was for Blacks to pay more in taxes for school support than was returned, with the balance going to White schools. Black communities embarked in what is termed the "Second Crusade," the campaign to raise money to build and support their own schools. Limited public funds were often combined with community contributions and philanthropic support, but more often than not Black communities financed and owned their own common schools (Anderson, 1988).

In a pattern that was to be repeated in rural communities throughout the South, in 1921 the Black community of Coffee County, Alabama, for example, donated 10 acres of land, raised $700 in cash, and pledged an additional $1,500 to build a school building. Community members provided building material and labor (Anderson, 1988, p. 161). These were extremely poor people, and they gave pennies, nickels, dimes, and all of the cash they had for the educational good of community children. "The school attendance rates of black elementary children increased from 36 percent in 1900 to 78 percent in 1940, and the corresponding rate for whites went from 55 percent in 1900 to 79 percent in 1940" (Anderson, 1988, p. 181). This was significant. Out of the second crusade came a literate Black population that played prominent roles in promoting the economic and social welfare of Americans of African heritage.

Up until the 1920s there were few public high schools for Black youth except for some in urban areas. Edward Krug (1972) reported in 1920 only 1.5% of Black youth attended high school, and a decade later the increase was only to 3% of Black youth. This contrasted to over 49% of the White high school age cohort attending in 1930. Few Blacks in rural areas went to school, not to count secondary schools. And in urban areas there was little interest among White southerners to provide secondary education for Black youth. Southern states pushed for the expansion of secondary education for Whites, but not for Blacks. In Georgia, for example, there were 4 high schools for Whites in 1904 with an increase to 122 by 1916. There were no schools for Black youth even though they made up 46% of the secondary school population. Similarly, in 1916, Mississippi, South Carolina, Louisiana, and North Carolina had no secondary schools for Black youth (Anderson, 1988).

With the increased flow of Blacks out of the rural South to urban southern and northern areas, however, secondary education started opening up. Many Black youth moved to cities without their parents. The accumulating numbers of Black youth forced action as northern philanthropists joined with southern school officials to found Black secondary schools. By 1925, there were a combined total of 143 secondary schools in the 11 former Confederate states, up from 21 in 1915. Many Black students continue to attend private schools, schools established through philanthropic grants, and others attended secondary education departments in the 28 land grant colleges and state normal schools.

The struggle between proponents of an industrial education and supporters of a "literary" curriculum continued, with what appears to be a clear preference on the part of students, parents, and local Black leaders for an academic curriculum. Proponents of academic education were quick to point out youth eventually secured "Negro jobs" as construction helpers, cooks and dishwashers, "yard boys," laundry men, and farm laborers, and none required secondary, if any, education. Academic studies held the promise of advancement through higher education for at least some. In Little Rock, Arkansas, for example, Black parents vigorously protested the pending building in 1928 of the Negro Industrial High School. They wanted an academic school for their children. One parent summed up the protest sentiment: "Our people here have been waiting patiently over a span of years for a real high school, one that would not be a subterfuge; one that would give a thorough educational training and literary background, and a curriculum upon which a college education could be well predicated" (Anderson, 1988, pp. 196–210). Black parents wanted their sons and daughters to have a chance to become a member of the talented tenth.

Something socially significant happened in the 1920s: Whites discovered Black American culture. A body of Black music emerged that expressed the cultural vitality of African Americans; black poets such as Langston Hughes and Sterling Brown defined the sense of Black being; and novelists and playwrights joined with composers, poets, and musicians to nurture in New York City the cultural explosion that became known as the Harlem Renaissance. Peter Carroll and David Noble (1988) suggested Afro-American music "had an effect on the composed and restrained patterns of ragtime; on the immediacy of the blues, where the human voice spoke in song; and on the improvisation of jazz, where the musician conversed with his listeners through his instrument" (p. 326). But the music, poetry, literature, and art also expressed to America Black despair, pain, sorrow, and joy and creativity. As the great Black jazz player Charlie Parker said, "Music is your own experience. If you don't live it, it won't come out of your horn" (Carroll & Noble, 1988, p. 326). White America started to gain some understanding of Black America.

The "Second Crusade" paid dividends. There developed a relatively small educated intellectual and professional class within reach of Black communities, and coupled with limited but greater affluence that provided confidence and resources, the stirrings of the civil rights movement became evident. Black school superintendents, principals, and teachers; writers and journalists; accountants, lawyers, and doctors; college presidents and professors; and scores of young professional men and women organized Black communities. Blacks had a limited degree of political power by virtue of numbers and an effective professional leadership, and they organized to achieve social justice. The stirrings of what became the civil rights movement of the 1950s and 1960s are evident in the late 1920s. Individuals such as Mary McCloud Bethune, a leader for women' rights, continued to play a national role; Black leaders honed their organizational skills, and a sense of purpose spread throughout Black communities. But the Great Depression and the following Second World War derailed early civil rights efforts. Nevertheless, the groundwork to build on was constructed.

The Great Crash: Education in the Time of Turmoil

Not only economic but also social and psychological disequilibrium was an outcome of the Great Depression that lasted for a decade after the October 1929 crash, with economic recovery only as the nation prepared for the impending armed world conflict. Unemployment had been rising since 1928, but with the stock market dive, the rate rose to over 30%. Those fortunate enough to have jobs had to take pay cuts and reduced hours as production slumped all across the country. On the average, wages fell by one third, but mortgage payments and credit card debt stayed the same, and even though prices fell for food and consumer goods, people did not have money. Consumer demand dropped, adding momentum to the downward economic spiral.

Those living on farms had food, but often no money and little opportunity to earn. They could not pay electrical bills, repair equipment, buy seed and fertilizer, or meet mortgage payments and tax bills. They lost everything they owned to debt piling up. In urban areas there were spectacular newspaper stories of suicide, men that could not face the psychological trauma of losing the wealth that was the very source of their identity; some men no longer able to face hungry children and wives disappeared, abandoning respectability and responsibility to join the faceless army of the unemployed: catching rides on freight trains, living under bridges and in abandoned houses, willing to work for pennies or food, or in desperation begging for handouts, or stealing. Some became drunkards. Some ended up in jail. Some returned home years later, psychologically broken. Some never came home. The young were trapped in unemployment. In 1932 there was an estimated 200,000 to 300,000 teenage tramps wandering across the country trying to survive. Around 10% were female. The unemployment rate among youth doubled or tripled that of adults. Blacks and young women had the most difficult time finding employment (Angus & Mirel, 1999; McElvaine, 1984).

Many took desperate measures to feed themselves. Violence against individuals and local government increased and spread fear and alarm. Groups of men attacked city halls demanding relief. People sold cherished possessions for a little food or money to pay the doctor bill for a seriously sick child. Families were broken up and children sent to different relatives. Children were sent out into the street or put into foster homes to make room for younger siblings. Weeds were used to make soup; men searched through garbage cans and dug in dumps to find something to eat. Robert McElvaine (1984, p.80) recorded the plight of one elderly woman who took off her glasses when preparing her meal to avoid having to see the maggots infesting the rotting food she was eating.

Officials urged the unemployed to look for odd jobs, sell apples or pencils on the street, or start gardens to feed themselves. Some communities set aside plots for family gardens to ease hunger. Community leaders urged "make-work" efforts and "household helper" schemes so those with money could help those without earnings. Neighbors bartered with local, small town merchants and with each other because none had any money. Soup kitchens and bread lines were established in cities and towns so the hungry could have a meal. Charity groups gave away used clothing, shoes, and blankets. Churches organized support groups to administer to the destitute. State institutions filled to capacity with children parents could no longer rear. One individual proposed to collect the leftovers from the tables of the affluent to feed the destitute. Another suggested enlisting restaurants to join in feeding the hungry with "the side dishes of vegetables, half-bowls of soup, half cups of coffee, portions of rolls" and all else that was left on the plates of dinners. The campus eating clubs at Princeton University collected food scraps and sent them to the poor (Carroll & Noble, 1988; McElvain, 1984).

Public Schools: The Struggle for Stability

Public schools contributed. For example, in Toledo, Ohio, teachers initiated a work relief program; needy students were paid for typing, performing office work, and assisting teachers. Of the over $800 paid out, the teachers themselves contributed more than half. In Seattle, teachers gave free afternoon classes to unemployed adults, and in Detroit the public schools organized the Committee on Social Services to raise money and provide hot lunches, shoes, clothing, eye examinations and glasses. But schools and teachers faced difficult times and often could do little (Krug, 1972).

Schools were directly impacted. Enrollments shot up while at the same time tax income dropped. More individuals attended school at all levels. At the high school level the increase was overwhelming. Of the high school age cohort, around 49% were attending in 1929; a decade later the increase was to 68%. At the same time, school income dropped by a third. The bulk of school income came from local property taxes, but the tax base was seriously eroded at the same time schools needed additional income to cope with the ever-increasing student load.

School officials scrambled to cope. Struggles ensued with teachers over reduced wages. Some school districts, unable to consistently pay salaries issued script: IOUs for payment at some future date for services rendered. Class sizes were enlarged and some subjects were eliminated in order to reduce the number of teachers. Some faculties were pared down by a third. No new teachers were hired. Physical education was secure. Class size could be expanded to 60 students by adding more kick-ball groups or enlarging the exercise group. Glee club was inexpensive because it required little more than sheet music and the number of students could be easily increased. Band was expensive because it required musical instruments, so it was a target for elimination. Shop and science were expensive because costly equipment was needed and laboratory enrollment was restricted to 24 students; cuts were made and labs gave way to larger-enrolled lecture classes. What were considered "fads and frills" were hit the hardest: kindergartens, special low-enrollment classes, foreign language, and vocational courses. Building programs were stopped, and repair and maintenance curtailed (Angus & Mirel, 1988; Tyack, Lowe, & Hansot, 1984).

Conflict developed between school administrators and boards of education. Boards wanted to cut expenses; administrators wanted to save staff and programs. Local boards of education typically represented the interests of community businessmen struggling to survive in the difficult economic times. To board members this was a time to cut school budgets and taxes: lop off programs, fire teachers, increase class sizes, take in fewer students, and forget about special classes and dropout rates. Fighting a rear-guard action, the National Educational Association and the American Association for School Administrators created in 1935 the Educational Policies Commission (EPC). Its purpose was to preserve school budgets and counter cuts. The activities of the EPC continued up into the 1950s. But in the immediate term, the EPC turned its attention to the federal government.

Public school officials hoped that with the election of Franklin Roosevelt in 1932 federal financial relief would be given to the nation's public schools. The formation in 1933 of the National Youth Administration fostered hope. Work-study positions were financed in high schools, colleges, and universities to enable youth from poor families to continue in school. But hope turned to disappointment with the failure of the efforts of the EPC to gain additional federal policy support for public education. Distrusting the effectiveness of public schools, Roosevelt addressed issues of youth education and employment outside of the public school establishment. For example, after a protracted struggle with public school interests, administration of the Civilian Conservation Corps (CCC) was granted to the U.S Army. The CCC camps potentially could be run by local schools, providing sources of much wanted revenue (Angus & Mirel, 1999).

There were two results from federal rejection. Public school educators were angered and disappointed. Education functions they performed, such as academic instruction, vocational training, guidance, and placement were now assigned to federal agencies. The possibility of federal aid for public schools was closed. Communities had to cope on their own. The second policy influence was long term. The Roosevelt administration's decisions signaled a shift in public policy from the domination by public schools of public money, to the educational use of public funds by constituency groups outside the orbit of public education. This policy shift continues at local, state, and federal levels as can be seen today by the enormous sums of money allocated to labor departments, poverty agencies, special needs groups, youth organizations, and private contractors for training and educational purposes. Education and training and the way it is delivered are cast in broad terms.

Curriculum Change and Cha[llenge]

Two curricular changes were advanced that continue to characte[rize educa]tion today. The most debated, *essentialism*, was the idea instruct[ion center on a] body of relevant content rather than on traditional literary stu[dies and the] cultural heritage of the nation. According to its leading proponent[s led by Bagley of Columbia] University, school should stress "modern" knowledge over the [past as a] way to promote economic and social regeneration. To be sure, rig[or was impor]tant, but essentialists considered the focus of subject matter shou[ld be on] useful knowledge. In this way, instruction is less intellectual but more useful while maintaining a core of studies organized as separate subjects for everyone. There were certain things every pupil needed to master in the modern world, Bagley (1939) asserted.

There were differences among supporters of essentialism, but the core subjects tended to be clustered around reading, math, science, "some acquaintance with the past," art, and health instruction (Kliebard, 1987, p. 231). At a time of financial crisis, essentialism was appealing. It was difficult to continue support for literary studies designed for a small proportion of the student population. Also, there were too many separate subjects offered, and all could not be supported. Essentialism had potential to collapse school studies for everyone into a reduced core, and at the same time save money.

The idea that there is a core of essential learning appropriate for everyone gained a strong hold on American education. Following World War II, emphasis on subject-centered instruction and the testing movement reflected essentialism, recurring talk about "going back to the basics" embodied essentialism, and today the idea of "core standards" is pure essentialism.

Another focus of curriculum change was the problem surrounding what was termed "the new fifty percent." The depression years brought into high schools more pupils inadequately prepared who did not want to be in school and who had limited aspirations. Formerly, these students would have gone directly into the labor market during or following the elementary school years. As suggested earlier, child labor laws, compulsory attendance laws, and the fact that they could not find work combined to push them into secondary schools, but now with the flow into high schools was depression at a troublesome rate. They did not want to or could not adjust to school studies. These individuals were characterized as "dull," "dull normal," or "with poor mental equipment" (Krug, 1972). And according to the test makers, not much could be done because their IQs were genetically fixed. They were products of nature. Earlier they would have been characterized by Thorndike or Termin as "mentally deficient" or "borderline moronic."

Echoing frustrations heard around the country, the assistant superintendent of Detroit schools, for example, voiced the opinion that one third of students attending high school is "congenitally incapable of doing high school work as it is now organized." But he did not favor excluding them from school: "these stupid children" needed "further training in citizenship, in morals, in health, and in the social arts" (Krug, 1972, p. 111). One response was to add more commercial and technical studies to keep students in school, but vocational educators complained that unprepared, poor performing students with little interest in school were eroding the onal studies. They were not performing much better than in academic classes. and Jeffrey Mirel (1999) observed educators quickly came to the conclusion ex- ocational education was not the answer. "Indeed, depression era educators believed ther the academic nor vocational tracks could successfully accommodate the new wave udents" (p. 72). Educators turned their attention to formulating a curriculum option for what was increasingly referred to as the "new fifty percent" (Butterfield, 1934).

It was estimated that roughly 25% of attending students profited from what was basically college preparatory studies. These were the future engineers, lawyers, doctors, writers, bankers, clergy, and teachers. Another 25% were best suited for vocational studies, the future mechanics, carpenters, plumbers, accountants, stock raisers, walnut growers, and stenographers. It was thought the remaining 50% needed little academic or occupational preparation because they would fill modest jobs requiring minimum advanced preparation: mail carriers, truck drivers, warehouse workers, street cleaners, parking lot attendants, farm laborers, and factory workers. What should school offer these students? They tended to do poorly in academic as well as vocational subjects, and vocational teachers complained uninterested, poorly performing students degraded the quality of offering.

Three instructional tracks were formulated that continue to form the core of high school studies: college preparatory, vocational, and general for the remaining 50% of students of unknown, but probable modest life roles. The general track largely consisted of what became known as "life adjustment" studies. In "consumer math" students learned basic arithmetic, and applied it to exercises on constructing a family budget, paying mock bills, filling out tax forms, and maintaining a bank account. In "consumer English" students practiced reading the newspaper, and applied basic grammar and language in simple stories, and read poems and short stories and wrote letters and filled out forms. Students in the general curriculum took courses on how government worked, civics, family living, health and hygiene, and current events. They were scheduled into craft courses, art and glee club, and they took physical education. The general track was thought to create good citizens capable of filling a constructive social and economic role, happy individuals, content with family life, responsible and aware of social responsibilities. And as Termin had earlier argued for, studies were not "academic."

David Angus and Jeffrey Mirel (1999) observed the curriculum change to accommodate the new 50% marked a significant policy alternation in American public education. What emerged was a "custodial high school" designed to keep youth out of the labor market and engaged in activities to shape constructive social behaviors and useful economic skills. Efficiency advocates were supportive. Hereditary evolutionists were supportive. The Educational Policy Commission was solidly behind the new policy thrust. Schoolmen lined up behind the shift in objectives. The debates between G. Stanley Hall and Charles Elliot over the elite curriculum outlined in the work the Committee of Ten were irrelevant, if even remembered. There was little support, or even discussion for the education of an elite. The objectives of education "for citizenship, for worthy home membership and for effective use of leisure time" outlined in the *Cardinal Principles* are what dominated educational thinking.

The shift to the general track for the new 50% was an effort to increase the holding power of the public school that went beyond the depression years. The fundamental social and economic transformation that extended beyond WWII and deep into our time required keeping students in school in order to counter potential serious problems for society. The custodial function is strongly present in schools of today. But high dropout rates; poor school performance that result in perhaps 20% or more of high school completers remaining functionally illiterate; substantial differences in quality within and between schools; high costs but poor individual and social returns on the public school investment—these and other indicators point to the limitations of the comprehensive school concept formulated by Clarence Kingsley and the National Commission on the Reorganization of Secondary Education. One limitation was a result of not being able to anticipate the difficulty of bringing together such divergent student populations into one comprehensive institution and provide all with a meaningful, relevant, quality education. Another was a result of not fully recognizing the necessity of also addressing the conditions of poverty, of broken families and communities, of bigotry, of the great disparities of wealth, and of class and ethnic tensions that fundamentally impinge on the school and its ability to serve all students.

George Counts: Constructing a New Social Order

The depression threatened to shred the economic, social, and political fabric of the nation. Like the population in general, educators expressed alarm, and they turned their efforts to addressing conditions they saw threatening social cohesion. The Education Policy Commission gingerly tiptoed around issues relating to the failure of the capitalistic system. The new journal, *The Educational Frontier*, faced issues head-on and called for the reconstruction of the broken society through public schools. It was George Counts, however, who gained national attention with his 1932 pamphlet *Dare the School Build a New Social Order*. With a doctorate from the University of Chicago, Counts built an impressive career of social analysis and criticism. He responded to the fear of violent social dislocation and advancing communism by arguing American schools could help shape a new society built on a more socialistic model that rounded off the hard edges of capitalism. Unregulated capitalism was "cruel, wasteful and inhuman," and unless an alternative was found society itself could implode. A new social and economic system based on "democratic collectivism" with less individualism and competition had the potential to eliminate poverty and class tensions, and address the perplexing issues associated with advancing industrialism, Counts claimed. Teachers, Counts urged, must "reach for power" and use schools to give birth to a new society (Bowers, 1969; Cremin, 1961; Krug,1972).

George Counts's vocal critics branded him as a communist. But Counts had a surprising number of supporters in the education, journalism, and political communities who saw reason in what he was saying. Unless the American economy could be fixed to eliminate the capitalistic excesses of inequality and destructive social and economic tendencies, a possible outcome was uncontrollable social violence and political collapse. Reform was better than total collapse. Schools and teachers turned to aligning instruction with social outcomes promoting more social cooperation and less individualism (Bowers, 1969).

In the 1930s, in the depths of the Depression, the ideas of Counts attracted a following. With the outbreak of the Second World War, thoughts of forging a new social order quickly disappeared as the nation tooled up for the war effort. Unemployment evaporated, and patriotism replaced social reform concerns. The power of the production system was praised. But Counts's influence continued after the war to haunt public education. Schools were accused of sheltering individuals that were advancing subversive influence. As the "red scare" enveloped the nation in the 1950s, critics bent their effort to rooting out educators from the public schools that if not red, were an incriminating pink.

References for Part Five

Allen. F.L. (1931). Only Yesterday; An Informal History of the 1929s. New York: Harper & Row.

Allen, F.L. (1952). The Big Change; America Transforms Itself 1900-1950. New York: Harper & Row.

Anderson, J.D. (1988). The Education of Blacks in the South, 1860-1935. Chapel Hill: The University of North Carolina Press.

Angus, D.L., & Mirel, J. (1999). The Failed Promise of the American High School 1890-1995. New York: Teachers College Press.

Ayers, E.L. (1993). The Promise of the New South. New York: Oxford University Press.

Bagley, W.C. (1939). The Significance of the Essentialist Movement in Educational Theory. Classical Journal.

Bennett, C.A. (1937). History of Manual and Industrial Education 1870-1917. Peoria, IL: The Manual Arts Press.

Berlin, I. (2010). The Making of African America. New York: Viking.

Berthoff, R. (1971). An Unsettled People; Social Order and Disorder in American History. New York: Harper & Row.

Bowers, C.A. (1969). The Progressive Educator in the Depression: The Radical Years. New York: Random House.

Boyer, R.O., & Morais, H.M. (1971). Labor's Untold Story. New York: United Electrical, Radio and Machine Workers of America.

Bureau of Education, Bulletin No. 18. Washington, DC: U.S. Government Printing Office.

Butterfield, E.W. (1934). The New Fifty Per Cent. Junior-Senior High School Clearing House.

Callahan, R.E. (1962). Education and the Cult of Efficiency. Chicago: University of Chicago Press.

Carroll, P.N., & Noble, D.W. (1988). The Free and the Unfree; A New History of the United States. New York: Penguin.

Cavalli-Sforza, L.L. (2000). Genes, Peoples, and Languages. Berkeley: University of California Press.

Commission for the Reorganization of Secondary Education (1918). Cardinal Principles of Secondary Education. Bulletin No. 35. Washington, DC: U.S. Bureau of Education.

Cremin, L.A. (1961). The Transformation of the School. New York: Alfred A. Knopf.

Cremin, L.A. (1988). American Education; The Metropolitan Experience 1876-1980. New York: Harper & Row.

Curti, M. (1959). The Social Ideas of American Educators. Totowa, NJ: Littlefield, Adams and Co.

Curtis, S.J., & Boultwood, M.E.A. (1965). A Short History of Educational Ideas. London: University Tutorial Press.

Dewey J. (1896). *University of Chicago Record.* The University School.

Dewey, J. (1916). The Need of an Industrial Education in an Industrial Democracy. *Manual Training and Vocational Education, 17*(6), 409–414.

Dewey, J. (1917). The Need of an Industrial Education in an Industrial Democracy. Proceedings of the Second Pan American Scientific Congress. Section IV, Part I. Washington, DC.

Drost, W.H. (1967). David Snedden and Education for Social Efficiency: Madison: The University of Wisconsin Press.

DuBois, W.E.B. (1903). The Talented Tenth. In R.L. Vassar (1968), Social History of American Education. Vol. II: 1860-the Present. Chicago: Rand McNally and Co.

Dworkin, M/S. (1959). Dewey on Education. Classics in Education No. 3. New York: Teachers College Press.

Eliot, C.W. (1905). The Fundamental Assumptions in the Report of the Committee of Ten (1993). Educational Review, 30, 325–343.

Ellis, E.R. (1996). Echoes of Distant Thunder. New York: Kodansha International.

Fisher, B.M. (1967). Industrial Education. Madison: University of Wisconsin Press.

Furnas, J.C. (1969). The Americas: A Social History of the United States 1587–1914. New York: Putnam's Sons.

Gould, S.J. (1981). The Mismeasure of Man. New York: Penguin Books.

Grob, G.N., & Beck, R.N. (1963). American Ideas. London: Collier-Macmillan.

Hall, G.S. (1904). Adolescence: Its Psychology and Its Relation to Physiology, Anthropology, Sociology, Sex, Crime, Religion and Education. Vol. 2. New York: D. Appleton.

Higham, J. (1970). Strangers in the Land Patterns of American Nativism 1860–1925. New York: Atheneum.

Hofstadter, R. (1955). The Age of Reform. New York: Vintage Books.

Holbrook, S.H. (1985). The Age of the Moguls. New York: Harmony Books.

Johnson, P. (1997). A History of the American People. New York: Harper.

Karier, C.J. (1967). Man, Society, and Education. Glenview, IL: Scott, Foresman and Co.

Katznelson, I. (2013). Fear Itself; The New Deal and the Origins of Our Time. New York: Liveright Publishing Corporation.

Kevles, D.J. (1995). In the Name of Eugenics. Cambridge: Harvard University Press.

Kevles, D.J., & Hood, L. (1992). The Codes of Codes. Cambridge: Harvard University Press.

Kliebard, H.M. (1987). The Struggle for the American Curriculum 1893–1952. New York: Routledge.

Krug, E.A. (1964). The Shaping of the American High School. Madison: The University of Wisconsin Press.

Krug, E.A. (1972). The Shapings of the American High School 1920–1941. New York: Harper and Row.

Lewis, D.L. (1993). W.E.B. DuBois Biography of a Race 1888–1919. New York: Henry Holt and Company.

Lukas, S.A. (1997). Big Trouble. New York: Simon & Schuster.

Mayhew, K.C., & Edwards, A.C. (1966). The Dewey School. New York: Atherton.

McElvane, R.S. (1984). The Great Depression. New York: Times Books.

Morrison, S.E. (1965). The Oxford History of the American People. New York: Oxford University Press.

Munsterberg, H. (1913). Psychology and Industrial Efficiency. Boston: Houghton Mifflin Co.

Olson, S. (2002). Mapping Human History Genes, Race and Our Common Origins. New York: Houghton Mifflin Co.

Report of the Commission on Industrial and Technical Education. Boston: State of Massachusetts.

Snedden, D. (1910). The Problem of Vocational Education. Boston: Houghton, Mifflin Co., 1910.

Spain, D. (2001). How Women Saved the City. Minneapolis,MN: University of Minnesota Press.

Spring, J. (2008). The American School. New York: McGraw-Hill.

Starr, K. (1996). Endangered Dreams the Great Depression in California. New York: Oxford University Press.

Thorndike, E.L. (1911). Individuality. Boston: Houghton Mifflin Co.

Tyack, D. (1974). The One Best System; A History of American Urban Education. Cambridge, MA: Harvard University Press.

Tyack, D., & Hansot, E. (1982). Managers of Virtue Public School Leadership in America, 1820-1980. New York: Russell Sage Foudation.

Tyack. D., Lowe, R., & Hansot, E. (1984). Public Schools in Hard Times. The Great Depression and Recent Years. Cambridge: Harvard University Press.

Woodward, C.V. (1957). The Strange Career of Jim Crow. New York: Oxford University Press.

Part Six
Education and The National Agenda

Introduction

There are great turning points in history. World War II was one. The modern world that was in its infancy in the early 1900s became one of sober maturity following the most destructive military clash the world had ever experienced. Hardly any region of the world was spared carnage: 60 million human lives extinguished. Too many killed. Too many villages, towns, and cities destroyed beyond count, too many lives torn apart. Those remaining experienced a radically altered world.

The United States largely escaped direct warfare at home, but the massive armament and manpower buildup to support extensive combat involvement in the European and Asian theaters irrevocably changed society. Men and women, young and old, Whites and Blacks, Indians, Asians, and Latinos were united as never before, as they joined in combat and on the homefront to maintain the war machine. Men between 17 and 35 were expected to enlist, and as the full productive energies of the nation were turned to the war effort, older men and women labored on the homefront to build ships, tanks, and airplanes; to make explosives, prepare food rations, produce radios; and to experiment in research labs to perfect destructive devices. Seventeen-year-olds left school and went off to enlist, Navaho Indians enlisted as code specialists, Chinese Americans served as interpreters, farmboys from Mississippi, Vermont, and Kansas, and sons of factory workers in Bridgeport and Oakland, and sons of Polish immigrants in Chicago drove tanks and charged bunkers, and killed and got killed. Blacks flew airplanes built by "Rosie the Riveter." Women flew planes from factories to military fields. Women, who never worked before outside of the home, filled the civilian workforce by the thousands; they experienced the liberation of earning a paying wage. Poor Whites, Blacks, and Latinos left the pine forests, sweatshops, and cotton and lettuce fields, and got good-paying defense jobs as discrimination barriers dropped. And all shared the anxieties over loved ones at the front, and the sorrows of lost lives. After the war, few wanted to go back to the old way of life that in any case was gone.

The war ushered in an age of science, technology, and engineering. Industrial production was key to winning the war. The United States produced more tanks, ships, guns, bombs, and planes than the Axis powers combined. But it was more than just quantity of material that won the war. There was an endless stream of scientific and technical breakthroughs that produced advances in radio, radar, and sonar. Better and faster planes, more powerful shells and bombs, new plastics, and stronger and lighter metals were produced. Antibiotics were introduced. Better ways of machining metal were perfected, more powerful engines developed, better fuels formulated, and the scope of electronics extended. All of these scientific and engineering advancements were transferred into the postwar economy; they revolutionized the way people worked and lived, and fed yet more scientific and technological innovation that opened a new age.

An outcome of the war was the realization that a new age had emerged, one in which the productive force of the nation was trained people who could continue to fuel the economy with scientific and technical advancement. This required the extension of schooling so that the potential of human resources could be fully employed. The opportunity to go to college was extended, driven by a new awareness of the importance of higher education but also by public demand. Horizons were expanded. More women wanted to go to college, and both boys and girls from modest-income families perceived that they too could climb the social and economic ladder through more education. Tuition fees were kept low at many state colleges. Two-year "junior colleges" linked with high schools proliferated so that returning youth who left high school to go to war, upon returning, had an opportunity to complete high school and possibly matriculate into a four-year college program. Two-year normal schools were converted to four-year coeducational colleges. State and private schools expanded, and everywhere small college became big. Enrollments for both women and men shot up in colleges across the country, accommodating a new kind of student population: Youth of the working class, women, and more minority youth sought out higher education. Income and class were no longer impediments. Youth of any income level could find higher education opportunity somewhere if they were fortunate enough to learn how to navigate the pathways to schooling.

The G.I. Bill, passed by Congress, had the dual outcome of keeping returning service personnel off the labor market to avoid a labor glut and making it possible for youth who formerly could not afford college to attend. The returning poor boy from a family engaged in day labor living in a rural shack could now go to college and fulfill his dream of becoming an engineer. There also was an extended effort to identify bright students and provide them scholarship incentives to attend the best research institutions in the country. The highly intelligent schoolgirl from a modest urban New Jersey home could realize her dream of earning a PhD in organic chemistry, a field formerly considered closed to women; or the precocious rural California farmboy could knock the dirt off his hightop shoes and enter into the sacrosanct halls of an elite university to become a leading scientific researcher. Or the Japanese son of a family interred during the war in a concentration camp in remote eastern Colorado could find scholarship help to complete his studies as a medical doctor, and the bright African American boy excelling in physics could earn a PhD at the top state university. America knew it needed to make the best use possible of its human resources. By removing barriers of class, ethnicity, and income, and making it possible for the bright to pursue higher education, the nation increased markedly its wealth of human resources. This was an insight of fundamental importance. Human resources continue to drive the prosperity of the nation.

A period of affluence was ushered in. A degree of wide relative affluence never before realized materialized as men and women banked the wages they earned from defense work, and continued to earn "good" money in the booming economy. With rationing there was little to spend on, but with victory the country went on a spending binge. Families bought homes, often little "ticky-tacky" cheaply constructed boxes, but this meant that for the first time many could bask in the pride of home ownership. They bought cars, stoves, new fangled washing machines, miracle soap that took out the "ring around the collar"; and they now had radios and clothing and all kinds of consumer items. But only 46% of households had telephones, and 52% of farm families had no electricity (Patterson, 1996).

Americans also had babies—many babies. During the depression years couples tried to avoid the expense of children and birthrates dropped. During the war, birthrates remained low as men and women were off fighting or struggling with rationing. With victory, the 12.1 million men still in uniform at the close of the war in 1945 came home. Birthrates soared, and so did the profits of merchants as a baby industry was launched. In 1946 alone, 3.4 million babies were born; in 1947, there were 3.8 million births, and the number increased until 1964 when it leveled off. During this 18-year period, a total of 76.4 million new lives were added to a population of 140 million. Prosperity continued as consumer demand drove spending up into the 1960s (Patterson, 1996).

No new school buildings were constructed during the war years. From the early 1950s on, schools were built at a hasty pace to house all of the arriving schoolchildren. Over a 15-year period in California, for example, a new elementary school opened up every Monday morning. High schools followed the construction binge, and colleges similarly experienced a facilities shortage. And teaching jobs opened to thousands of American youth now going to college to earn degrees, some among the first ever in their families. Of the college age population, 21% had earned a BA by 1955.

More than a facilities shortage challenged educators. Debates resurfaced over the form and substance of American education, and this continued to be largely centered in the high school. Studies for college-bound students were reasonably well defined along the *Essentialists'* lines that Bagley and others had once advanced. But it was the 50% of the school population identified in the 1930s as low achievers and the disinterested—now considered 60%—that now provoked the most achromous discussion. These students generally did not like school and did not perform well. How could the custodial function of secondary education best be continued? An ill-fated national "life adjustment" movement after the war met resistance as a barrage of criticism was launched by educators alarmed at what they considered a dilution of the academic quality of high school instruction. Similarly, vocational educators were alarmed over the practice of scheduling poorly academic performing students thought to be of lower mental ability into vocational education. Vocational educators did not want to be a part of a custodial curriculum. But soon the subject field was being referred to as a "dumping ground." The outline was thus sketched for what was to be a continuing debate in American education to the present.

The war also brought to the surface long-simmering social issues that the nation failed to address in the contentious 1920s and the desperation of the depression years. Pockets of deep poverty persisted. Racial tensions aroused apprehension and fear. Religious intolerance divided communities and homes. Class divisions fostered resentment over the special privileges of the few. But with a renewed sense of national purpose and a time of relative affluence, citizens were receptive to the plight of others and the national failure to act. The stalled civil rights movement of the 1920s reignited and the leadership within the Black community caused America to examine its inner soul: Could the nation dare to build a more egalitarian and just society?

The Focus of Part Six

Part Six covers the continuing struggle in education to come to terms with a complex, diverse society changing at a rapid pace, and to redefine the public education system that evolved out of the early 1900s. American society is extremely complex. Educational discourse is similarly complex, and tends to be dominated by one group or another at a particular time, but this does not mean that there are not other counterviews commanding public support. It is the continuous churning of ideas that creates such a dynamic society. No one viewpoint can dominate without going through a process of redefinition and accommodation in response to counter assumptions and beliefs. Nor can one set of school practices be considered appropriate for all. And it is the practice in local schools that bend and shape educational ideas to achieve practical results. So it is with education in our time.

The national education agenda was dominated after the war and up to the national 1960 election by what can be described as "conservative" thought, although this term is not precise and unitary in belief. All conservatives do not think alike, and some views overlap with liberals. But the term continues to be used. Conservative thought occupied the center of the national education stage during the latter 1940s and 1950s, but "liberal" (again, an imprecise term) education advocates continued to make their views heard, even if from the stage wings. With the political shift in 1960, liberal views took place at the front of the national stage and dominated public educational discourse through the Kennedy and Johnson administrations. The national education actors shifted position with the Nixon administration, and the 1970s are best described by a mixed chorus of voices for education renewal, with conservatives and liberals each stepping forward to recite their respective parts.

In Chapter 15 we examine the initiatives conservatives took to reshape American education along lines that addressed their concerns and beliefs. We examine their accomplishments and enduring influence. In Chapter 16 we examine liberal influence on society and education. The concluding Chapter 17 focuses on the remarkable and continuing influence of the Reagan administration on shaping American education policy to the present. The two Bush administrations and the Clinton and Obama administrations continue to reflect the powerful influence of what can be termed the "conservative restoration."

Chapter Fifteen
To Protect the National Good

Education historian Lawrence Cremin (1961) observed that by the end of the war the American public had moved away from the ideas promoted by national leaders during the flowering of the progressive movement prior to World War I; and the revolutionary call by George Counts and others associated with him in the 1930s to use the schools to shape a new social order did not sit well with Americans now interested in stability and intent on building "the good life" from the surrounding material comforts that now seemed within reach. Progressive voices were not stilled, but they were often muffled by other concerns that occupied the public's mind.

Conservatives had an appealing agenda. Although they differed among themselves, there nevertheless were six largely interlocking school reform interests that represent the scope of conservative thought. First, conservatives wanted to continue to use schools as the tool of efficiency to help drive the economic machine generating immense American wealth. Material comforts would continue to be in reach of Americans. Liberals agreed with strengthening economic development because it helped to make people better off. But conservatives chafed at the idea of spreading educational opportunity widely because of the public cost and associated increased taxes. Conservatives tended to want to limit and redirect the scope of educational opportunity to address the more academically inclined; liberals wanted to expand the reach of education throughout all of society.

Second, conservatives expressed alarm over the apparent failure of American schools to adequately prepare students to compete with the Soviet Union in the cold war. They wanted to strengthen science and math education, and thus not only improve the intellectual quality of college graduates but also increase the national output of engineers, scientists, and mathematicians (Rickover, 1959).

School critics attacked the overall low intellectual quality of high school instruction. A third outcome that conservatives wanted was to limit the range of high school courses, and focus on preparing youth for college admission in a select number of subjects. This meant getting rid of the custodial function for the "new 60%," reducing vocational offerings, and eliminating the whole idea of unification established in the *Cardinal Principles*. All three of these outcomes were interlocking and at the level of school application reinforced one another.

In related concerns, conservatives wanted to root out from public schools what they thought were subversive ideas and practices that had been building up throughout the 1930s. American schools needed to reflect "American" values. A fourth outcome, then, was to cleanse the schools of contaminating influences. This outcome dovetailed with the fifth concern to counter the strong movement in the direction of inclusiveness and diversity. Educational integration was contested. Echoing the testmakers of the 1920s, conservatives argued that mixing youth of different ethnic and ability levels led to disastrous social consequences. Finally, conservatives wanted to limit educational funding in general, and balked at increases designed to spread services to populations on the fringe of mainline America (Katz, 1989; Nelson & Roberts, 1963).

Economic Progress and Cold War Warriors

Following victory over Germany and Japan, the uneasy alliance with the Soviets to fight Hitler became a contest of political will and economic and military might as tensions escalated. Client states were created in previously German-occupied Eastern European countries. An armed border Winston Churchill termed the "iron curtain" was erected across Eastern Europe and the Soviets declared their intention of conquering the west and spreading Marxist-Lenin ideology across the world. American policymakers faced two related challenges: (1) to keep the economy strong in the face of communistic propaganda, which stated its superior economic system would soon outpace the capitalistic system, but in any case was doomed to fail from its own internal inconsistencies (The proletariat will rise up and revolt, said the Soviets.); and (2) to build up American military capacity to keep ahead of the Soviets (Future wars would be different, the American public was told.). The obliteration of hundreds of thousands of human lives with two atomic bombs dropped on Hiroshima and Nagasaki signaled a possible future life of horror if the society gained a decisive edge. "[The] United States is in danger," stated James Conant, president of Harvard University and member of the National Defense Research Committee (Spring, 1976, p. 41).

Building Intellectual Capacity

The most decisive action—one that resulted in massive benefits to the long-term economic, military, and scientific development of the United States—was the formation of the National Science Foundation (NSF). Marked changes resulted in American education as thousands were provided with educational opportunity. Early in 1945, Vannover Bush, head of the recently formed U.S. Office of Scientific Research and Development, and James Conant, then-president of Harvard University, advanced a proposal for the federal funding of an agency solely focused on support of basic scientific research. Conant was able to convince a reluctant president Truman to support the proposal, which became the National Science Foundation in 1950. The NSF contributed to both economic and military advancement. The important condition was that NSF funded basic research conducted in universities free from any specific link with industrial and military research. Researchers concentrated on fundamental scientific questions independent from any practical application. "Basic knowledge" was advanced.

An immediate impact of the NSF was to ensure talented young men and women had the opportunity to pursue advanced science and mathematical studies in colleges across the country. They were given financial support for their studies. Efforts were later extended to undergraduate support, and to support for high school science studies. Large numbers of bright math and science students were recruited and supported through funding in universities all across the country. University researchers build highly productive research teams. Fundamental scientific advancements were made through NSF grants. The only rival in importance to the social and economic welfare of the nation was the Morrell Land Grant Act of 1862.

By the late 1940s and early 1950s, there was a stepped-up effort throughout the country to support talented youth to pursue college studies in science, engineering, and mathematics. High school science and math teachers and guidance counselors were on the lookout for promising students. Newspapers, popular magazines, and radio talk shows took up the cause of strengthening the science and engineering capacity of the nation: more and better-prepared students had to be produced. High schools strengthened science programs and early identified talented youth; they worked with community leaders and sponsors of scholarship funds to find ways to support additional education for more students. Thousands of the bright young, often the first ever in their families, went on to college as the character of higher education itself changed. Science, math, and engineering departments grew to dominate colleges. The function of human capital development triumphed.

A major early element in the enhancement of the nation's human capital supply was the passage by Congress of the Servicemen's Readjustment Act of 1944, known as the G.I. Bill of Rights. Policymakers feared that the country would drop back into an economic depression following the end of the war. The 4 million in arms were returning to civilian life. The machines of war production would stop, thousands would lose jobs, and returning GIs would flood the labor markets. A depression followed the end of World War I, policymakers observed; however, it did not happen this time.

There was so much pent-up consumer demand and ample saved money that the economy boomed. Military production was kept going by the cold war; and the long-term benefits to young people of the G.I. Bill countered any unrealized, fizzled economic fears. Millions of youth now could afford to go to college, contributing to the overall strengthening of the human resources of the nation. The G.I. Bill funded tuition, books, and living expenses. In 1945, more than 1 million former GIs were in attendance, a doubling of the college population. Over 7.8 WWII servicemen benefitted, and subsequent college funding was available for participants in future military conflicts (Spring, 2008). These were individuals that constituted a growing, educated middle class. They became accountants, bankers, social workers, businessmen, engineers, nurses, and doctors; and thousands and thousands became schoolteachers and principals, staffing the expanding school systems. Throughout the country by the late 1940s, and up into the 1950s, a climate of greater support was created for talented youth to pursue studies in science, engineering, and mathematics; and concern grew for strengthening the quality of public education for everyone.

Protecting the Nation: The War Hawks

The efforts of those working to strengthen the quality of education found support among those concerned with defense weakness. Largely ignoring the strong movement underway to produce more and better trained scientists and engineers, as the 1950s unfolded what best can be termed "war hawks" issued dire warning that the Soviets were quickly matching and would soon overtake American military capability. Public schools were at fault because of the poor quality of math and science instruction. Not enough engineers and scientists were turned out with the ability to compete with the best Soviet scientists. We would lose the contest for military superiority because we were falling behind in the military innovation that was driving what became known as the "arms race."

In the 1950s there was a steady drumbeat of criticism directed at American public schools. A lead drummer was Vice Admiral Hyman Rickover, noted as the "father of the nuclear navy." Rickover warned the country that it was losing the arms race with the Soviets. The United States could not keep up because of the anti-intellectual atmosphere in schools created by professional educators; schools are the weak link in the national defense chain, Rickover (1959) claimed. In the eyes of Rickover, schools failed to teach students "fundamental principles" and "how to think." More rigorous studies were required, with the primary emphasis on instructing the most intelligent students. Rickover emphasized, "Talented children are this nation's reservoir of brain power. We have neglected them too long" (1959, p. 208).

Educators came in for fierce criticism. Rickover did not like them: Arrogant, inflexible, narrow-minded, and ill-informed, professional educators were not committed to maintaining high-quality standards, he claimed. The main flaw in the American high school, according to Rickover, was that they were locked into the comprehensive school model. Any effort to prepare the most intellectually promising students was thwarted. It is impossible to educate slow, average, and exceptional students in the same educational setting because overall standards decline as instruction is slanted to slower and average students. Exceptional students also learn that they do not have to work as hard because they remain ahead of other students simply by their superior intellectual aptitude. Their full academic potential remains undeveloped. Sort out students and establish separate high schools for superior students, Rickover urged, if American was to retain any chance for competing with Soviet brainpower in the struggle for economic and military domination (Angus & Mirel, 1999).

The military thought that it had a lock on nuclear weapons, but by 1951 the Soviets tested an atomic bomb; similarly, after development of the hydrogen bomb, the Soviets soon had their own. The event that shocked the nation was the launch of *Sputnik I* in October 1957, the small sphere that circled the earth, twinkling as the sun reflected off its shiny, polished surface and sounding an eerie beeping signal to announce its presence. There followed the launch of a dog, and then a man to circle the globe. The Soviets matched U.S. nuclear capability, and now they appeared to have missile superiority. How could all of this have happened? Poor public school instruction, critics warned. Soviet schools were turning out better scientists.

Reacting quickly, Congress passed in early 1958 the National Defense Education Act, authorizing the largest amount of federal aid to education below the collegiate level to date. This was a Republican bill; previously they fought the extension of federal aid to public schools on the grounds that it was unconstitutional. Now they danced to the tune of Rickover's drumming. Leading up to the formulation of the NDEA, Eisenhower outlined a number of recommendations: support for a nationwide system of testing to identify high-ability students, including support at the school level for guidance, counseling, and testing programs; incentives in the form of scholarships to persuade students to pursue science and professional studies; the hiring of more math and science teachers; support for the purchase of equipment to improve science, mathematics, and foreign language instruction; and graduate fellowship programs to support the preparation of more college teachers. All of these recommendations became in varying degree part of the NDEA. Also included was a fivefold increase in support for science teaching activities funded under the NSF. Included additionally was funding for a massive national curriculum development effort (Ford & Pungo, 1964). Out of this emerged the "new mathematics" based on set theory and functions, the new biology, physics, and in time just about every school subject of any real or constructed relevance to national defense.

The NDEA reflected the political bias against public education earlier noted in the Roosevelt administration in the 1930s. In the hearings leading up to passage of the NDEA, officials of the National Education Association, for example, urged a general appropriation of federal money to be used under the discretion of local administrators; they knew best what schools needed. But the overwhelming tone of the hearings was that federal funding should be specific, categorical aid with spending decisions taken off the hands of educators. In addition, educators had no voice in the massive national curriculum reform efforts that produced the new math and revised curricula in science and other subjects. Private think tanks and university professors were allocated the role. And as Joel Spring (2008, p. 404) observed, the "NDEA became a means by which the federal government could control local educational policy simply by offering money for the establishment of specified educational programs."

A consequence of keeping educators away from policy decisions was that the national curriculum revision effort floundered, not because of ineffective administration, but because the materials produced were decidedly not teacher or student "friendly." The developers of the new curricula had little understanding of student learning or of classroom instructional requirements. Again, there was little value for the general school population in learning advanced concepts of math and science. The value of the new math and science, for example, was limited to a select population of students contemplating higher education. Surprisingly, test comparisons with more "conventional" instruction showed no achievement advantage. The instructional material was a wonderful example of subject matter knowledge, but not in a form that was easily transformed into effective classroom application.

With the disappearance of federal funds, much of the innovative curriculum work disappeared. The National Defense Education Act today stands as a monument to the difficulty encountered when attempting to shape national curriculum outcomes in such a vast decentralized public educational "system" such as found in America. Can "one size," imposed from the top down, fit all? This was the question the NDEA appeared to answer in the negative.

Arthur Bestor: Restoring Intellectual Integrity

Arthur Bestor and fellow critics who asserted American education was failing because of its poor overall intellectual quality joined those concerned with poor school performance, weak science and math instruction, and the lack of curricular coherence within schools. In his highly quoted work, *American Wastelands*, Bestor argued that the influence of progressive educators, tracing their origin back to the turn of the century and John Dewey, resulted in a significant watering down of studies. His criticism was bolstered by Mortimer Smith's work, *The Diminished Mind: A Study of Planned Mediocrity in Our Public Schools*, and Albert Lynn's work, *Quackery in the Public School,* as well asother accounts blaming progressives for the alleged failings in public schools. Echoing Rickover, the central source of failings was found in the work of Clarence Kingsley and the 1918 Report of the National Commission on the Reorganization of

Secondary Education. The *Cardinal Principles* established the organizing concepts of selection and unification. The idea of differentiated studies, Bestor claimed, resulted in academic studies pushed aside for other studies of lesser intellectual quality. Moreover, the former higher quality studies themselves became degraded by the indiscriminate mixing of lower ability students in courses designed for the more intelligent. Unification meant the school day was filled with all kinds of diverting activities that took time from academic studies. Students were having fun in school, but they were not sufficiently developing their intellectual abilities (Cremin, 1961; Ravitch, 2000).

Bestor, a historian at the University of Illinois, was particularly incensed by the efforts of the college of education and the state to place emphasis in schools on a "life adjustment" curriculum for students considered not interested or able to pursue "academic" studies. By 1950, total national high school age enrollment peaked at 87% of all eligible youth, but educators continued to be perplexed over what to do with what was considered the 60% or more poorly performing students. Charles Processor, a nationally recognized educator and David Snedden's former associate director for vocational education in Massachusetts, as well as a leading voice in the formulation of the 1917 Smith-Hughes Act, persuaded the U.S. commissioner of education to sponsor national efforts for establishing life adjustment programming. Conferences and workshops were organized, commissions formed, pilot programs instituted, and teacher training implemented. A "general" national curriculum was formulated that emphasized healthy living, family and social relations, citizenship, and vocational interests. Students took coursework in family budgeting, human reproduction, civics, consumer math, consumer English, and applied science, along with art, music, physical education, and practical arts subjects such as home economics and industrial arts (Zeran, 1953). The life adjustment movement quickly spread across the country as school principals and teachers thought they found an answer to providing an education that was relevant and meaningful to a student population that American schools continue to struggle with today.

Bestor, along with like-minded colleagues, formed in 1956 the Council for Basic Education, organized to attack pubic schools and professional schools of teacher education in colleges as anti-intellectual. Reflecting an essentialists' view, it was argued that schools had to discard the notion of a differentiated curriculum and the idea of unification and return to a common academic core program for all students—that is, mathematics, science, history, English, and foreign languages. The fault for the poor intellectual quality of education, Bestor claimed, rested with colleges of education and professional educators. In teacher education programs students did not obtain a rigorous grounding in their respective subject fields. Their days were filled with teacher preparation courses that lacked substance and intellectual respectability. Consequently, schools were staffed with teachers that did not focus on the intellectual development of students. The influence of colleges of education had to be reduced to providing only instruction on "how to teach," and the larger university itself should be the site of the remaining education of the prospective teacher. Above all, agreeing with Rickover, Bestor affirmed, the purpose of all education is to promote intellectual training, that is, "the deliberate cultivation of the ability to think." Lawrence Cremin (1961, p. 344) concludes, taken together the cumulative writing of Bestor "constituted by far the most serious, searching, and influential criticisms" leveled against American education.

The combined assault on public education of the supporters of more and higher quality math and science instruction, of the movement to pass the NDEA, of the war hawks, and of the critics aligned with Bestor lamenting the deterioration of intellectual quality in public education, all had a lasting influence on American education. The perception persists that teachers are poorly prepared, lack intellectual qualities, and are unmotivated. The perception that America's schools lack quality persists. Perhaps the most consequential long-term influence was on the thinking of a mid-life, Hollywood actor making a career change with a move into politics. Ronald Reagan was reorienting his political life as he made the switch from a Roosevelt Democrat to a conservative Republican, and was receptive to the debate over the character of American education swirling within the political world. When Reagan took office in 1980, his educational policies reflected the beliefs of Rickover and Bestor, and the framework for educational reform Reagan advanced duplicated the concept of a core curriculum promoted by Bestor almost two decades earlier.

The Commie Hunters

To the cold war warriors it was obvious that there were Soviet spies at work and that American institutions were weakened by the infiltration of Soviet agents and sympathizers. The latter 1940s and up through the 1950s can be characterized as a period of intense criticism directed at public education. The most vocal and vicious critics were conservatives who banded together under the banner of patriotism to combat the threat of perceived "un-American" influences they claimed were spreading throughout schools. They endlessly alleged schoolchildren were being indoctrinated through subversive ideas that spread communistic beliefs. They matched the patriotic zeal of the cold war hawks. These two groups reinforced each other in creating a high level of public apprehension: Soon mushroom clouds would be sprouting all over the land as the Soviets flung their superior intercontinental missiles and nuclear weapons at our cities in a country that had been disarmed from within by a fifth column of treasonous citizens and poor schools.

Rather than demobilization after the Axis defeat, there was an armament race. Both sides built huge stockpiles of lethal weapons with the power to annihilate one another. The advent of nuclear weapons and the development of intercontinental missiles made the world a dangerous place. American politicians used the Soviet threat to secure and hold office by affirming that they would build up American military power and root out destabilizing and threatening subversive influences. They would protect America. The young former naval officer and future president, Richard Nixon, for example, won a California congressional house seat by promising he "would keep America safe from communism." The tactic was so successful he extended it to gain his 1950 senate election victory against the incumbent Helen Gahagan Douglass by asserting she was a closet communist: She was a "Red," Richard Nixon informed alarmed voters.

Nixon, like others, achieved national recognition as a "commie fighter" through the televised hearings of the House of Representatives Committee on Un American Activities. Individuals were called to testify on either past or current associations and activities with organizations considered communistic in intent. The Senate held similar hearings organized under the initiative of Senator Joseph McCarthy of Wisconsin. McCarthy had presidential aspirations, and he basked in the glow of national attention. Combined, the two committees treated a captivated American audience to great theater as witness after witness was grilled on imagined and real past activities. Screenwriters, directors, and actors were major targets. The hearings generated considerable national attention. Government officials were subjected to intense examination. Leading educators drew attention. Witnesses had to either "come clean" or face contempt charges. Individuals uncooperative or with a suspect past record were "blackballed" and lost jobs. The proceedings became so distasteful and the outcomes so nasty that the political value diminished. McCarthy unwittingly helped to put an end to the ongoing national circus when he announced he was going to investigate subversive activities in the military. He overstepped. The Senate hearings stopped.

Doubt and apprehension thickened with the shock over the creation by the Soviets of their own nuclear weapons and what appeared to be superior missile capability. How could the Soviets—who were portrayed in cold war propaganda as half inebriated, vodka drinking, crude buffoons—ever perfect such scientific and technical complex weapons? One answer the war hawks projected before the public was failing schools. The other answer was that there were subversives and spies who were feeding national defense secrets to the Soviets. This assertion drew public support that in turn supported the "commie hunters" and the activities of politicians benefitting from public fear that they helped to generate and spread. A "witch hunt" ensued as universities, government laboratories, research facilities, and public instructions of all kinds were scoured for evidence of spying. Public schools did not escape scrutiny.

Civilian groups such as the John Birch Society and citizens' councils mobilized to fight civil rights legislation and Supreme Court decisions that they contended reflected "communistic influence." They spread an atmosphere of suspicion and distrust. Public education was attacked directly. Publisher Lucie Cardin Crain, for example, issued a quarterly newsletter, the *Educational Reviewer*, with the specific purpose of weeding out of schools subversive textbook material that was poisoning the minds of pupils. Milo McDonald's American Education Association worked in school districts across the nation spreading doubt and dissention, and destroying community morale (Nelson & Roberts, 1963; Patterson, 1996). Allen Zoll founded the National Council for American Education, which still exists. Zoll's organization set out to purge community schools of communistic influence. Periodic updates were sent to members on how to detect subversive influences in schools. For a fee, teams were sent to organized community groups to facilitate local school inspections: School library collections were sorted through and "unsuitable" material destroyed; the classrooms of suspect teachers were observed; textbooks and curricula were scrutinized; and pressure exerted to fire teachers and administrators considered not supportive enough of "American values." Zoll said, "We set out to raise hell in schools, and we did."

Reflecting the influence and methods of the House and Senate investigating committees, individual states mandated the use of "loyalty oaths." Lists of organizations that were considered sympathetic to communism and antagonistic to capitalism were compiled. Individual teachers had to verify they were never members. If they were, they could not teach and were blackballed for life. During the "red scare" as previously suggested, the earlier activities came into sharp public focus of George Counts and other educators who advocated using schools to shape a new social order, one that was less individualistic and capitalistic, and more socialistic. In the 1930s, thousands joined organizations that appeared to offer alternatives to the economic system that had produced such a shattering national and world catastrophe. Young, idealistic college students in particular were quick to join causes that appeared to offer the promise of shaping a better future. Many became teachers with the booming expansion of schools following the war, and continued to express support for a social reconstruction role in schools. Their idealism caught up with them in the contentious 1950s as some were forced out of education. Conservatives did not easily forget George Counts, his colleagues, and the actions of young idealists rushing to join what later were labeled as subversive organizations. Conservatives spread a fog of doubt over the nation's schools concerning the loyalty of educators.

Of Money, Religion, and Diversity

Yet another strand of criticism came from a more diffused source: taxpayer groups. In the postwar years, the primary source of public school support was local property taxes. The rapid expansion of schooling translated into increased tax rates and bond issues to finance capital growth. Who paid for the increased costs? The more affluent elements in communities bore the economic brunt of expanded educational opportunity, and they balked at paying for the educational opportunities for the children of different social classes and ethnicities that would primarily benefit from their tax dollars. They resisted paying for expanded programming and building programs. Desegregation and busing particularly rankled.

These were store and wealthy company owners, corporations, and individuals of means. They had more taxable assets and paid more taxes, but their use of public school resources was proportionally limited. They also had political influence and used this influence to organize resistance to increases in school expenditures. The already considerable criticism directed to public education was used to bolster claims that taxes should be kept low and school resources limited. Super patriotic organizations in the name of countering "soft pedagogy" and combatting subversion worked to keep school taxes low. The nationally respected school superintendent of schools, Willard Goslin, for example, became a target because he was highly successful in passing bond issues for the expansion of schools. A coalition opposed to taxes managed to force his resignation over the charge that he was "pink" and soft on subversives in the Pasadena, California, school district he headed (Spring, 2008).

Throughout the country "school development councils" were formed to keep taxes down by eliminating "fads and frills." Mass meetings were held, boards of education coerced, and teachers intimidated, always with the threat lurking in the background of a deeper probing into the loyalty and efficiency of administrators and teachers. The nursery school, guidance program, special education, teacher workshops, and school construction expansion were limited or curtailed (Cremin, 1961; Spring, 2008). And this was a time of unprecedented national wealth.

Resistance to school funding and change also was rooted in conservative religious groups. The 1954 Supreme Court *Brown v. Board of Education Topeka* desegregation ruling was met with resistance, and provoked a backlash among religious groups. They contended that the integration of schools would bring Black and other ethnic students with completely different values into what were formerly rather homogeneous, White school environments that projected their own values. Their children were now exposed to values and behaviors that they contended were corrupting and counter to their deeply held beliefs.

But there was a second blow. Protestant groups had long exercised considerable influence on public schools. In many communities they controlled school boards and were able to insert religious instruction and prayer in schools regardless of the principle of separation of religion and state. But with the *Brown* ruling and the influence of the civil rights movement in related court cases, decisions went against religious groups and prayer, and religious instruction was effectively removed from public schools. This caused outrage among some parent groups. More than 100 years earlier Horace Mann predicted parents would withdraw support from public education if they no longer thought schools conveyed their values and beliefs. They did, as conservative Protestants searched for alternatives to public education. At the same time, many opposed increased educational funding for public schools that they no longer wanted their children to attend. They joined with other critics to devalue public schooling.

James Bryant Conant: Bridging the Divide

From a modest background James Conant became a renowned chemist and the first scientist appointed as president of Harvard University, a position formerly exclusively preserved for esteemed persons from the liberal arts. Toward the latter years of his career as president from 1933 to 1953, and after his retirement he turned his creative mind to national education issues. He was the most commanding figure on the national educational stage following the war and up to Ronald Reagan. His influence continues. Conant was one of the rare individuals who could bring warring factions over social and educational issues together in compromise that achieved practical results and mutual benefits, while not compromising his own beliefs (Karier, 1967). People listened to Conant.

A large part of this national stature stemmed from the crucial national leadership positions he accepted leading up to, during, and after the war: Conant was a member of the National Defense Research Committee, which eventually oversaw the development of the atomic bomb; an instrumental figure in the founding of the Educational Testing Service; advisor to the Atomic Energy Commission; chairman of the National Science Foundation; board member of the Office of Defense Mobilization; and high commissioner for Germany and later ambassador. After retirement he successfully solicited funding from the Carnegie Foundation to study American schools. His resulting books, *The American High School Today*, *The Junior High School*, *Slums and Schools*, and the *Education of American Teachers*, among others, conversed on ways to reform and strengthen education.

Conant received the support of conservatives because of his work in getting the G.I. Bill passed, and along with Vannover Bush, successfully founding the National Science Foundation. He repeated the message that the human resources of the nation must be developed through education, and especially the individual intellectually talented must be identified and mathematical and scientific abilities groomed to the fullest. The cold war warriors liked what he said.

His work among national defense committees also made him a patriot in many eyes. And as a common man who distinguished himself professionally as a scientist, he was living proof of the power of rigorous intellectual training. And as a chemist, he understood science.

But the educational argument Conant and all of the critics focused on was the functionality of the comprehensive school model and its suitability in the new world taking shape. Conant took a position outside and beyond what conservatives as well as liberals took, and the fact that he promoted counterviews did not lose him the support of others because they saw in him a powerful voice for ideas they believed in, and a voice for formulating a compromise putting to rest the ideological warfare between conservatives and liberals. He shifted the national school discourse from ideological positions to one based on studies of what was actually happening, or not happening, in the nation's schools. As a pragmatist, he stressed that educational dialogue had to focus on what was possible and worked, not on what one believed.

Conant fully agreed that achieving and maintaining educational excellence was critical to the economic and military welfare of the nation, and he supported the identification and selection of the most talented students to be singled out for superior academic training. But he departed from Rickover, Bestor, and others who ultimately wanted to disassemble the common school model based on specialization and unification. Conant argued that the common school played two essential roles and the institution needed to be strengthened, not eliminated. First, in the comprehensive high school, the rich range of possible educational opportunities gives students multiple ways to build on their potential. Small high schools restrict options so they should be consolidated, and vocational education should not be given in separate systems of schools following what Snedden attempted to implement in Massachusetts, because student options are severely limited. Possible paths of upward mobility are cut off by too early career specialization. Second, critics wanting to disassemble the comprehensive school model are essentially promoting an elitist and fundamentally un-American attitude about public responsibility toward education, Conant asserted. The comprehensive school stands as a mark of democracy (1959).

The most contested arguments were over the low quality of instruction, and the life adjustment curriculum in particular, that was lowering academic standards. By filling the school with courses and programs of low intellectual quality and rigor, critics claimed a general "watering down" of academic quality across all subjects occurred. As noted, Bestor wanted all students regardless of background, ability, or interests to pursue a core of academic studies related primarily to college admission. He provided no satisfactory answer to the large number of students that potentially would struggle, perform unsatisfactorily, or drop out. His best answer was to have struggling students do extra work outside of school. Rickover wanted a separate school for superior students. Based on his studies of schools across America, Conant observed, however, that high schools were doing reasonably well, the comprehensive school model was basically sound given the diversity of the school population, and the differentiation of studies should be preserved. But Conant thought the education of the gifted was being neglected. The academically talented student did not have a sufficient range of challenging subject offerings, and did not work hard enough. Reflecting the ideas of Bagley and other essentialists, he urged schools to require for all students mandated courses in the core subjects of foreign language, math, and science, but provide two tracks, one for the academically gifted (top 3%) and a second one for the remaining students. His idea lives in the form of gifted and talented programming for superior students (Conant, 1959).

He also proposed strengthening school counseling and guidance. Students can be better sorted, he urged. This would better help to address the human resource requirements of the country. This also would enable identifying the gifted, but at the same time help to discourage overly ambitious parents from insisting on enrolling mediocre-performing students into advance work. He wanted to strengthen the prerequisites for advanced academic work. He advocated individualizing student courses of study. Ability grouping was stressed, and in this way, more programs could be provided for the academically talented while at the same time special courses could address the concerns of slow learners. He supported offering more science courses for everyone, but with different offerings for student with low math skills. At the same time, Conant advocated honors programs that equally recognized academic, commercial, and vocational students. Reflecting an awareness of the unification function set out by Kingsley and others, he wanted to have mandatory twelfth-grade social studies courses composed of a cross section of all students learning together about the fundamentals of the American form of government and economic system (Conant, 1959).

Conant offered a compromise to the raging debates and made people feel comfortable about the American high school. David Angus and Jeffrey Mirel (1999) best sum up his work: "Rather than boldly challenging the educational status quo, Conant embraced it. By making recommendations that barely diverted from conventional educational philosophy and practice, he helped restore the shaken confidence of school leaders and gave them a plan of attack that could effectively neutralize local critics" (p. 115). As Conant took a center position on the national educational stage, the song he sang then continues to resonate today. The high school of today is very similar to the one Conant envisioned.

Liberals could identify with Conant because he wanted a good society, a free society, a pluralistic one that was socially mobile, open, and free of class and ethnic divide (Karier, 1967, p. 252). As the decade of the 1960s came, Conant in *Slums and Suburbs* (1961) turned his attention to schooling for the poor and to the squalor of the ethnic slum school. The nation was flirting with "social dynamite," he warned. Tensions were building up in the cities that would soon explode. He urged increases in urban school funding to reconstitute quality programming, more employment opportunities for youth, vocational guidance to age 21, more practical job training in school, and more on-the-job training. But he struggled over the question of de facto segregation in urban schools. He did not have any good answers. This issue was left to others as the liberals moved to center stage with the election of John F. Kennedy.

Richard Nixon and the Search for Order

With the election of Richard Nixon after the eight years of the Kennedy and Johnson administrations, the Republicans regained a prominent position on the national education stage. But the issues had profoundly changed. The nation was in a state of crisis and on the edge of imploding. The civil rights movement turned inward, with fighting within; the murder of the two Kennedy brothers and Martin Luther King Jr. shocked and traumatized; cities burned with protests and revolt in the Black ghettos; communities struggled with efforts to finally realize the promises of the 14th and 15th amendments; the young rebelled and discarded the religious and social values of their parents; and the Vietnam antiwar protests spread from college campuses across the country to envelope citizens everywhere. And protest and counter protest turned violent. The country learned to distrust its government that lied; and deep fissures developed within a society that could not completely mend (Morrison & Morrison, 1987; Patterson, 1996).

Nixon ran on a winning platform that had three main promises: Stop the war in Vietnam, end busing, and bring social order to the nation. His "secret plan" to end the war remained secret and the United States extracted itself from the war only shortly after Nixon was forced from office; to end busing was a campaign ploy to attract and hold votes and impossible to realize. But Nixon directly addressed the promise of realizing social order, and schools were his major tool.

Nixon contended that the cause of social discord and violence was the unreal aspirations created in the minds of citizens by Democrats promising a better life that could not realistically be achieved. Youth especially were lulled into thinking they could attain with little effort more in life than was even a remote possibility. The young had to develop life aspirations based on a realistic understanding of their ability and the kinds of schooling, career preparation, and work required to achieve personal goals. Nixon said schooling could be used to create in the minds of individuals a realistic understanding of the work-world through career education, the major educational initiative of his administration. Career education aimed at no less than a fundamental reordering of the structure and purpose of public education (Spring, 1976).

Nixon was not alone in his thinking. An inherent assumption of the life adjustment movement that peaked out by the end of the 1950s was the majority of youth entering high school, the 60%, had modest career aspirations. They were not going to excel in school or enjoy the career benefits of the higher achieving youth. They were not going to become lawyers, doctors, accountants, pilots, engineers, or the mathematicians and scientists Rickover wanted, or pursue the academic studies Bestor thought best for all students. Rather they would become grocery clerks, taxi drivers, or security guards; they would work in factories packing fruit and vegetables or attending machines turning out plastic parts or attaching electronic components. The function of high schools was changing. Schools were less concerned with being "an institution commonly associated with increasing social mobility to one deliberately trying to get young people to limit their aspirations and accept menial roles in society" (Angus & Mirel, 1999, p. 83).

But the Kennedy and Johnson administrations raised aspirations. Civil rights opened opportunity and the War on Poverty countered joblessness, was the claim promoted. A hallmark of the Kennedy years was the hope he generated in the creation of a better society, a new beginning in which citizens bonded together to create the "New Frotier," a time of ever-expanding promise. Lyndon Johnson, one to think in expansive terms, promised poverty could be eliminated, and social justice achieved. The Great Society could establish opportunity for everyone. Instead, America descended into chaos after the 1964 election. The grand expectations did not materialize.

Following the interlude of the Kennedy and Johnson administrations, concern reemerged over the unrealistic aspirations of youth destined for modest roles in society. The national economy slumped and inflation spiraled out of control with the spending excesses of the Vietnam War coupled with the war on poverty; counter to what Lyndon Johnson asserted, the country could not have "guns and butter" at the same time. The economic frontier was closed, some said. But the reemerging concern over redirecting the career aspirations of the young had a new dimension: Emphasis shifted especially to the poor and minorities. Both groups, often one and the same, were a central focus of the civil rights movement and the war on poverty. The aspirations of these two groups especially had to be reoriented. Career education was one way to do this, Sydney Marland, Nixon's commissioner of education, claimed.

Learning to Work

Career education was organized around two major concepts applied to all levels of education: integration and articulation. Integration meant that on all grade levels the subjects of instruction were integrated in some way with work. The fifth-grade student, for example, learning simple uses of arithmetic would also find out how it was applied by postal workers or mechanics, and would practice similar uses. Similarly, students in English wrote essays on "my trip to the factory" or researched and wrote an essay on the career track and qualifications related to becoming a dentist. Articulation meant that instruction at one level fed into the next level in a seamless sequence of learning about careers to the point were choices are made and specific education and training is given. Reaching back to the work of G. Stanley Hall and the idea of development tasks, the "mastery" of certain key learning was thought essential to the successful movement to the next level of career development. Little schoolchildren, for example, engaged in "career awareness" experiences before moving on to the next stage, "career exploration." The practice of "curriculum infusion" was promoted, meaning that career education was not a new subject separately added to studies, but rather all courses in the school were refocused to include career education elements. Promoters of career education thought infusion would create less resistance by not threatening to eliminate existing programming.

Marland used all of the discretionary funds that he could muster and ploughed them into career education workshops and grants to persuade colleges, high schools, and elementary school systems to convert studies to include career education. Additional arguments for career education were made. By stressing work preparation, "stagflation" could be eased, the combination of slow economic growth coupled with inflation in the early 1970s economy; the nation's productivity could be increased, the foreign deficit lowered and the rising unemployment rate among college graduates checked. In other words, in addition to a social control function, schools could also perform through career education a timely economic stabilizing role (Angus and Mirel, 1999, pp. 135–138).

By 1973, half of the states appropriated funds so local schools could implement career education programming, and Congress opened the federal purse wider to ensure that "every child should, by the time he has completed secondary school, be prepared for gainful or maximum employment and for full participation in our society according to his or her ability." The movement spread quickly across the country; it "boomed' according to one supporter (Angus & Mirel, 1999, p. 137). But what goes up, comes down, and sometimes fast. By the start of the

Jimmy Carter administration and the end of the 1976-77 school year, federal and state funding were gone and career education programming swiftly dropped as local school districts failed to provide funding. Educators were uncomfortable with "diluting" academic instruction with career objectives, especially since the voices of Rickover, Bestor, and others in the 1950s urging the strengthening of academic instruction were not completely stilled. Alarmed critics pointed out that schools could not do both (Grubb & Lazerson, 1982; Herr, 1976).

Success and Failure

Career education was another example of an attempt to implement wide-scale, massive curriculum reform on a national level in a remarkably short time. To effectively imbed new ideas and change conventional school practices takes decades, not months or even a few years. And change that generates organically from local efforts to address programing challenges has a greater chance of succeeding. Local jurisdictions often cannot see the value of initiatives that are prescribed from a distant source unconnected with their own pressing priorities. But probably the major error among career advocates was the failure to distinguish between the character of the knowledge and skills associated with work, and formal knowledge. Work makes selective use of formal knowledge, while formal academic instruction attempts to create an understanding of the total underlying intellectual structure that gives meaning to the associated concepts, themes, principles, theorems, and laws. The builder, for example, uses parts of geometry to lie out the dimensions of a roof dormer; the student of geometry studies the theoretical underpinning of the complete field. Colleges and universities were not willing to accept high school credits for biology applied to horse farming or advanced English concentrated around the reading of material on occupations. They wanted students who studied the "real" stuff.

Richard Nixon was a brilliant but extremely complex individual. Even those close around him never fully understood his personality. He was humorless. And he was politically ruthless. He was extremely competent and knew how to run government, but his moral compass seemed to be broken and he did not always know where to draw the lines of permissible action. This got him into serious trouble of his own making, and resulted in forced resignation; his highly honed instinct for political survival failed him. But Nixon was not an ideological conservative, and he knew when to be flexible and support ideas that had merit, which called on all of his skills at political maneuvering to counter the resistance of conservatives in his own party.

Nixon, above all, was a political pragmatist who knew how to work with Democratic congressional majorities to pass legislation that he considered worthwhile and politically expedient to support. "Liberal" legislation gestating in the wrappings of the Great Society, for example, acquired final form and passage in the Nixon administration in the 1970s. During his time in office, Nixon signed an impressive amount of legislation that came out of the 1960s. The two best examples are support for Amerindians and women's rights. He supported extension of the Voting Rights Act of 1965, and continued funding for the National Endowment of the Arts and Humanities. He signed the National Environmental Policy Act, which led to setting up the Environmental Protection Agency. He did not dismantle the War on Poverty programs. He approved hikes in food stamps funding (Blum, 1991; Patterson, 1996).

But Nixon also worked hard to squash social and political movements he did not agree with and that would give him political trouble. He disliked hippies, antiwar activities, and civil rights advocates. He was extremely conservative on race relations. Sensing a political opening, he repeatedly used the "race card" to gain tactical political support. He tried to erase gains. He worked to change the composition of the "liberal" Supreme Court to "conservative" by supporting southern segregationist judges. He delayed desegregation through funding decisions and the support of court actions. He used the FBI to destroy the Black Panthers. Threatening civil rights leaders were "silenced." He challenged court-ordered busing with delaying tactics. He fanned the anxieties of working-class Whites and segregationist southerners, groups he thought he could bring into the Republican fold. His policies and those of his attorney general, John Mitchell, helped to create a national political backlash so that by the early 1970s the civil rights movement that was already limping along was pushed further on the defensive, and struggled to garner public support. The cause of racial desegregation continued to stall in the 1970s (Patterson, 1996, p. 735).

Chapter Sixteen
The Harvest of Good Intentions

Social concern over economic progress cannot be easily separated from apprehension over poverty. The two are intertwined. They feed on each other. While conservative critics of public education primarily wanted school reform to focus on maintaining a strong economic posture, the essential concern of the more "liberal" element among reformers was to address long-standing issues of poverty and inequity in America. They saw this not only essential for social stability, but also necessary for the continuing economic progress of the nation. Liberals agreed with conservatives about the importance of economic progress, but they disagreed on how it best can be advanced and maintained. Liberals believed the issue of poverty itself could not be separated from the growing momentum of the civil rights movement, which to be sure, was centered in African American leadership, but eventually encompassed many social groups. It was the dispossessed in society who needed help irrespective of ethnicity, gender, skin hue, or religion. The civil rights movement had two intertwined thrusts: freedom from discrimination and the reduction of poverty among the less privileged.

Civil Rights Movement

The origins of the civil rights movement extend back before World War II. W.E.B. Du Bois as editor of the NAACP publication *Crisis,* for example, kept up a steady beat in the 1920s and 1930s for the advancement of social justice. Young graduates of Black colleges in the 1920s provided a growing core of professionals who assumed leadership positions in communities struggling for civil rights. In the latter 1920s, a national campaign grew in intensity to enact a federal anti-lynching law. As earlier recorded, the KKK was on a rampage across the South and Midwest, intimidating, burning, and lynching with no legal recourse in local courts. Black leaders emerged to resist; but civil rights were put on hold with the Great Depression. There was no national political will. This was not the time to promote civil rights for Blacks when millions of Whites were struggling with destroyed lives, poverty, and hunger. But as the nation turned to the war effort, conditions changed.

Black leaders such as Mary McLeod Bethune and A. Philip Randolph, for example, worked with federal leaders to achieve civil rights for Black citizens. Contributions from all citizens were needed in the pending war. Bethune was successful in developing a close relationship with Eleanor Roosevelt and convincing her of the importance of promoting civil rights for not only Black women but for all women. Randolph, as president of the Porters Union, the largest African American labor organization in America, had considerable political clout. He was successful in courting Franklin Roosevelt, who wanted to keep the Black vote that he had just taken away from Republicans. Joining with Bethune, they advocated for affirmative action in employment for men and women of all ethnicities. Franklin Roosevelt issued an executive order opening employment in all places where federal money is used. In addition, Randolph wanted federal action to desegregate the military, but Roosevelt was successful in arguing for a delay until any hostilities were concluded. President Harry Truman fulfilled Roosevelt's promise by desegregating the military as soon as World War II was concluded. A desegregated military was a step toward a desegregated society.

There were a number of conditions following the war that made civil rights a possibility. First was the status of the Black community itself. As a result of the war effort, Blacks too had employment in defense industries at good wages, and like others there was no place to spend the accumulating affluence. Black communities experienced a level of banked prosperity never before enjoyed. But this was not just a passing interlude like the one that occurred in World War I. During the 1930s and up through the 1950s, a new national union was on the labor stage, the Congress of Industrial Organization (CIO). Unlike the older American Federation of Labor (AFL that was organized along craft lines, the CIO was organized vertically. All occupational categories in a given industry, such as auto or steel, were organized in one union. This produced considerable bargaining power. Employers could not divide and rule. Also, unlike the AFL that was a segregated union, the CIO was inclusive from its very first days. After the war, the employment conditions of Blacks as well as others continued to be protected. With greater employment security and economic stability, Blacks engaged with confidence in civil rights activities. Booker T. Washington was partly right: Economic stability is an essential condition for the civil rights advancement of a people.

Leadership was another critical condition within the Black community. The opening up of educational opportunity through the second crusade of the 1920s produced a generation of educated Americans of African heritage positioned to lead the postwar civil rights movement. They came primarily from two sources: education and religion. The preparation of teachers, school principals, and superintendents of schools created a cadre of individuals positioned to be community leaders. Similarly, the Black ministry was a source of recognized leadership, and along with an array of lawyers, doctors, businessmen, editors and writers, and academicians, a core of professional leaders contributed considerable weight to the movement. DuBois also was right: Leaders are essential.

Challenge to the Past: Cultivating National Consensus

Successful social and political movements in the United States require the broad support and participation of citizens across the social, ethnic, and economic spectrum. Although total political consensus is next to impossible to attain, a strong, broadly based majority is essential to achieve change. Americans felt good after the war. The population enjoyed a level of broad prosperity never before experienced. In a united effort they vanquished the Axis powers in the name of democracy. They were ready to rally behind the effort to achieve greater social justice. Jeffrey Mirel (1993), for example, found when he examined the social legislation voting records in Michigan there was community support across all socioeconomic and racial strata.

The civil rights movement gained strength around the edges through the participation of ethnic and social groups not fully sharing in the bounty of the new, evolving order—namely, the low-paid Chicano field worker from the San Joaquin Valley in California, the Native American in South Dakota resisting forced relocation, the Chinese American sweatshop worker in New York City wanting better wages, and the White factory worker in Milwaukee angry that he could not even afford to buy his child a tricycle for Christmas. These people wanted better opportunity and a decent life. And it was not just the disposed that wanted opportunity and equity. The middle-class small business owner in Detroit, basking in economic security, deep in his soul knew he should do something to help others realize the bounty of the American dream. There was considerable national momentum behind the civil rights movement.

Public opinion was strongly swayed by the findings of a study commissioned by the Carnegie Foundation in the depths of the Depression. Poverty and its link with ethnicity were potentially explosive issues. The foundation commissioned a group of researchers under the direction of highly respected Swedish sociologist Gunnar Myrdal, to investigate poverty and its connection with race in America. The onset of World War II delayed the work, and its findings were not released until late 1944. The final report, *The American Dilemma,* deflated the nation's sense that it was a just society and challenged citizens to take action (Myrdal, 1944).

Myrdal and his colleagues reported that there was a significance gap in what Americans liked to believe about themselves and the reality of poverty and suffering surrounding them that they chose to ignore. Poor citizens were pushed into the margins of society and largely hidden from obvious view, but the unfairness and discrimination they encountered continued to eat away at the psyche of a nation that knew it was not living up to its professed ideals. This psychological dissonance was at the center of social tension, hostility, and violence, the report asserted. America had to learn to live up to its ideals. These were strong words.

Regarding the concept "cycle of poverty," the report offered an explanation of the deep, persistent poverty in America that continues from generation to generation: Children in poverty experience substandard housing, have less nutritious food, lack medical care, suffer from more sickness, and attend poor-quality slum schools where attendance and student achievement is low, and students therefore lack a competitive position in the labor market. Work is intermittent, pay is low, money is short, and the cycle continues on into the next generation. The concept of the cycle of poverty achieved wide recognition, and became central to the formulation of the War on Poverty in the Kennedy and Johnson administrations. Education was considered to be the key element to break the cycle. In the meantime, the work of Myrdal and his team fueled discussion about poverty and racism in America and what could be done. The report helped generate public awareness that society had to act.

World War II and the subsequent cold war were major elements in generating responsiveness to the civil rights movement. The war was fought against the Axis powers in the name of protecting freedom and democracy. Yet, how can the United States in the world's eyes occupy such a high moral position when in fact a large part of its population lives in abject poverty, is denied social justice, does not have the right to vote, and lives daily under unconstitutional laws that generate fear and violence and destroy any individual sense of dignity and worthiness? The Soviets were quick to proclaim they were the legitimate defenders of social justice, equality, and the rights of citizens. And their economic system served all, and not the selfish interest of a few capitalists. The Soviets contended they were the future of the new world order, not the Americans. In words of James Patterson (1996, p. 82), there was recognition "somewhat rudely forced on a reluctant nation" that America's vision of democracy rooted in the past was extremely shallow. This was a theme Myrdal and his colleagues stressed in slightly different terms.

Wrestling with History: Martin Luther King Jr.

Following the war, hesitant steps were taken along the path of civil rights. Immigration laws, for example, were opened slightly to allow 105 Chinese annually to enter the United States, and the 1882 Exclusion Act was repealed. Similar legislation restrictions for Asian Indians and Filipinos were removed, but the quota also remained small. However, family reunion provisions made it possible for more to come. Around 45,000 Japanese and 32,000 Chinese came in the 1950s. Importantly, naturalization restrictions on "race" codified in the 1790 Naturalization Act were removed so newly arriving, non-European immigrants could become naturalized citizens. At the same time, however, the primary immigration legislation, the 1952 McCarran-Walter Act, set quotas to prevent unwanted eastern and southern Europeans from emigrating while opening allotment so that 85% of immigrants were from northern "Anglo-Saxon" stock. It was not until 1965, at the peak of the civil rights movement, that congress passed new legislation basically eliminating most quotas (Patterson, 1996).

As briefly discussed in Part Four, the League of United Latin American Citizens was successful in challenging the segregation of Spanish-speaking schoolchildren in the 1946 *Mendez* and the 1948 *Delgado* court cases. In 1950, the Texas Supreme Court ruled to admit a Black plaintiff to an all-White law school, and in the same year, the state of Oklahoma was ordered to discontinue using segregated facilities within a graduate school of education. In 1953, five suits brought against segregated schools reached the U.S. Supreme Court, and *Brown v. The Board of Education of Topeka*, filed in 1951 and alphabetically first, became the landmark desegregation case. This was the beginning of the end of segregation in all public institutions.

The NAACP's legal team under Thurgood Marshall presented persuasive arguments. First, the assertion under the 1896 *Plessey v. Ferguson* Supreme Court ruling that separate facilities were equal simply was not supported by historical facts. Segregated schools are unequal. Public schools in the South, for example, typically spent $3 on White schools for every $1 spent on Black schools. In Mississippi, $52.01 was spent on every White schoolchild and $7.36 on every Black schoolchild, with similar disparities among other states. For transportation, 100 times more was spent for White children. Rural Black children could not get to school. Everywhere, in Black schools the teachers were paid less, textbooks were discards from White schools, the school year was shorter, and the faculties shabby (Patterson, 1996, p. 386). This situation was "purposeful and maligned neglect of black schooling, during which ignorance had been cultivated and sustained by public policy" (Ravitch, 2000, p. 374). In striking down segregated schools, the Warren court agreed.

Second, the NAACP argued that the times had changed. Perhaps Booker T. Washington was right. Blacks held a different position in society, and White society itself had changed. The war helped make this change, and probably the rising affluence within both Black and White communities was instrumental. The time had arrived for segregation to be eradicated. A third argument drew on the work of Gunnar Myrdal and Columbia University sociologist Kenneth Clark. Both emphasized the destructive psychological influence of segregation on individuals and on society. The Court largely bypassed "the niceties of legal precedent" and came out strongly emphasizing the urgent need to promote social justice. "In the field of public education the doctrine of separate but equal has no place," Chief Justice Earl Warren informed the public on May 17, 1954 (Patterson, 1996, p. 389). Now, Linda Brown, the daughter of Reverend Oliver Brown, a welder, like thousands of other children did not have to walk blocks away to attend an all-Black segregated school when a White school was only blocks from her home.

All of these events marked early civil rights actions, and were significant, but frustration grew particularly among African Americans over the slow pace of breaking down the barriers of discrimination that prevented citizens from realizing the most basic human rights to be free of fear and suffering and dream of a better future. The quickened pace of the civil rights movement in the 1950s was in response to the slow pace and inability of the nation's political leadership to eradicate the disgrace of racism. Outside forces were required. In Martin Luther King Jr. the Black community found an exceptional leader at an exceptional time in U.S. history. He was the glue that held a social revolution together—one that was conducted against strong opposition. He brought people from every walk of life, social class, religion, and color of skin and place of abode together in the crusade for social and economic justice. He turned the civil rights movement into a moral crusade for the soul of America. A reluctant U.S. government was prodded into action.

Eisenhower and Desegregation

The southern voting block played a key role in national politics. Democrats relied on southern votes to control congress; Republicans wanted to wean away southern influence to strengthen their own congressional power. Federal action on civil rights would inevitably change the political dynamics in uncertain ways. Unsure of outcomes, both parties were reluctant to take any action. The most cautious political action was to take no action and hold firm to the status quo (Katzenelson, 2013). Southern intransigences and violence, however, forced the Eisenhower, Kennedy, and Johnson administrations to act. It also brought the civil rights campaign together into a national movement.

Following the decisive Supreme Court's 1954 *Brown* ruling to desegregate the nation's schools "with all due speed," Eisenhower took what he thought was a politically safe course of action: He issued an executive order to direct local judges to oversee the implementation of desegregation, the same judges that had been denying Blacks justice all across the South for generations. Little happened.

But Eisenhower, like Kennedy and Johnson later, was prodded into action by the lawless challenge to federal authority as the world watched. The *Brown* decision emboldened the resolve of southerner segregationists to violently resist. There were eight unprosecuted lynchings in 1955 alone; Blacks attempting to register to vote were shot at point-blank range in broad daylight in Mississippi; 14-year-old Emmett Till was beaten to a pulp because he recklessly whistled at a White female grocery store clerk. (His mangled body, recovered from the Tallahatchie River, displayed by his mother in an open casket was shown around the world by media.) In Clinton, Tennessee, mobs of Whites terrorized Black children as they attempted to attend school; Autherine Lucy, a young Black woman, narrowly escaped lynching in 1956 as she attempted to register at the University of Alabama. (She was later officially expelled so she could not try again.) In Mansfield, Texas, the governor called out the Texas Rangers to restore order at the local school as a White crowd of several thousand organized a violent protest against entering Blacks. All Blacks were subsequently removed from the school (Patterson, 1996, pp. 390–398). There was no federal action; with predictable outcomes, matters were left in the hands of local and state authorities.

The actions of Arkansas governor Orval Faubus forced Eisenhower to finally take federal action. Faubus used the National Guard, a wing of the U.S. army, to prevent nine Black students from attending Little Rock High School. The calculus was changed. No longer could federal action be sidestepped by the observation that civil rights violations were lawless actions under the responsibility of individual state law enforcement and judicial systems. Faubus used the federal military to obstruct a federally mandated court ruling. Eisenhower had to act. He sent the Arkansas National Guard to the Barracks, and mobilized the army's 101 Airborne Division to fulfill the legal mandate to desegregate schools in America as the nation and world watched on television. A corner was turned. The precedent was set for federal involvement, even if reluctantly. But more violence followed (Branch, 1998).

Violence and the Moral High Ground

By 1960, civil rights rebellion had spread all across the South. The reaction of the White power structure was quick and brutal. Neither politician nor citizen could not ignore what was shown nightly on television screens in front rooms across the nation. Citizens watched high-pressure fire hoses trained on groups of children, tossing them into the air and inflicting serious injury when they fell to the ground; the nation cringed as policemen flailed with four-foot clubs men and women doing no more than quietly marching, knocking them senseless; they saw buses burned, and the bleeding and seriously wounded kicked and battered with no protection or medical help available. They saw killings, mangled bodies, and burnt bodies. The violence was indiscriminate. Children, women, and the elderly were not spared. White as well as Black protesters were beaten, some so severely that they later died. Black churches were bombed and burned. Thousands were jailed for nothing more then peacefully marching for the rights of all American citizens. All of this violence was sanctioned, overseen, and carried out by White political and law officials responsible for the protection of all citizens. Officers of the law played a dual role as members of the Ku Klux Klan perpetuating the very crimes they were charged in their official roles to prevent and prosecute (Branch, 1988, 1998, 2006).

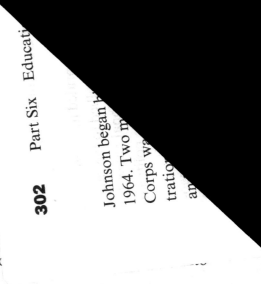

What Americans saw was repugnant and had no place in
decency. Gunnar Myrdal had also said as much. People all ac
with young people in particular traveling south to join in v
social justice. Money flowed into civil rights organizations, a
came to the conclusion something had to be done.

Civil rights is a moral issue. Martin Luther King Jr. follo
lence. This was the only policy with the potential of success.
would have countered Black violence with "official" violence
order. But by accepting the expected consequences of violenc
sive resistance the civil rights movement held the moral high gro
doing what was "right."

Part Six   Educat

302

Johnson began
1964. Two m
Corps wa
tratio
an

Kennedy, Johnson, and the Legislative Response

The Kennedy administration was reluctant to act and was a latecomer to the civil rights cause.
While voicing early support for the principle of civil rights, Kennedy had to keep his eyes
turned primarily on southern conservative Democrats to muster congressional support.
"Kennedy faced a line-up on Capital Hill that he expected would defeat major liberal initiatives"
(Patterson, 1996, p. 465). In actual fact, Kennedy got very little legislation passed. Conservative
Democrats teamed up with Republicans to scuttle most of Kennedy's legislative initiatives. By
the summer of 1963, his attitude changed as he realized civil rights was an issue that could not be
left unattended. Law was flaunted. The nation was tearing itself apart. Kennedy needed southern electoral votes, and even though it may cost him the 1964 election, in the summer of 1963
he had his administration begin drafting civil rights legislation as part of the "New Frontier."
His aim was to devote more attention to domestic policies that addressed civil rights, poverty,
and economic growth (Branch, 1988, 1998; Patterson, 1996). Following the mortal gunshot in
Dallas on November 22, 1963, the Lyndon Johnson administration picked up the pieces of the
yet unfinished civil rights legislation and recrafted them as the centerpiece of his "Great Society"
program to eliminate poverty and advance civil rights. He said he wanted to create a better and
just society. Johnson cast civil rights in the context of larger social legislation.

Johnson showed an impressive display of moral purpose and political ability as he achieved
passage of a spate of domestic legislation "liberals" had wanted ever since the election of 1960:
clean air legislation, more parks and national wilderness areas, consumer protection, immigration reform, and mine safety. Federal housing support was given, and food stamps for the poor
and Aid for Dependent Children were established as policy. The National Endowment for the
Arts and the National Endowment for the Humanities were created. The Higher Education Act
approved by Congress established guaranteed student loans and expanded college work-study
programs. The act helped to fund the growth of students entering college in the 1960s and supported graduate programs in colleges of arts and science. Youth from blue-collar and middle-
class families, and Black, Latino, and Asian families could realize dreams of going to college.
Medicare and Medicaid were passed, which provided health security for aged and disabled
citizens. And linking civil rights and poverty, far-reaching legislation was passed.

Addressing Poverty and Civil Rights

is "War on Poverty" with passage of the Economic Opportunity Act (EOA) of ajor provisions were the establishment of the Jobs Corps and Head Start. The Job s patterned after the Civilian Conservation Corps (CCC) of the Roosevelt adminis- and Depression years. Johnson wanted to use the Job Corps to counter unemployment d provide training for out-of-school youth. Most of the participants were school dropouts from lower income families. Like the CCC, the Job Corps was administered outside of public schools. On the other hand, Head Start, a preschool program for needy children, aimed at preparing economically disadvantaged children to enter into public school on relative equal terms with children from more affluent families. Thousands upon thousands of little children from poverty homes benefited from community Head Start programs as their entrance into public schools was eased.

The program continues to be politically popular, but its limitations are clear: After the Head Start interventions end following public school attendance, children lose ground, many soon to be relegated through the school's social-sorting process to lower-level programming where they tend to remain. But funding is not available to continue with similar in-school interventions to keep children from disadvantaged homes performing at a higher level. Nevertheless, Head Start remains a key part of preschool education for disadvantaged children.

The EOA opened a "Rights Revolution." Through the Office of Economic Opportunity, court suits were enjoined to litigate the grievances of individuals felt discriminated against. Minority rights in housing, work, and education were addressed. Johnson advanced the scope of litigation through an executive order to include gender as an element of discrimination. What we refer today as "affirmative action" became a tool of protest groups as a way to combat discrimination. Employment discrimination became a major target, with contractors using public money required to "take affirmative action to ensure that applicants are employed, and that employees are treated during employment without regard to their race, color, religion, sex or national origin." The employment prospects of disadvantaged individuals were advanced, and Blacks, American Indians, Asians, and "Spanish Americans" found support to enhance their job possibilities. Colleges were influenced in both hiring and admission practices. They struggled to design ways to diversify ethnic and economic diversity while at the same time protect the rights of all students. This struggle continued, and marked a "key trend that was to accelerate in coming years: the tendency of people to join groups in defense of their rights and seek legal redress in order to advance them" (Patterson, 1996, p. 641).

The Elementary and Secondary Education Act (ESEA) is the major piece of education legislation of the Johnson administration. Passed in 1965, federal assistance is intended to help children from economically disadvantaged homes, with the amount of federal assistance related to the level of poverty in the school districts served. The act also allowed federal funding to be provided to public and private schools, a sharp constitutional break from the past. To bypass the issue of the separation of the state and religion, federal support was supplied to parochial schoolchildren rather than to the parochial schools themselves. Catholic Kennedy could not have done this; Protestant Johnson could. The door was opened for public support for private schools regardless of religious affiliation (Blum, 1991; Patterson, 1996).

Five forms of assistance were provided through the ESEA. Funds were provided for the improvement of education programs for children from educationally deprived backgrounds. Local schools were granted money and latitude to best determine how to address the educational needs of children of parents at the bottom of the economic pile. Financial assistance was provided to improve library resources, and to purchase textbooks and instructional materials. Supplemental centers were financed to foster local educational innovations. Educational research was supported though funding for research and development centers. Finally, funds were available to state departments of education to strengthen administrative capacity, a clever move to generate support at the state government level.

State departments of education not only got a slice of the federal money pie, but their influence over local educational jurisdictions was increased; local funding flowed through them. Joel Spring (2008, p. 408) noted a distinct result of the ESEA was the enhanced power given "to state departments of education in relation to local school districts." But the ESEA also dramatically increased the involvement of the federal government in local education. Over 90% of school districts in the nation eventually received funding. Congress willingly appropriated money that went to their constituents. The ESEA has become a major way to provide ongoing federal aid to schools. Subsequent federal education funding tends to be tucked into revised authorizations of the ESEA, such as the 2001 No Child Left Behind Act.

The ESEA of today no longer even remotely resembles the original intent or form of the 1965 legislation. The original act as amended has funded four decades of federal involvement in public education. The presence of federal involvement was solidified. It marked "a historical change in the nature of financial support for schools in the United States" (Patterson, 1996, p. 571). The federal government invited itself in 1965 to the local school funding party and it did not go home.

The importance of the 1965 Voting Rights Act to the civil rights movement cannot be overestimated. The U.S. Justice Department was empowered to intervene in cases where 50% or less of a county's voting age population had been able to register or vote; local, state, and federal elections were covered; and in cases of violations, federal agents were authorized to conduct elections. Within a year, 46% of Blacks were registered to vote in the six southern states covered. And the influence of the Voting Rights Act spread both in the southern and northern areas to knock down discriminatory voting practices. Blacks now empowered in elections got representatives elected to town councils, served on school boards and juries, influenced the composition of law enforcement agencies, and helped determine the allocation of public money. Blacks achieved moderate control over their civic lives; and the character of southern politics changed (Patterson, 1996, pp. 585–587). White resistance was not ended, but change was irreversible.

The desegregation of schools continued to be a national issue throughout the Johnson administration, and as previously discussed, up into the 1970s and beyond. Reflecting ideas expressed six decades earlier by John Dewey, parents want and support the concept of community schools. A sense of identity and belonging is generated; neighborhood children develop meaningful relationships that continue throughout a lifetime; and community schools themselves reflect the pulse of the community. Housing patterns determine school social class and ethnicity patterns. Parents buy housing with careful attention to the character of the neighborhood school. Desegregation efforts threatened to destroy parental calculations, however.

Overall, nationally the pace was slow as school districts figured out ways to maintain de facto segregation. The North in particular lagged, and the nation discovered segregation was not only a southern issue. Courts stepped up action with court-ordered busing becoming one of the most contentious issues facing the nation in the early 1970s. The White population rejected busing by a ratio of 3 to 1, and the Black population by 47% to 45%. And as already noted, a volatile issue became more volatile with violent public backlashes that tore communities apart (Patterson, 1996, pp. 732–733). School desegregation and busing continued to be a consuming national issue throughout the early 1970s. The harvest of good intentions yielded bitter fruit.

From Great Society to Troubled Society

The Johnson administration lost control of the Great Society initiative, and he lost what may have been an exalted position in the pantheon of American presidents. Johnson was forced to step away from running for office again in 1968. Three forces converged to destroy his presidency: splintering within the civil rights movement and White backlash; the war in Vietnam and public revolt; and the social revolution. In the mid-1960s the three became fused in the public's mind.

The civil rights movement was remarkable in many ways. It succeeded against strong opposition. There was the opposition of the entrenched power structure in the South. Cheap Black labor was exploited for generations to create great wealth for the moneyed class. The civil rights movement threatened to remove all of the "tools" White southerners used to keep the Black population in a condition of subservience: Jim Crow laws; denying Black citizens the right to vote; limiting quality educational opportunity; keeping Blacks in low-level jobs and on the land; fostering racial hatred; and intermittent violence. The reaction to the civil rights challenge was sharp, nasty, and brutal.

A source of southern opposition was centered in the law enforcement and legal systems. Civil rights advocates had to battle against segregationist sheriffs, "law" officers, and judges in the South intent on derailing the movement. Largely hidden from view but effective and invasive, however, were the actions of J. Edgar Hoover to thwart the movement. He illegally used resources of the Federal Bureau of Investigation (FBI) on a personal crusade against King and the civil rights movement. And he refused to use power of the FBI to support federal laws and used his political power and connections to warn away potential large civil rights donors (Branch, 1988, 1998, 2006).

In a direct effort to discredit King, Hoover wiretapped all of the places he stayed, collecting as much smut as he could, and editing and compiling tapes sent to opposing leading political and media figures across the South. Federal congressmen and senators from the South were sure to receive tapes. In an effort to nationally discredit King, planted information was used to accuse him of being a "closet communist," and to paint the movement red: The civil rights movement was nothing more than a communist plot directed from Moscow to disrupt America, was the line Hoover spread. He was a destructive, negative force by virtue of the power of the FBI in his hands (Branch, 1988, 1998, 2008).

King, however, faced particularly difficult problems within the civil rights movement. Traditional, mainline African American groups complained that King and the civil rights movement were siphoning off donor funds that they normally relied on. The National Association for the Advancement of Colored People (NCCAP), for example, faced a dilemma: They had to express public support for King and others, but privately were annoyed because their funding was stalled. Donor money they relied on for years now went to the civil rights cause. Similarly, African American religious groups experienced a drop in funding and saw King as a competitor, and not necessarily a collaborator. The greatest internal threat, however, came from young Blacks who wanted faster progress, arguing the policy of nonviolence was not working fast enough (Branch, 1988, 1998; Marable, 1984).

In addition to King and the Southern Christian Leadership Conference (SCLC), other civil rights organizations were the scene. Some, such as the Congress of Racial Equality (CORE) initially promoted nonviolence and worked with King. The Student Nonviolent Coordination Committee (SNCC), under the chairmanship of John Lewis, worked cooperatively with King, although they were ready to use violence to gain voting rights. Others were not as restrained. Black leader Stokely Carmichael, for example, started preaching "Black Power" with the warning: "Its time we stand up and take over. Take over. Move on over, or we'll move on over you." The Black writer Le Roi Jones sneered at "white liberalism." James Baldwin in *The Fire Next Time* warned "Freedom now" or "Burn, Baby, Burn." The Black Panther Party in Oakland, California, became in the eyes of the FBI a domestic terrorist organization to be hunted down (O'Neill, 1971, p.173). Black activists across the country began promoting the slogan "Black Power" and organized paramilitary protection groups. Violence and the threat of violence became a poisonous reality.

Critics of King argued that the nonviolent, direct action tactics practiced in the South would not work in the northern and western city ghettos where desperation was concentrated. Urban social upheavals could not be easily controlled, and as predicted, massive black rebellions swept through cities across the nation from 1964 to 1968, randomly destroying life and property, provoked by poverty, poor schools, the violence of law officers, radical rhetoric, and the killing of civil rights leaders, most noticeably the killing of King in 1968. Cities burned (O'Neill, 1971; Marable, 1984).

A split developed among Blacks within the civil rights movement, but Whites also fled, perceiving they were not wanted, and also fearful. Some were forced out. A national White backlash occurred. Communities formed gun clubs and armed themselves; housewives took shooting lessons; and police departments equipped themselves with heavy weapons. And the political dynamics changed. Liberal politicians, such as then-governor Pat Brown of California, for example, were politically ruined and voted out of office. Lyndon Johnson was blamed for social unrest. Broad-based national support for civil rights could no longer be mobilized.

But the civil rights movement was remarkable in what it accomplished in the face of entrenched resistance, and eventual fragmentation. The harsh discrimination and violence Black citizens encountered primarily in the South was transformed from a southern, sectional issue to one of national focus. As Myrdal and his associates reminded Americans, racism and poverty were national issues of shared responsibility. It was the nation that had to act. The disturbing episodes of cruelty and brutality could not be easily erased from the minds of the American public. The inspiring rhetoric of civil rights leaders gave Americans a new vocabulary of moral redemption. Crucially important legislation was passed. National perceptions changed: The pluralism that Americans always lived with now commanded recognition and accommodation.

War, Protest, and Schools

Participants in the civil rights movement also played roles in the Vietnam War protest. The Vietnam War embroiled the nation in an overseas conflict that it could not win and that at the same time created deep domestic fissures that continue to exist to this day. More than any other single factor, it brought down Lyndon Johnson's presidency. In what was basically a civil war, the U.S. government backed a South Vietnamese government that was so inept and corrupt that it could not secure the support of its own people. The loss of human lives was tragic: 58,000 Americans and around 3 million Vietnamese. There was an additional 2 million lives indirectly lost as a result of the bombing of neutral Cambodia, the fall of the government, and the genocide of the Pol Pot regime (Karnow, 1983).

To the soldier and the American public there was no convincing explanation of why we were fighting in Southeast Asia, and there was no plan of how the war was going to end. "Progress" was gauged by how many enemy bodies were stacked up against dead American men and women. The generals assured the American public that when enough North Vietnamese were killed they would give up, but they did not calculate how many more American youth, perhaps in the hundreds of thousands, would be killed before this happened. And they seem impervious to the moral issues involved. The generals wanted more troops. By 1967, over 464,000 were in Vietnam, and antiwar protesters stormed the Pentagon. The young, those who were most likely to fight and die, rebelled. Civic discord erupted all across the nation (Blum, 1991; O'Neill, 1971; Patterson, 1996).

A rebellion occurred among young men eligible for the draft, and in the universities. Both blacks and poor Whites were drafted in disproportionate numbers, and they died in disproportionate numbers, but all young men eligible for the draft felt threatened. On college campuses, antiwar groups formed, and rallies and demonstrations often ended in violence as state governors called in National Guard units, almost guaranteeing that violence ensued. The nightly carnage on television from Southeast Asia, the civic disorder at home, and the growing opposition among the general population contributed to the inability of the Johnson administration to retain the public confidence required to conduct the war. A sitting president was forced from political life. Richard Nixon was elected in 1968 on the promise that he would "get us out of Vietnam with honor." But in 1970 he ordered the bombing of Cambodia, a neutral country. Protests erupted across the nation. The U.S. government lost control of civil society. We left Vietnam in 1974 with embassy and military officials fleeing in helicopters as the North Vietnamese surged into Saigon. It was not an honorable exit (Morrison & Morrison, 1987; Patterson, 1996).

The chaos of the protest impacted schools. At the university level blame was placed on "liberal" professors for inciting students. The accusation was they subverted the military effort.

Some were not granted tenure, forced out by lack of pay raises, harassment, and the slashing of department funds. Blame was assigned to subject fields in the liberal arts and social sciences that were considered the major source of protesters, and there was a decided shift in funding to "safe" fields such as mathematics, engineering, and science. At the same time, campuses became disorderly places, but more accepting places and exciting places with protest speeches, demonstrations, and sit-ins. There were serious discussions on foreign and domestic policy as topics of national concern came out of classrooms and became subjects of campus-wide discussion. Acts of civil disobedience were carried out. Students clashed with law enforcement. The chaos at the college level also filtered down into public high schools as younger students emulated older. Public high schools became unruly, difficult places to manage.

Protest, Pot, and the Counterculture

The civil rights and Vietnam War protests became intertwined and in the public's mind inseparable from what probably best can be termed a "social revolution" in thought. The civil rights movement caused Americans to think differently about themselves and others. Now the war and young people were causing Americans to think differently about the values that they held and the society in which they lived. In the 1950s, the book *Organizational Man* was a bestseller outlining in detail how a male prepared himself to enter and succeed in the corporate world. It even went into detail on the kind of wife one should marry to ensure a smooth climb up the corporate ladder. By the mid-1960s, however, young women were reading Betty Friedans' *The Feminine Mystique* (1963) and Helen Gurley Brown's *Sex and the Single Girl*. Boys were reading *Playboy*. The young also read Rachel Carson's *Silent Spring*, Jane Jacobs's *Death and Life of Great American Cities*, and Joseph Heller's *Catch-22*, and saw Stanley Kubrick's film *Dr. Strangelove*. The *Organizational Man* was forgotten. Rosie the Riveter's daughter was told she could go to college and become a social worker, and Brown told her she could have a lot of sex along the way. Young men were accommodating. The city boy wanted to become an organic farmer, not an insurance executive like his father. The son of an investment banker wanted to become a professional musician and play the trumpet in a band much to his father's displeasure. The daughter of the president of the local women's club ran off and married the son of a Mexican field worker she met in college and together they started a vegetarian restaurant. Many young people discounted the kind of life they saw their mothers and fathers were locked into and wanted a different kind that was yet undefined. They wanted "fulfillment." They rejected the values of their parents.

Both young men and women listened to Timothy Leary speak on the wonderful properties of lysergic acid diethylamide (LSD), and absorbed renditions of Bobby Dylan's "The Times They Are a-Changing" and "Desolation Row." Young women flaunted the new miniskirts and young men and women began living together, thus challenging parents. Hispanics, Native Americans, feminists, gays, and straights joined in massive rallies protesting police abuse, the domination of the corporate state, the war, and social injustice. College administrations were besieged with protests against the arbitrary rule. Sit-in and office occupations followed. Students wanted a voice in college life. "The New Left" emerged from campus protest. Some civil actions were romanticized, peaceful demonstrations, but most were radical and violent. The Students for a Democratic Society was formed, and soon split with the offshoot Weathermen preaching and acting on violent, antiwar social resistance. Violent crime, drug abuse, and alcohol consumption sharply increased, the illegitimate birthrate went up, and SAT scores dramatically fell (Blum, 1991; Patterson, 1996).

One element of the social revolution was the rejection of the values grounded in family and religious beliefs. This was combined with experimenting with and testing what were often radically different values. There were, as suggested, more open and substantially changed ideas about sex. In the minds of some, sexual liberation was combined with women's liberation, and the advent of the pill took fear of pregnancy away. The smoking of pot became a way of life for some; more sinister drugs also were freely available. The "filthy speech" movement became part of "free speech." There was a strong ecology movement that expressed concern about planet earth, and the *Whole Earth Catalogue* defined a healthier way of life and a kinder, gentler treatment of nature. Herb shops, and organic and vegetarian restaurants became alternatives to commercial vitamins and fast-food outlets. Guitar playing and Frisbees were good. Che Guevara posters were "neat." Baths were out and unwashed, unkempt long hair was in; starched white shirts and ties were out, and frayed, threadbare jeans with holes were in along with un-ironed and wrinkled clothes and beads. In an act of liberation young women burned their bras.

Some of the young "dropped out" and ran off and joined a commune where they talked endlessly of a new utopian lifestyle, got "high," freely copulated, had unexpected babies, failed in growing corn, beans and peas, and collectively spent the money a few received from their affluent fathers. Most ended up quarreling over the freeloaders among them, sex, work and money, and returned home to eventually work at a bank or car wash, join the church, sing in the choir, and take kids to soccer practice. Some ended up with wrecked lives.

By the end of the 1960s there was a different kind of nation, one less innocent, more conflicted, divided, and less certain. Schools were changed. Opportunity was extended. Head Start and the ESEA helped bring in and retain more children in public schools. Remedial and special education programs helped minority and poor kids make up deficiencies. There was a concerted effort to reduce the dropout rate and encourage youth to graduate from high school. Busing appeared to be a way to fulfill the promise of more equal educational opportunity, but in reality it ushered in a period of angst and public protest. Public schools became places of chaos and conflict. All of the disorder once only in colleges found its way into public schools: disobedience, protest, drugs, sex, challenge to authority, rejection of social and religious values, and the lack of achievement. Difficulties in maintaining order and achievement were compounded by court rulings that the academic, dress, and discipline codes public schools relied on could no longer be used because they were often applied in unfair and unequal ways. They discriminated and were in violation of civil rights. Public schools became difficult places to promote learning.

At the college level, policies formulated extended educational opportunity to a more diverse and a larger segment of the population, encompassing individuals formerly not encouraged to go on to college. Remedial programs, low tuition, student aid, loan programs, fellowship, and affirmative action brought working-class men and women, and youth from poor families and minority families, into higher education in even larger numbers. A trend starting with the end of World War II continued. Many dropped out, many failed, but many succeeded, motivated by an opportunity formerly closed to them. Course offerings also radically changed. No longer was it sufficient to offer a core of subjects that constituted what was thought to be the substance of "an educated man" as educators faced the necessity of addressing student demands for a more relevant, contemporary education. Black history, women's studies, human sexuality, ecology, pollution control, and contemporary politics became part what can be termed "boutique courses" designed to appeal to particular student groups. Achievement in school as measured by standardized tests dropped. Students spent less time concentrating on the subject fields tested; among some students, basic, fundamental skills were less developed; and as the breadth of the student population was extended there was an expected statistical regression to the mean.

The end of the 1960s saw a seriously fragmented nation. Deep rifts existed between different population segments that could not be closed and healed over, and continue to this day. Protestors were battered and beaten by gangs that saw them as easy, reprehensible prey. Parents were disillusioned, hurt, and saddened by a rejection that they could not understand. Citizens were alarmed over what appeared the disintegration of society before their eyes. Large segments of society stood by and watched, puzzled and uncertain about what to do; others redoubled efforts in churches, schools, and political organizations to reestablish values under attack. "The vast majority of Americans had little if anything do with campus rebels, counterculturalists, or anti-war protesters" (Patterson, 1996, p. 450). There were millions of upward mobile Americans during the longest period of uninterrupted economic growth the nation had ever seen. In this decade, wages were up, prices stable, unemployment dropped to 3.5%, and the poverty rate fell from 22% at the beginning of the decade to 12% in 1969.

The Changing Times

Some bitter fruit came out of the decade of good intentions, but also there was a sweet yield. There was a continuing consciousness that issues of poverty, discrimination, opportunity, and social justice could not simply be ignored. And the nation had to come to terms with its basic characteristic of ethnic plurality. Some of the most productive outcomes of the 1960s found legislative support in the early 1970s with a Democratic-controlled Congress and a Republican presidency.

Women, Civil Rights, Work, and Schooling

Women found legislative support. Like many others, young women believed they could change the course of history for the good. Women were a big part of the social revolution of the 1960s. They marched in the civil rights movement, travelled in the bus boycotts, and helped conduct voter registration drives; they were beaten and jailed; and they worked behind the scenes to stuff envelopes, cook meals for demonstrators, nurse the battered, and raise money (Branch, 1998). Women were a big part of the Vietnam antiwar protest. They signed petitions, took part in candlelit marches, and shouted, cursed, and broke windows in both organized and spontaneous demonstrations. They joined campus protests and occupied buildings. They sang antiwar songs and stuffed flowers in the barrels of soldiers guarding the Pentagon. Women were also part of the culture revolution that had no center but spread itself throughout all of society challenging middle-class values: They became hippies, agitators, and advocates. Some women joined cults. Some went politically far left, others far right (Blum, 1991; Patterson, 1996).

In the 1960s more women attended and graduated from high school than men, and women attended college in greater numbers but fewer than men. Women achieved higher status academically than men; but women also came to realize the barriers of discrimination were difficult to breach. To be sure, employment for middle-class women continued to open, but elite colleges continued to exclude women or exile them to segregated companion institutions. In 1982, Columbia was the last Ivy League university finally to become coeducational. In 1960, nearly 1.3 million women nationwide attended college in contrast to 2.26 million men. Few graduating women went on to earn higher degrees. In the same year, 8,800 men but only 1,028 women attained higher degrees. Women were discouraged from enrolling in engineering or science programs, and women had a difficult time obtaining admission to medical, law, and business schools. Colleges exclusively for women had "feminine curricula" featuring flower arranging, ceramics, interior decorating, cosmetics, and grooming (Patterson, 1996).

Women went to work in greater numbers. During the war effort, a full 35.8% of the civilian workforce was comprised of women. After dipping in the 1950s, the employment of women was up to 37.8% in 1960, marking a continuing trend resulting in over 50% of the labor force today comprised of women. But women were rarely hired to fill corporate executive positions and women were paid less than men for the same job and equal qualifications. Promotions were more difficult to realize.

The social movement was rife with bias toward women. Women complained they were relegated to subservient roles: They cooked, made beds, washed clothes, and cleaned toilets for men. Few women filled leadership roles in the civil rights antiwar protest movements. They could march and sing, but were told it was best not to want to lead rallies and speak. Young men in the social movements may have been more sensitive to women's rights, but they considered leadership a male prerogative and displayed patronizing, domineering behavior. Young women soon learned that inequality manifested itself not only in ethnicity, but also in gender (Blum, 1991; Patterson, 1996). Many women reacted in outrage and organized.

Young and older women working together in towns and cities, and especially on college campuses, organized in a spirit of solidarity to agitate for their rights. They broke into a militant faction that declared war on men, and a moderate faction that did not necessarily consider themselves "feminists" or sexual liberation advocates: They just wanted fairness. Local issues took on national import, as women's liberation became a major political issue.

Earlier, Kennedy established the Commission on the Status of Women, issued an executive order to end sex discrimination in federal employment, and signed the Equal Pay Act, but it had no provisions for emforcement. Overall, these were weak measures, but "they unintentionally aroused expectations that encouraged a much more self-conscious feminist movement after 1964" (Patterson, 1996, p. 463). One of the most important groups, the National Organization for Women (NOW), was formed in 1966, and companion local groups formed. Organized women groups demanded equal rights in marriage, laws, education, and work. Reproduction rights became a national issue. Stopping sexual harassment became an issue. Women were effective in building the case against discrimination. Polling in 1962 showed only about one-third of American women considered themselves discriminated against; by 1970 half did, and by 1974 two-thirds of women across the nation thought they were victims of discrimination (Patterson, 1996, p. 644).

One of the most notable education achievements of the women's movement was passage of Title IX of the 1972 Higher Education Act. Its impact cannot be overestimated. Gender equality in educational employment and programming was provided. The act applied to all educational institutions from preschool and elementary, high schools, technical and professional schools, to colleges and universities, both public and private. To counter restrictive court decisions, the 1987 Civil Rights Restoration Act amended Title IX to include all activities in educational institutions reviving federal aid. The most visible public impact was on women's sports. Joel Spring (2008, p. 44) reports at the high school level female sports participation went from 7% in 1972 to 37% by 1990; at the collegiate level the percentage gain was from 15.6% in 1972 to 34.5% in 1993.

Less visible but significant was hiring. Inclusive searches for faculty and administrators had to be carried out. No longer could personnel be hired through an "old boys" network. Curricula, textbooks, and tests came under close scrutiny; "non-sexist" materials were developed. Public school vocational and home economics enrolled both girls and boys.

In colleges "women studies" were added, and science and engineering opened to more women; efforts were expanded to recruit more women admissions. Women were encouraged to go to law and medical school. Women medical school graduates increased from 8.4% in 1969 to 34.5% in 1990 (Spring, 2008, p. 447).

Perhaps the most significant impact of the women's movement was the change in public attitude. The nation could no longer continue to treat half of its population as less capable, less deserving, and subservient to male perceptions of superiority. Civil rights for women were a moral issue, but it also was a pragmatic issue. There was a slow recognition that by denying women the right to fully develop their talent, individuals were discriminated against, but the nation also lost. Society was denied the full social and economic benefit from the considerable unused, latent talent that was suppressed through discrimination against women. Women can manage companies equally, or better than men. They can fly airplanes, drive trains, walk in space, troubleshoot computers, raise cows, weld, repair cars, and design buildings and monuments. The new world of science, technology, and communications emerging from the postwar period needed to apply the talents of women to do more than scrub, wash, cook, clean, and change diapers.

Immigration, Latin Americans, and Bilingual Education

The Latino population benefitted from the 1960s. There was a revolt against low wages and poor working conditions, particularly in agriculture where there was no job security, no benefits, and uncertain seasonal work. The movement for "brown power" is best represented in Cesar Chavez's success in organizing California field workers. Joining with Filipino laborers, the United Farm Workers were organized and went on strike against the table grape growers of Delano, California. Much wider strike actions were set off, and la huelga (the strike) succeeded after five years. Growers were finally brought to the bargaining table through the national boycott of grapes. In the meantime other nonviolent strikes were more successful, and demonstrated to Mexican Americans the potential for achieving fair working conditions and pay (O'Neill, 1971). Many of the leaders of the Latino revolt, like Cesar Chavez, were veterans of World War II and no longer willing to wait for unfulfilled promises. Eva Hernandez, for example, explained, "The war had provided us the unique chance to be socially and economically independent, and we didn't want to give up this experience simply because the war ended. We, too, want to be first-class citizens in our communities" (Takaki, 2008, p. 388).

Latino youth were embolden in the 1960s and led organized boycotts for better and diversified schools, and more relevant studies. In the 1960s, Mexican American students demonstrated in schools in support of using Spanish in schools, the teaching of Mexican American history and culture, the serving of Mexican food in cafeterias, and the hiring of more Spanish-speaking teachers. In California, 57% of pupils in 1966 with Spanish surnames were attending segregated schools, and in 1973 two-thirds of Mexican heritage children were still attending segregated schools in Los Angeles. Throughout the nation, secondary segregation, the practice of segregating and isolating students on the basis of language or "special needs," was widespread among Latino students. The Mexican American Legal Defense Education Fund (MALDEF) was established in 1967 to combat de facto segregation, unequal funding, and unjust punishment for student participation in civil rights activities (Spring, 2008, p. 436).

In a legal case that had long-term national consequences brought by the MALDEF, the Supreme Court decided in the *Rodriguez v. San Antonio Independent School District* ruling in 1973 that inequality in funding was not a constitutional issue because schooling was a function of states. School districts in the state of Texas with primarily enrollment of Mexican students received less funding than did White enrollment districts. To this day, the unequal funding of schools within and between districts remains probably the most intractable issue impaction on student achievement and educational quality (Spring, 2008).

An outcome of the drive for educational opportunity, Mexican, Puerto Rican, and Native American as well as other communities pressed for bilingual education. The issue became national through the efforts of groups such as La Raza Unida, formed to protect the rights of Mexican Americans. They wanted bilingual education in schools to preserve and protect the cultural and language heritage of Spanish-speaking pupils. The Bilingual Education Act of 1968 was passed by Congress.

Bilingual education is defined by contrasting views and practices. To some its purpose is to "wash" the cultural heritage and language use out of what is considered a subordinate group. Bilingual education is considered part of the process of deculturalizing students by replacing their historical, cultural, and language heritage with that of the dominant culture. Deculturalization does not always implies assimilation because in a continuing national political struggle some groups are considered best left on the outside looking in; they are assigned to an identity limbo with limited integrated social and economic participation.

On the other hand some groups—Native Americans, Spanish-speaking Mexicans, Puerto Ricans, Cubans, Salvadorians, and other Latinos—advocated a more inclusive form of bilingual education, a vision of a truly multicultural and multilingual society. They favor a bilingual education similar to the cultural views of W.E.B. Dubois that seeks to strengthen and preserve the heritage of individuals, not to erase it, while at the same time build pathways of full participation in mainstream society. These two views continue to dominate national discussion of bilingual education: Is it a tool used to erase an individual's cultural heritage and replace it with the dominate cultural influence? Or is bilingual education a tool used to help individuals to preserve their language and cultural heritage while developing the English language skills, cultural understanding, and school achievement that enables one to ease into mainstream society?

Three basic instructional models dominate bilingual education (Newman, 1994). The purpose of *structured immersion* is to help limited-English-proficiency students gain language skills as quickly as possible with the minimal use of the indigenous language. The teacher always speaks English and students are encouraged to always use English. Its use is a form of deculturalization. Proponents cite not only lower instructional costs, but argue that unless ethnic students learn good English skills they are at an educational and labor force disadvange. The *transitional bilingual model* is a compromise. Students in some subjects, such as social science or music, are taught in their mother tongue to help retain use and ease the transition into English; but other classes are given in English along with English as a second language (ESL) classes in the practice of reading, writing, and speaking. ESL instruction is given alone in some schools. In both models it is best to start instruction early in the elementary grade years.

A third model is *bilingual/bicultural maintenance*. At each grade level students take classes in both languages with teachers fluent in both. The purpose is to develop greater language proficiency in both the mother tongue and English. The theme of multicultural richness runs through all instruction. Supporters claim greater understanding is developed of the multicultural world we live in. A major criticism is that the student does not develop high language proficiency in either language. And what about schools with multiple language groups? The cost of many low enrolled groups is prohibitive.

Bilingual education is not politically neutral. Conservatives tend to support structural immersion because of lower instructional costs, the alleged efficiency in teaching English, and the lack of interest in maintaining elements of cultural and historical heritage. It also best supports movements to make English the official language of the nation. The transition model gets support from conservatives because of its goal to develop English language proficiency quickly, while at the same time the cultural aspects of the transition model appeal to liberals. The transition model was supported by both the Ford and Carter administrations. The most politically controversial model is bilingual/bicultural maintenance. Increased pluralism can be politically destabilizing. Bilingual education will continue to be at the front of national policy issues as the population itself is increasingly "brown" in tone.

Amerindians: Toward Education Self-Determination

Amerindians as an identifiable ethnic entity were on the verge of dissolution by 1950. The census enumerated only 343,000 in a nation of 151 million. The civil rights movement helped to reverse ominous trends by stimulating Indian activism and enlisting outside support. The American Indian Movement (AIM) was formed to fight civil rights abuses. Indian citizens lobbied before

Congress and testified at hearings; some became militant. A group took over and trashed the Bureau of Indian Affairs (BIA) offices in Washington, D.C. A group calling itself "Indians of All Tribes" seized the former prison island Alcatraz in San Francisco Bay, demanding its conversion to an Indian cultural and education center. The village of Wounded Knee on the Oglala Sioux Pine Ridge Reservation in South Dakota was taken over, and gun battles were fought with federal marshals sent to close the reservation. After a 72-day standoff, the long-standing treaty rights were reconsidered. A march on Washington, D.C., called the "Trail of Broken Treaties," was organized in 1972 (Reyhner & Eder, 2004).

Indian parents and children demonstrated and boycotted at BIA-run schools across the country. Instructional quality was extremely poor; the range of studies was limited and Indians claimed instruction was exclusively designed to erase Indian identity. Indians observed there was little of cultural value for Indian children from reading about Dick and Jane, Baby Sally, and their dog, Spot. Some groups organized on reservations across the country to demand that Whites controlling school boards and employed as principals and teachers be replaced with Indians. Common practice was for school board members to be appointed among operators of trading posts and BIA employees (Reyner & Eder, 2004).

From the time at the turn of the century when the decision was made to make Native Indians "White" through government-run boarding schools, and through the breaking up of reservations and opening up of former Indian land to White speculators through the allotment and guardian systems, Native Americans as an identifiable people were entangled in a long, slow downward trajectory leading to poverty and dissolution. Public reaction was strong enough to force the federal government to do something, but it was not until after the close of World War I that action was taken. Earlier, the Institute of Governmental Research at Johns Hopkins University (later the Brookings Institute) conducted a study under the guidance of Louis Meriam on the causes of Indian poverty and the loss of cultural identity. The Meriam Report issued in 1928 had one overriding conclusion: The policies of the U.S. government were the major factor in the destruction of Amerindians as a people. As a result of the report, advocates of Indian welfare both outside and inside of government rallied to the cause of righting what was considered a grievous national wrong (Reyhner & Eder, 2004, pp. 207–210).

Like many social causes, however, efforts to reconstruct the economic and cultural life of reservation Indians came apart with the Great Depression of the 1930s. An opportunity was lost. And Indians on and off reservations kept losing large parts of their land heritage through legal and illegal means (Debo, 1970). By the end of World War II, efforts to strengthen the independence and self-determination of Native Americans came under fire mainly by conservatives bent on ending government support and taking reservation land not yet taken. A "termination" policy was established by Congress. It was justified on the basis of making individual Indians "free" from tribal authority and government control (Patterson, 1996; Reyhner & Eder, 2004). As Patterson (1996, p. 377) suggested, "the miserable condition of most American Indians in the 1950s, as throughout United States history, testified to the continuing strength of white ethnocentrism and institutional discrimination in the country."

"Set the American Indian free" was the cry of supporters of termination as they calculated how to take over former reservation land. Reservations were to be disassembled, and land distributed to families, and some sold on the open market; individuals were given job training, with cash payments for land given up when relocated in urban centers. Some tribes, such as the Menominee of Wisconsin and the Klamath of Oregon, along with other smaller groups, were eliminated. Termination was considered the "final solution" to the "Indian Problem" (Patterson, 1996; Reyhner & Eder, 2004).

Political action caused a reversal of the government's termination policy. White and Indian activists joined to vigorously protest the destructive treatment of Native Americans, and the federal government backed away from the termination policy that was formally ended by Richard Nixon in 1969. But movement to reconstitute Indian life was already strongly underway, and Nixon's executive action affirmed what was already a political fact. A Pan-Indian movement had taken hold. In 1961, 450 Indian delegates from 90 tribes met in Chicago to draft a *Declaration of Indian Purpose*, a document opposing termination. John F. Kennedy opened a change in Indian policy by including tribal representatives in federal decision making. The Navajo Rough Rock Demonstration School was established in 1966, a joint effort of the Office of Economic Opportunity and the BIA to show that local Indian communities could run their own schools. Indians also benefited from the Bilingual Education Act, passed as part of the ESEA in 1968 and other Great Society legislation directed at overcoming discrimination and poverty (Reyhner & Eder, 2004).

Congress, perhaps atoning for its previous termination policies, formulated educational policy giving greater tribal involvement in running schools. The 1969 report of the Senate Committee on Labor and Public Welfare, *Indian Education: A National Tragedy—A National Challenge,* was important in this effort. The foundation was constructed for two important pieces of legislation. The Indian Education Act was passed in 1972. The Office of Indian Education was established and helped to set guidelines for protecting the rights of Indian youth, including the right to freedom of religion and culture. Support to local schools was provided through federal financial assistance to "meet the special needs" of Native children. The piece of federal legislation, however, that had the greatest impact on the shifting to Native American parents greater involvement in the education of their own children was the 1975 Indian Self-Determination and Education Assistance Act. Individual tribes were given the authority to contract with the federal government to operate education and health programs. In the case of local districts that received funds through the 1975 act, but that did not have a majority of Indians on school boards, provision had to be made for a separate school committee comprised of parents of attending Indian children. The committee had authority over the federally funded programs (Spring, 2008).

In 1979, Congress passed a resolution to protect the religious freedom of American Indians. The resolution aimed at maintaining the surviving traditional cultural and religious beliefs from three centuries of Christian missionary proselytizing efforts. This was a huge step away from termination. Additional movement in the direction of greater educational self-determination was the 1988 Tribally Controlled Schools Act. Tribes obtained grants to operate their own schools. Finally, in 1990, the Native American Languages Act committed the federal government to work to preserve the language heritage of Amerindians.

After 160 years, Americans of Native heritage could freely speak their own language in schools that they had the authority to run. But they could not fully recapture the past. There were fewer, and they were poorer, and as Joel Spring (2008, p. 434) observed, tribes had to re-discover and recreate languages and traditions that had been largely destroyed by government policy and human greed.

Busing and Alternative Schools

Richard Nixon may have promised that he was going to end busing during his 1968 presidential campaign, but court-ordered desegregation was not going to go away, and neither was the major tool, busing. In the 1954 *Brown* desegregation decision, the Supreme Court mandated desegregation to proceed with "all deliberate speed," but in follow-up court deliberations no date was set to get this accomplished. It was left up to federal district judges to supervise desegregation, and most of the federal judges in the South were southerners sympathetic of existing conditions. As late as 1964, nearly 10 years after *Brown*, only 2.3% of Black children in the South attended desegregated schools (Patterson, 1996).

The Kennedy and Johnson administrations spurred Congress on, resulting in the civil rights legislation of 1964 and 1965. Both the justice department and the courts became more aggressive in tightening affirmative action. Court-mandated busing was stipulated, and the busing spread across the country as a means to accomplish school desegregation. The reaction was explosive, especially in the North. The cry was the courts and federal government were forcing lower-class Blacks into orderly, White neighborhoods. The cherished ideal of the "neighborhood school," an offspring of John Dewey's belief in the school as community, was now being destroyed, protesters lamented. "Black kids did not fit into White schools." A volatile issue turned more violent as barricades, mobs, and marches were used to thwart integration. There were nasty incidents all across the country (Blum, 1991; Patterson, 1996).

In both the North and South, resistance took several forms. "White flight," the movement into what appeared to be a "safe" community was one, but busing destroyed the best-laid plans because no one knew for certain how busing would be implemented. More affluent communities, however, tended not to be targets for busing. Some school districts formulated "freedom of choice" options, which were not really options because Blacks were discouraged from attending White schools, afraid, or they did not have the required transportation. The Prince Williams County school district in Virginia disbanded public schools to avoid integration. Public financial aid, however, was given to private segregated schools.

At the political level primarily in the South, school districts were redrawn so that Black students resided in separate districts from White students. The shape of school districts took on strange forms as boundary lines wound in complex patterns around and through communities, thickening and shrinking according to ethnic housing patterns. The court mandate for schools to approximate the racial composition of school districts was fulfilled. Throughout the country, oddly formed school districts continue to exist and the practice has been expanded in areas with high concentrations of Latino students (Blum, 1991; Patterson, 1996).

A development at the local school district that had influence on quelling public resistance to busing was the alternative school movement. Magnet schools were established. There are two kinds. In one kind the curriculum focus of the total school is concentrated on a cluster of studies in one subject field, such as the performing arts and music, science and technology, or health professions. Today there even are "back to basics" magnets. Students throughout the school district elect to apply and gain acceptance through various kinds of entrance examinations. The ethnic balance achieved in the integrated magnet school is expected to significantly contribute to the overall ethnic balance of the district. There is less pressure to balance out other district schools.

The second kind is a magnet school within a school. A comprehensive high school within an area of predominantly one-ethnic concentration contains a separate magnet program open to all district students. The expected result, for example, is that a considerable number of White and Asian students will elect to enroll in a science and math magnet housed in a predominately Black-enrolled high school. District ethnic enrollments all level out.

The impact of magnet programs as well as other related options had the impact of defusing public resistance to busing. The volatile, bitter fights of the 1970s were tamped down. Parents felt they had options for their children. Parents felt they had choice. The magnet idea was even extended to the elementary grades. Magnets are a voluntary form of desegregation, and one attractive feature is that programs are offered that are otherwise not available in other district schools. But perhaps as Joseph Newman (1994) observed, the biggest disadvantage is that segregation by social class is increased as segregation by ethnicity is decreased. In many school districts "magnet schools have filled up with middle-class students, leaving working-class students in neighborhood schools everyone regards as second-class" (p. 229).

The idea of providing schooling alternatives is politically potent. Politicians get elected by promising parents choice. Choice tends to be promoted as a way to offset what are considered failing public schools, but there continues to be undertones of resistance to ethnic inclusion. By the early 1990s, however, busing ceased to be such a public volatile issue. In national polling, 41% of the population supported busing for purposes of desegregation. Among those most likely to experience busing, 60% of 18- to 24-year-olds were favorable, and 51% of 25- to 29-year-olds expressed support. Among families with children being bused, 71% thought the experience "very satisfactory." But relatively few students in the United States were bused: Only about 4% of children were bused for the sole purpose of integration, and the average time of busing one way was only 15 minutes. Far more children in rural areas were bused just to get to school, and for a longer trip (Newman, 1994).

Busing has been largely defused as a political issue, although in some states there are strong movements to return to more segregated patterns of public schooling. Many parents today feel that they have more alternatives available through private schools, home schooling, and charter schools. This may be one reason. Acceptance of the ideas of multiculturalism and diversity probably has had a moderating influence. Shifting demographics may be influential. At the same time, there is a strong national movement in the direction of finding alternatives to public supported community schools. There is evidence indicating, however, that de facto segregation is increasing largely because of the White population moving from urban centers to the suburbs. The courts have ruled that school districts are not required to correct ethnic imbalances due to neighborhood population transitions. An additional factor is ethnic rebalancing is no longer on the larger national political screen. President Reagan, the two Bush presidents, and

Clinton and Obama shifted political emphasis to improving the quality of education below the collegiate level for everyone through improved instruction and accountability measures. There is considerable less interest in desegregation as a way to improve American education for everyone (Ravitch, 2013).

Students with Special Needs

Schoolchildren with special needs were brought to the attention of the nation through the civil rights movement. As recounted in Part Five, concern by educators in the 1920s over the increasing numbers of students entering public schools with physical problems, learning difficulties, and emotional behavioral problems resulted in instituting special education programs. In the postwar years it was evident to parents that services were not adequate for their children. State laws excluded so-called handicapped and retarded children from public schools, and the services that were provided tended to be inadequate. Common practice was to keep students with physical, hearing, or seeing conditions home, and to schedule students with lesser handicapping conditions into classes isolated from the "regular" school. There was no interaction with other than handicapped students. Concerned parents turned activists.

Local schools tended to be unresponsive, and advocates for the handicapped became politically organized and turned to the courts. As an example, Joel Spring (2008) records the combined activities of the Pennsylvania Association for Retarded Children (PARC), the National Association for Retarded Children, and the Council for Exceptional Children, as well as lobbying groups for the handicapped, to obtain favorable legal rulings that in turn could be used to obtain supportive state and federal laws. Legal action was filed in 30 cases against individual state governments. It was not until 1975, however, that the federal government stepped in with the Education for All Handicapped Children Act, Public Law 94-142.

Several major accomplishments were realized. Public school systems all over the country conducted training and retraining for faculty in order to conform to the requirements of the act. No longer could students with handicapping conditions be shunted off into separate, isolated rooms. Students with handicapping conditions had to be instructed in "the least restrictive environment," which often meant "regular" classrooms with "regular" teachers serving the general school population. School facilities had to be accessible: Stairs were replaced with ramps to handle wheelchairs, elevators were installed, lighting changed, rooms repainted, and many other large and small changes that contributed to a more accessible, clean, and functional physical setting that all students profited from. Educators began to realize that there was a much wider range of handicapping conditions that required attention than previously recognized, and that those students required individually tailored and different interventions. Specialists were assigned to give informed assistance.

In order to address the complexity of handicapping conditions, the act required the development of an individual educational plan (IEP) for each student. The IEP is an outcome of a joint meeting with the local educational agency and parents to determine the kinds of services to provide. A reading specialist, a specialist in autism, a social worker or psychologist may be included, depending on the dimensions of the student's individual handicapping condition.

The IEP is a means of reaching agreement on the kinds of interventions to be initiated and the responsibilities of both the school and parents. It provides a framework and timetable for advancing the educational progress of the individual student.

The Education for All Handicapped Children Act has given hundreds of thousands of children an opportunity to pursue learning that they formerly did not have. It has raised public awareness, and helped to develop the understanding that students with special needs require the support and assistance of everyone in schools and communities. It is a civil rights law, and handicapped citizens have greater assurance of "equal treatment" under the law. Above all, the act signaled a meaningful shift in public attitude about social responsibility. But challenges continue to surround the implementation of the act.

Classroom teachers struggle to implement the concept of least restrictive environment. They lack qualifications or experience to handle all of the variations of handicapping conditions students bring with them into the classroom; and some handicapping conditions manifest themselves in behavioral problems. Ideally, classroom help from specialists is available, but budget constraints often eliminate any assistance. Then again, when students are assigned to "special classes" they may fall behind "regular" classroom instruction because of the remedial character of the work. They can never catch up because the "regular" students have moved ahead and beyond the scope of the remedial work. Schools continue to struggle with these issues.

Accountability and the Community School Movement

One outcome of the 1960s was the community school movement. The movement originated in the New York City area primarily among Black parents sensitive to the fact that they had little influence with the large school bureaucracies running the schools their children attended. They wanted a say in school matters, particularly in those concerning issues of their cultural heritage and courses of study. They saw vestiges of discrimination and racism in the schools for Black pupils that were primarily staffed by White principals and teachers, but disturbingly, they saw studies that almost solely reflected a White perspective. Joel Spring (2008, p. 468) best summed up the community school movement when he observed, "In many ways, it was an attempt to capture the nineteenth-century ideal of democratic localism according to which the schools were to reflect the values and desires of their users." Black parents wanted more influence and power over the hiring of principals and teachers, curricula, use of money, and the running of schools. In short, they wanted authority vested in local, community boards with Black membership.

Local parents at the Intermediate School 201 in Harlem and in the Ocean Hill-Brownsville section of Brooklyn gained some control over the schools their children attended, but eventually in ongoing battles with elite school boards, an administrative bureaucracy intent on retaining power, and teacher unions, they lost and control reverted to the central authority. In the meantime, the community control movement spread across the country, and its identity as a ethnic concern changed to becoming more inclusive as parents across ethnic and socioeconomic lines demanded more local influence in running local schools. One response was for large bureaucratic school organizations to establish satellite administrative units bounded by ethnic, social, or economic concerns. These units maintained more local influence, but at the same time the central administration retained its control over money and policy. Local parents did not achieve the degree of influence they wanted, and the community school movement was therefore blunted.

A response by professional educators that had a deep and lasting influence on American schools was the accountability movement. Professional educators perceived a threat in the community school movement to their independence as well as jobs, and they countered. They built the case that public schools should be run by professionals held accountable for student progress: It was professionals who were best positioned to make school decisions, and to track student performance over time—in other words, educational experts knew how to select, administer, score, and interpret test results that not only gave parents vital information on the progress of their child but also demonstrated the quality of instruction, the learning progress, and the critical importance of keeping schools in the hands of professionals. The use of tests, especially standardized instruments, spread across the country as educators sought to reinforce the importance of keeping schools in the proper hands. Accountability would be achieved.

Widespread testing had several results. It kept public education in the hands of educators—the experts knew best. It also made standardized testing central to school activities, restoring some of the influence testmakers of the 1920s had lost over the decades. Underlying concepts of behavioral psychology that support testing were locked into the curricular framework. School districts had a way to standardize classroom instruction through district-wide course guides and to measure and compare instructional results based on outcome measures.

But soon two troubling results came to the front. The test results were shocking. In reading, for example, gains did not occur and many students continued to lose ground and performed below grade level. Although many students entered school with low reading ability, they did not catch up. In was not unusual to find that a student entering the second grade at a 1.8 reading level when tested at the end of the school year was only reading at a 2.4 grade level and clearly not ready to go into the third grade. General overall expected gains simply did not occur. Over all of the subject areas and grade levels tested, poor results were found. To be sure, bright spots were found, but the national picture was grim.

Another result was that testing began to dominate over other instructional concerns as if more testing would improve school performance. But particularly troubling to professional educators was the practice of critics to use the poor test results to point to the failure of public education. Some argued that declining school performance was the result of integration, of the poor quality of teacher preparation programs, of the need to sack teachers and administrators in poor performing schools, or of the urgency to find private alternatives to the monopoly of public education. The criticism of Bestor and Rickover, and others of the 1950s, found new life in the 1970s. The nation continues to be engulfed in the presence of testing.

Jimmy Carter: Capturing the Liberals

Along with other social groups, teachers discovered a new militancy in the 1950s and 1960s. These were prosperous years, but teachers struggled to achieve salary increases comparable to others in the workforce. And there was rapid inflation that made it hard for teachers to balance the checkbook every month. Aggravated by the sense of powerlessness, teachers turned to the use of strikes. Teachers belonging to the National Educational Association (NEA), the oldest and largest teacher organization in the nation, also revolted against the leadership.

Since its organization in 1851, the NEA was primarily run by men holding leadership positions as state superintendents of schools, district superintendents, and noted college professors of education. By 1910, a rival teacher organization emerged, the American Federation of Teachers. The AFT was affiliated with the American Federation of Labor. It was a labor union run by teachers, and to this day its strength is in industrial cities with strong union presence. The NEA leadership comprised of men in administrative positions was challenged by the large number of women teachers staffing public schools for the over 18 million pupils attending. Women teachers by a large margin made up the majority of dues-paying membership but they had little influence on NEA policy or operations. Also, women felt that the male administrators running the organization did not work for the best interests of classroom teachers; it was an "old boys" network that worked to enhance its own interests. The male leadership stopped the revolt by securing a change from floor votes at the national conventions to proportional representation by delegates; they were apportioned according to state membership levels with state educational administrators controlling delegate selection. Until the 1960s, the NEA was firmly controlled by what was considered the elite leadership of American education. Teachers revolted and took over the NEA.

In the 1950s and 1960s the AFT and its local affiliates organized under the United Federation of Teachers and demonstrated its ability to secure better working conditions, better pay, and greater job security for teachers. Strike action or the threat of strikes backed by other unions was an effective tool. NEA-member teachers observed and grumbled, and grumbling turned to action, and action turned to revolt. By the early 1970s, the NEA was in the hands of teachers. Administrators bolted and formed their own national professional organizations, resulting in three major consequences.

The NEA became more representative of the interests of classroom teachers. In the 1979–80 school year, for example, at a time when the national inflation rate was at an all-time high with interest rates hovering around 20%, NEA affiliates struck 208 times; AFT affiliates struck 34 times. Teachers won concessions through the possibility that was acted on or not of militant labor action. In contrast, when the NEA was under the control of school elites it tended to work quietly though political action and lobbying. They probably were more successful than they appeared in securing tenure rights, retirement, health, and sick leave benefits (Newman, 1994).

The second, long-term consequence was the loss of national political power. Up until the teacher revolt, the NEA was considered to be the national voice of public education. Its leaders were national and state leaders. When a president or a governor wanted to formulate education policy, the head of the NEA was consulted; when a politician wanted to run for office, the NEA was consulted on winning education policy. The NEA helped to influence laws, policies, state tax rates and bond issues, school reform, the appointment of local, state, and national leaders, and about any issues impinging on education. Everything changed with the teacher revolt. The governor of Oklahoma, for example, was not going to consult the sixth-grade teacher in Topeka and president of the NEA on education policy, or the school board members in Raleigh were not going to give much attention to a speech by the high school biology teacher and president of the NEA.

The NEA has worked to regain national stature and influence. Political action committees (PACs) are formed; candidates favorable to public education are supported; NEA members staff telephone banks, distribute literature, and ring doorbells for candidates. NEA-member teachers reach into almost every community in America, and influence local, state, and national elections. But the NEA of today does not talk with the same authority of the NEA controlled by the "old boys" network. Unlike then, there is no one voice that is considered to represent the voice of American education.

The third consequence had long-term damaging results to public education. The NEA dropped any pretense of political neutrality. The AFT was always in the "liberal" column. It grew out of the progressive education movement around the turn of the century; key leaders were women; it supported Democratic political candidates; it backed the civil rights movement, the war on poverty, and women's rights; and it endorsed Kennedy and Johnson and continues to endorse Democratic political candidates. The NEA in contrast attempted to preserve a stand of political neutrality and bipartisanship.. With teacher control, however, the NEA swung left. During the 1976 election, Jimmy Carter approached the NEA with the following proposal: If the NEA broke its former policy of political neutrality and supported Democratic candidates across the country at the local, state, and national levels, he would create a cabinet office of secretary of education. In addition, the NEA would be given a primary voice in the selection of the first secretary of education and in educational policy during his administration. A good deal? The NEA thought so and decisively shifted to the Democratic political column where it has remained ever since. What was a short-term boost in national stature turned into a political mistake, however, following the Carter defeat and the election of Ronald Reagan.

Chapter Seventeen
The Conservative Restoration

Ronald Reagan remains a key educational figure in the last quarter of the 20th century. His administration effectively shaped educational policy that continues to define the borders of national education discussion. Reagan appealed to people. He conveyed a warm, caring personality, and to a people weary of the conflict, chaos, rancor, and bitterness of the previous two decades he expressed confidence in a "new morning in America," one that promised a more tranquil, safe, and prosperous society. Reagan used the education policy of his administration as a primary political tool. Education was key to shaping his electoral success: He embraced within his administration's policies responses to the contentious issues the nation had been struggling with since the close of World War II.

There are two sources of influence that shaped Ronald Reagan's educational beliefs. The first source is in the immediate postwar years. In his younger days, Reagan was a Roosevelt Democrat, but by the time he took the position as president of the Screen Actors Guild in the mid-1940s, his political beliefs had gone through a transformation. He became active in politics and became a Republican where he found a ready reception for his considerable speaking abilities and warm, commanding personality. During this formative period he was exposed to the beliefs that public school teachers were suspect, and included among their ranks closet commies and individuals who were overly "liberal," as Allan Zoll and others had contended; he followed the arguments that public schools were the weak link in the defense chain, with poorly qualified and unmotivated teachers; and the arguments of Arthur Bestor for more intellectual rigor in schools impressed him. He carried these impressions acquired during this formative period with him throughout his life and into his presidency—that is, public schools were seriously lacking. The chaos of the 1960s surrounding American education only deepened his newly acquired beliefs.

On a strictly political level, the influence of Jimmy Carter in persuading the leadership of the National Education Association to support Democrats was a second decisive influence on the formation of Reagan's educational policy. As suggested in Chapter Sixteen, while the NEA was under the leadership of school administrators, it followed a nonpartisan position in political elections. But under the leadership of classroom teachers, the NEA came out in the 1976 elections for Democrats as part of a political bargain with Jimmy Carter. This worked fine in 1976, but not in 1980. The NEA represented the largest and most influential organization of public school teachers in America, and now it supported Democrats. Republicans had no choice but to politically attack public schools and cultivate in the 1980 election educational constituencies outside of public education. Reagan did this brilliantly.

Policy, Education, and Politics

The Reagan administration very effectively used education as a political tool to appeal to specific constituency groups and bring them into the Republican column. To those against "big government" he pledged to "get government off our backs." Among other actions, he slashed the federal education budget. He also pledged to eliminate the newly formed cabinet position under Jimmy Carter of secretary of education and return the federal government's education functions to the Interior Department. This was good politics, but it did not happen.

To the Protestant religious right he promised that he would back a constitutional amendment to support prayer in schools. The fact that the probability of this happening was close to zero did not matter. He won votes just by the act of coming out in favor of school prayer. Similarly, he promised to provide tax credits to parents disaffected with public schools so that they could send their children to private alternatives. He supported "choice."

Educational choice is a powerful political idea. It is extremely broad in its appeal. Parents want the best education for their children, and if for any reason they are dissatisfied with the public community school the idea of government financial help to offset the cost of private schooling is appealing. To the parent angry over integration and busing, choice means that a private school with children exclusively like their own is a possibility. To the parent wanting to shelter their religious beliefs, choice is appealing. To the parent apprehensive over the lack of school discipline, drugs, bullying, and disorder, choice means that a private alternative may be an option. Parents want the choice to send their children to schools with higher academic standards, more appropriate curricula, better teachers, safer environments, different student mixes, and values that they believe, among other reasons.

Reagan's use of the idea of choice brought him votes from what were normally three Democratic constituencies. The very poor have few educational options for their children often trapped in what are dangerous, unruly, resource poor, and substandard education environments. Completion is an achievement, but the diploma often is meaningless because it represents so little. But there are few alternatives for the poor. The idea of choice and financial help offered hope. Reagan cared. They voted for him.

One of the most frustrated parent groups among the middle class wants better public schooling for their children, but they cannot afford housing in "good" school areas. They also cannot afford the full cost of private school fees. The idea of tax credits is appealing because it offers the possibility of enough additional resources to make private schools a viable option.

The idea of choice swung Catholic voters Reagan's way. The majority of private schools were Catholic and the majority of children attending were Catholic. The additional funding from tax credits could potentially bolster the finances of individual schools through enrollment increases and at the same time help Catholic and non-Catholic parents alike to take advantage of private schooling.

Reagan also used another powerful political term: "family values." His administration would reestablish family values in public schools. Religious conservatives were pleased. Although the values he was referring to were never defined, this was a big part of the political appeal of the term. Anyone who believed that public schools did not represent their own belief could take heart that Reagan was on their side. But in addition, Reagan was indirectly hinting at the reestablishment of the social and moral order that in his eyes had been shredded during the tumultuous 1960s. In his eyes, "lax academic standards were correlated with lax behavioral standards and neither should be ignored" (Ravitch, 2000, p. 411).

Reagan focused on the preparation of high-ability students for college through improved instructional quality. This appealed to upper-middle-class parents with aspirations to send their children to college. Now, their child could be positioned to score high on admission examinations, and along with the promise of tax credits, the possibility of enrollment in a high level but more expensive college seemed within reach. A constituency that already supported him came out even stronger.

Setting the National Agenda

Reagan cut the national education budget, but how was the Reagan administration going to achieve fundamental changes in American education with a significantly reduced federal educational budget? The federal government typically exerts leverage on states and local school districts through federal grants. Now the money was gone. His administration turned to a low-cost, creative, and effective strategy: public persuasion. For a relatively small amount of federal money ($300,000), the National Commission on Excellence in Education (NCEE) was constituted to study the condition of American public education. Its report, *A Nation at Risk*, caught the attention of the nation and formed the foundation for an endless stream of criticism aimed at public education.

The criticism seemed well founded given the reported results. American students lagged behind in international comparisons of student achievement; functional illiteracy rates were high, topping 40% among minority groups; standardized test scores showed a continuing downward trend since the 1960s, with verbal scores dropping over 50 points and mathematics scores over 40 points; the number of students scoring in the superior range declined. Science scores showed a steady decline, and enrollment in basic college remedial courses in mathematics and English showed increases (NCEE, 1983).

Playing the tune with a few modified notes that Hyman Rickover and Arthur Bestor and colleagues composed in the early 1950s, the report claimed that the nation was in great danger of losing the economic war with Japan and Germany because of the poor quality of education. America could not compete in the global marketplace. It lacked sufficiently educated engineers and scientists. American schools were intellectually inferior and teachers poorly qualified. They lacked a sufficient understanding of the subject fields that they taught. For the first time in history, the report asserted, the current generation of students was less educated than the pervious one. Academic standards had to be strengthened, teacher selection and training improved, and curricula refocused.

Appealing to business leaders and upper middle-class Whites, a proposed remedy was to create a core curriculum along the lines Bestor advanced in the early 1950s: All students take four years of math up through trigonometry and calculus; four years of English; three years of a foreign language; four years of science, and instruction in the emerging field of computer use.

History was not included, but the arts were for the purpose of transmitting the cultural heritage of the country. A better-trained workforce would result, giving employers a deep labor pool to dip into; parents with college aspirations for their children liked the idea of higher quality academic preparation. But how could schools be persuaded to adopt the proposed core curriculum without the leverage of federal money?

The administration kept up a drum beat of criticism leveled against public schools in order to create public opinion favorable to change: The quality of schooling in America is poor; teachers are limited in ability and poorly prepared; public schools lack intellectual rigor; the new core studies are essential. If something is said often and loud enough it does not matter if it is factual: People believe. The Reagan administration also used the political apparatus of the Republic Party to support the election to state and local school boards of favorable candidates. Coalitions of business, state, and local leaders were formed to pressure school officials. In state after state, graduation requirements were established that reflected the core requirements. Subjects considered nonessential were cut back or eliminated to make room for core studies.

But the same flawed assumption that characterized the writings of Bestor in the 1950s was evident in the report *A Nation at Risk*: The core was designed to prepare students for college admission when three-fourths of graduating high school students never completed college. How many non-college-bound students, for example, ever used calculus or French? What happened to the idea of a comprehensive school? In a real sense, the report advanced an unarticulated shift away from the comprehensive high school model with differentiated studies, to one with a single primary purpose: college preparation. College-bound students from more affluent families became the focus of high school instruction to the neglect of lower income and ethnic students who were relegated to what was considered lower status programming.

Local school officials were confronted with an immediate problem. Graduation requirements reflecting the core subjects applied primarily to the academically advanced students, not to the majority who did not plan on achieving higher education; some students did not take the requisite core subjects, and often they failed tests required for graduation. Local educators immediately developed "variations within subject domains in order to meet the letter but not the spirit of new, stiffer graduation requirements" (Angus & Mirel, 1999, p. 195). Lower achieving students continued to be scheduled into what were basically custodial programs with new titles. Different levels of math or English, for example, were given, all "qualifying" for meeting core graduation requirements. Again, "equivalent" substitutions were identified. For example, auto shop or cosmetology counted for science.

The national educational mood changed. The idea of the comprehensive school model continued to be challenged with calls to limit course diversity. Mortimer Adler, for example, in his widely publicized *The Paideia Proposal*, urged "we should have a one track system of schooling, not a system with two or more tracks, one of which goes straight ahead while the others shunt the young onto sidetracks not headed toward the goals our society opens to all." Ernest Boyer, in his study conducted for the Carnegie Foundation, concluded the comprehensive high school was a "troubled institution," and like Bestor before him, argued its function should be narrowed to "academic course work for *all* students." Theodore Sizer, one-time dean of the graduate school of education at Harvard, and John Goodlad, dean of the graduate school of education at the University of California–Los Angeles, came to similar conclusions (Angus & Mirel, 1999, pp. 166–167). Said Goodlad (1984, p. 88), schools "dare not neglect the academic and intellectual aspects" of studies. At the same time, Goodlad and his researchers, drawing on their study of school populations, concluded that lower income and minority students consistently were scheduled into lower tracks, while Whites tended to be consistently placed in higher-level studies. But his conclusion was high schools should implement a "common core of studies which students cannot escape through electives, even though the proposed electives purport to be in the same domain of knowledge" (p. 297). In almost every state, national dialogue and mandated core graduation requirements resulted in limiting programs of study and narrowing course options, a striking movement away from the idea of a differentiated curriculum serving different student populations.

Jeannie Oakes, who formerly worked with Goodlad, carried out some of the most cogent work on tracking practices. Based on a study of 14,000 students spread between 25 junior and senior high schools, and an extensive literature review of tracking and differentiated studies for the National Science Foundation and the Rand Corporation, Oakes found substantial evidence that the practice of placing low-ability or non-college-bound students in "lower level" nonacademic courses is detrimental. Academic achievement is low and opportunities are foreclosed. Counter to the ideas that dominated most of educational planning from the time of the 1918 report by the National Commission on the Reorganization of Secondary Education, Oakes as well as others concluded differentiated studies work to the disadvantage of students relegated to custodial kinds of courses, and decidedly promotes educational inequality. Said Oakes,

> Students bring differences with them to school. Schools, most specifically through counselors and teachers, respond to these differences. Those responses are such that the initial differences between students are likely to widen. Students seen as different are separated into different classes and then provided with vastly different kinds of knowledge and with markedly different opportunities to learn. It is in these ways that schools exacerbate the differences among the students who attend them. And it is through tracking that these educational differences are most blatantly carried out (1985, pp. 111–112).

All through the second half of the 1980s school districts across America struggled with implementing graduation requirements patterned after the core requirements outlined in *A Nation at Risk*. More students enrolled in "academic" courses, but the overall test scores of students did not improve, and many had difficulty meeting the core graduation requirements. Dropout rates increased, and graduation rates decreased. Parents complained. Why should their child be denied a diploma because he or she failed trigonometry? The core graduation requirements were simply irrelevant to many students or they exceeded their ability to cope given their backgrounds and home and community environments. Controversies over the form and substance of American secondary education continued to simmer as George H.W. Bush ascended to the presidency and assumed the mantle of Ronald Reagan.

George H.W. Bush: The Education President

When George Bush ran for election in 1988, he proclaimed that he wanted to be known as an "education president," but by midterm his staff reminded him that he had done very little to warrant the title and a new election cycle was fast approaching. He immediately took a number of initiatives that attracted public note. In the two remaining years he was not able to secure sufficient funding for his proposals, but his ideas influenced Bill Clinton, and were later reflected in the No Child Left Behind legislation of his son, and continue to be reflected in national educational discussion and the educational policies of the Obama administration. He influenced public discourse. The nation was engaged in sorting through the implications of Reagan's policies, and his initiatives sparked lively debate.

In 1989, Bush invited the state governors to an education summit held in Charlottesville, Virgina, for the purpose of beginning the creation of a national system of assessments and standards. With then governor of Arkansas, Bill Clinton, chairing the summit, six national goals to be achieved by the year 2000 were decided upon: Two related to promoting higher academic achievement, and the other four applied to high school graduation rates, school readiness, adult literacy, and eliminating substance abuse and violence in schools (Ravitch, 2000). "Goals 2000" was a political statement. Follow-up implementation plans were incomplete and little public money was available. However, the Department of Education in 1991 and 1992, with the collaboration of the National Endowment for the Humanities and the National Science Foundation, awarded grants to groups, to develop voluntary national standards in seven subjects as a way to advance academic achievement: science, history, geography, the arts, civics, foreign language, and English. Around the same time, the National Council on Educational Standards and Testing (NCEST) was created.

When Clinton took office, his first major education legislation was the Goals 2000 Education Act. Grants to states to develop standards were available, and a certifying federal board was to be established. But after inaction on the part of his administration, the Republicans upon gaining control of Congress in 1994 abolished the program. Federal and state efforts already underway to establish standards floundered with considerable infighting, and descended into chaos. Diane Ravitch (2000, p. 433) observed, "The abortive effort to create national standards revealed the deep fissures within academic fields, as well as the wide gap between avant-garde thinkers in the academic world and general public." The movement for standards and educational accountability limped along, to be reenergized with the election of George W. Bush and the No Child Left Behind legislation. His father had provided the initial push in the direction of national standards.

President George H.W. Bush supported a number of policy positions adopted by Reagan, but he put his own twist on them. He supported prayer in the school, for example, and alternatives to public schools. But choice was to be supported through vouchers rather than tax credits as Reagan proposed to do. Vouchers have appeal because they give parents partial support for the cost of private school expenses, thus opening options to public schools. Bush also came out strongly for support of business interests. Earlier under the Reagan administration the task force Education for Economic Growth was formed, and its *Action for Excellence* report advocated a closer link between schools and business. Partnerships were to be a major collaborative tool, and business interests were to participate in setting school goals, the report stressed. These recommendations were acted on in some communities. Bush took a further step: He invited business into public schools; they would establish and run them.

Looking for Profit: The Entry of Business

The main argument Bush made was that the private sector had the experience and knowledge to efficiently run schools. His first initiative was the establishment of the New American Schools Development Corporation. The source of funding was to be primarily from the private sector in cooperation with the federal government. The board of directors was mainly comprised of large corporate heads; educators were not included. The task of the board was to raise money from private sector sources to support the establishment of 535 model schools, distributed among state congressional districts. Congress balked at putting in money. The cost over time would be enormous, and the program could never be eliminated because every congressional representative had a vested interest preserving the model school in his or her district. The millions in private corporate donations did not come in; corporations want to make money, not give it away and this was a gigantic undertaking with an extended commitment. The $60 million plus raised was not enough.

An offshoot of the thrust for more business involvement in public schools was the establishment of private companies to directly run public schools under contract with local school boards. Typically, the facility is provided by the school district. The company provides management, staffing, and instruction, with the expectation that student achievement gains will be demonstrated. Usually the same amount of public funds normally allocated for each student on a daily average attendance basis is the amount contracted by the company. For example, in 1992, Educational Alternatives Inc. (E.A.I.) contracted with the Baltimore City Schools to run nine schools, and in 1994 the school board of Hartford, Connecticut, hired E.A.I. to manage the school district. In 1994, the Edison Project contracted with the Wichita, Kansas, school board to run two elementary schools and signed agreements with school boards in six other states (Spring, 2008). What was the result?

School buildings were cleaned up and school environments became generally pleasant and orderly. But, achievement levels were no higher than the public administered schools and usually dropped over time. The defining issue, however, was teacher costs could not be lowered enough to make a profit. Companies found that they could not make a profit running instructional programs with the same student populations public schools typically served and with the same amount of money. After a flurry of private-for-profit efforts in the early 1990s, most of the companies terminated the effort and went out of business. There were exceptions, such as the Edison Project, which struggled to make a profit but had access to deep financial resources among shareholders and tended to contract to run schools with select populations. But the idea endures that the private for-profit sector can run schools better than professional educators.

His emphasis on privatization was a lasting aspect of Bush's education policy. Public education is big business. Schools are lucrative markets for books, computers, sports equipment, and cafeteria lunches in addition to thousands of items from pens and paper to chalk, maps, videos, and test sheets. What evaded private business was the actual running of schools for profit. By 2000, the dynamics changed. Private companies figured out how to make money running charter schools with the use of technology to replace instructional costs. More than 150 years ago, the common school movement had to battle against private school interests that monopolized public schooling; today, the battle is rejoined as private for-profit interests seek to capture an ever-growing part of the public education purse, a topic discussed in a following section.

Vocational Education: Preparing for Work

Policies of the Reagan administration impacted directly on vocational education. In 1968, the long standing Smith-Hughes Act was significantly amended. There was a shift from federal funding based on occupational fields, such as metal machining and small crop growing, to funding directed to categories of individuals, such as working women, unemployed youth, and the handicapped. The influence of the civil rights movement is obvious. Following the publication of the *Nation at Risk*, however, many vocational programs were pushed out of high schools in the name of more academic rigor and budget savings. In addition, the courses left were increasingly used to accommodate the custodial programming needs of floundering, "non-academic" students. Not only the number but also the quality of vocational programs dropped. The idea of addressing the educational interests of specific social groups also fell by the wayside. Schools responded in several ways.

One was to develop district-wide "career centers" for students to pursue work in specific technical fields, such as computing, health occupations, or building construction. There are two variations. Students can attend all day, participating for one half of the school day in the academic component, and one half in the technical. The other variation is for the student to take academic classes in a parent school, and the technical in the career center. Around the county there are some outstanding programs, and in some cases students can continue on to pursue a college degree. Another variation is the establishment of "career academies," vocational and technical magnet programs within a comprehensive high school serving the district population. These programs tend to be high quality.

The transfer of vocational and technical programming up into community colleges has been the most widespread national trend over the past two decades. Vocational offerings formerly found in high schools are now offered on community college campuses. Considerable program flexibility is achieved. High quality programming is given. All kinds of collaborative career preparations can be done with local employers. Programming configurations can vary. Students pay part of the cost, and they are self-selected. Students make the decision to enroll. But as high as 50% or more of students matriculating into community colleges are stuck in qualifying remedial courses and cannot gain entrance into the regular programs. An example is the case of the graduates of the Chicago City Schools, a district with high numbers of low-income and minority students: 69% of entering community college youth were unprepared for college-level reading; 79% for writing; and 95% for math (Schneider, 2011, p. 137). They carry their poor high school performance with them as the day of accounting arrives and they "washout."

There is a big hole in American education, and hundreds of thousand of young people fall through it. A disproportionate number are from minority groups, and a majority from moderate- and low-income families. Of the youth population in America, 20% to 30% do not have skills necessary to pursue a fulfilling, productive life. A boy or girl who cannot read, write, or use simple math, or who does not have self-discipline or hold shared values often is locked out of full participation in society. Diane Ravitch (2000, p. 466) cautions, "The society that allows large numbers of its citizens to remain uneducated, ignorant, or semiliterate squanders its greatest asset, the intelligence of its people."

Clinton, School, and Work

Bill Clinton agreed with choice, privatization, standards, and the use of education as a tool of economic development. He supported closer ties with business. Perhaps his concurrence indicates how strong the conservative lock was on the minds of the educational public. This was a Democrat president basically endorsing Republican policy. During the two short years Clinton had before losing the majority in Congress, he achieved few lasting educational legislative accomplishments. The short-lived Goals 2000 Education Act included what was termed "life-long learning," with funding for preschool, adult education, and increased Head Start funding. He was concerned with improving skills of the general workforce, and particularly for the need to boost the quality of education for poor children and create a smoother path to college attendance (Spring, 2008). His main initiative to promote human capital development was the School-to-Work Opportunities Act (SWOA). It was innovative in the flexibility it provided to local schools.

The intent of SWOA was to strengthen the relationship between community schools and local business. But rather than a top-down federal mandate, local school districts had considerable programming flexibility to design cooperative education interventions that fit local priorities and dovetailed with local business interests. Local school districts submitted for federal approval a full plan with a detailed accountability component outlining how program objectives will be implemented and outcomes measured. One local school district, for example, may plan to use SWOA funding to structure remedial programming for newly employed youth lacking basic skills. Other plans submitted by school districts may include cooperative work experience programs, structured career exploration options, strengthening of vocational counseling, on the job training, sponsored speakers programs, among other combinations of school and employer cooperative programming.

The act was signed in May 1994. Typically it takes as much as two years for new federal legislation to take hold at the local level. The SWOA was authorized by Congress for four years, and when it was resubmitted for reauthorization, the Republican-controlled Congress in a display of partisanship voted it down. The SWOA had the potential to open up programming for what was a school population basically left out of the new educational calculations of the Reagan and Bush administrations. It was at the beginning stage of perhaps opening up what may have been meaningful ways to address the non-college-bound youth population through increased collaborative programming with community business establishments. It may have been a way to insert more educational value into what continued to be custodial programming for large numbers of students not otherwise served well by American schools.

George W. Bush and Children Left Behind

George Bush tucked his major educational initiative into the reauthorization of Title I of the 1965 Elementary and Secondary Education Act (ESEA) in the form of what he called the "No Child Left Behind" initiative (NCLB). The 1965 ESEA legislation focused on culturally disadvantaged youth, but as Joel Spring (2008, p. 487) noted, the NCLB act "dramatically changed the coverage of the 1965 legislation from a specified group of students needing help to all students in all public schools." It also changed emphasis from strengthening local instructional programming to making judgments about school quality and imposing "punishment" on principals and teachers of low-performing schools. It is corrosive in form and practice.

In abbreviated form, the following provisions were advanced (Ravitch, 2010, pp. 97–98):

a. All public schools receiving federal funds are required to test all students from third through eighth grades annually and high school students once in math and reading.

b. Test scores are disaggregated by ethnicity, income, disability, and limited English proficiency. The purpose is to ensure each set of group scores can be monitored.

c. States can choose their own tests, but three performance levels have to be indicated: basic, proficient, and advanced. States also have to indicate with timelines how they will achieve 100% proficiency in reading and mathematics by the school year 2013–2014.

d. All schools are expected to make "adequate yearly progress (AYP) toward the goal of 100% proficiency," and schools that do not make adequate progress for every separate group will be classed as "a school in need of improvement (SINI)."

e. SINI schools are warned the first year. Failing the second year requires schools to offer all students the option to transfer to a "successful" school with transportation cost covered by the school district. Third-year failure results in the requirement to provide free tutoring to low-income students. Fourth-year failure results in required "corrective actions" such as staff and curriculum changes, and lengthening the school year. Fifth-year failure is particularly onerous. Schools are required to restructure in one of several ways: convert to a charter school; replace the principal and teachers; turn control over to private management; or relinquish control to the state. A provision that borders on the absurd is the mandate that all students in every state must reach proficiency in reading and mathematics by the year 2014. Not surprising, Arne Duncan, Obama's secretary of education, waved the 2014 deadline and substituted alternatives.

f. All states are required to conduct biennial testing in reading and mathematics in the fourth and eighth grades using the federal National Assessment of Educational Progress. The results have no consequences for individual schools or districts, but they serve as a way to nationally compare the progress of states.

What has been the result? Since individual states use different tests to access AYP, comparisons of state results are not meaningful. Some states set low standards and some higher. The National

Assessment of Educational Progress, however, shows nationwide results on a common scale. Overall, the results are not impressive. Diane Ravitch (2010, pp. 109–110) reported NCLB did not achieve rapid test score improvement: "To the contrary, test score gains on the National Assessment of Educational Progress—the only national yardstick for this period—were modest or nonexistent." In fact, in some cases, such as fourth-grade reading and mathematics and eighth-grade reading, test scores went up more in the proceeding years than after implementation of NCLB. In the case of comparisons of the school performance of Black and White students, the achievement gap showed a greater narrowing before than after NCLB. Similarly, in the case of the lowest performing students in bottom 10th percentile, there were greater gains before than after, and in some cases there were no yearly changes after NCLB (Ravitch, 2010, pp. 109–110). NCLB did not generate expected changes in student achievement as measured by the NAEP.

The provisions in NCLB to "fix" failing schools or provide alternatives to parents have had limited results. Schools complain there is not enough financial support forthcoming to address the challenges they face. The tutoring services specified in the law are rife with problems and unattractive to students. Within the framework of No Child Left Behind it was recognized schools in low-income and ethnic areas would struggle to overcome failing status, but there is no recognition of the need to address the attending home and community problems that impact on low school achievement. Then again, parents have the theoretical option to send their children to higher performing schools, but generally it is not possible: Seats simply are not available. But also, parents appear to be reluctant to send their children out of neighborhood schools into unfamiliar surroundings, even when free transportation is provided. This is especially true in the case of English-language learners. At the same time, some excellent community schools are classed as failing because one particular student group scores low, so for most parents there is no reason to seek an alternative. Alternatives, such as charter schools, private school management firms, and the use of "turnaround specialists" yield weak results with failing schools (Ravitch, 2010).

The strategy that seems to work best is to change the composition of the student population, replacing low-performing students with enough high-achieving students to balance out test results. Schools also practice "banding," concentrating test preparation efforts on the group of students just above and below the passing mark; this practice is thought to yield the highest probability of elevating the total school's AYP score. Nevertheless, the Center on Education Policy (CEP) in Washington, D.C., noted regardless of the strategies used, "failing" schools continue to fail. Some children are left behind (Ravitch, 2010, p. 105).

A growth industry grew up around NCLB. Local school districts hired consultants by the score to help find out how to raise test scores, "turn around specialists" advertised they could help save failing schools, and firms by the thousands vied for a cut of the federal money to offered remedial programs or the disadvantaged in failing schools. Big money, in the hundreds of millions, was made through testing.

What has been the influence on the everyday school experience of pupils? The focus of schooling has shifted from children to test preparation. The consequences of failing to achieve AYP benchmarks are so threatening to school administrators and teachers that the challenge of providing a meaningful, full, creative, interesting, and exciting education is cast aside to accommodate the threat of high-stakes testing: The curriculum is narrowed; scheduling time for math and reading is increased and for other subjects reduced; teaching history, science, art, music, and geography is curtailed. Recess time is reduced, and physical education scaled back to 30 minutes once or twice a week; and as test time approaches, other scheduled subjects give way to extra test preparation (Valli, et al., 2008).

Practice in test-taking skills takes precedent over knowledge and understanding. Drill and practice are the primary instructional methods; standardized worksheets replace creative instructional activities; and teaching to the test pushes aside creative instructional practices. The school day revolves around the testing schedule (Ravitch, 2010; Valli et al., 2008).

Overall, NCLB has had a corrosive influence on American education. Teachers are subjected to enormous stress; the curriculum is narrowed and diluted, training is substituted for education, subject matter is superficially covered; recall trumps knowing, individual differences are shoved aside. Simplistic reasons are given for low performance, equally simplistic solutions are mandated, and school life is transformed in disturbing ways. "Although NCLB was surrounded with a great deal of high-flown rhetoric when it was passed, promising a new era of high standards and high accomplishments," it fell short (Ravitch, 2010). "Its remedies did not work. Its sanctions were ineffective. It did not bring about high standards or high accomplishments. The gains in test scores at the state level were typically the result of teaching students test-taking skills and strategies, rather than broadening and deepening their knowledge of the world and their ability to understand what they have learned" (p. 110). And the practice of closing down low-performing schools is demoralizing, selective, and punitive. At the same time, billions of dollars have been sunk into NCLB with contractors, consultants, and test-makers realizing large amounts of money through an industry formed around schools struggling with the implementation of a seriously flawed political initiative that leaves lots of children behind.

Bilingual Education

Both the Reagan and Bush administrations were not favorable toward bilingual education. They would have liked to have eliminated it if they could. The Reagan administration came out strongly against the bilingual/bicultural model, and undercut bilingual education because of its link with political issues of ethnic empowerment, cultural diversity, and social justice. Attempts were made to derail support through appointments to government committees, such as the National Advisory and Coordinating Council on Bilingual Education. The immersion model was advanced as most appropriate for developing the language skills essential for moving youth into the social and economic mainstream (Spring, 2008).

A strong link was developed with right-wing Republican groups, such as U.S. English, Save Our Schools, and the Heritage Foundation to advocate for making English the "official" language of the nation. By 1988, in a long, ongoing, and continuing political debate, 17 states passed legislation making English the official language. Robert Dole, the Republican candidate for president in the 1996 election, promised he would introduce an amendment to the Constitution making English the "official language" of the nation. The impact was directly counter to the 1965 Voting Rights Act, giving citizens the right to voting information in their own language. The practical outcome is to limit the minority ballot count.

The administration of George W. Bush came out strongly against bilingual education. Their position was that there should be no support for the preservation of minority languages. English acquisition is the goal of NCLB, and embedded in the legislation is a change in the name of the federal Office of Bilingual Education to the "Office of English Language Acquisition, Language Enhancement, and Academic Achievement for Limited English Proficient" (Spring, 2008). But the change in title does not reduce the educational complexity and political volatility surroundings minority pride and rights. Joel Spring (2008) reported the reaction of Humberto Garza to a ruling by Los Altos, California, city govertnment that mandated the speaking of English on the job. Revealing deep-seated past wounds, he exclaimed, "Those council members from Los Altos should be made to understand that they are advocating their law in occupied Mexico. . . . They should move back to England or learn how to speak the language of Native Americans" (p. 440). With emigrants continuing to come in from the South, issues surrounding bilingual education are not going away.

The Obama Administration: Rushing to the Top Slowly

Arne Duncan earned his place as superintendent of Chicago Pubic Schools by building a reputation for budget cutting and closing schools. Liberals expecting relief from the drumbeat of testing, accountability, and teacher blame, were surprised and disappointed by the policies developed by the Obama administration following Duncan's appointment as secretary of education, but they should not have been. As Chicago superintendent of schools, Duncan endorsed much of NCLB, and the education policy he formulated with Obama in many ways went beyond what NCLB wanted to accomplish. Using $5 billion in economic stimulus money, "Race to the Top" was an initiative designed to change the dynamics of public education. Competition was launched among states for federal money; winners were expected to demonstrate the adoption of new common standards and tests, the expansion of charter schools, the implementation of teacher evaluation based on student test scores, and the implementation of strategies to "turn around" lower-performing schools. A preferred step was the firing of underperforming staff and closing schools.

Eleven states and the District of Columbia won grants in the first competition. But the impact was considerably more widespread. All competing states rushed to position themselves for future grants so that considerable leverage was generated for the kinds of change advocated in Race for the Top. Schools all over the country joined in expanding use of standardized testing as the best way to judge student progress and the professional competency of teachers and principles; the founding of charter schools was promoted as a means of achieving school choice and competition; the use of merit pay was implemented; and the use of school closings as a way to improve low-performing schools was carried out. Federal funds did not have to be granted; the possibility of obtaining funds was enough to stimulate change.

Explicit in Race to the Top was a fundamental shift in the way Democrats administered federal funding. Rooted in the concept of the cycle of poverty formulated by Gunnar Myrdal

50 years earlier, the administration of federal money was seen as a way to help various social groups break the grip of poverty and secure a place in mainstream America. Education money tended to be proportionally distributed by formula grants to school districts with high poverty rates and high needs. Race to the Top money in contrast was distributed to states based on competition, with the more affluent best positioned to obtain grants. They could hire professional grant writers. The needy were left needy, and at the same time schools with high numbers of disadvantaged students made up the bulk of low-performing schools. They were left out of the race. The rush to the top for those near to the bottom of the economic scale was, indeed, slow. "Race to the Top abandoned equity as the driving principal of federal aid" (Ravitch, 2013, p.15).

Perhaps the most pervasive influence of Obama's educational policies is the commanding support given to private interests over the use of public money. The doors of public education are opened wide to private business. Private interests today sponsor most of the major "reforms" on the national education stage, and most are designed to generate profit for those who know how to capture the levers of control. Large major foundations work hand in hand with education publishers, entrepreneurs, Wall Street hedge funds, and small specialty companies under the approving eyes of the U.S. Department of Education to advance initiatives to create a large, money-generating, market-based system of national education. The Gates Foundation, for example, partnered with Pearson Publishers, a large multinational company based in the UK, to develop online instructional material to teach the national Common Core standards. The Common Core standards will cost billions to implement nationally and the potential profits are great. Some estimates are the amount will reach $16 billion. Investment firms are thick in the charter school movement that is seen as a lucrative profit-making venture, and tech and service firms make billions supplying all kinds of new educational products and technologies of unproven worth (Ravitch, 2013).

Private advocacy groups representing business interests have large amounts of money available (Ravitch, 2013). The Gates Foundation is the largest and is joined by the Bradley Foundation, the Robertson Foundation, the Michael & Susan Dell Foundation, Walton Family Foundation, and Fisher Foundation, among others. Education, money-making and politics are joined. Wall Street hedge fund managers created Democrats for Education Reform and were instrumental in getting Arne Duncan appointed secretary of education. Jeb Bush created the Foundation for Excellence in Education, which supports vouchers, for-profit charter schools, for-profit online instruction, testing, and accountability. Major corporations and philanthropists fund the American Legislative Exchange Council (ALEC). It writes model legislation for politicians to bring to their state legislatures. Reflecting the educational views of Ronald Reagan 30 years ago, the ALEC does not like public schools or teacher unions. It supports privatization, likes vouchers and charters schools, especially for-profit and cyber-charter schools, and it wants to eliminate tenure, seniority, and teacher certification. The ALEC helps parent groups formulate petitions to pressure government officials to turn public schools into charter schools (Ravitch, 2013).

All kinds of think tanks are involved in public education. The American Enterprise Institute, the Center for American Progress, the Center for Reinventing Public Education, the Friedman

Foundation for Educational Choice, the Goldwater Institute, the Heritage Foundation, and Policy Innovators in Education Network, among others that are politically left, right, and center. But they work closely together in formulating policy, co-sponsoring conferences and issuing publications that not surprisingly reflect the ideology of the corporate sponsors. They are joined by state and national groups such as Education Equality Project, Education Reform, Educators 4 Excellence, National Council for Teacher Quality, New Leaders for New Schools, New Schools Venture Fund, Stand for Children, among a host of other groups agitating for change.

But "change" means drastically alternating the educational picture so that the major players are private sector actors. "Many of these groups have overlapping membership on their boards and are funded by the same foundations...They exist in a giant echo chamber, listening and talking only to one another, dismissing the concerns of parents, teachers and communities" (Ravitch, 2013, p. 22). Unlike the educational ideas of James Conant several decades ago, "reform" proposals are not grounded in a careful study of American education, society, and the vital link between the two, but rather are based on rather narrowly defined interests that are shifting the focus of education to private entrepreneurship. We are witnessing a greening of American education, and "green" refers to money, not grass.

A Less Than Bright Morning

More than three decades ago Ronald Reagan promised a "new morning in America," one free of the divisiveness and rancor of the 1950s and 1960s, and one of prosperity and dreams fulfilled. He advocated far-reaching educational changes: A reduction in federal support; tax credits to support choice; privatization and alternatives to public education; a core curriculum for everyone; and higher academic standards for everyone. But highly significant was the shift in policy away from the use of schools to help ameliorate debilitating social and economic conditions surrounding the less fortunate in society. The focus was away from educational interventions directed to specific groups of children and youth, and in the direction of strengthening the economy. Reflecting his formative years in the 1950s, the primary focus of public education in Reagan's eyes was on economic development objectives, and this mainly involved bolstering the academic achievement of the more talented.

George H. W. Bush continued the policies of Reagan and added his own twists. He invited private sector entrepreneurs to run schools for profit; and he launched the standards and accountability movement that dominates public education today. Private sector involvement in public education soared with the beginning of the new century, but with a difference: Money was now made through the attending services the private sector provided to enable schools to fulfill federal funding mandates. The mandates themselves generated large amounts of money for educational entrepreneurs. Testing alone is a multibillion-dollar industry. In the last two decades a large education marketplace has been created that profit-making firms have rushed into.

Both the No Child Left Behind and the Race to the Top initiatives have a probable long-term detrimental influence on the financial and educational health of local schools. Schools in lower income districts are particularly vulnerable. An original infusion of federal money funds all kinds of programs and services, and costly mandates such as testing are required. But the federal funds come with a cost. Ancillary services, upkeep, specialists, and consultants accrue costs that usually are taken from the regular school budgets, thus displacing money formerly used elsewhere. What formerly were strong programs can be weakened because financial support is taken away and used to fund mandates.

More pernicious is the long-term consequence of a relatively large short-term infusion of grant money. The newly built educational capacity through outside funding cannot be sustained without the infusion of additional local funding once the outside cycle is completed. Federal money, for example, is allocated for capacity building, and not for long-term sustaining support. Unless a new, additional source of local funding is generated along with the use of outside money there are detrimental results: Local schools cannot build adequate capacity to fully support the use of the funding; "reform" elements introduced through outside support cannot be sustained; and other programming elements within the school are reduced in importance or eliminated to free up funding for what may turn out to be often costly but yet unproved initiatives. And for local schools, the response to federal mandates can be costly in more than money terms: It can result in considerable internal dislocation within schools.

The Reagan policies that have dominated public education for the past three decades also reflect the belief that social and economic progress is best accomplished through the upper strata of society. Attend to their interests, and the benefits accrue to everyone as they trickle down into the lower strata. And education policy is bounded by the marketplace. In stark contrast is the belief that the roots of human poverty and need are grounded in the lack of education and employment opportunity, income inequality, and discrimination (Katz, 1989). Reflecting the perspective of the Social Gospel of the 1880s, it is society itself that needs to be healed. Schooling is conceived as a way to intervene in the interest of the larger society to ameliorate conditions of inequality, poverty, and need.

The educational policies of the Reagan era have been constructed around the contention that focusing on accountability and raising standards helps all students. It is no longer necessary to think in terms of specialized programming to address individual school populations. At the same time, we know failing schools are characterized by disadvantaged students, an inconsistency that is compounded by the support of choice and alternative schools, a political outlet for more affluent parents disaffected by the quality and substance of public education.

Charter Schools: The Wedge of Privatization

The idea of charter schools is appealing. Reflecting the spirit of the community school movement in the 1960s and early 1970s, school units are formed that are under the control of a separate, local board. Typically, a charter is granted by the local school board to operate a semi-independent school with public money, but local and state education requirements remain in place. Parents have choice: They can influence the hiring of principals and teachers, the curriculum, and the outcomes. And many charter schools have a specialized focus, such as math and science, foreign language immersion, or college preparation. Enrollment is selective, with a lottery system commonly used. Parents are attracted to the idea of charter schools because they offer an alternative to public schools considered disruptive and characterized by low-quality instruction. Parents also like the idea of charter schools because values more akin to their own can be promoted. Charter schools, however, have gone through a transformation. They have become a source for private money interests to generate large profits from public school money. There are several ways this is done.

Charter school executives receive large salaries to manage a single school or relatively small groups of schools, ranging annually anywhere between $300,000 to $500,000. But even when salaries appear more in line with local public school administrators, looks are deceiving: Large amounts of money are generated through subsidiaries controlled by the private founders of the schools. A company that is owned by the very individuals charged to operate the school sells materials, supplies, and services to the school. There are also all kinds of real estate "deals" made to rent, lease, or buy school facilities by individuals with a stake in the school. School managers lease property that they own to the very same schools that they are charged to oversee. It is big business that is subsidized with federal loans and tax breaks.

Charter schools supported through tax dollars cannot generate profit. But for-profit "management" companies are employed to operate schools for a hefty fee. The "non-profit" chain Success Academy Charter Schools, for example, pays salaries and bonuses of around $400,000 annually, and charges 15%, or an amount equal to $2,000 per student for management fees paid from public money (Ravitch, 2013, p. 171). But profits also are hidden by the large amounts of instructional material sold to charter schools that are captive to the management staff who are operating schools while they are at the same time supplying costly school resources.

The greatest breakthrough that is rapidly propelling the charter school movement is the substantial reduction in teacher costs achieved through the use of online instruction. An insurmountable constraint private firms faced during the early privatization push by the George H.W. Bush administration was the inability to lower instructional costs. Teacher costs are the most expensive part of school operations. Some companies tried using inexpensive computers with teacher aides to replace teachers, but achievement fell. Others gave up; sufficient profit could not be generated with the same amount of per-pupil funding public schools received. But with the potential of online instruction, money prospects opened. In what is termed "blended" or "hybrid" learning, students spend large numbers of hours in "virtual classrooms" in front of a computer screen following programmed instruction, typically from home or in large rooms supervised by a teacher aide. Periodic "live" group instruction is given, but the hours typically do not match the computer hours. Enormous teacher savings are realized, and additional profits are generated by the software and courseware supplied by the school management company. Publishing companies, like Pearson, are developing an extensive market for their educational products through captive markets controlled by the extensive charter school network they are building. It is no surprise "public" charter schools are a "hot market." Wall Street investors, hedge fund operators, speculators, and entrepreneurs are rushing into the charter school business with the encouragement of federal educational policy.

How good are charter schools? Can they replace teacher-staffed public schools? Some schools are a fraud. They cannot deliver what they promise, and probably never intended to. Disappointed parents walk away with nothing but frustration, while businesspeople walk away with money in their pockets. Overall, charter schools have not produced superior results, and they generally produced results similar to public schools with similar student populations. There are excellent charter schools, but caution has to be used because some charter schools with stringent academic and behavior demands also tend to have high dropout rates, leaving a core of potential high achievers. Some schools also have extensive admission procedures that function as a screening device. Some charter schools will not accept disadvantaged students and English-challenged students. Most charter schools do not accept students with disabilities. On the other hand, there are good community charter schools that work hard to deliver quality education. They try to fill a community gap not filled by hard-pressed public schools. But charter schools can also siphon off some of the best performing students from public school, leaving a noticeable void.

By 2012, at least 42 states had laws authorizing public-supported charter schools. There are 6,000 charter schools enrolling over 2 million K-12 students. This is about 4% of the national school enrollment. In some big cities, charter schools make up a substantial part of school enrollment, perhaps as much as 50% or more with 18 city school districts enrolling 20% of school children in charters (Ravitch, 2013, pp. 158–159). The movement is moving fast and is here to stay. A question the American public has to face is, Can the profit motive also produce quality public education? Charter schools do not have to be profit-making, but the movement has been taken over by those who see profit.

Common Core State Standards and Reform

Since the first Bush administration, standards have been on the national education agenda. NCLB embedded standards in the public's psychic, and criteria for qualifying for Race to the Top funding force states to adopt "a common set" of standards it they want to qualify for consideration. States have to "collaborate" in establishing "benchmark" standards supporting college and career readiness objectives. In effect, a national system of standards independent of local schools is being created through a federal funding mandate. Constitutional restraints prevent the federal imposition of standards, but the outcome is the same because in order to quality for funding under the Obama administration it is "understood" the Common Core Standards are what will be acceptable. They are sanctioned by the U.S. Department of Education. The driving force is the National Governors Association, the Gates Foundation, and Pearson Publishing, a multinational corporation as mentioned earlier (Ravitch, 2013, pp. 314–315). Individual states have no option but to accept the standards if they want to be eligible for the federal educational largeness, and the potential amounts of money are so huge that states cannot but conform.

What will the Common Core Standards accomplish? We do not know. They have not been field-tested. But any set of standards is selective; there are limits to what can be included, and there will be a national narrowing and "normalizing" of school studies to reflect the Common Core Standards, even though some states already have more "superior" sets of standards in place (Ravitch, 2013, p. 315). Because of the selective character of standards, the question of who develops standards is crucial. Standards are value statements attesting to what is important for students to learn or not to learn. The failure in the 1990s to establish national "voluntary" standards, for example, was largely a result of the inability to resolve questions of what is most important to teach. It is doubtful whether the Common Core Standards can develop and maintain consensus over the long term when federal money is no longer available to apply the leverage necessary to bring states into conformity.

The public education stage today is crowded with all kinds of "reform" initiatives. These range from workplace learning, online universities, distance learning, and private learning centers to home schooling and national for-profit charter school chains. There is a proliferation of educational videos of every kind for populations ranging from toddlers, to language learners, auto mechanics, cooks, mathematical students, and exercise enthusiasts. Students can learn phonics and counting skills, calculus, French, and physics. There are test preparation and tutoring materials available. All kinds of computer-based learning software is available. Students can take an incredible journey into the inside of electrons, or back in time to the Constitutional Convention, or to the distant stars; they can dissect the internal organs of a frog or construct the design of a building. The way we think about teaching and learning is changing, and will continue to change as we look ahead.

Looking Ahead

Society faces a pivotal point, a turning in the direction of a new world that is becoming one based on the incredible power of the digital revolution, on the biological probing of the very elements that make up the substance of life, and on the human ingenuity that advances medicine, creates stronger materials, improves fuels, generates new sources of power, creates greater crop yields, and helps us to work faster and better. It is a world based on education and knowledge. Intellectual power has replaced physical power as the productive force of society. We live in a knowledge age, and education in the broad sense is the force that propels society.

It was on the building blocks of education that our society was constructed. Public schools are the great triumph of more than 150 years of educational history. Nicholas Lemann (1999) captured the spirit of national achievement when he stated,

> The idea of educating everyone at public expense ranks with political democracy as one of the United States' great original social contributions. Both ideas rest on a belief that ordinary people are capable of more than the leaders of previous societies would have thought possible. The best and most distinctive tradition in American education is the tradition of pushing to educate more people. That is what Thomas Jefferson was doing when he tried unsuccessfully to establish public elementary schools in Virginia; it is what Horace Mann did when he finally got taxpayers to support public schools in Massachusetts; its was the effect of the GI Bill (p. 350).

The challenge of "pushing to educate more people" continues. The recent decades have seen a reformulation of the meaning of public education. Education almost solely means promoting academic achievement for what is in reality is a select group of students. Academic achievement is a laudatory and crucial objective. It is a purpose traditionally associated with social and economic conservatives, extending back to the social efficiency proponents of the early 1900s, but today it is a perspective widely shared. Today, however, the moral responsibility and social necessity expressed during the Great Society of the 1960s of advancing opportunity for the underclass is largely pushed into the background. The moral guideposts that Gunner Myrdal, Martin Luther King Jr., Rosa Parks, or Cesar Chavez gave to the nation are largely overlooked.

Creating opportunity tends to be equated with the academic advancement of a relatively affluent segment of the population destined for higher education. The underserved tend not to benefit from the standards, the testing, and charter schools, and the slogans and educational products pushed onto schools by the promoters of educational "reform" empowered through the largeness of federal money. While there are modest academic gains in some schools among the underserved, and there are isolated examples of remarkable gains, the overall gains are not enough to suggest that a shift from concern about access, economic security, equity, and social justice to a refocusing on the economic development function of public education is fully justified. And educational interventions designed for an affluent school population cannot be assumed to produce lasting results in schools for the underserved without also coming to terms with the debilitating social and economic conditions facing children of the less fortunate.

Not only does the nation face the challenge of strengthening the academic performance of the upper strata of the student population, but it also faces the challenge of "pushing more people" into the realm of academic excellence. The full promise of American education is yet to be realized.

Part Six References

Angus, D.L., & Mirel, J.E. (1999). The Failed Promise of the American High School, 1890–1995. New York: Teachers College Press.

Blum, J.M. (1991). Tears of Discord: American Politics and Society, 1961-1974. New York: W.W. Norton and Company.

Branch, T. (1988). Parting the Waters: America in the King Years. New York: Simon & Schuster.

Branch, T. (1998). Pillar of Fire: America in the King Years, 1963-65. New York: Simon & Schuster.

Branch, T. (2006). At Canaan's Edge: America in the King Years, 1965-68. New York: Simon & Schuster.

Collins, A., & Halverson, R. (2009). Rethinking Education in the Age of Technology. New York: Teachers College Press.

Conant, J.B. (1959). The American High School Today. New York: McGraw-Hill.

Cremin, L. (1961). The Transformation of the School. New York: Alfred Knopf.

Debo, A. (1970). A History of Indians in the United States. Norman: University of Oklahoma Press.

Ford, G.W., & Pungo, L. (1964). Structure of Knowledge and the Curriculum. Chicago: Rand McNally.

Goodlad, J.I. (1984). A Place Called School. New York: McGraw-Hill Book Company.

Grubb, W.N., & Lazerson, M. (1982). Education and the Labor Market: Recycling the Youth Problem. In H. Kantor & D. Tyack (Eds.), Work, Youth and Schooling. Stanford, CA: Stanford University Press.

Herr, E.L. (1976). The Emergence of Career Education: A Summary View. Washington, DC: National Council on Career Education.

Karier, C.J. (1967). Man, Society, and Education. Chicago: Scott, Foresman and Company.

Karnow, S. (1983). Vietnam, A History. New York: Viking Press.

Katz, M. (1989). The Underserving Poor. New York: Pantheon Books.

Katzenelson, I. (2013). Fear Itself. New York: Liveright Publishing Corp.

Lemann, N. (1999). The Big Tests. New York: Farrar, Straus and Girox.

Marable, M. (1984). Race, Reform and Rebellion: The Second Reconstruction in Black America. Jackson: University Press of Mississippi.

Mirel, J. (1993). The Rise and Fall of an Urban School System: Detroit, 1907-81. Ann Arbor: University of Michigan Press.

Morrison, J., & Morrison, R. (1987). From Camelot to Kent State. New York: Times Books.

Myrdal, G. (1944). The American Dilemma. New York: Oxford University Press.

National Commission on Excellence in Education. (1983). A Nation at Risk: The Imperative for Educational Reform. Washington, DC: Government Printing Office.

Nelson, J., & Roberts, G. Jr. (1963). The Censors and the Schools. Boston: Little, Brown and Company.

Newman, J.W. (1994). America's Teachers. New York: Longman.

Oaks, J. (1985). Keeping Track: How Schools Structure Inequality. New Haven: Yale University Press.

O'Neill, W.L. (1971). Coming Apart. New York: Time Books.

Patterson, J.T. (1996). Grand Expectations. The United States, 1945-1971. New York: Oxford University Press.

Ravitch, D. (2000). Left Back. New York: Simon & Schuster and Co.

Ravitch, D. (2010). The Americn School System. New York: Basic Books.

Ravitch, D. (2013). Reign of Error. New York: Alfred Knopf.

Reyhner, J., & Eder, J. (2004). American Indian Education. Norman: University of Oklahoma.

Rickover, H.G. (1959). Education and Freedom. New York: Dutton.

Schneider, J. (2011). Excellence for All. Nashville, TN: Vanderbilt University Press.

Spring, J. (1976). The Sorting Machine: National Educational Policy Since 1945. New York: David McKay Company.

Spring, J. (2008). The American School (7th ed). New York: McGraw-Hill.

Takaki, R. (2008). A Different Mirror. Boston: Little, Brown and Company.

Valli, L., Croninger, R.G., Chambliss, M.J., Graeber, A.O., & Buese, D. (2008). Test Driven High-Stakes Accountability in Elementary Schools. New York: Teachers College Press.

Zeran, F.R. (1953). Life Adjustment in Action. New York: Chartwell House.